PRECARIOUS DEMOCRACIES

RECENT TITLES FROM THE HELEN KELLOGG INSTITUTE FOR INTERNATIONAL STUDIES

Scott Mainwaring, *series editor*

The University of Notre Dame Press gratefully thanks the Helen Kellogg Institute for International Studies for its support in the publication of titles in this series.

Kenneth P. Serbin
Needs of the Heart: A Social and Cultural History of Brazil's Clergy and Seminaries (2006)

Christopher Welna and Gustavo Gallón, eds.
Peace, Democracy, and Human Rights in Colombia (2007)

Guillermo O'Donnell
Dissonances: Democratic Critiques of Democracy (2007)

Marifeli Pérez¬Stable, ed.
Looking Forward: Comparative Perspectives on Cuba's Transition (2007)

Jodi S. Finkel
Judicial Reform as Political Insurance: Argentina, Peru, and Mexico in the 1990s (2008)

Robert H. Wilson, Peter M. Ward, Peter K. Spink, and Victoria E. Rodríguez
Governance in the Americas: Decentralization, Democracy, and Subnational Government in Brazil, Mexico, and the USA (2008)

Brian S. McBeth
Dictatorship and Politics: Intrigue, Betrayal, and Survival in Venezuela, 1908–1935 (2008)

Pablo Policzer
The Rise and Fall of Repression in Chile (2009)

Frances Hagopian, ed.
Religious Pluralism, Democracy, and the Catholic Church in Latin America (2009)

Marcelo Bergman and Laurence Whitehead, eds.
Criminality, Public Security, and the Challenge to Democracy in Latin America (2009)

Matthew R. Cleary
The Sources of Democratic Responsiveness in Mexico (2010)

Leah Anne Carroll
Violent Democratization: Social Movements, Elites, and Politics in Colombia's Rural War Zones, 1984–2008 (2011)

Timothy J. Power and Matthew M. Taylor
Corruption and Democracy in Brazil: The Struggle for Accountability (2011)

For a complete list of titles from the Helen Kellogg Institute for International Studies, see http://www.undpress.nd.edu

PRECARIOUS DEMOCRACIES

Understanding Regime Stability

and Change in Colombia and Venezuela

Ana María Bejarano

University of Notre Dame Press • *Notre Dame, Indiana*

Manufactured in the United States of America

Library of Congress Cataloging-in-Publication Data

Bejarano, Ana María.
Precarious democracies : understanding regime stability and change in
Colombia and Venezuela / Ana María Bejarano.
    p.   cm. — (From the Helen Kellogg Institute for International Studies)
Includes bibliographical references and index.
ISBN-13: 978-0-268-02226-6 (pbk. : alk. paper)
ISBN-10: 0-268-02226-7 (pbk. : alk. paper)
1. Political stability—Venezuela. 2. Political stability—Colombia.
3. Democracy—Venezuela. 4. Democracy—Colombia. 5. Venezuela—Politics
and government—1999– 6. Colombia—Politics and government—1974–
I. Title.
JL3881.B45   2011
320.9861—dc22

                                       2011009411

For Federico

CONTENTS

ILLUSTRATIONS

ACKNOWLEDGMENTS

This project began as a Ph.D. dissertation at Columbia University. Many seasons and travels later, it has acquired the form of this book. Lisa Anderson helped shape the first version of the research proposal and supervised the research until its successful completion as a dissertation. She has been a role model in more ways than one. Doug Chalmers accompanied me throughout the project, pushing me along on several occasions when I wanted to throw in the towel. It is to him that I owe the comparative thrust of this book. Despite her late arrival in the evolution of my dissertation, Consuelo Cruz soon became a vital source of inspiration and encouragement. Throughout my time in New York, Margaret Crahan generously provided warm friendship as well as intellectual support.

In Colombia and Venezuela I counted on various institutions and the friends and colleagues therein. Among them, I should mention the Department of Political Science at the Universidad de los Andes in Bogotá, where I returned to work as a professor and researcher, and the following individuals: Andrés Dávila, Francisco Leal, the late Dora Rothlisberger, and Maria Emma Wills. Catalina Acevedo, Felipe Botero, Fernando Pieschacón, and Renata Segura helped with the collection of data at different stages of this project. Gonzalo Sánchez, then-director of the Instituto de Estudios Políticos y Relaciones Internacionales (Institute for Political Studies and International Relations) at the Universidad Nacional, helped raise funds for the project and offered a stimulating working environment at the institute during 1995. My deepest thanks go to the Centro de Investigación y Educación Popular (CINEP; Center for Popular Research and Education) for its institutional backing from 1994 to 1998. Its director at that time, Fernán González S.J., mentor and lifelong friend, is in great measure responsible for the successful culmination of this project. Without Fernán's affectionate and wise advice, and without CINEP's generous institutional and financial support, it would surely have been abandoned midway.

In Venezuela I must thank the Centro de Estudios del Desarrollo (CENDES; Center for Development Studies) at the Universidad Central de Venezuela, in particular staff members in the Sociopolitical Area who took me on my first field trip in that country. On a second trip the Instituto de Investigaciones Económicas y Sociales (Institute for Economic and Social Research) at the Universidad Católica "Andres Bello" and its researchers welcomed and helped me in generous ways. During my next trips to Caracas, the Instituto de Estudios Superiores de Administración (IESA; Institute for Higher Studies in Administration) provided an ideal place to further this investigation. The support of its researchers, especially Miriam Kornblith, Rafael Rodríguez, and María Antonia Martínez, and its excellent collection offered unparalleled conditions for this purpose. The Centro Gumilla (Gumilla Center) allowed access to its valuable collection of the *Revista SIC*. Last but not least, the Centro por La Paz (Center for Peace) at the Universidad Central de Venezuela and its director, Ana María San Juan, provided steady and generous support throughout the project.

My gratitude goes to all those who generously offered their time for interviews, as well as for informal consultations regarding all the questions, big and small, that arose as I was building my interpretation of the Venezuelan case and establishing the contrast with Colombia. It is difficult to express with mere words the immense appreciation I have developed during this time for Venezuela, its geography, its history, and, most of all, for its people. I especially cherish the friendship and hospitality offered by Miriam Kornblith, Sergio Meza, Nolly Raven, Manuel Rachadell, Francisco Suniaga, and Maria Eugenia Vethencourt. Beyond all gratitude are the affection and intellectual support offered by Margarita López Maya, Luis Lander, and Edgardo Lander. Through their eyes I learned to know and love Venezuela. Edgardo, whom I had the good fortune to meet in New York when writing the first draft of my dissertation, was one of its most assiduous and generous readers.

Such a prolonged research effort would have been impossible if it were not for the financial support of various institutions. A grant from the Tinker Foundation financed my first field trip to Venezuela in summer 1992. The Instituto Colombiano para el Avance de la Ciencia

(COLCIENCIAS; Colombian Institute for the Advancement of Science) funded a second short trip to Venezuela in summer 1993. A grant from the Latin American Program of the Woodrow Wilson Center (the Venezuela Fellowship Award) financed my fieldwork in Venezuela during 1994 and 1995. Research on Colombia during 1994, 1995, and 1996 was conducted with the financial and institutional support of CINEP. COLCIENCIAS partially funded fieldwork in Colombia during 1995. A grant awarded during the V Convocatoria de Becas de Doctorado COLCIENCIAS–BID (Fifth Convocation of Doctoral Fellowships COLCIENCIAS–IDB) allowed me to fly back to New York in fall 1996 to begin writing my dissertation. The Centro por La Paz funded my last research trip to Caracas in December 1999. Thanks to the resources granted by each one of these institutions, I was able to count on, as Virginia Woolf would put it, a room of my own.

That "room" was also possible thanks to the generous support of various people and institutions that welcomed me and my family on leaving Colombia in January 2000. In spring 2000, thanks to an invitation from Doug Chalmers, ILAIS became again a home away from home. Meg Crahan reappeared on the scene, lending a hand in many more ways than I can tell. In fall 2000 a most generous welcome was extended by Scott Mainwaring and his colleagues at the Kellogg Institute for International Studies at the University of Notre Dame. Thanks to Scott's encouragement and unparalleled generosity, I was able to join one of the most exciting research environments in North America. A generous invitation extended by Jeremy Adelman from Princeton University's Program in Latin American Studies (PLAS), together with a visiting fellowship at the Center for International Studies and lectureships in the Department of Politics and the Woodrow Wilson School of Public and International Affairs made possible our stay in Princeton from 2001 to 2003. Since then I have counted on the support and resources offered by the Department of Political Science at the University of Toronto.

Over the years this book has benefited from the comments and suggestions of many generous readers. I wish to thank Jo-Marie Burt, Miguel Carter, Catherine Conaghan, Erica Cosgrove, Antoinette Handley, Jonathan Hartlyn, Judy Hellman, Lisa Hilbink, Paul Kingston, Scott Mainwaring, Sarah Pralle, Ed Schatz, Martín Tanaka, Judith Teichman, and Laura Wills, as well as the anonymous reviewers for the University of

Notre Dame Press. Jonathan Hartlyn and Scott Mainwaring deserve special mention for their enlightened advice and unwavering support through the most trying phases of this effort. During its final stages, Ingrid Carlson provided excellent research assistance, in addition to many suggestions that greatly improved the manuscript.

Many things have happened in my life since I first embarked on this long journey. There is, however, one I am most thankful for, because it gives meaning to everything else, and that is Federico. To him I dedicate this book, with all my love.

ABBREVIATIONS

Colombia

AD-M19	Alianza Democrática M-19 (M-19 Democratic Alliance)
ANAPO	Alianza Nacional Popular (Popular National Alliance)
ASI	Alianza Social Indígena (Indigenous Social Alliance)
AUC	Auto-Defensas Unidas de Colombia (United Self-Defenses of Colombia)
CRS	Corriente de Renovación Socialista (Current of Socialist Renovation)
ELN	Ejército de Liberación Nacional (National Liberation Army)
EPL	Ejército Popular de Liberación (Popular Liberation Army)
FARC	Fuerzas Armadas Revolucionarias de Colombia (Revolutionary Armed Forces of Colombia)
FN	Frente Nacional (National Front)
FSP	Frente Social y Político (Social and Political Front)
MAQL	Movimiento Armado Quintín Lame (Quintín Lame Armed Movement)
M-19	Movimiento 19 de Abril (April 19 Movement)
MRL	Movimiento Revolucionario Liberal (Liberal Revolutionary Movement)
MSC	Movimiento Sí Colombia (Yes Colombia Movement)
MSN	Movimiento de Salvación Nacional (Movement of National Salvation)
NFD	Nueva Fuerza Democrática (New Democratic Force)
NL	Nuevo Liberalismo (New Liberalism)

PC	Partido Conservador (Conservative Party)
PCC	Partido Comunista de Colombia (Communist Party of Colombia)
PDA	Polo Democrático Alternativo (Alternative Democratic Pole)
PL	Partido Liberal (Liberal Party)
PRT	Partido Revolucionario de los Trabajadores (Revolutionary Workers' Party)
PSC	Partido Social Conservador (Social Conservative Party)
PSUN	Partido Social de la Unidad Nacional ("Partido de la U") (Social Party of National Unity)
UP	Unión Patriótica (Patriotic Union)

Venezuela

AD	Acción Democrática (Democratic Action)
CN	Convergencia Nacional (National Convergence)
COPEI	Comité Político Electoral Independiente (Political Electoral Independent Committee)
COPRE	Comisión Presidencial para la Reforma del Estado (Presidential Commission for State Reform)
CTV	Confederación de Trabajadores de Venezuela (Confederation of Venezuelan Workers)
EN	Encuentro Nacional (National Encounter)
FCV	Federación de Campesinos de Venezuela (Federation of Venezuelan Peasants)
FDN	Frente Democrático Nacional (National Democratic Front)
FDP	Fuerza Democrática Popular (Popular Democratic Force)
FEDECAMARAS	Federación de Cámaras y Asociaciones de Comercio y Producción (Federation of Chambers and Associations of Commerce and Production)
LCR	La Causa Radical (The Radical Cause)
MAS	Movimiento al Socialismo (Movement toward Socialism)

MBR200   Movimiento Bolivariano Revolucionario 200 (Bolivian
         Revolutionary Movement 200)
MEP   Movimiento Electoral del Pueblo (People's Electoral
         Movement)
MIR   Movimiento de Izquierda Revolucionaria
         (Revolutionary Left Movement)
MVR   Movimiento Quinta República (Fifth Republic
         Movement)
PCV   Partido Comunista de Venezuela (Communist Party
         of Venezuela)
PJ   Primero Justicia (Justice First)
PP   Polo Patriótico (Patriotic Pole)
PPT   Patria para Todos (Fatherland for All)
PRVZL   Proyecto Venezuela (Project Venezuela)
PSUV   Partido Socialista Unido de Venezuela (United Socialist
         Party of Venezuela)
UPA   Unión para Avanzar (Union to Advance)
URD   Unión Republicana Democrática (Democratic
         Republican Union)

Map 1. Colombia and Venezuela

Caribbean Sea

PANAMA

Barranquilla

Maracaibo

Caracas

Valencia   Maracay

Mérida

VENEZUELA

GUYANA

Medellín

Pacific Ocean

Bogotá

COLOMBIA

Cali

ECUADOR

BRAZIL

PERU

South America

INTRODUCTION

Venezuela's long-acclaimed democracy started to crumble in February 1989. Had this book been written before that time, Colombia and Venezuela would have provided the perfect pair for a contrasting comparison: whereas Venezuela boasted a well-established democratic regime, Colombia's barely survived amid serious restrictions and shortcomings. As Venezuela's democracy started to confront challenges that threw its continuity into question, however, the contrast became increasingly blurred. These South American nations have drawn closer together over the past two decades as both have been rocked by political turmoil.

While most standard explanatory arguments about democracy in Colombia and Venezuela point to similarity, my comparison emphasizes difference. This book seeks to highlight and explain divergence in the patterns of regime evolution in two cases that, due to a tendency to converge at certain crucial moments of their institutional histories, have traditionally been interpreted as following a similar trajectory. The differences between these two cases, I argue, are not only puzzling but also revealing. They throw into question commonly held assumptions about the impact on democratization of staple-led models of development or modes of transition. I draw a nuanced picture of the factors involved in democratization, as well as a more detailed mapping of regime trajectories as complex political processes.

Since their democratic transitions fifty years ago, the political regimes in Colombia and Venezuela have evolved in different directions, creating a complex pattern of convergence and divergence. They first converged in the late 1950s when they underwent simultaneous "pacted transitions." After 1958, however, these two fledging democracies evolved in significantly divergent ways: whereas Venezuela soon became an inclusionary and competitive political system, Colombia remained stunted by the restrictions imposed by the National Front pacts. In the late 1980s and early 1990s they converged again, this time as a result of political crises. The first decade of the twenty-first century has seen these two neighboring democracies diverge again, as they have confronted their crises in very different ways. Figure 0.1 shows the evolution of these two democracies over time based on Freedom House scores.[1]

Political trajectories do not move along straight, predictable lines. No matter how stable they may seem, political regimes suffer setbacks, experience cycles, and take unexpected turns. Alas, the neatly paired comparisons that may be drawn by focusing on more discrete periods of time become extremely difficult to obtain when comparing half a century of political development. Should we then content ourselves with the apparent impossibility of conducting systematic comparisons over time?

As I struggled with the challenges imposed on my initial "most similar systems" research design by actual changes on the ground,[2] I stumbled, somewhat serendipitously, on a research strategy that provided a way out of my dilemma: following Jared Diamond, I call it the Anna Karenina principle.[3] The famous opening lines of *Anna Karenina,* Tolstoy's great novel, read as follows: "All happy families are alike; each unhappy family is unhappy in its own way."[4] In this deceptively simple

Figure 0.1. Colombia and Venezuela: Regime Convergence and Divergence

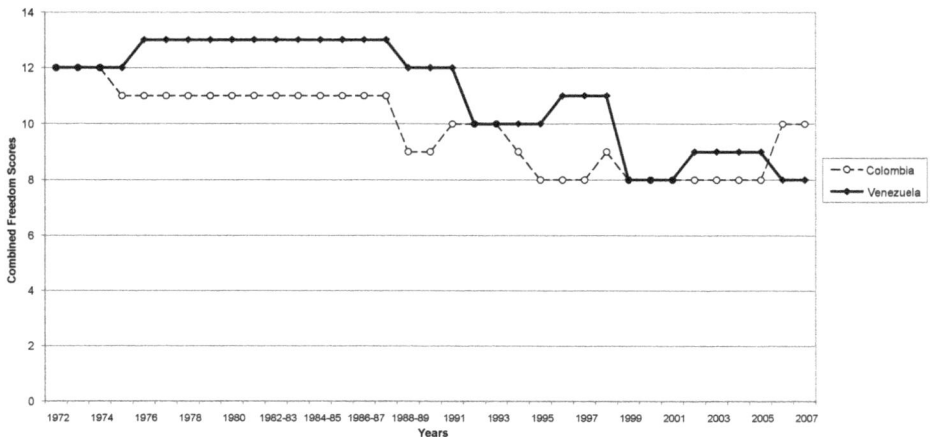

Source: Freedom House Scores, 1972–2007, available at www.freedomhouse.org

sentence Tolstoy is making a universal statement: in order to be happy, families must succeed in many respects, not just one; failure to achieve any of those essential components can doom a family, even if it has all the other necessary ingredients for happiness (Diamond 1999: 157). It does not take long to realize the powerful analytical device hidden in this simple statement. Like many other complex social phenomena, democracy is a multifaceted proposition: in order to build and sustain a democratic regime, a society needs to meet a bundle of conditions. The absence of one of them can throw the complex artifact into disarray, thus making for regimes that fail to achieve the basic characteristics of a well-established, functioning democracy. Success, indeed, requires avoiding many separate causes of failure. Thus, to paraphrase Tolstoy, while all happy democracies are alike, each unhappy democracy is unhappy in its own way.

What the precise ingredients for a happy democracy are is of course a matter of heated debate. For the purposes of this book, I rely on a widely accepted procedural view of democracy that focuses on four key attributes: (1) inclusion of the majority of the adult population through universal suffrage; (2) selection of the top political leadership (at the very least the executive and legislative powers) by means of regular, competitive, free, and fair elections; (3) respect for and effective protection of civil rights and liberties; and (4) the ability of elected authorities to govern without being subject to external controls or vetoes by nonelected actors, such as the military.[5] Significant restrictions on or the absence of any of these core elements will therefore yield an unhappy democracy.[6] The beauty of the Anna Karenina principle is that it makes us aware of the fact that the missing ingredients can vary from case to case, as well as over time, and therefore prompts us into a systematic investigation of that variation. This is exactly what this book seeks to do: it is an effort to distinguish the many ways in which Colombia's and Venezuela's unhappy democracies differ from each other and to provide an explanation of the reasons why, despite their many similarities, these two precarious democracies have evolved in divergent and sometimes unexpected ways.

Colombia and Venezuela have often been bracketed together as a particular subset of cases within the Latin American region. The two are not only geographically close (see map 1) but also, at first glance, have marked similarities: they were both subdued by military dictatorships during the 1950s, both experienced democratic transitions in the same pacted mode at exactly the same time, and both came out of these transitions with stable, enduring, democratic regimes. In addition, both countries have recently experienced political turmoil and institutional decay. Beneath these similarities, however, there are crucial differences in the evolution of these two political regimes. These differences, I argue, not only merit explanation but also throw light on the conditions that help democracy emerge and endure, and eventually decline and break down.

In contrasting the post-transition trajectories of these two regimes over the past five decades, I focus on three divergent outcomes. The first is related to the degree of civilian control of the military and the limits placed on the military's influence on policy matters. Since the late 1950s, and for the first time in Venezuelan history, the military became subordinate to civilians, who in turn asserted their authority in most realms of public decision making. By contrast, in Colombia, despite the fact that power was also devolved in 1958 from the military to civilians, the latter experienced enormous difficulty gaining full control and asserting their authority in crucial matters such as defense and security. The second divergent outcome has to do with the ability to neutralize and incorporate armed challengers on the left and thus secure the state's monopoly over the use of force. Again, in stark contrast, whereas in Colombia an internal armed conflict pitching the state against various irregular forces persists to the present, Venezuela not only managed to quell a disloyal opposition by defeating the guerrillas in the late 1960s but also, and most important, managed to turn the disaffected former guerrillas into a loyal opposition on the left, fully incorporated into the polity. The third and last divergent outcome has to do with the consolidation of an inclusive and competitive political society. In part as a result of the incorporation of the radical left, in the 1970s and 1980s Venezuela managed to create a pluralistic, representative, and competitive party system that allowed for the active participation of a diversity of parties on the left, despite the continuing dominance of the two main center parties. On the other hand, the Colombian party system remained dominated by two-century-old political parties, and the formation of a loyal opposition on the left was thwarted by both formal exclusion and the expansion of the armed left. Despite their common origins as pacted democracies, differences in these three crucial dimensions mark the distance that separated Colombia and Venezuela's democratic trajectories between 1958 and 1998.

Since the late 1980s these two long-standing democracies have been shaken by deep political crises that have compromised their survival. Still, amid the simultaneous decline of these democracies, the differences remain apparent: whereas Venezuela's democracy struggled to survive the challenges posed by a declining oil rent, the progressive weakening of its state, the collapse of its party system, and the ideological polarization that ensued, the Colombian crisis is more aptly characterized as the slow and gradual decay of a regime that had trouble overcoming certain "birth defects," or restraining conditions, inherited from its pacted transition. That these two democracies have simultaneously faced deep trouble should not obscure the fact that their twin crises are fundamentally different in nature.

My hope, of course, is not only to point to those particular features that make these two democracies precarious, or unhappy, yet different. I also seek to account for those differences. That these two countries followed different democratic trajectories is puzzling given their apparent commonalities—most notably, the simultaneity and almost identical nature of their democratic transitions. Why did they diverge after having undergone such similar transition processes? This question becomes even more puzzling in light of the two regimes' previous evolution: for over a hundred years since independence, caudillo and military rule had been a constant in Venezuela, with only one ephemeral democratic experiment, the Trienio years, from 1945 to 1948. In sharp contrast, since the 1830s Colombia shows an impressive record of civilian rule, grounded in periodic (if not completely free and fair) elections, with very few and brief interruptions—rare episodes of military rule in a case where some form of elected civilian government has been a constant. Why then was Venezuela more successful at establishing a democratic regime after 1958 than Colombia? And why have they recently displayed divergent forms of decay?

To answer these questions, I build on and critically engage a large body of literature written over the past two decades on democratization. With the "third wave" of transitions from authoritarian rule for the most part over, the field of Latin American politics started shifting in the 1990s: the previous emphasis on democratic transitions gave way to new preoccupations, mainly centered on the durability and performance of these fledging democracies. Starting in the early 1990s there was an out-pouring of studies concerned with the dilemmas and challenges of demo-cratic consolidation.[7] By the mid-1990s, however, the term *consolidation* came under attack by one of its early proponents: Guillermo O'Donnell wrote a searing critique in the *Journal of Democracy* that not only sparked a fascinating intellectual debate in that journal but also did away with the use of the very concept of consolidation.[8] O'Donnell's critique cen-tered on the teleological nature of the concept, as well as its ethnocentric implications: because it tacitly implied that all democracies were on the road to becoming mature democracies (such as the ones that exist in the global Northwest), studies focusing on consolidation had difficulty ac-counting for those cases (such as most countries in Latin America) where a problematic mixture of democratic institutions and antidemocratic practices had become, nonetheless, deeply institutionalized. Despite ef-forts by some to clarify the meaning and uses of the concept (see Schedler 1998), the debate over "consolidation" became entangled in a contro-versy between a minimalist notion (where consolidation was equated with stability or duration, thus becoming superfluous)[9] and a number of maximalist—though often highly imprecise—definitions of what it meant for a democracy to become consolidated.[10] In the end the concept of consolidation was abandoned, probably for the better.[11]

With the shift away from democratic consolidation came a new em-phasis on the "quality of democracy."[12] This new approach has yielded little progress in the way we conceptualize the variation among existing democracies: for some, the quality of democracy refers to the perfor-mance of a given set of democratic institutions (Altman and Pérez-Liñán 2002); for others, the quality of democracy should be viewed from the perspective of outcomes (in particular, in terms of the extension of de-mocracy to the realms of the economy and the society).[13] The notion of the quality of democracy suffers from exactly the same teleological prob-lems O'Donnell found in the concept of consolidation: it poses, again, whether explicitly or implicitly, that democratic regimes inherently move through levels or stages from lower to higher degrees of democratic quality. Neither does it escape from the ethnocentric trap: there is, again, the tendency to associate high-quality democracies with those developed in the northwestern quarter of the globe, leaving again a residual category ("low-quality democracies") to encompass all those regimes that have emerged and developed elsewhere. In terms of conceptual clarity, the "quality of democracy" debate has so far added very little: instead, it seems to have gone full circle, by adding an ever-increasing list of attributes and dimensions that should be considered in measuring a democracy's quality.[14]

The disappearance of "consolidation" as a well-received term in debates on democratization, as well as the many drawbacks affecting the emerging focus on the "quality of democracy," has left us without a unifying paradigm for the study of politics in post-transition Latin America. As Hagopian noted more than a decade ago, since the heyday of the transition studies "the Latin American field has not followed with as compelling a framework for studying politics *after* regime change" (1993: 465; original emphasis). That we lack a unifying paradigm, a common umbrella to cover the rich variation among currently existing democracies, may be for the better: instead of trying to cluster them in a unsatisfactory dichotomy pitting consolidated versus unconsolidated regimes, we are forced to observe even more attentively the processes whereby democracies evolve and the trajectories they follow and to become more adept at defining with greater precision in what respects and to what degrees democracies do vary. Some authors have classified their cases according to an electoral democracy/liberal democracy dichotomy. Others have proposed new typologies: among the most useful suggestions is the proposal by Mainwaring, Brinks, and Pérez-Liñán (2001) to add a new type, semidemocracy, to the classic division of regimes into democratic or authoritarian ones. Still, the type "semidemocracy"—being the most populated one—encompasses too many "diminished subtypes of democracy" (Collier and Levitsky 1997), thus leaving us without a clear way to differentiate between them.

My proposal is to disaggregate the bundle of dimensions encompassed in what we call the full package of "democracy" and then use the Anna Karenina principle to make a distinction between different types of unhappy, or precarious, democracies. The research strategy that guided my comparison of Colombia and Venezuela builds precisely on this idea: by unpacking the multiple components of democracy and disaggregating the various dimensions on which issues of quality and performance can be assessed, it becomes possible to identify the dimensions or components that may be weak or missing in each particular case. Once such attributes are identified, we not only have a more accurate way to describe currently existing regimes, but we are also better able to compare and contrast cases that do not obtain the full package implied by standard definitions of liberal democracy.

This book picks up where debates on democratic consolidation and the quality of democracy have left us: short of easy labels with which to classify a series of borderline cases, it aims at uncovering significant variations among them, thus making them susceptible to classification and explanation. The argument also builds on the conviction that democratization is better conceived as an ongoing process, a continuum rather than a dichotomy, which admits intermediate stages, moments of advance as well as moments of regression. Rather than use the problematic concept of consolidation, my argument falls back on an older alternative, that is, the notion of institutionalization, conceived as the post-transition development of a regime that is able to fulfill and reproduce the procedural conditions of political democracy.[15]

There is no need for this process to be unilinear or for the concept to have a teleological flavor. Democratic institutionalization is rather conceived as a contentious process whereby the institutions typical of democracy may or may not become resilient and self-sustaining. The process consists, to a great extent, "of eliminating the institutions, procedures and expectations that are incompatible with the minimal workings of a democratic regime" (Valenzuela 1992: 70), thereby permitting the beneficent ones to develop further.[16] It involves a struggle between actors who benefit from and lose due to these formal and informal undemocratic arrangements and hence "unfolds through precedent-setting political confrontations that alter or revalidate the institutional and procedural environment in its perverse or beneficent aspects" (71).

In sum, I propose to view the institutionalization of democracy as an ongoing contentious process—a struggle among political actors who continuously clash over the shape of the institutional architecture framing their interaction. Such a struggle does not take place in a political vacuum, however, but within the constraints imposed by the historical and institutional context, inherited from the preauthoritarian period, the authoritarian experience, and the transition process. It is a multifaceted process, occurring simultaneously in different arenas or dimensions that interact, sometimes reinforcing each other, sometimes neutralizing or even reversing previous achievements. As such, it cannot be understood as a unilinear and smooth progression of the entire political regime, from unconsolidated to consolidated democracy. Finally, as the Venezuelan case abundantly shows, it is by no means inevitable, irrevocable, or a historical necessity: there is always the possibility of political change occurring in the opposite direction, what some have called "deconsolidation," or better put, political decay.

A Contrasting (and Long-Overlooked) Pair of Cases

Colombia and Venezuela make an interesting pair indeed. Not only did they share the same Hispanic colonial experience,[17] but also, from 1821 to 1830, they formed part of the same country, Gran Colombia. After its dissolution and the emergence of Venezuela, Colombia, and Ecuador as three separate political entities, some basic similarities endured: the division of the newly independent elites into Liberal and Conservative Parties was a common feature in these countries, as it was in most of Latin America during the nineteenth century; the struggle among competing regional elites was the cause of frequent civil wars throughout the century;[18] state formation was slow and made difficult by the scarcity of resources that these societies could muster (see Centeno 2002); both remained basically poor, agrarian societies, dependent on the boom-and-boost cycles of their main agricultural products for export, namely, coffee and cocoa (see Bergquist 1986b).

They also share a common feature regarding their population: in contrast to other countries in Latin America in which a significant portion of the population defines itself as direct descendants of ancestral indigenous cultures (e.g., Mexico, Guatemala, Ecuador, Peru, and Bolivia), Venezuela and Colombia have small indigenous populations (estimated at 2 percent in each case), and a significant majority of the population is made up of mestizos, people of mixed indigenous, African, and Spanish heritage.[19] The majority of the population in these two countries speaks Spanish and is Catholic.[20] In consequence, there are no salient ethnic, linguistic, or religious cleavages in either Colombia or Venezuela that could explain variation in political outcomes.[21] The absence of deep-seated cleavages that could threaten the shared notion of national unity means that by the beginning of the twentieth century both countries had achieved a well-delineated and largely undisputed national identity. Therefore, the lack of national unity cannot be posed as the cause of differences between these two democratization processes.[22]

Interestingly, despite these and many more common historical features, the political trajectories of Colombia and Venezuela have differed in important ways. It is precisely that divergence which this book seeks to emphasize and explain. Following independence, and as a result of the tumultuous politics characterizing much of the nineteenth century in Latin America, two different forms of rule emerged in these two agrarian societies: whereas Venezuela became an autocracy, Colombia became an oligarchy.[23] From independence until the turn of the twentieth century, Venezuela had only three civilian presidents (Vargas, Rojas Paúl, and Andueza Palacio), whose governments, taken together, lasted fewer than four years (López-Alves 2000: 198). After the last of the civil wars in Venezuela, the triumph of Cipriano Castro's Andean army led to the installation of a long-enduring autocracy headed first by Castro (1903–8) and later by his lieutenant, Juan Vicente Gómez (1908–35). On his death Gómez was succeeded by two military strongmen: General Eleázar López Contreras (1935–41) and General Isaías Medina Angarita (1941–45). After a brief interlude, characterized by an attempt to establish a radical version of democracy by force under the so-called Trienio (1945–48),[24] Venezuela returned to military rule, first under a military junta (1948–50) and then under the personal rule of General Marcos Pérez Jiménez (1950–58). In sum, before 1958 Venezuela never experienced a period of "oligarchic" democracy but only three years of an experiment in radical democracy.

By contrast, in Colombia an even-handed competition among regional elites was conducive to a competitive oligarchy that became an "oligarchic democracy" on the establishment of universal male suffrage in 1936.[25] From 1830 to the late 1800s Colombia had a string of civilian governments, with only three failed attempts (by Urdaneta, Melo, and Mosquera) to establish military rule that together did not amount to more than three or four years. Throughout the nineteenth century elections and civil wars were the main mechanisms for achieving power and forming a government in Colombia. From 1910 to 1946 (when a new episode of violence broke out), elections became accepted as the only mechanism for doing so. In Colombia oligarchic civilian rule has been the norm and caudillo or military autocracy the exception.

Taking the previous regime trajectory as a predictor of regime evolution, one might expect to find a lasting dictatorship in Venezuela and a stable democracy in Colombia. In 1958, however, both experienced a transition to democracy, and, paradoxically, it was in Venezuela that a more inclusionary and competitive democracy emerged, while only a limited semidemocracy took root in Colombia. How can we account for this counterintuitive outcome? Why did democracy thrive in the case where one would have least expected it (Venezuela) and become stunted in what seemed to be the most favorable case (Colombia)? What accounts for their divergent forms of institutionalization? How do we explain their divergent forms of decay?

Unfortunately, for the most part, the literature on Latin American politics has left us without a clear understanding of how to locate Venezuela and Colombia from a comparative perspective. Despite the fact that they have been, together with Costa Rica, Latin America's most enduring democracies, they have largely been neglected in the comparative literature on the region.[26] Because of the stability of their democratic regimes they used to be mentioned only in passing as divergent cases from the rest of the region throughout the 1960s and 1970s. Most analysts addressing the wave of democratization that swept the continent in the 1980s have also overlooked them, focusing instead on cases where democratization occurred much more recently.[27]

Despite the number of studies on the subject, students of democratization in Latin America have yet to draw out the full implications of Costa Rican, Colombian, and Venezuelan models of democracy. These long-enduring democracies have many lessons to offer, especially with regard to the long-term evolution of democratic regimes once they are successfully installed. They provide a sufficiently long time span to assess the predictions that have been formulated on the basis of much more recent democratization experiences. Indeed, they offer a unique opportunity to test, revise, refine, or modify a whole set of propositions put forth during the past two decades of studies on democratization.

The comparative study of Venezuela and Colombia,[28] I argue, contributes to the ongoing debate about the prospects and dilemmas of democratization in Latin America and other regions of the world. Not so long ago, a conspicuous interpretation of Latin American politics saw the region as condemned to an endless pendulum movement between authoritarianism and democracy. By focusing on the Colombian and Venezuelan cases, where democratic institutions managed to endure for over four decades, and by exploring the causes of their stability as well as their enduring shortcomings, this study contributes to an understanding of the conditions under which—short of achieving the full package of a happy democracy, and in the absence of an open authoritarian regression—precarious democracies may evolve and endure. Once considered enigmatic exceptions to Latin America's authoritarian swing, Colombia and Venezuela may now be regarded as potential models—both in their accomplishments and in their limitations—of the future of democracy in the region.

Explaining Divergent Democratic Trajectories: The Notion of Structured Contingency

Colombia and Venezuela belong to what Huntington (1991a: 12–36) has labeled the "second wave" of democratization, which took place between 1945 and 1962. Many of the cases belonging to that wave soon fell prey to authoritarian regression. Democracy managed to survive in Colombia and Venezuela. As a consequence they have been classified as "successful" instances of democratization.[29] A closer study of these two cases yields some interesting results. First, they show that successful transitions do not necessarily lead to the institutionalization of happy democracies. Second, they reveal that the long-term evolution of a democracy does not depend as much on the mode of transition (which was similar in both cases) as it does on other factors.

In a suggestive piece titled "Democracy Is a Lake" (1994), Charles Tilly summarized the two opposing views on how and why democratization happens by drawing a contrast between those who see democracy as an "oil field" (i.e., a product of structural change) and those who conceive of it as a "garden" (i.e., an artifact of elite manipulation). He then proposed to think of it as a "lake": "although it has distinguishing properties and a logic of its own, it forms in a variety of ways, each of which retains traces of its singular history in the details of its current operation" (14). Tilly's lake metaphor is an ingenious way to stress the need to find a middle ground between structural explanations of regime change and those based on individual agency and to integrate them in sound, productive, and systematic ways.

In lieu of Tilly's lake metaphor, I like to think of democracy as a work of architecture, whereby if the design and details of the construction are consequential to the final outcome, so is the terrain where the building is planned and constructed. This is the image conveyed in my mind by Terry Karl's notion of "structured contingency," coined in her article, "Dilemmas of Democratization in Latin America" (1990). Even in situations characterized by high levels of uncertainty—as regime change tends to be—the decisions taken by actors respond to a series of limits and possibilities set by the existing socioeconomic structures and political institutions. The margin of liberty is not unlimited, yet it still exists. Conversely, the preexisting structures and institutions do not predetermine the results, but they do indeed condition them. In Karl's words:

> What is called for, then, is a path-dependent approach which clarifies how broad structural changes shape particular regime transitions in ways that may be especially conducive to (or especially obstructive of) democratization. This needs to be combined with an analysis of how such structural changes become embodied in political institutions and rules which subsequently mold the preferences and capacities of individuals during and after regime changes. In this way, it should be possible to demonstrate how the range of options available to decision makers at a given point in time is a function of structures put in place in an earlier period and, concomitantly, how such decisions are conditioned by institutions established in the past. (1990: 7)[30]

Building on Karl's notion of structured contingency, I argue that long-standing political institutions (e.g., the state, political parties, and the party system) play a crucial role as bridges between structural factors and the strategic choices made by elites during critical junctures. "Between the constraints imposed by societal interests and class struggles and the opportunities presented by individual choices and elite bargains are the political institutions that link the structures to the agents, knitting them together in complex ways" (Anderson 1999b: 10–11). These institutions, in particular, the state and political parties, at once embody the legacies of historical battles and shape the way in which current political struggles and bargains are carried out. In other words, economic structures and social transformations do not have an immediate impact on politics, unless there are political institutions and organizations that are able to translate those underlying forces into the political arena.

The role of political institutions as bridges helps explain how socioeconomic structures become "translated" into actual strategic decisions and political outcomes. Thus my explanation emphasizes long-standing political-institutional variables: the timing and pace of state formation, the nature of political parties and the timing of their emergence, and, above all, the relationship between states and parties. Political institutions not only translate the impact from the social and economic realms into the political; they also act as the living testament of the past, embodying the legacies of previous trajectories and choices. They thus exert a continuous influence, providing a thread of continuity even after critical junctures (such as the transitions) have significantly altered the course of political trajectories.

My work thus sides with those arguing in favor of a fundamental role for institutions in social causation, especially those working on the variant called "historical institutionalism."[31] In my view, historical institutionalism and the notion of structured contingency combined make the most suitable analytical approach to the emergence and evolution of democracy. I conceive of democracy neither as an "oil field" nor as a "garden" but as a social construction whose designers must pay due attention to the building's structural foundations. It is the interplay of structures, institutions, and agents that finally shapes strategic decisions and their outcomes. Many have tried to short-circuit this complex explanatory path by jumping directly from structures to outcomes or by overlooking the causal impact of background conditions and placing all explanatory power on short-term elite choices and calculations. In my explanation, socioeconomic structural transformations, as channeled by preexisting institutions (i.e., states and parties), add up to a historical-institutional account of the kinds of struggles, the nature of the setting, and the types of decisions that become available to political actors in times of change.

The causal argument built in the following pages thus points in two different but interrelated directions. It first turns to the distant past in search of clues beyond the immediate chronicles of the transition and points at important historical disparities with a long-term impact on both the transition process and its aftermath. As indicated by the apparent paradox of previous regime evolution, in searching for these clues it is necessary to look beyond regime-level variables. In addition to the obvious dissimilarity in socioeconomic evolution, differences related to the state and political parties but most important to their mutual relation emerged as avenues for accounting for the divergence between Venezuela and Colombia in the post-1958 period. This book therefore calls for the recovery and full use of political history as a key to our explanation of contemporary political processes—not political history understood in the conventional sense, as a narrative of heroes and epic battles, but rather as a genealogy of political institutions such as the state and the party system. With regard to the state, it is important to take the timing of its emergence and consolidation into account, as well as the vehicles by means of which it managed to assert control over territory and population. Among other things, differences in the timing and experience of state consolidation are key to explaining whether parties become (or not) appropriate vehicles for the representation of social cleavages and conflicts. Taken together, states and parties go a long way toward explaining variation in regime trajectories.

My explanation also confronts issues raised by the transitions' literature, more specifically, the role of the mode of transition as a predictor of future regime evolution. A careful look at Colombia and Venezuela makes it evident that their pacted mode of transition does not suffice to explain the complex and not always predictable ways in which a regime may evolve after a transition has been completed. In order to account for differences in the patterns of regime evolution, a more nuanced analysis is needed. My argument thus becomes more finely grained and explains divergent regime evolutions as a consequence of differences discovered when unpacking the notion of pacts: their degrees of exclusion and inclusion, the nature and scope of the institutional constraints imposed on the various dimensions of democracy, and, finally, their degree of institutional entrenchment.

These two distinct institutional legacies (from the past and from the transition) are then used to explain why between 1958 and the late 1980s Colombia's and Venezuela's democratic trajectories diverged. They also help us throw light into the processes of erosion and decay that have affected these two democracies since the early 1990s. The strategy yields a complex and nuanced comparative historical account of the evolution of these two regimes during the second half of the twentieth century. Such an account differs from two alternative approaches to the study of democratization: the so-called structural approach, primarily concerned with the role of socioeconomic factors as determinants of political outcomes, and the voluntarist, elite-driven approach, which is mainly interested in the short-term consequences of actors' strategic decision making.[32]

Structural Explanations of Regime Evolution

It would be very tempting to solve the puzzle posed by the divergent evolution of democracy in Colombia and Venezuela with an explanation that hinges mainly on structural factors. According to this view, democracy is a rare species, the outcome of a unique convergence of long-term structural processes not susceptible to willful manipulation by interested political actors. The main problem with explanations of this type is that even though a focus on structures may produce compelling accounts of why, they often seem unable to explain when and how socioeconomic developments translate into regime transformations. That is, they usually fall short in terms of their capacity to specify the actual mechanisms whereby structural forces get translated into actual political outcomes.

Furthermore, a careful exploration of the staple-led development hypothesis in the cases of Colombia and Venezuela leads to an even more puzzling question: as many authors studying oil politics have concluded, oil is not so much a good predictor of democracy as it is of authoritarianism (see, e.g., Ross 2001). Oil-rich regimes tend to be state-centered and tend not to become democratic (Huntington 1991b). The more resources state elites control independently of socioeconomic classes, the more likely it is that authoritarian regimes will take hold and persist over time (Rueschemeyer, Stephens, and Stephens 1992; Kitschelt 1992: 1030). Yet, despite all these predictions, oil-rich Venezuela managed to build a democratic regime that lasted for over four decades.

On the other hand, the comparison of Colombia with other coffee-producing countries is also a puzzling one: while Costa Rica, for example, was able to build a resilient democracy, Colombia has gone from one type of limited democracy to another. Thus, not only Venezuela but also Colombia challenge resource-driven explanations of democracy, especially those focused on the political impact of their primary commodity exports. What, then, is the ultimate role of structural factors? My conclusion is that by neglecting the organizational, institutional, and political factors that mediate between structures and agents, some structural explanations fall short of offering a satisfactory account of regime change.

The Mode of Transition Hypothesis

From the perspective of those who see democracy as the contingent outcome of elite bargaining and negotiation, elites can make democracies grow, given the right values, beliefs, attitudes, and strategic choices. O'Donnell, Schmitter, and Whitehead's (1986) influential volume offered an argument of this kind when accounting for the democratizing wave that starting in the mid-1970s extended from southern Europe to South America under unfavorable structural conditions. According to their model, transitions from authoritarianism to democracy happen through a game of strategic decisions between actors who suffer from few structural constraints (see also Di Palma 1990; Higley and Gunther 1992). For these authors, the crucial issue is the ability of elites to manipulate a highly uncertain setting and their capacity to create agreements that lead to the creation, maintenance, and reproduction of a democratic set of rules.

This kind of actor-oriented explanation has been charged with abandoning the structural approach in favor of a short-term view of democratization, as well as with overlooking the social forces from which elites draw their strength and capacity to negotiate, thus making democracy look like the artifact of relatively simple and self-interested action on the part of the elites. It is nonetheless important to acknowledge their view of regime transitions as exceptional moments in which structural conditions seem to be temporarily suspended, thus allowing for more fluid political exchanges and less constrained contingent choices.

My criticism focuses on the assertion that the specific modality of transition is the main predictor of the regime's subsequent evolution and trajectory. Among others, Stepan (1986) and Karl (1990) have forcefully argued that the specific path taken by a regime in the course of its transformation away from authoritarianism (the "mode" of transition) holds the key to understanding the subsequent evolution of a democratic regime. However, arguments that overemphasize the mode of transition as a predictor of regime development suffer from several problems. They may assign more importance to the juncture of the transition than it really deserves, at the cost of ignoring or overlooking the importance of long-term (i.e., socioeconomic or political) factors, which have a distinct impact on the future evolution of a democracy (Cavarozzi 1991; Hartlyn 1994). Likewise, placing the main focus on the transition juncture tends to ignore the contingent nature of politics, that is, the extent to which democratic evolution depends on contemporary factors, not necessarily related to the transition period, such as the opportunities or hurdles that appear as the political process unfolds (see Hartlyn 1994).

The comparison between Colombia and Venezuela, where transitions to democracy followed the same "pacted" mode, calls into question the alleged impact of the mode of transition on subsequent regime trajectories. If that hypothesis were true, Colombia and Venezuela's political regimes would have evolved in very similar ways after their transitions in the late 1950s. Yet this was not the case. While admitting that transitions are indeed critical turning points at which actors purposely change the institutional structure framing their interaction, the comparison of these two crucial cases of pacted democracies leads to a more nuanced conclusion: instead of the overall "mode" of the transition, it is the blueprint for a new institutional arrangement crafted during the transition that holds the key to its long-term effects. In particular, I argue for the importance of the degree of inclusion or exclusion provided by the new institutional architecture, the scope and nature of the restrictions introduced by the new rules of the game, as well as their degree of entrenchment in the political process. In other words, what really matters for the subsequent evolution of a democratic regime are the transition's institutional legacies rather than the overall mode of transition.

In sum, both the structural and the process-oriented approaches to regime change suffer from serious shortcomings when it comes to explaining regime development over time. In Kitschelt's felicitous words, "Whereas structural approaches explain too much, . . . 'transitology' explains too little" (1992: 1033). An excessive emphasis on a contingent and elitist outlook on democracy runs the risk of being too instrumental and voluntaristic, as well as neglecting the historical, structural, and institutional constraints that frame political interaction. On the other hand, an exaggerated emphasis on structural factors risks overlooking the elements of individual and collective agency present in the configuration of the political framework within which social life evolves. There is good reason to attempt to bridge the structural/procedural divide. In my view, a focus on the genealogy and evolution of political institutions provides precisely that much-needed bridge.

Organization of the Book

Chapter 1 acknowledges that there is a place for structural factors in explanations of how democracies come about and evolve over time, especially those that focus on the social consequences of economic configurations. However, the narrower political economy arguments, in particular, resource-driven explanations focused on coffee in Colombia and oil in Venezuela, are not only insufficient but also, at times, misleading. I argue that these nations' economic structures helped the development of coalitions of social and political forces that were critical to advancing democracy in the second half of the twentieth century, with new urban middle sectors playing central roles with varying degrees of independence vis-à-vis the landed elites and different allies in each one of these two cases.

In chapter 2, I contrast the sharp discontinuity in Venezuelan socioeconomic and political patterns from the nineteenth to the twentieth century with Colombia's notable continuity. The consolidation of a central state and the emergence of the oil industry account, to a great extent, for Venezuela's capacity to make a clear break with the past, whereas in Colombia the persistence of the Liberal and Conservative Parties provided a remarkable degree of political continuity. I also argue that the differing evolution of parties in the two countries is more a function of variations in stateness than of social structures. The divergent patterns of state and party development meant that Venezuela, by the 1950s, was endowed with a more autonomous and resource-laden state and more modern and representative political parties than was the case in Colombia.

The third chapter revisits the literature on democratic transitions, focusing on pacted transitions from authoritarian rule, which involve formal agreements across the civilian political opposition to limit competition and constrain change in certain policy areas, thus providing significant guarantees to key social and political actors. Rather than uncritically accept that all pacted transitions may significantly compromise further democratic development, I argue that pacts can vary in significant ways, with different implications for the kinds of institutional blueprints and legacies they engender. The final section of chapter 3 unpacks the category of pacts and introduces a series of innovative analytical distinctions that help explain their impact on subsequent democratic evolution; these have to do with their degree of inclusion or exclusion, the nature and scope of restrictions imposed by the agreements, and the duration and degree of institutional entrenchment of the agreements. These differences are then employed to account for the contrast between the Colombian and Venezuelan post-transition democratic trajectories.

In chapters 4 and 5 I examine the extent of democratic institutionalization achieved by the regimes in the two countries. Chapter 4 explores the degree to which these two democracies managed to limit the use of force, first by examining civil-military relations and then by analyzing efforts to eliminate and incorporate challengers on the left of the political spectrum. Chapter 5 focuses on the evolution of political society, paying particular attention to the institutionalization of a pluralistic, inclusive, and competitive party system. It highlights dramatic differences between the two countries in this crucial dimension of democracy.

The book concludes with an exploration of the nature of the contemporary crises confronted by Colombia and Venezuela, those same crises that opened the gates for the arrival of Alvaro Uribe and Hugo Chávez to the presidency of their respective nations. Here I argue that the contemporary crisis in Colombia is much more tightly linked to the nature of its pacted transition than is true in Venezuela.

The complex patterns of regime evolution in Venezuela and Colombia can be made intelligible through a comparative historical analysis. The recent travails of democracy in these countries are better understood from a vantage point that privileges political history, especially the history of institutional evolution, rather than long-term structural factors or short-term calculations. While I argue for the importance of the past, I do not advocate using a framework that privileges the so-called structural or socioeconomic determinants of politics. I prioritize political institutional variables, such as the state and political parties, as the carriers of political experience from one historical era to the next. To the extent that it highlights continuities from the past, my analysis emphasizes path-dependence. Nevertheless, it also acknowledges that long-prevailing political practices may be purposively changed at certain critical junctures,[33] such as transitions, by the actors engaged in the struggle for institutional redesign that characterizes episodes of regime change. In short, this book makes the case that a comparative historical institutional framework—focused on the institutional legacies from the distant past as well as on those from more recent critical junctures—provides the best means to account for the divergent trajectories followed by these two democracies in the second half of the twentieth century.

For those readers interested in the fascinating presidents of Colombia and Venezuela, Alvaro Uribe and Hugo Chávez, respectively, this book may prove a disappointment. As mentioned above, this book's main contribution is a sustained comparative historical analysis of Colombia's and Venezuela's divergent democratic trajectories over the past fifty years; it is therefore neither about Uribe nor about Chávez. Part of the argument, precisely, is to challenge those accounts that are predominantly or exclusively focused on individual personalities, or short-term events. What those same readers may find in these pages is an explanation of why, and how, Colombia and Venezuela arrived at a point where their societies were ready to put their trust and confidence in the hands of these two highly controversial figures. Sitting at opposite ends of the ideological spectrum, Uribe and Chávez epitomize two radically different responses to the political impasses faced by these democracies since the late 1980s. Whereas Uribe is usually associated with the right, Chávez is a self-declared socialist, a pioneer in the recent leftist turn in Latin America. They are both extremely popular in their own countries. Even after the disclosure of paramilitary-related scandals in Colombia, Uribe's popularity remained at an all-time high. In Venezuela, despite surprisingly stubborn poverty indicators combined with rising levels of criminality, Chávez remains the most popular political leader in decades. A lot of ink and paper has been spent describing these leaders' contrasting styles and radically divergent positions vis-à-vis critical issues such as free trade or the role of the United States in the region. Much less, however, has been devoted to explaining how it was that the two oldest and allegedly most stable democracies in South America gave rise to such polarized politics and mercurial leaders. This book is precisely an effort to do so. It traces the evolution of these two democracies, from their emergence in the late 1950s until the crises that provided fertile terrain for the emergence of Uribe and Chávez. While quality and style of leadership remains a crucial factor in political life, this study is built on the conviction that historical legacies, sociopolitical coalitions, and institutional architectures provide a fuller explanation of contemporary politics in Colombia and Venezuela, and elsewhere.

Part I
HISTORY MATTERS

History matters. It matters not just because we can learn from the past, but because the present and the future are connected to the past by the continuity of a society's institutions. Today's and tomorrow's choices are shaped by the past. And the past can only be made intelligible as a story of institutional evolution.

—Douglass C. North, *Institutions, Institutional Change and Economic Performance*

CHAPTER ONE

Oil versus Coffee

Searching for the Structural Foundations of Regime Type

In attempts to solve the puzzle of Colombia's and Venezuela's divergent democratic trajectories despite seemingly identical transitions, one of the most appealing explanations focuses on the structural factors favoring or impeding democracy. While I do not dismiss the explanatory power of socioeconomic factors altogether, I find some resource-driven ("sectoral") explanations of regime type insufficient. By deriving political outcomes from economic structures in a mechanical fashion, such accounts can miss the complexity that makes politics fascinating and sometimes unpredictable. On closer scrutiny, the assumption that economic forces determine political outcomes may not only be overly simplistic, but also misleading. Colombia and Venezuela present resource-driven explanations with a puzzling paradox: despite oil being a good predictor of authoritarianism, Venezuela developed a durable democracy, whereas Colombia, with a coffee economy based on a relatively democratic distribution of land (at least in the coffee-growing areas), has faced great difficulties building a democratic order.

Following in the tradition of Moore's *Social Origins of Dictatorship and Democracy,* authors such as Charles Bergquist (1986a, 1986b) take a more complex and indirect route toward explaining politics, by putting class structures and class alliances at the center of the analysis. I find these class-based accounts much richer and more nuanced. And yet, because of their predominant focus on socioeconomic factors, they still miss an important part of the story. As Bergquist (1986b: 376), one of its most accomplished proponents recognizes, there is a crucial aspect of these societies that is not captured by the structural paradigm, and that is the independent influence of states, parties, and party systems on the very political outcomes under scrutiny. I take up this missing part of the puzzle and devote the next chapter precisely to these institutional factors (the state, parties, and the relationship between the two) as variables with an independent effect on the evolution of political regimes.

The Structural Determinants of Regime Type

From a socioeconomic perspective, Colombia and Venezuela looked very similar at the end of the nineteenth century: both economies revolved around the production of agricultural goods for export, with coffee a main staple in both cases and cacao a major export in Venezuela. In 1900 coffee was close to half of both nations' total exports: in Colombia, it amounted to 49 percent; in Venezuela, 43 percent. The second most important export commodity was gold (17 percent) in the case of Colombia and cacao (20 percent) in the case of Venezuela (Thorp 1998: 347). Starting in the third decade of the twentieth century, however, the countries took divergent paths of economic development and integration into the world economy due to a variation in the primary commodity for export: whereas Colombia's economy became strongly anchored in coffee production, Venezuela's quickly turned to oil.[1] Figures 1.1 and 1.2 clearly illustrate the contrast between these two nations' export sectors. Although surprisingly similar up to the 1920s, they look strikingly different from the 1930s onward.

Since the late nineteenth century and throughout the twentieth, Colombia's economic development remained closely tied to the export of coffee (see Palacios 1983, 1995; Bergquist 1986a, 1986b; Ocampo 1987; Palacios and Safford 2002). Even the incipient process of industrialization through import substitution, which took off during the first decades of the twentieth century, was predicated on the foreign income accruing from coffee exports. This predominantly agrarian mode of economic de-

Figure 1.1. Colombia: Share of Principal Commodities in Total Exports of Goods

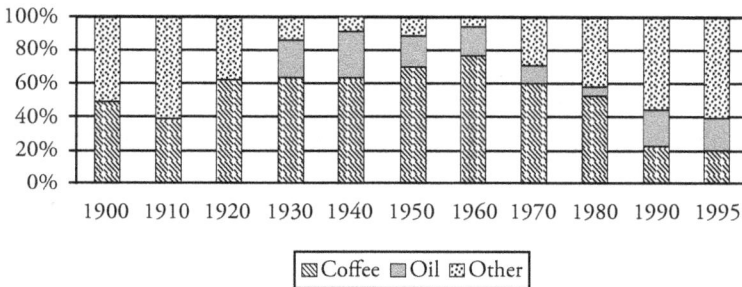

Source: Data from Thorp 1998: Statistical Appendix, Appendix VII, p. 347.

Figure 1.2. Venezuela: Share of Principal Commodities in Total Exports of Goods

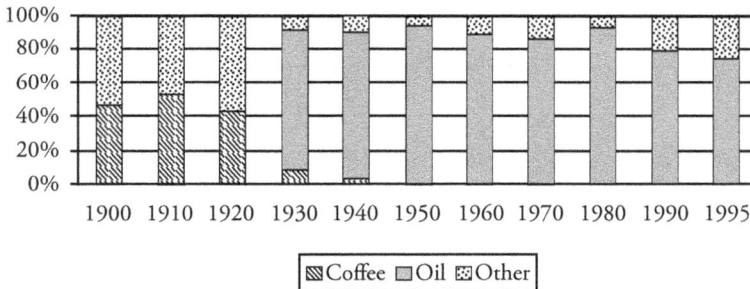

Source: Data from Thorp 1998: Statistical Appendix, Appendix VII, p. 347.

velopment had a number of typical effects on society and politics. Colombia's society remained predominantly rural, traditional links between landlords and peasants remained strong, urbanization was relatively slow-paced, and new social groups and sectors emerged only gradually while remaining strongly linked to the landed oligarchy.

By contrast, since the mid-1920s Venezuela has undergone an accelerated process of economic and social transformation. By the 1930s oil had become the main product in the Venezuelan economy and the main income source for the Venezuelan state.[2] The central role played by petroleum had a number of characteristic impacts on Venezuela's economy and society: the importance of agriculture diminished rapidly, and there was no immediate need for industrialization through import substitution since exports could pay for a wide range of imports. There were instead strong incentives for the development of the service sector of the economy, and an incipient commercial and industrial sector associated with oil production prospered, leading to a boom in the construction industry, urban commerce, and the service and financial sectors. This, in turn, had a visible impact on the country's social structure. It accelerated the urbanization process, thereby contributing to the substitution of traditional relations, typical of an agrarian structure, for wage relations of a capitalist type; it also produced a pattern of population concentration around the areas where oil income was concentrated and distributed. The increasing contrast between the two cases is clearly illustrated by a few social indicators. Figure 1.3 illustrates the faster pace of urbanization in Venezuela compared to that of Colombia, and table 1.1 offers a clear sense of these two economies' changing structure of production, together with their impact on the sectoral distribution of their labor force.

Figure 1.3. Urbanization in Colombia and Venezuela (percent of total population)

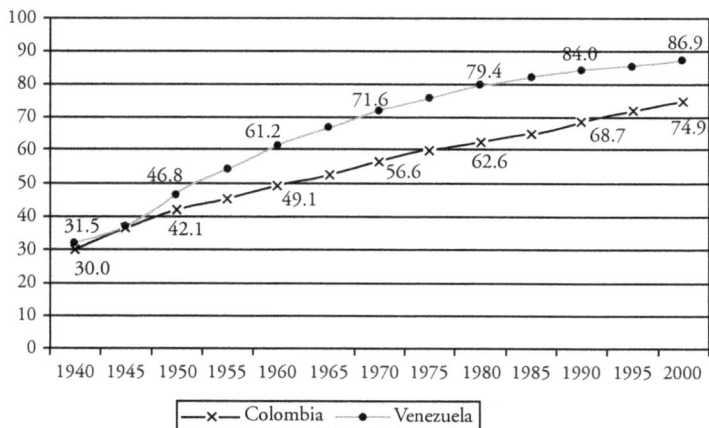

Sources: Data for 1950–2000 for Colombia and Venezuela, United Nations, Population Division of the Department of Economic and Social Affairs of the United Nations Secretariat, World Population Prospects: The 2006 Revision and World Urbanization Prospects: The 2005 Revision, http://esa.un.org/unpp (accessed 2007); for 1940 and 1945 for Venezuela, the Oxford Latin American Economic History Database (OxLAD), http://oxlad.qeh.ox.ac.uk/search.php (accessed in 2007). Data for Colombia for 1940 are actually for 1938 and are from Ocampo 1987. Data for Colombia for 1945 are an estimate based on Ocampo 1987 and the United Nations.

Table 1.1. Structure of Production and Distribution of Labor Force in Colombia and Venezuela

	Agriculture				Industry				Services			
	% GDP		% labor force		% GDP		% labor force		% GDP		% labor force	
	CO	VZ	CO	VZ	CO	VZ	CO	VZ	CO	VZ	CO	VZ
1935–39	47	22	...	...	10	33	...	...	...	...	...	...
1940–44	45	18	...	...	12	34	...	...	...	...	...	...
1945–49	42	11	...	...	14	38	...	...	...	...	...	...
1950	38	8	...	...	22	47	...	...	40	45	....	...
1960	34	7	51	35	24	49	19	22	42	44	30	43
1965	33	7	...	...	26	49	...	...	41	44	...	...
1970	27	7	41	25	28	43	...	...	45	50	...	...
1975	25	7	...	...	28	41	...	...	47	52	...	...
1980	24	7	26	15	29	35	21	28	47	58	53	57
1985	23	6	...	...	28	35	...	...	49	59	...	...
1990	22	6	24	12	29	44	...	...	49	50	...	...
1995	16	5	...	...	31	46	...	...	53	49	...	...
2000	15	5	22	10	29	49	18	22	56	46	59	68

Sources: For structure of production, author's calculation for 1950–2000 based on data from United Nations, *Comisión Económica para América Latina (CEPAL), América Latina y el Caribe: Series regionales y oficiales de cuentas nacionales 1950–2002, División de Estadística y Proyecciones Económicas*. For 1935–49, data from Mitchell 2003. For distribution of labor force, data for Venezuela for 1960 and Colombia for 1980 from The World Bank, *World Development Report 1984*. For 1970 and 1990, data from Oxford Latin American Economic History Database (OxLAD), http://oxlad.qeh.ox.ac.uk/search.php.data (accessed 2007). All other labor force data from World Bank, World Development Indicators Online, http://data.worldbank.org/indicator/ (accessed 2007).

Note: "Agriculture" includes agriculture, hunting, forestry, and fishing. "Industry" includes mining and quarrying; manufacturing; electricity, water, and gas; and construction. "Services" includes wholesale and retail trade, restaurants, and hotels; transport, storage, and communications; finance institutions, insurance, real estate, and business services; and community, social, and personal services. For 1935–39, for Venezuela years included are 1936–39.

Together with figures 1.1 and 1.2, these data sets show the increasing disparity between Colombia and Venezuela at the time of their respective transitions to democracy: by the 1950s they displayed a growing contrast in terms of the structural foundations of their societies and polities. Could this be the key to explaining their divergent political trajectories? It would be very tempting to explain the variation in political outcomes in these neighboring countries on the basis of differences between their socioeconomic trajectories during the first half of the twentieth century. Some authors strongly believe that differences in the structure of the primary export sector account for much of the divergence observed in the historical trajectories of these two societies in the second half of the twentieth century.[3] I argue that while it is crucial to understand the longer-term patterns of social and economic transformations underlying these two countries' contemporary histories, variation in these factors alone does not fully account for their divergent political trajectories after the late 1950s. Furthermore, a superficial contrast focused solely on a few economic variables (such as export commodities) can lead to erroneous conclusions. For, if anything, Venezuela's oil abundance should have condemned it to the antidemocratic effects that usually accompany the "resource curse" (Ross 1999, 2001); Colombia's coffee-based economy, in contrast, seemed at first glance much more favorable to the building of a democratic order. However, this is essentially the opposite of what occurred.

The Economic Foundations of Democracy: Exploring the Staple-Led Development Hypothesis

In one of the most influential accounts of democracy in Venezuela, Terry Lynn Karl (1986) presents a persuasive structural explanation of political change.[4] In the Venezuelan case, she argues, "petroleum is the single most important factor explaining the creation of the structural conditions for the breakdown of military authoritarianism and the subsequent persistence of a democratic system," a claim to which she immediately adds, "An oil-mediated integration into the international market created the necessary structural conditions for a party system" (1986: 197).[5] Karl attributes both the disappearance of "sultanistic authoritarianism" and the emergence of democracy in that country to oil: "The long-term impact of oil, a commodity which initially served to buttress existing regime arrangements, undermined the social basis for authoritarian rule, laying the groundwork for political change" (199). Even though military rule was restored in 1948 after a brief and failed experience with democracy, her confidence in the socioeconomic transformations brought about by an oil-induced model of development remains unabated: "It was merely a matter of time before the disjuncture between an outmoded polity and an increasingly complex economy and society reached crisis point again" (206).

It would be tempting to accept this structural explanation for the emergence and persistence of democracy in Venezuela and apply it to the problems confronted by democratic development in Colombia and elsewhere. Karl's underlying hypothesis lends itself to the kind of contrasting comparison that I draw in this book. Her main claim is as follows:

> In primary commodity exporters dominated by a single product, this staple affects social class formation, the rise and decline of different groups, the structural potential for organization and consciousness, the development of the state, the relative importance of various political actors, and finally, the types of socio-political alliances that can or cannot be forged. Over time, staple-led development can discourage the emergence of certain regime types at a particular moment while increasing the likelihood of the appearance of other types. (1986: 197)

According to this line of reasoning, resource-rich Venezuela was better endowed to undertake democratic rule, while resource-poor, agricultural Colombia was bound to face a harder time achieving the kind of socioeconomic structure and flow of resources that tend to make democracies possible. Although compelling, this type of resource-driven explanation of political development may turn out to be not only overly deterministic but also even seriously flawed. A comparison of Venezuela with other oil-exporting countries and of Colombia with other coffee-exporting countries throws light on why different export commodities should not be taken as the single most important factor explaining regime change.

Oil and Democracy in Venezuela

Oil has certainly played a crucial role in Venezuelan politics but not necessarily on the side of democracy.[6] As early as the 1930s oil accounted for 82 percent of the total export of goods in Venezuela. This share increased throughout the century, reaching a peak of 90 percent in 1980 (Thorp 1998: 347). As Bergquist (1986b: 208) writes, "In terms of its long-term ability to provide a large and expanding supply of foreign exchange and government revenue, the Venezuelan petroleum economy has had no equal among the export economies of Latin America." As a result many scholars have attributed the making and unmaking of Venezuela's democracy to its oil-dependent economy. However, if instead of comparing it with the rest of Latin America, one places Venezuela in the context of other major oil-producing countries—especially those in the Middle East—its political development stands out as an anomaly.

None of the major oil-exporting countries in the developing world has managed to develop a stable, competitive regime such as the one found in Venezuela in the three to four decades after 1958.[7] Instead, in most oil-exporting countries, oil has favored existing regime arrangements rather than undermined them; it has allowed authoritarian rule—whether patrimonial, single-party, or military—to persist and stabilize itself, especially in the Middle East but also in Asia and Africa.

Since the 1970s scholars specializing in these regions, especially those concerned with politics in the Arab oil-exporting countries, have developed a series of arguments stating exactly the contrary to the pro-democratic oil-based argument that has emerged around the Venezuelan case. Oil, they argue, not only buttresses existing authoritarian arrangements but also is inherently inimical to democratic development. The availability of oil has acted as a structural hindrance to democratization in that region of the world (Luciani 1987, 1994; Beblawi 1987; Gause 1994). Ross (2001) has carefully tested and added empirical weight to the oil-hinders-democracy hypothesis advanced by scholars of the Middle East.[8] Chaudhry (1997: 3) has put it in the starkest terms: "The boom decade [referring to the oil boom between 1973 and 1983] did not change a single political regime in the Arab world: indeed, in the vast majority of cases, the same political leaders who ushered in the boom were still in charge in 1996." In fact, the only possibility these authors see of opening, liberalizing, and eventually democratizing those polities is a fall in oil prices, the fiscal crisis of the state, and the related opportunities that may open for civil society groups and opposition parties to take advantage of state weakness.

This is the mirror image of the political economy argument that has long portrayed Venezuela's oil-induced development as conducive to democracy and the economic and fiscal crises caused by a drop in the oil prices as the main cause for its more recent ailments. Given the evidence coming from other major oil-exporting countries, one is forced to conclude that something must be wrong with the argument linking oil and democracy as applied to the case of Venezuela. If oil undermined Juan Vicente Gómez's grip on Venezuelan politics and society—as Karl argued in 1986—why has it not undermined the social bases for the various types of authoritarian regimes, from the most patrimonial monarchies to the most repressive sultanistic dictatorships, in the Middle East? Seen from the oil-hinders-democracy perspective, it seems as if Venezuela became democratic despite oil, not thanks to it.[9] In my view, Venezuela's democratic development is an anomaly in need of further explanation rather than a structurally determined outcome.

Coffee and Democracy in Colombia

By contrast with Venezuela, the many shortcomings of Colombia's democracy have often been accounted for by resorting to political-institutional factors (rather than socioeconomic ones), especially the role of the two traditional parties and their recurring pattern of conflict and negotiation.[10] Only a few scholars have attempted a structural explanation of Colombia's political trajectory, and they often place the structure of coffee production and its social implications—in terms of working-class formation and mobilization—at the center of their accounts. Clearly, the predominance of coffee production for export goes a long way toward explaining the evolution of Colombia's society and politics in the twentieth century, as demonstrated in the excellent work of the historians Charles Bergquist (1986a, 1986b), Marco Palacios (1983, 1995) and Frank Safford (2002). At the turn of the twentieth century, coffee already accounted for half of the total export of goods from Colombia; this share reached its peak in the 1960s, when it accounted for 75 percent of total exports.[11] The structure of the coffee export economy seems useful for explaining the late emergence of the labor movement, the inability of the left to place it under its control, and the ease with which the traditional parties first incorporated (in the 1930s) and then demobilized and repressed the most militant sectors of the labor movement (in the mid- to late 1940s).[12]

However, despite its centrality, coffee production for export seems insufficient for explaining the evolution of the political regime, the democratic breakdown of the late 1940s, and the process of redemocratization in the 1950s. Even Bergquist (1986b), who places a clear emphasis on the structure of the export sector and its attendant class configuration, recognizes that it is a combination of the structure of the coffee economy and the political system inherited from the nineteenth century that explains Colombia's political trajectory in the 1940s and 1950s. That is, even someone who is clearly convinced of the explanatory power of class-based analysis recognizes the importance of political variables for offering a full explanation of Colombia's political development.

If viewed from a political economy perspective, Colombia's political trajectory only adds to the puzzles encountered so far. An interesting comparison can be drawn between Colombia and other coffee exporters such as Brazil and the Central American nations regarding the impact of coffee on social evolution and political development, especially its effects on state formation and regime evolution.[13] A look at the literature on coffee and politics, however, makes the task of building a causal explanation of regime change with coffee production for export as the main independent variable seem rather daunting: no single parsimonious hypothesis could possibly account for the variation between Costa Rica's strong and stable democracy, Colombia's limited or restricted democracy, Brazil's punctuated history of regime change, and the various forms of authoritarianism characteristic of most Central American coffee-exporting countries (Guatemala, El Salvador, Honduras, and Nicaragua).

As shown in the excellent comparative analyses of Central America by Williams (1994), Paige (1997), and Mahoney (2001), coffee production for export, while accounting for some broadly similar socioeconomic consequences, does not seem to be a good predictor of either democracy or authoritarianism. Instead of deriving any political implications directly from coffee production, all these authors take great care to emphasize that coffee is only a common background condition and does not explain the variation in political outcomes among these cases. By contrast, they propose a variety of intervening variables—the social organization of the coffee industry, the role of public institutions, sociopolitical coalitions and/or elite ideologies—to explain why these similar coffee-exporting economies yielded such divergent political histories.

Despite the diversity of explanatory variables proposed by these authors, there is one issue on which most of them agree: one key difference among coffee exporters is the structure of land tenure within which coffee production takes place. If there is one common hypothesis in all these studies it is that whereas land-concentrated, hacienda production of coffee tends to be inimical to democracy, a structure of coffee production based on small peasant-owned farms should be conducive to a democratic outcome.[14]

Again, a comparison of Colombia with other coffee producers shows how much of an outlier Colombia is in relation to this generalization. Most analysts of the Colombian economy (Palacios 1983, 1995; Bates 1997; Palacios and Safford 2002) agree that Colombia's coffee expansion in the twentieth century was based on numerous, small-landholding peasants. This puts Colombia together with Costa Rica, Venezuela, and the Mexican state of Veracruz on one side of the landowning structure divide and Brazil, El Salvador, Guatemala, and Chiapas on the other, where various types of haciendas predominated as the basic unit of coffee production.[15] Nonetheless, Colombia did not follow the political trajectory that would be expected from a peasant-based, smallholder coffee economy. A relatively dispersed structure of ownership and production, composed by myriad independent, propertied coffee producers—apparently similar to the one found in Costa Rica—should have led, by most predictions, to a relatively dispersed power structure favorable to democracy. However, it first witnessed the emergence of an oligarchic democracy, which later broke down, leading to the bloodshed known as La Violencia (1948–58), and finally to a severely restricted version of democracy.

In closing this brief exploration of the staple-led hypothesis, we are thus faced with a paradox: despite oil being a good predictor of authoritarianism, Venezuela managed to build an inclusionary, competitive regime, while Colombia, with a coffee economy based on a relatively democratic distribution of land, faced enormous difficulties building a democratic order in the second half of the twentieth century. Given this paradoxical outcome, we ought to conclude that neither oil nor coffee nor any other staple can, in and of itself, account for the prospects of democratic development or regime change in any single country. Echoing Mahoney's (2001) critique of explanations of Central American political development grounded in the distinction between coffee republics and banana republics, my own findings tend to confirm his claim that "a limited focus on commodity differences has proved unable to explain twentieth-century regime outcomes" (18). Whether a specific export commodity is conducive to democracy or not depends not only on its social consequences, to which I now turn, but also and more importantly on the interaction of socioeconomic structures with political institutions such as the state, as well as on state-society relations as mediated by political organizations such as political parties. My study thus emphasizes the role of states and parties to a much greater degree than work that focuses on the impact of varying types of economic structures on political development.

Bourgeois, Peasant, and Middle Classes: Exploring Class-Based Hypotheses

One of the most obvious differences between Colombia and Venezuela is the social configuration spawned in each country by diverging models of economic development. In both cases the history of economic evolution has left indelible marks on their social and class structures, which some authors (e.g., Bergquist 1986b) have rightly pointed to as a key variable in explaining political development and change. In this section I explore the social implications of the two staple-led models of development discussed above, throwing light on the contributions as well as the shortcomings of arguments focused on social variables, in particular, class structure, as explanatory factors of regime change.

One of the long-term structural changes set in motion by oil in Venezuela was the acceleration of the decline of its agricultural sector. As Bergquist (1986b: 212) notes, "By 1950 Venezuelan agriculture supplied only one-fifth of the national market for food and industrial agricultural commodities. The rest was imported." This transformation had an important impact on social structure: the decline of the landowning elite and the parallel decline of a significant peasant population (see fig. 1.3). Oil quickened the pace of urbanization by promoting migration to the oil-producing zones as well as to the area surrounding the capital, Caracas. According to Bergquist, "Between 1920 and 1940 the population of the oil-producing states grew faster than the other parts of Venezuela, save for the Federal District (where the nation's capital, Caracas, was located)" (211).

The expanding volume of foreign trade also fostered the growth of urban import businesses, banks, and commercial services, which in turn spawned the emergence of new urban middle sectors made up of white-collar workers in the service sector, professionals, civil servants, students, intellectuals, and politicians. These middle sectors, which formed the new Venezuelan parties of the 1930s and 1940s, hold the key to the democratization of Venezuela in the second half of the twentieth century. The parties mobilized key social groups and forged the progressive alliance that finally brought democracy to Venezuela. That alliance, spearheaded by the urban elites, included two additional social sectors: a small but strategically placed working class[16] and a transitional peasantry. Oil production is a capital-intensive and technologically sophisticated enclave industry that depends on capital goods and technology much more than on labor. Thus the labor force employed in oil production tends to be small. However, the fact that the oil export sector provides most foreign exchange as well as the highest percentage of state revenue endows its workers with strategic bargaining power. The adjective *transitional,* as applied to the peasantry, means that the majority of the rural population was in the process of disappearing as smallholding peasants and was becoming urban workers and marginalized dwellers (see Powell 1971). These qualities were critical to determining the political behavior of these social sectors and their disposition to become crucial allies of the urban middle sectors in the fight against dictatorship and for a democratic political order.

Both Karl (1986) and Bergquist (1986b: 195, 204) stress the fact that oil spawned the social forces that undermined Gómez's dictatorial rule and promoted democracy in Venezuela. Whereas Bergquist puts all the emphasis on the working class, Karl pays more attention to the role of the middle sectors. Neither of them gives much importance to the crucial role played by the peasantry, organized mainly by Acción Democrática (AD; Democratic Action) into a powerful political actor, a fact stressed by Powell (1971). My account differs from all these authors in calling attention to the fact that it was not any of these social sectors alone but their powerful alliance forged and consolidated through the parties that eventually brought democracy to Venezuela.[17] Given the small size of the Venezuelan working class, especially the sectors engaged in oil production, it would be illusory to think that it was the oil workers alone who achieved the transformation of Venezuela's society and political order.[18] It was, instead, the workers together with the transitional peasantry and led by the urban middle sectors that spearheaded the struggle for democracy. My point, again, is that what mattered most was not a single, particular class or social sector but the coalition formed by these forces and crystallized in the vehicle of the multiclass populist party.

There is certainly a clear contrast between Venezuela's social configuration and the one we find in Colombia by the end of the 1950s; in the latter a landed oligarchy was entrenched, a majority of the population still lived in the rural areas (see fig. 1.3), the working class was small and weakly organized (see Bergquist 1986b), and both the bourgeoisie and the urban middle sectors had strong links with the landed elites. Two crucial differences between these two cases stand out regarding their social structures: the first is the persistence of a powerful landed upper class in the Colombian case versus its virtual disappearance in Venezuela; the second one is the different role played by the new urban middle sectors, who saw their capacity for maneuvering limited in the face of powerful landed interests.

In Karl's (1986: 200) words, "If the condition of the landed upper class is a key variable in the type of political outcomes that arise in the transition from agrarian societies, as Barrington Moore has argued, this class in Venezuela experienced a rapid transformation with the foreign introduction of an oil enclave. . . . Venezuelan landowners sold their property to the oil companies, converting themselves into the commercial and financial urban bourgeoisie that had once been their nemesis." Thus Moore's (1966) thesis concerning the landed upper classes and their negative impact on the prospects for democracy seems to hold, in the sense that their weakening and eventual disappearance in Venezuela constituted a facilitating condition for democratization in that country. By contrast, the persistence of a powerful landed oligarchy in Colombia could help explain not only the more conservative character of its transition but also many of the difficulties confronted in the years since its transition to democracy in 1958.

However, Moore's famous dictum, "no bourgeoisie, no democracy," does not seem to hold in either one of these cases. Oil tends to delay industrialization, and thus Venezuela became, just like Colombia, a late industrializer. In contrast to some Southern Cone cases where industrialization took off early in the twentieth century and was given a strong boost by the external shocks of World War I and the Great Depression, both Colombia and Venezuela began their industrialization processes relatively late. This tended to slow down the formation of those social classes commonly associated with capitalism (the bourgeoisie and the working class) and thus also delayed the onset of pressures to expand political participation, which usually accompany the process (see Collier and Collier 1991). Colombia's and Venezuela's respective bourgeoisies were weak: in Colombia the commercial and industrial bourgeoisie remained strongly linked to the landowning class, and like the state, it also depended on income from coffee exports (see Leal 1984). In Venezuela the landowners transformed into an incipient commercial and financial bourgeoisie, soon becoming a rentier class, closely linked with and dependent on state protection for survival.

By the same token, Rueschemeyer, Stephens, and Stephens's (1992) statement—summarized in the phrase "no working class, no democracy"—does not seem to hold in either case. In both Colombia and Venezuela the working class was small and became organized later compared to other major Latin American countries (Bergquist 1986b; Collier and Collier 1991). Rueschemeyer, Stephens, and Stephens's hypothesis could apply in the Venezuelan case only but with strong qualifications: as noted above, Venezuela had a very small but strategically placed working class, which became organized and mobilized by the political parties (first by the Communist Party of Venezuela [PCV] and later by AD).[19] Venezuela's workers were effective because of their alliance with organized peasants and with political parties, which were also excluded from the political system, and together engaged in mass action as well as in deliberation and negotiation, thus resembling Ruth Berins Collier's (1999: 168–69) "joint projects" scenario—a coalition of progressive middle sectors with labor. By contrast, the workers in Colombia were not as strong or organized, and they were definitely subordinated to the two traditional parties. They did not engage in either mobilization or negotiation, thus producing a more conservative transition in which the middle sectors predominated while the workers provided electoral support. In sum, while Colombia witnessed what can more clearly be labeled "democratization from above," in Venezuela there was certainly a much more intensive process of participation "from below."[20] In neither of these cases however, was there a strong organized working class that could accurately be portrayed as the decisive actor in the process of democratization—as was true in some of the European cases during earlier waves of democratization (see Rueschemeyer, Stephens and Stephens 1992; Collier 1999).

As stated by Collier (1999: 1), the working class is by no means "the only subordinate class, politically excluded group, or mass actor that has fought for democracy." Instead, in both Colombia and Venezuela a delayed industrialization process turned the middle sectors into the pivotal force behind the democratization process. There is, of course, nothing inherently democratic about the middle classes: "middle class movements played this role not because of any innately pro-democratic orientation on their part. . . . Rather, the reason for their prominence . . . is that, in class and political struggles among workers, employers, and the national state, urban middle classes occupy a uniquely strategic position" (Andrews and Chapman 1995: 17). It is their function as social "hinges" that drives the middle classes to build alliances in order to emerge as crucial actors on the social and political scene. Thus they can play a critical role in democratizing processes: when confronted with deeply entrenched landowning oligarchies in agrarian economies they can search for allies among rural and urban workers, as well as among the urban poor. They can also rapidly turn against their former allies, when they come to perceive an organized working class or a mobilized and radicalized urban mass as their social enemies; they then build alliances with the oligarchy and the military favoring military coups and dictatorships against the popular sectors (as was the case in the Southern Cone). Again, their behavior and power do not derive as much from an inherent or predetermined socioeconomic location or ideological outlook as from their strategic location as social pivot or hinge.[21]

In sum, unlike Moore's (1966) prediction about the role of the bourgeoisie, or Rueschemeyer, Stephens, and Stephens's (1992) characterization of the role of the working classes, the existence of democratic outcomes and their variations in Colombia and Venezuela are best explained by the role played by the new urban middle sectors, organized in political parties, as the pivotal actors in the making of the alliances, coalitions, and compromises leading to democracy (see table 1.2). In my view, the search for the "true revolutionary," "most progressive," or "most democratic" class (in which scholars have often engaged) seems rather fruitless. I contend, instead, that it is not one single class or social group that brings about democracy (or revolution, for that matter) but rather an alliance or coalition of social and political forces. Following in the steps of Huber Stephens (1989) and Yashar (1997), my analysis places a strong emphasis on coalition building and the role of sociopolitical coalitions in bringing about political and institutional change. In both Colombia and Venezuela, given that the working class was small and weak and organized late, the middle sectors that emerged as a result of the process of economic development and social modernization in the first half of the twentieth century became the crucial actors in the democratization process.[22] In both cases, as we shall see, they made use of a critical political instrument—political parties—to build their democratic coalitions. The struggle was made easier in Venezuela because of the weakness of the landowning classes and the related availability of a transitional peasantry to form a "radical populist" alliance (Collier and Collier 1991). In Colombia, by contrast, the upper landed classes retained much of their economic, social, and political power, and the peasantry, while large, was much weakened and disorganized by decades of interparty warfare in the countryside. Thus the coalition spearheaded by the middle sectors was much narrower and therefore more prone to accepting a more restricted form of democracy. Table 1.2 summarizes my findings regarding the role of different social classes in Colombia and Venezuela's democratization processes.

One should be careful, however, not to draw quick conclusions, deriving political consequences automatically from social or economic

Table 1.2. Colombia and Venezuela: Social Configuration by the Mid-Twentieth Century

	Working Class	*Bourgeoisie*	*Peasantry*	*Landowners*	*New Urban Middle Sectors*
Colombia	Small and weak	Strongly linked with landed oligarchy	Significant; disorganized, decimated by violence	Strong	Strongly linked with landed oligarchy
Venezuela	Small but strategic and well organized	Dependent on the state	Small but organized and mobilized by parties (AD and PCV)	Weak	Independent; no allies among dominant classes

configurations and short-circuiting the longer path that goes from socio-economic structures to institutions and on to contingent political choices and outcomes. The story of how these socioeconomic configurations led to democratic transitions and came to produce divergent patterns of regime evolution is by no means simple or mechanical. The process was, instead, strongly mediated by the emergence and evolution of two key political institutions: political parties and the state. As the next chapter makes abundantly clear, socioeconomic changes cannot produce democracy in the absence of institutions of political intermediation that are able to "translate" those transformations into political outcomes.

Structural Explanations and Their Limits

Perhaps the most controversial argument in this chapter is the one that downplays the role of oil in the making of Venezuelan democracy, since by implication it throws into question those explanations of regime change that attribute heavy weight to economic factors, especially to resource-driven models of development. This may appear to be a difficult argument to make given that the two cases under consideration differ a great deal in terms of their socioeconomic structures. However, comparisons among cases with similar structural features but different political outcomes lend support to my argument for the central role of political factors in democratization. A comparison of Venezuela with other oil-producing countries shows that in the absence of political mediation petroleum is not conducive—some even argue it is inimical—to democracy. Likewise, coffee is not able to adequately explain the political evolution of cases as dissimilar as Brazil, Colombia, and Costa Rica and other Central American republics. My main claim here is that even though a focus on "deep" socioeconomic or structural factors to explain divergent post-transition trajectories may be warranted and to a certain extent instructive, the incorporation of political variables is absolutely essential to explain variation in political development in Colombia and Venezuela.

In the next chapter I argue that the key to an explanation of regime change in these two cases lies first and foremost with the political parties, which in Venezuela were more modern, more organically tied to its population, and more representative of contemporary social cleavages than their Colombian counterparts. The Venezuelan political elites could also count on a coherent, autonomous, resourceful state that—if placed under the control of civilians—could back up and sustain a normative order, including the rules of the democratic game. Thus, instead of explaining the divergence in outcomes in Colombia and Venezuela's democratic evolution after 1958 exclusively as a result of differences in their socioeconomic configurations, I propose a framework in which economic factors are construed as causes of variation in the political sphere via the mediation of political institutions that translate economic and social change into actual political outcomes.

CHAPTER TWO

Beyond Oil and Coffee

The Political Foundations of Democratic Rule

It is not just the history of social and economic transformations that matters. This chapter calls for the recovery and full use of political history—understood not as a narrative of heroic leaders and epic battles but rather as a story of institutional evolution—as central to our understanding of contemporary politics. In particular, it makes the case for a focus on the emergence and consolidation of two crucial sets of political institutions, the state and the party system, which together shape the political choices and resources available to leaders in times of change, thus influencing subsequent regime trajectories.

As argued in the previous chapter, explanations based exclusively on socioeconomic structures seem insufficient and at times even misleading. Also insufficient are accounts primarily based on contemporary events and their short-term consequences (e.g., the crumbling of dictatorships, the mobilization of oppositions, the signing of party pacts). My account of the emergence and evolution of democracy in Colombia and Venezuela therefore challenges two conventional explanations of regime change and democratization: on the one hand, those that are strictly focused on socioeconomic determinants; on the other, those solely concerned with the short-term consequences of recent political events. A central premise of this chapter, therefore, is that to explain many significant political phenomena it is not enough to chart socioeconomic structures and their consequences; it is also necessary to observe how "the strategic behavior of leaders is shaped by and in turn shapes political institutions" (Shefter 1994: 3).

I seek to show how two important political institutions—the state and parties—shaped and in turn were shaped by the actions of leaders who negotiated institutional designs while pursuing their strategic interests.[1] These political institutions, I argue, play a major role in translating socioeconomic realities into political outcomes; they also embody the continuous influence of the past in the present.

Many authors have emphasized the role of parties in political outcomes in Latin America.[2] A few others have emphasized the role of the state.[3] My account draws from all these sources while making an additional contribution: it makes the argument that the timing and the sequence of the emergence of the state and the parties critically influence their behavior and interaction.[4] Neither the state on its own nor the parties by themselves provide a complete account of the fate of democracy. Rather the establishment of a central state is considered a prerequisite for the consolidation of competitive party politics. Thus the timing and sequence of their emergence and their interaction over time have a decisive impact on the prospects of building a long-lasting democratic polity.

State Consolidation and Regime Outcomes

States have been active participants and independent determinants of social, economic, and political transformations, not only in Latin America, but also in other regions of the developing world. As such, they need to be taken into account as independent variables in their own right.[5] Responding to a previous tendency to ignore the state when considering issues of democratization, the literature has recently emphasized the importance of the state for democracy. Rueschemeyer, Stephens, and Stephens (1992: 9), for example, concluded that "consolidation of state power was an essential prerequisite for democratization." In their view, it is not only the balance of power in society but also the structure, strength, and autonomy of the state apparatus and its relation with civil society that crucially affects democracy's future prospects. The consolidation of state power is a basic precondition for democratization, for without it there can be no institutionalization of contestation. For democracy to emerge and take hold, "overt challenges to state authority had to end, particularly challenges in the form of armed resistance, and the state had to be able effectively to claim a monopoly on the use of organized force" (Huber Stephens 1989: 285).[6]

Below I consider two crucial aspects in the evolution of the state in Colombia and Venezuela that, in my view, had a clear impact on subsequent political trajectories: the timing of state consolidation (relative to the timing of party formation) and the vehicles by means of which states managed to assert their control over their territories and populations. I argue that differences in the timing and experience of state consolidation are crucial to explaining variation in the subsequent patterns of regime evolution.

State Consolidation in Colombia and Venezuela

A relative lack of interstate wars, the economic legacies of the colonial period (including continued economic dependence and lack of economic integration), plus the sheer size of the territory, its geographic difficulties, regional diversity, and relatively low population densities, all contributed to delaying national unification and state centralization in Latin America.[7] As a result, "consolidation of the state apparatus and the establishment of effective control over a geographically defined continuous population were rather problematic. . . . In contrast to Western Europe, the tasks of consolidating state power and establishing a stable form of elite rule were more difficult, completed later than in Europe (if at all), and thus temporarily closer to the incorporation of newly emerging groups into the political system" (Huber Stephens 1989: 293).[8]

Against this common backdrop, however, there was some significant intraregional variation: the time it took for the different countries to solve the common challenges of border conflict, regional autonomy, power centralization, and the enforcement of rules varied from case to case. Throughout the nineteenth century state institutions in Chile, Argentina, and Mexico "grew stronger and were able to monopolize coercion, but others such as Uruguay, Colombia, and Venezuela remained weak and maintained only a feeble presence in the countryside" (López-Alves 2000: 2). In Colombia significant accumulation of power in the hands of the central state, in the wake of a sustained period of export expansion (based on coffee), did not happen until the beginning of the twentieth century.[9] In Venezuela high regional and economic diversity among the elites and the strong caudillo legacy from the independence wars delayed effective unification also until the beginning of the century. Significant export growth, based on coffee and cocoa, did not occur until this time (Huber Stephens 1989: 297–98).

Many scholars of Latin America have considered the period between 1870 and 1914 a key to explaining the political and economic trajectory of the region's states. These years have become the preferred testing ground for theories stressing the impact of the world economy and export expansion on power centralization.[10] My findings suggest that this period was indeed crucial not only for the reasons usually emphasized in political economy accounts but also for political reasons. It was in that period that the basic institutions of the state became consolidated throughout most of Latin America. In some cases, such as Colombia, where a party system also solidified in the second half of the nineteenth century, the modal patterns of interaction between the state, political parties, and social forces became a central and lasting feature of the political landscape.

In nineteenth-century Latin America political parties and the military were the main vehicles for nation building and state formation (López-Alves 2000). Although Colombia and Venezuela resemble each other in terms of the weakness of their states during the nineteenth century and their late consolidation in the early twentieth, they diverge markedly in two crucial respects: the timing of their emergence relative to that of political parties and the principal vehicle through which they achieved control over their respective jurisdictions. Whereas the parties, having predated the state, became the main vehicles for state formation in Colombia, it was the military caudillos (veterans of the independence wars) and later the army that played that role in Venezuela. The difference, I would like to emphasize, is not to be found in the material bases of state power since in both cases the late-nineteenth-century expansion of the coffee economy provided the impetus for the integration of the national economy into the international market, in addition to supplying the resources with which to build the foundations of a central state (see figs. 1.1 and 1.2).[11] Rather, I argue, the main difference between Colombia and Venezuela resides in the routes by which national unity and state consolidation were achieved: in Venezuela the main vehicles of state formation were first the regional caudillos and then the national military; in Colombia the mechanisms through which elites organized and institutionalized their competition for power were the two traditional parties. To quote from López-Alves's (2000: 2) pioneering comparative study on state making in Latin America: "a political elite, alongside the traditional coalition of landed and mercantile interests, crafted the state in Colombia, Chile, Uruguay, Argentina, and Peru; in Venezuela and Paraguay, however, the military and associated militias virtually created the state."

The process of centralization of state power was slow in both cases. In Venezuela the backbone of the state was formed by the military, with the nineteenth-century political parties fading away before the turn of the century. By contrast, in Colombia it was the parties that subordinated all other organized political actors, whether the state as a whole or the military, well into the twentieth century. López-Alves (2000) has argued that these divergent routes of state formation go a long way toward explaining regime outcomes in Latin America; in the two cases under discussion, they would account for the emergence of a restrictive democracy in Colombia and the persistence of autocracy in Venezuela. While I concur with López-Alves's description and analysis of the two cases, I disagree with his conclusions, especially with regard to their longer-term implications for regime evolution.[12] It may be true that a stronger state backed by a strong military paired with weak parties did not bode well for the emergence of democracy in Venezuela in the first decades of the twentieth century. Nevertheless, in the longer term, once Venezuela's modern parties appeared on the scene, the political-institutional landscape became much more favorable to pluralism and competition. Thus in the second half of the twentieth century a solid state provided a strong foundation for the representative and competitive party system that came to characterize Venezuela from 1958 to 1993. By contrast, the combina-

tion of a weaker state with a weaker military and strong parties characteristic of Colombia turned out to provide a very problematic foundation
for the longer-term development of a democratic order. The implications
of these two divergent routes toward state consolidation are spelled out
below.

Colombia

The Colombian experience of state formation from the early nineteenth century until well into the twenty-first century has been marked
by serious difficulties in centralizing power and monopolizing the use of
force. The latest cycle of violence gripping the country since the mid-
1980s is witness to the fact that Colombia's traditionally weak state has
not been able to gain control over its entire territory and population even
after two hundred years of independence.[13]

The centralization of power in Colombia has been slow, even when
compared with other Latin American states. Some historians (e.g., Palacios and Safford 2002) have pointed to the country's rough geography
and its derivative, regional diversity as a main reason for this. Indeed,
Colombia is home "to several ecosystems and rural economies that, at
times, did not even connect with one another commercially, much less
socially" (López-Alves 2000: 13). Efforts to centralize power and project
authority over the territory and population faced daunting obstacles due
to the country's complex geography, its regional and ecological diversity,
size, and population density.[14] David Bushnell (1993: 36) has dramatically captured the obstacles to state making and nation building in Colombia: "No part of Spanish America had so many obstacles to unity, so
many obstacles to transportation and communication per square kilo-
meter."

The Colombian central state remained weak throughout the nineteenth century. Indeed, as noted by López-Alves (2000: 19), "in countries
such as Colombia and Uruguay, the state was only one among many
competing organizations trying to extract resources and loyalty from the
population." The extreme political weakness of the Colombian state was
dramatically evidenced by its fiscal situation: as late as 1871 a well-known
political figure, Salvador Camacho Roldán, commented with great dis-
may that Colombia's total revenues were half those of El Salvador, a third

of Mexico's, a fourth of Venezuela's, a fifth of Chile's, and a sixth of Costa Rica's and Argentina's. In this regard Colombia was superior only to Honduras.[15]

It was not until the late nineteenth century that the country experienced intense power centralization and army building under the conservative coalition headed by Rafael Núñez, leader of La Regeneración, the so-called regeneration period.[16] Indeed, in Colombia "effective consolidation of state power and a first sustained period of export expansion, based on coffee, were delayed until the early twentieth century. Consequently, it was only after the end of the War of a Thousand Days in 1903 that the Conservative and Liberal oligarchic factions started to overcome their deep historical enmity and establish a viable system of elite contestation" (Huber Stephens 1989: 294–95). Coffee expansion at the end of the nineteenth century enhanced the capacity of this coalition of state makers to put in place reforms aimed at building a relatively centralized locus of national power (see Palacios 1983, 1995; Bergquist 1986a). For all its efforts, however, the coalition's relative success in creating the semblance of a central state did not do away with the parties or create an independent standing military. The central state remained weak, with little autonomy from the landed gentry, and the first standing army in Colombian history would have to wait until the early twentieth century (see Pizarro 1987a).

After the century's turn Colombia's weak state was epitomized by the loss of Panama. Dramatically debilitated after the last and fiercest of the civil wars of the century (the War of a Thousand Days) and defenseless against a regional rebellion, Colombia's central state had no option but to surrender the province of Panama (with an area of 77,082 sq. km) to an incipient independence movement, backed by the United States, in 1903.

The explanation for the secular weakness of the Colombian state lies in part in the structural factors noted above. The most important part of the story, however, rests on the responses elicited from political elites as they confronted these difficult structural conditions. It is therefore crucial to examine party formation and interparty competition. Two recognizable parties emerged in the 1849 elections and rapidly grew to be useful nationwide networks of elite representation and competition,

based on family and clientele.[17] From the mid-1800s they not only exercised "unmediated party rule" (as in Uruguay; see López-Alves 2000: 97)
but also became the key vehicles for nation building and state formation
in Colombia. For most of the nineteenth century and into the twentieth,
the Colombian state was "unable to reach down into the rural population, but the parties could and did" (López-Alves 2000: 101). In Colombia, as in Uruguay, political parties became state makers to such an extent
that it was difficult to separate them from the state, and competition between the two parties shaped the entire polity.[18]

The parties were central not only as mechanisms of participation
and representation but also as instruments of control, including the re-
cruitment of peasants into militias, which were later turned into standing armies. In other words, parties were not only the basis on which
citizenship and the nation were built; they were also the main vehicles
for army and state building. The main political parties, Liberals and
Conservatives, developed as durable organizations before most state institutions became consolidated. More than just the means for elite participation and representation, the Colombian parties became a substitute
for an almost nonexistent state: they solved conflicts and imposed order;
they settled disputes; they mobilized the wider population and incorporated them into politics. At times they also doubled as the coercive apparatus of the state, controlling territory and population, substituting for
the standing army or controlling it, and keeping private militias at their
disposal whenever they needed to control insurrections from below or
confront competing sources of regional authority and control. Eight civil
wars and more than fifty local and regional rebellions during the nineteenth century attest to this fact.[19] Indeed, party and state strength, including that of the army,[20] evolved in an inversely proportional fashion
in Colombia (Leal 1984: 28–53; López-Alves 2000: 135). As I discuss
below, this relationship affected not only state formation but also the nature of the parties and party system from then on: two political parties
emerged and consolidated early, the military and the state remained
weak, strong regionalism persisted, and the incorporation of the popular
sectors occurred through the parties rather than the state.[21]

An additional characteristic feature of Colombia's institutional landscape has been the enormous power of the Catholic Church. What is

peculiar about Colombia's path to modernity, alongside the notorious preponderance of its parties and the weakness of its state, is the central place occupied by the church throughout its republican history until well into the twentieth century (see Abel 1987; González 1997b). Despite its nonpolitical nature, the institution of the church has played a crucially important role in Colombia since colonial times, providing a measure of social control that at times the state could not.[22] At the end of the nineteenth century, when the process of state consolidation was under the aegis of liberal coalitions in most of Latin America (Mahoney 2001), in Colombia a conservative bipartisan coalition, with the strong support of the church hierarchy, gained control of the state (see Bergquist 1986a). This so-called República Conservadora lasted from 1886 to 1930. Thus, in Colombia, state consolidation, the expansion of the coffee export economy, and its incorporation into the world market all happened under the auspices of this conservative coalition. This fact partly explains the "conservative" character of Colombian politics throughout the twentieth century compared to the rest of Latin America.

In the final balance, though the subordination of the military to the parties, the slow pace of state consolidation, and the relatively low degree of centralization of power vis-à-vis regional elites favored the emergence of a relatively stable civilian regime in Colombia during the twentieth century—a regime characterized as an "oligarchic democracy" (Wilde 1982) or a "protodemocracy" (Solaún 1980)—the persistent weakness of the state also meant that in the long term democracy would not be able to establish firm roots. The theme underlying the many attempts to build and consolidate a democratic regime in Colombia was in the twentieth century, and remains in this century, the secular weakness of the state and its incapacity to broadcast power throughout the territory and population (see Bejarano and Pizarro 2004, 2005).

Venezuela

There is heated debate among historians of Latin America over the degree of continuity or discontinuity in the region's history and whether contemporary Latin America can be read and interpreted on the basis of its colonial heritage and distant past.[23] It is useful to keep in mind, however, that degrees of continuity or discontinuity are not uniform throughout the region; there are significant variations from case to case. Colombia and Venezuela are telling illustrations of this point.

Whereas Colombia's social, economic, and political development can be read as a slow, gradual process of evolution out of the past, with few dramatic ruptures or discontinuities, contemporary Venezuela has little resemblance to nineteenth-century, much less colonial, Venezuela. Neither its economy nor its society, state, or political parties can be interpreted as having evolved from the distant past. Venezuela stands out in Latin America for how little the colonial period and the nineteenth century shaped the modern scene. The long struggle for independence from Spain began a series of armed conflicts and civil wars that together wrecked the basis of colonial wealth and destroyed the small local aristocracy. Administrative decay and regional fragmentation were other consequences, making the central state mostly nominal throughout the nineteenth century and political parties little more than armed bands, often with marked regional bases and loyalties (Kornblith and Levine 1995: 39; see also Urbaneja 1978: 12–13). In Venezuela and in Argentina, "nineteenth-century tradition was interrupted, their political pasts separated from the present in a way that has no parallel in the Colombian case, due to massive migration and to discontinuities in their parties' histories," to mention only two features (Deas 1999: 28). In the words of Dan Levine (1973: 14), "Modern political life began for Venezuela in 1936. The forces unleashed, the organizations created, and the positions assumed in that year set the pattern for subsequent political change and conflict."

Venezuela's dramatic transformation owes a great deal, obviously, to the development of the oil industry and its impact on society and politics—a fact emphasized by Karl (1997) and Coronil (1997), among others. There is, however, a political dimension in the country's transformation that began well before oil became the center of Venezuela's economy: the disappearance of the nineteenth-century Liberal and Conservative Parties, the consolidation of a powerful centralized state, and the central role played by the military in that process. Again, I wish to stress precisely this political dimension, if only to emphasize the incomplete nature of the structural explanations that tend to dominate in some accounts of Venezuela's political development.

After independence the balance of power in Venezuela tipped in favor of military caudillos and the military rather than civilian elites. Throughout the nineteenth century, neither the parties nor the army took the lead in the process of state formation; rather, as López-Alves (2000: 195) writes, "armed groups under the leadership of war veterans did, and the period of independence evolved into the most intense war-making situation of the cases considered [i.e., Uruguay, Colombia, Argentina, Venezuela, and Paraguay]." Most of the commanders of the Bolivarian liberation army were of Venezuelan origin, and after the separation of Venezuela from Gran Colombia (1830) deep divisions emerged among these generals, with no single group achieving permanent control. The decentralized caudillo armies were clearly an avenue for social mobility as well as a vehicle for the incorporation of the population into politics. Caudillo rule was, however, very unstable. As the long tenures of José Antonio Páez (1830–63) and Antonio Guzmán Blanco (1870–88) demonstrate, these "gifted caudillos" were able to build the semblance of a state, but these were not institutionalized forms of rule and they did not survive their founders.[24] Furthermore, throughout the nineteenth century "links between these armies and the central state remained loose, thus failing to create a central army as in Paraguay" (López-Alves 2000: 195).

A central army did not emerge until the early twentieth century in Venezuela, and the centralization of power was slow, as in Colombia. While similar in this regard, the main difference between the two cases remains the dominance of military elites as state builders in Venezuela, as opposed to the dominance of party leaders and organizations in Colombia. As in much of Latin America, post-independence Venezuela saw the rise of two parties, the Liberals and the Conservatives. Unlike in Colombia, however, these parties never took root, and whatever little party activity existed was severely affected by the Federal War (1859–63)[25] and finally dismantled during the Guzmán Blanco dictatorship. Throughout the nineteenth century military caudillos largely substituted for parties. As López-Alves (2000: 197) recounts, "Party building did not prosper, and civilians remained the weaker partner in ruling coalitions." By the close of the century the traditional cleavage dividing Liberals and Conservatives had all but disappeared from the Venezuelan political landscape.

Miguel Angel Centeno (2002: 109) has aptly summarized the process of consolidation of a central state in Venezuela at the turn of the twentieth century: "Guzmán Blanco established centralized control and the fifty years of *Andinos* established political peace."[26] During Guzmán Blanco's tenure "the state grew stronger in terms of the administration of services and tax collection, but it remained unable to monopolize coercion" (López-Alves 2000: 202). This would happen only after 1899, when Cipriano Castro seized power at the head of a coalition of Andean landowners and military leaders. Under the leadership of Castro, the so-called Revolución Restauradora (Restoration Revolution) became a turning point in the process of state making in Venezuela. Important steps toward state consolidation were taken under Castro, when the caudillos lost significant influence as "independent war machines" (López-Alves 2000: 203) as a consequence of the superior military might of the Andean army. Castro did not negotiate or share power with other caudillos, and the construction of a central standing army began. It later became consolidated under the long authoritarian rule of his lieutenant, Juan Vicente Gómez (1908–35). Gómez "imposed his authority over local strongmen, built a stable system of national finances and administration, professionalized the military, improved the physical infrastructure connecting Venezuela's regions, and thus laid the foundations of Venezuela's modern, centralized state" (Yarrington 2003: 10).

Castro's and Gómez's rule marked a fundamental break with the past. Until then, argues Steve Ellner (1995: 98), "Venezuela was even more fragmented and subject to continuous internal warfare than its Latin American neighbors. Gómez established a centralized state that . . . has been altered in form but not in substance over the years." Castro's and Gómez's main contributions to state consolidation were the elimination of caudillo warfare and the formation of a national army.[27] What remains debatable is the common claim that Gómez's success in centralizing political and military structures depended on "deriving enough revenue from the oil industry to finance the expanded bureaucracy and new projects" (Ellner 1995: 98)[28]—a claim that suffers from a basic flaw in terms of timing: oil came after, not before, state consolidation. Any explanation of state formation in Venezuela has to confront the critical problem of timing, for as Yarrington (2003: 11) has put it, "By the time oil wealth began to flow freely in the 1920s, Gómez had already been in power well over a decade, his hold on Venezuela had become virtually unbreakable, and the system that would continue until his death in 1935 was largely in place." Admittedly, in Gómez's time the Venezuelan state was by no means a modern, legal bureaucratic state but a patrimonial one (see Karl 1997). However, the fact remains that the three main tasks central to state building (i.e., differentiation from society, centralization of authority, and monopolization of coercion) had already been achieved in Venezuela by the time oil became its main source of revenues—in the second half of the 1920s.

Rather than oil, it was the expansion of coffee production for export that provided the material basis for state consolidation in Venezuela during the first quarter of the twentieth century.[29] In both Colombia and Venezuela the process of creating a viable post-independence state and consolidating its control over the rest of society lasted beyond the turn of the century, "for only then was the mutually supportive dynamic of export expansion and consolidation of effective state power under the aegis of export interests fully consummated" (Bergquist 1986b: 202). It was coffee, in both countries, that first provided a stable link with the international economy and a stable foundation for a viable state. Bergquist writes, "By the end of the [nineteenth] century coffee accounted for about three-fourths of Venezuela's expanding volume of foreign exchange and contributed . . . the bulk of the government's revenue" (203). The growing importance of the coffee economy finally propelled a regional ruling class (i.e., Castro and his followers, called the Andinos) from the Andean coffee state of Táchira into contention for national political power. "Beginning in 1908 . . ., after a decade of depression, coffee prices began a steep upward spiral that continued for two decades. . . . [D]uring this period [which coincides with Gómez's rule] the value of coffee exports more than doubled" (203). Thus, as in Colombia, the expansion of coffee production for export, not oil, initially provided the material basis for state formation in Venezuela.[30]

This is not to deny the profound impact the emergence and development of the oil industry would have on Venezuela's state and society. Since the late 1920s and early 1930s oil has endowed the central state with a source of income that offered enormous distributive possibilities as well as autonomy from the economic elites—two features that the Colombian state sorely lacked.[31] Oil certainly added to the impetus of state centralization and consolidation in Venezuela; however, it did not cause it. By the time oil emerged as an important source of revenue, there was already a central state and a standing army, products of the centralization efforts initiated by Guzmán Blanco in the 1870s and continued under Castro and Gómez. What Gómez did, of course, was to cleverly use the advantages provided by oil income, notably the autonomy from the domestic economic elites, to further the process of centralizing authority in the hands of the central state, increasing its coercive power and beginning a serious expansion of its administrative apparatus.[32]

To paraphrase Centeno's (2002) argument regarding the impact of wars on state making, neither war nor export expansion, in and of itself, produces states. Both need a preexisting political logic to yield the expected outcome. The discovery of oil and the rise of the oil industry in Venezuela did not make the Venezuelan state; instead, oil provided additional resources with which to boost a state that was already in the making when oil became the main staple of Venezuela's economy. By then the basic tasks of centralization and pacification had already been accomplished. What really mattered was that the organizational and political bases of the state were in place before the advent of the oil bonanza.

What, then, are the implications of this pattern of state formation for the prospects of building a democratic regime? As López-Alves (2000) has argued, a strong military did not bode well for the future of democracy in Venezuela. Instead, it portended the protracted influence of the military in Venezuelan politics, where democracy was absent throughout the first half of the twentieth century, save the brief and failed experience of the Trienio years (1945–48). However, as I discuss below, the consolidation of a strong state in the early twentieth century set the stage for the emergence of modern representative parties such as Acción Democrática, the Communist Party of Venezuela (PCV), and the Social Christian Comité Político Electoral Independiente (COPEI), which mobilized and incorporated the various interests in Venezuelan society. Because the establishment of a central state is conceived here as a precondition for the emergence and consolidation of competitive politics, the Venezuelan experience of state and party formation turned out to be, quite paradoxically, more favorable for democracy than the one observed in Colombia.

I have argued that in state formation and consolidation Colombia and
Venezuela did not differ in terms of timing (both were late) or in terms
of material bases. Major differences appear in the extent to which the
state was successful at centralizing power and monopolizing the use of
violence and of the main vehicle used by state makers to do so, political
parties in Colombia versus military caudillos and, later, the army in
Venezuela. Venezuela's state makers were more successful than their Colombian counterparts in terms of wresting power from the regional elites
and concentrating it at the center during the first decades of the twentieth century. Simultaneously, they also were more successful in eliminating the use of violence throughout society and monopolizing coercion
in the hands of the state.[33] Since the consolidation of Gómez's rule, any
inclination to political violence had practically disappeared from the
Venezuelan repertoire of political action. Gómez and his correspondents,
however, had a much more critical view of the Colombian government's
capacity to govern its territory: they saw it as "a 'lyrical' government,
without administrative energy or command power, upon which not
much could be trusted."[34]

Once the core of a viable state had been established, oil served the
purpose of endowing the Venezuelan state with abundant resources,
thereby helping it achieve a degree of autonomy from the landed elites,
accelerating the pace of bureaucratization and enhancing the state's administrative capacity. By contrast, the Colombian state has remained
much more dependent on the extraction of resources from entrenched
economic elites; especially the landed elites. Therefore, at the moment of
the transition in the late 1950s, the Venezuelan parties could count on a
coherent, autonomous, resourceful state apparatus that was potentially
"usable" by the civilian elites in order to uphold the newly created rules
of the game. By contrast, the Colombian state, historically much weaker
than its Venezuelan counterpart, had been partially destroyed by civil
strife and spiraling violence during the decade referred to as La Violencia. At the moment of the transition to democracy, the starting point in
the Colombian case was a negative-sum situation with a very weak and
precarious state and a very weak and fragmented civil society. Both had
to be rebuilt almost from scratch. That consolidating state authority and
control over the territory and society remained an incomplete task in

Colombia—whereas it was achieved with relative success in Venezuela—has contributed to the difficulties of institutionalizing contestation witnessed to this day.

The consolidation of state power is a necessary but by no means sufficient condition for the creation and stabilization of a democratic regime. In addition, a set of vehicles for participation and representation, namely, two or more political parties or a party system, must emerge and become stabilized. Any explanation of the emergence or trajectory of democracy would be incomplete if it did not take into account the emergence of political parties and the consolidation of a party system and their intereaction with the state.

Parties and Party Systems: Patterns of Conflict and Cooperation

It may seem superfluous to state at this point that the emergence of at least two political parties and the institutionalization of competition between them constitute a decisive democratic breakthrough. The argument has been made by major scholars of democracy such as Dahl (1971) and Sartori (1976) and has recently been pressed even further by Mainwaring and Scully (1995) and Mainwaring (1999b). Parties make institutionalized, nonviolent, intraelite competition possible; this obviously reduces the chances for appeals to military intervention in politics, which in turn makes the transition to and stabilization of democracy possible. On the other hand, parties play a crucial role in the incorporation of subordinate classes, a process that is crucial for the transition to a full democracy. Both contestation and inclusion are vital dimensions of democracy (Dahl 1971), and parties contribute significantly to making them possible.[35]

There are, of course, different types of parties and party systems. Following in the steps of Collier and Collier's (1991) celebrated study, my comparison of Colombia and Venezuela makes the case that these differences are consequential for the long-term evolution of democracy. Two visible contrasts between the Colombian and Venezuelan parties receive attention here. First, whereas Colombian parties have typically been classified as elitist, based on clientelistic exchanges of votes for patronage (see Archer 1995), the Venezuelan parties have been variously classified as ideological, programmatic, mass based, and even, by one account, "radical populist" (Collier and Collier 1991). Second, whereas polarization and conflict have characterized the interaction between the two traditional parties in Colombia, competition and cooperation have been the hallmarks of the relationship between parties in Venezuela. This apparent contrast between the parties and party systems in the two countries is of great consequence for my explanation of regime evolution.

Huber Stephens (1989: 323–24) makes the distinction between ideological or programmatic mass parties and traditional clientelistic ones while proposing a political economy explanation of the emergence and role of political parties: "In mineral export economies, ideological mass parties emerged and mobilized alliances between middle and working classes. . . . In agrarian export economies, clientelistic parties emerged and promoted alliances between the middle classes and sectors of elites and/or the military, while appealing for popular support on a patronage basis."[36] I propose instead a political explanation of party building and strength that puts the emphasis on the timing and sequence of state and party consolidation. In his article "The State as a Conceptual Variable" (1968), J. P. Nettl argued that the state has a fundamental role in determining the character and strength of parties, as well as their capacity to actually represent social cleavages.[37] Variation in stateness (or the degree of state consolidation), according to Nettl, has considerable influence on the form and strength of parties.

> In empirical terms, the existence of a strong state has considerable effect on the development of parties. It can be shown that where states exist, parties tend largely to be the institutionalization of social cleavage—and this usually means a multiparty system. Where no state exists, however, parties carry a much larger functional weight. They become engines of authority-legitimation (not now provided by the state); where this is the case the structured articulation of interests and/or cleavages in party terms is inhibited. . . . The very absence of the state has often been largely responsible for transforming parties of representation into vehicles of government. (1968: 517)

This clever conceptualization of the relationship between state and party strength greatly contributes to making sense of the different trajectories observed in the cases under consideration here. While Nettl's first hypothetical case fits Venezuela rather closely (with a strong state preceding the formation of the parties), the second hypothetical case (parties substitute for the state and claim parity with if not priority over it) fits Colombia's experience quite well. As predicted by Nettl, this difference had strong implications for the extent to which parties in Colombia and Venezuela came to effectively represent salient societal cleavages.

As Shefter (1994: 4) argues, a state-centered analysis "is useful for understanding the conditions under which strong political parties will develop."[38] Shefter's central argument is that "the *relationship* between political parties and public bureaucracies is of crucial importance in shaping the behavior of politicians. The relative *timing* of democratization and bureaucratization has crucially influenced the character of political parties both in Europe and America" (xi–xii; emphasis added). The relative strength of the state and parties and the timing of their emergence have major consequences for the structure of political parties and for the electoral strategies they are able to pursue: "If political parties are the stronger institution, they will be in a position to extract patronage from the bureaucracy and to distribute it to the cadres who conduct their campaigns and the voters who support their candidates; if parties are weaker than bureaucracies, they must find some alternative means of mobilizing popular support" (61). In addition, the relationship between the state and parties hinges on whether the parties are formed by elites within or outside the incumbent regime at the moment of their formation. This leads to Shefter's basic distinction between "internally mobilized" and "externally mobilized" parties. While internally mobilized parties are formed by "elites who occupy positions of authority within a regime . . . in order to gain, retain or exercise power,"[39] externally mobilized parties "are established by leaders who do *not* occupy positions of power in the prevailing regime and who seek to bludgeon their way into the political system by mobilizing and organizing a mass constituency" (5; original emphasis).

Nettl and Shefter provide an interesting vantage point for an interpretation of the contrast between Colombia's and Venezuela's parties:

while the Colombian parties were internally mobilized and preceded the emergence of a consolidated state, remaining stronger than the state at least until the second half of the twentieth century, the Venezuelan externally mobilized parties emerged after the consolidation of a relatively powerful and resourceful state but also remained without access to it until the late 1950s (except for a very brief hiatus between 1945 and 1948).

In terms of their origins, the main difference between the Colombian and Venezuelan parties is the timing of their emergence. While the Colombian parties emerged in the mid-nineteenth century, Venezuela's parties began only after Juan Vicente Gómez's death in 1935.[40] As noted above, Colombia presents a stark contrast with Venezuela in terms of the former's greater degree of continuity with its past; indeed, the latter experienced a rupture with its past in the early twentieth century. These different degrees of continuity or discontinuity are related, to a great extent, to the parties' own history: more than any other institution, the two traditional (Liberal and Conservative) parties weave a thread of continuity throughout Colombian political history. While those parties were the main actors controlling and exercising political power in Colombia from the 1850s onward, Venezuela's parties only had a short glimpse of access to state control during the brief Trienio period.

Colombia

At the beginning of the twentieth century, after the last and most debilitating of Colombia's civil wars, President Rafael Reyes launched a major effort to build and strengthen the Colombian state (see Mesa 1980). Despite his efforts, his own power and the power of the state remained severely limited by the Liberal and Conservative Parties, which came out of the civil war with their status intact as the most important institutions for social and political control in the country. The short-lived civilian dictatorship led by Reyes (1904–9) was overthrown by a bipartisan coalition called the Unión Republicana, which reasserted bipartisan control of the state and the electoral process from 1909 onward. As in Uruguay, and unlike Venezuela, the opposition party did not disappear but alternated in periods of one-party hegemony, reinforcing the two-party system (see Oquist 1978; Abel 1987).

Due in part to the weakness of the state, the elite Colombian parties held sway over Colombian politics from the mid-1800s until the last quarter of the twentieth century (see Oquist 1978). Relative to all other institutions—the state, the army, and even the Catholic Church—the two traditional political parties were by far the most important political institution in Colombia for more than a century.

They emerged in the mid-nineteenth century as expressions of cleavages that divided the elites along religious lines (the proper role for the church in society and politics), regional lines (the periphery vs. the center, otherwise expressed as a preference for federalism vs. centralism), and their opposite conceptions of how to deal with the legacies of the colonial past (those willing to preserve them vs. those wishing to make a radical break from them). Some authors have tried to present the Liberal and Conservative Parties as representatives of different social classes (Colmenares 1968; Leal 1984), with the Liberals representing the emerging commercial, industrial, and financial bourgeoisie and the Conservatives representing the more traditional landed oligarchy. Safford (1977) and González (1997a) have made a convincing case against this interpretation, arguing instead that ideological, religious, and regional cleavages seem to be more relevant in explaining the origins of party competition in Colombia. Although the original divisions eventually disappeared, party identities not only remained but also became stronger over time, aided by the violent history of interparty competition and conflict. The two parties ended up forming two different political "subcultures" (Sánchez and Meertens 1983), or sectarian identities, with strong emotional appeal, though not necessarily tied to socioeconomic cleavages. For most of their existence the two parties' membership has comprised all classes while their national-level leadership historically has been drawn from the elites.

Both parties were built on a predominantly agrarian society. As discussed in the previous chapter, in Colombia there was a significant peasant population and a strong landed oligarchy with a great degree of influence on society, as well as on the state (see fig. 1.3 and table 1.2). A peculiar characteristic of the evolution of parties in Colombia is that these rural bases of support were not concentrated in one single party; they were shared by both parties, with both the Liberals and the Conservatives having a strong hold in rural areas and a strong representation of the landed oligarchy among their leadership.[41] This is one of the reasons that the democratization process may have yielded a more conservative outcome in the Colombian case: the two parties that took part in the negotiated agreements of the late 1950s kept strong ties with the landed oligarchy. By its very nature the sociopolitical coalition behind the Colombian transition was more prone to preserving the interests of the privileged elites than to representing and incorporating the excluded sectors of society.

In terms of the patterns of interparty conflict and cooperation, abundant literature shows that the relationship between the two traditional parties in Colombia followed a consistent pattern of conflict and confrontation from the mid-1800s to the mid-twentieth century.[42] Although the country holds one of the longest records of electoral competition in Latin America,[43] there is a parallel history of violence and interparty warfare. Some authors have emphasized the recurrent use of coalitions between the traditional parties as the defining feature of the Colombian party system and political process.[44] Some have even considered it natural that the crisis in the late 1950s would have been overcome by a bipartisan coalition, given an alleged historical tradition of conciliation in the Colombian political system.[45] But one should not lose sight of the fact that the majority of the coalitions before the Frente Nacional (National Front) pacts were only tactical and transitory, with the parties cooperating merely for defensive tactical purposes when faced with political crises. Moreover, coalition governments usually served as a bridge between one hegemonic period and another: "Partisan hegemonies in Colombia, generally, need a transitory coalition government before their consolidation" (Oquist 1978: 14). The propensity toward bipartisan coalition coexisted with a contrary inclination to impose governments that completely excluded the opposition party, also a historical feature of the Colombian party system. To a certain extent, the survival and reproduction of the Colombian political parties depended on a convulsive combination of these two predispositions. As Abel writes:

> It is possible to extrapolate two traditions in Colombian politics starting in the decade of 1840s . . . ; one tradition of conflict between the two parties at the national level, . . . and one tradition of cooperation between the conciliatory factions of the rival parties in

order to modify the radical position of the intransigent factions. The relationship between these two traditions constituted the main key for the survival of the two parties throughout the nineteenth century, and it can be said that it continues until today. (1987: 17)

The following dates provide evidence of the balance between the co-operative and conflictive tendencies of parties in Colombia. Between the years 1910 and 1958,[46] there were intermittent coalition governments in 1910–14, 1930–34, 1945–46, 1946–47, and 1948–49. In other words, bipartisan coalition governments came into being and functioned during a little over one quarter of those forty-eight years. Each of these periods reflected moments of high political tension, when the system was on the verge of a crisis, deep divisions between the elites arose, or a threat from below emerged. Bipartisan coalitions substituted for military interventions: the traditional parties' strength and their propensity to coalesce in the face of critical junctures certainly account, to a large extent, for the scarcity of military interventions in Colombian politics (Leal 1984). Instead of long-lasting cooperative solutions, however, most of these coalition governments were a prelude to the building of a hegemonic government: the Republican Union (1910–14) preceded the Conservative hegemony, which lasted until 1930; the National Concentration (1930–34) preceded the Liberal hegemony, which lasted until 1946; and the various coalitions between 1945 and 1949 preceded the rebuilding of the Conservative hegemony (1946–53).

Despite its tradition of electoral competition, Colombia cannot show a clean record of open, free, and fair elections. Initially there were formal restrictions on suffrage (partially lifted in 1936 when universal male suffrage was granted). There was also a history of fraud, as well as a recurrent dynamic of interparty conflict that threatened the electoral process at each and every turn. A common way to avoid open confrontation was for one of the two parties to completely abstain from participating in electoral contests, which simultaneously was a way to sabotage the elections.[47] During the presidential elections of 1922, 1930, and 1946—the only three electoral episodes between 1922 and the regime's breakdown in 1949 in which the two parties openly competed for the presidency—there was partisan violence. In short, from 1922 until the time of the transition there was not one single presidential election in which the parties could compete openly and peacefully.

For the purposes of my argument, it is important to emphasize the tendency toward antagonistic conflict because of what it implies as an obstacle to the institutionalization of a loyal opposition and the consolidation of a competitive party system. The extreme levels of intensity and antagonism reached by the partisan division in Colombia hindered the creation of a common terrain—a political community—within which political adversaries could establish a relationship based on a common normative framework. Much to the contrary: from their inception until the late 1950s the two parties framed their relation as one of mutual exclusion, behaving like enemies.[48] The absence of this notion of a common, shared terrain between the parties has long prevented the toleration of an opposition party with all its prerogatives, legal and political. The existence and survival of the opposition came to depend instead on the incumbent party's benevolence or need to share power and disappeared automatically as soon as this party (whichever one of the two) foresaw the opportunity to gain absolute control of the state apparatus and exclude its enemy. Amid such convulsive alternation between coalition tactics and warfare, it was impossible to build and solidify a set of rules of the game that could turn the opposition into a permanent, legitimate institution.

Colombia's two main political parties have thus played an enduring and significant, if not always positive, role in the country's political development. In part because of their early emergence and in part because of the social coalitions that stood behind them, they have generally been more predisposed to act as "vehicles of authority legitimation" (Nettl 1968) and to defend the interests of the elites rather than incorporate and represent the excluded. The kind of representation they have offered, moreover, has mostly been of a clientelistic type rather than ideological or programmatic. Because of their clientelistic nature, they have acted as central pillars of the political system, contributing more to stability than to change. Yet given its tradition of hostile, sectarian competition and violent conflict, Colombia demonstrates that "the breakthrough/close down cycle of radical mass parties could also occur with clientelistic parties when mobilization levels were sufficiently high and party leaders had lost control over their organization" (Huber Stephens 1989: 309).

Venezuela

The last civil war of nineteenth-century Venezuela (the "Restoration Revolution") was won by the last of the great caudillos, Cipriano Castro. Castro was later ousted by his own lieutenant, Juan Vicente Gómez, who became Venezuela's omnipotent ruler between 1908 and 1935. The Conservative Party had disappeared from the political landscape after the Federal War (1858–63). In the last quarter of the nineteenth century the antagonism between Venezuela's Liberals and Conservatives faded out of existence, and Gómez's long reign put an end to what remained of that country's partisan tradition (Kornblith and Levine 1995: 40; Deas 1999: 44–47). Gómez strengthened the central state as an institution of social and political control, and the caudillos saw their power wither away with the disbanding of their regional militias. Perhaps with the sole exception of the weak and very circumscribed social influence retained by the Catholic Church, Gómez managed to centralize and concentrate all power in his own hands.

In Venezuela the Gomecista state predominated over any other social or political organization, and the nineteenth-century party tradition simply disappeared. Venezuela remained a state-dominated society during Gómez's rule. During the 1930s the young student leaders who were exiled after the student demonstrations of 1928 traveled to Costa Rica, Colombia, postrevolutionary Mexico, the United States, and Europe, where they came into contact with new political ideas and modern, mass-based parties.[49] The new parties that were born in Venezuela after Gomez's death and the return of the exiles in 1936, were inspired by the European-style modern mass-based parties.[50] One of their most important characteristics is that they kept no ties whatsoever to the traditional oligarchic parties of the nineteenth century. Nor was the population in Venezuela tied to those traditional partisan identities. The newly emerging social groups had little connection to older elites or to political structures of the past. Their needs and demands found no legitimate vehicle of expression, thus opening the way for organizers of new movements.

In the words of the historian and former Venezuelan president Ramón J. Velásquez, Venezuela was "like plowed land waiting for the seed."[51] In the Venezuela of the 1920s and 1930s there was plenty of available political space to build a qualitatively different type of party, more modern in organizational structure and more closely tied to the new groups emerging out of Venezuela's rapid social transformation, with an ideological discourse and a program that addressed the concerns of the excluded.[52] Because they emerged after the successful centralization of power in the hands of the state and also because they were externally rather than internally mobilized, the modern Venezuelan parties (not only AD and COPEI but also the URD and the PCV) had greater incentives to mobilize, organize, incorporate, and represent a wider range of interests that had no representation under the Gomecista regime.

Venezuela's social and political configuration was thus more favorable to the emergence of parties that were not the natural representatives of the oligarchy and had a higher stake in incorporating and representing the excluded. As Karl (1986: 200) has argued, one of the most important political effects of the oil-induced decline of agriculture in Venezuela was the elimination of a rural basis of support (a strong landed elite or a significant peasant population) either for a conservative political party, which could shift the political spectrum to the right, or for a peasant revolution. The Venezuelan parties that emerged in the 1930s became instead the forgers and carriers of a new progressive coalition between the new urban middle sectors, the organized working class, and the mobilized peasantry. This is what gives them, according to Collier and Collier (1991), their character as "radical populist" parties.[53] Given that they mobilized outside the established political system, with few political allies, while facing substantial resistance from the incumbent regime, their leaders had no alternative but to build a strong party organization.

Thus while it is true that the social transformations brought about by the oil industry provided the middle class in Venezuela with autonomy vis-à-vis the landed elite and the potential to pursue a reformist course in alliance with the workers and the peasants, the role of leaders, the kinds of resources at their disposal, and the degree of resistance encountered in their quest for political power should also be a central part of the explanation. Besides the impact of the oil economy on party politics in Venezuela, "the activity of political organizers and leaders, many of whom had returned from exile in 1935, was of crucial importance for strengthening civil society and its political articulation" (Huber Stephens 1989: 311).

During the 1930s and the 1940s, the formative period of the Venezuelan parties, the parties competed to capture the "available masses," especially the oil workers and the peasants.[54] Gradually AD won the competition for the allegiance of the organized working class. In addition, AD was for a long time the sole organizer and main beneficiary of the peasant leagues, which later would form the Federation of Venezuelan Peasants (FCV) (Powell 1971). Parties may have competed to build their own bases of support, but since political power was overwhelmingly concentrated in the hands of the dictatorial regime, they could not compete for access to or control of the state. In Venezuela political parties emerged under the authoritarian regime, mobilized from without, and finally crystallized as the vehicles that made possible a new opposition coalition among the emerging urban middle sectors, the small but strategic working class, the transitional peasants, and even some sectors within the military. In particular, "the leaders of AD engaged in intense organizing activity which enabled them to ally with sectors of the military and force a breakthrough by coup to full democracy in 1945" (Huber Stephens 1989: 312). The 1945–48 attempt to bring democracy via a coup d'état was the first effort on the part of this new coalition to upset the ancien régime.

When AD came to power for the first time in 1945, it was the most successful party in Venezuelan politics: it had managed to organize the unorganized—the peasantry—and it had won the contest against the PCV for the control of the trade unions. AD successfully translated its social power into electoral majorities and easily swept all elections convoked during the Trienio years (see table 2.1).

Riding into power on this indisputable electoral support, the AD succumbed to the temptation of majoritarian rule. Its leadership calculated that it could afford to underestimate its adversaries, including the church, the business elites, and the military. Moreover, its attempt to build a hegemonic party system rapidly alienated even those who could have been its most important allies: the newly emerging parties, COPEI

Table 2.1. Venezuela: Electoral Results, 1945–1948

Year	Type of Election	AD	COPEI	URD	PCV
1946	Constituent Assembly	78.4	13.2	4.3	3.6
1947	Legislative elections	70.8	20.3	4.3	3.6
1947	Presidential election	74.4	22.4	–	3.2
1945–48	Average	74.5	18.6	4.3	3.4

Source: Data from Levine 1985: 55–56, tables 1 and 2.

and URD, which had a stake in creating and maintaining a competitive political system. The Trienio's experiment in majoritarian democracy was crushed under the weight of its radical policy postures (which alienated the elites, the church, the U.S.-backed oil companies, and the military) but also under the weight of increasing conflict between the ruling party and the emerging opposition parties.[55]

Immediately after the 1948 coup the AD and its affiliated organizations, the FCV and the Confederación de Trabajadores de Venezuela (CTV), were banned by the military regime. Its leaders were forced to go underground, and many of them were imprisoned, exiled, or killed during the dictatorship. A few years later very little of AD's previous organizational apparatus existed; the remnants barely survived as clandestine networks of students, workers, and political activists. Two years later, in 1950, the PCV was also outlawed by the dictatorship. Its militants joined AD's cadres in the underground network. They were soon to be joined by still another party, the URD, after the 1952 electoral results (which favored the URD) were rigged in favor of dictator Pérez Jiménez's continued rule. Finally, in the last period of the dictatorship, even the conservative Social Christian party, COPEI, was driven underground by increased repression by the authoritarian regime.

Unity among the parties came as a by-product of government re-pression. Unity took shape in two different spaces: one was the underground network in Venezuela, which was responsible for much of the mobilization that led to the dictator's downfall; the second was a network of political exiles, which was active in Costa Rica, Mexico, Puerto Rico, the United States, and Canada.[56] Even though there were tensions between the exiles and the underground networks, the parties were able to unite and collaborate in a common cause, namely, the toppling of the Pérez Jiménez dictatorship.

As a consequence of the political learning process that occurred during the decade of dictatorship (1948–58),[57] the possibilities for inter-party coalition and alliance building among the parties grew. A broad multiparty coalition[58] not only managed to build a party alliance but also was able to bring other social forces—the church, business associations (grouped under FEDECAMARAS), and the CTV—into the antidicta-torship coalition. Acting clandestinely, this coalition was able to garner enough strength to challenge the military government and overthrow Pérez Jiménez. They would soon become the protagonists of one of the most successful and lasting episodes of democratic institution building in twentieth-century Latin America.

Although the parties in Venezuela experienced competition, conflict, and divisions, there was never the kind of deep-seated, widespread violence among their leaders or the rank and file that was the hallmark of Colombian politics. They became the main victims of state repression under Pérez Jiménez, and this obviously made their partisan activities more costly, risky, and difficult. Most of them had to work underground, under very difficult conditions. Simultaneously, however, state repression acted as catalyst for a new era of cooperation between the parties, one that would take into account the lessons of the Trienio's failure, as well as the lessons derived from a decade of military rule.[59]

In sum, owing to the parties' emergence after the consolidation of state power and also to the more modern social structure spawned in Venezuela by the oil industry, Venezuela's political parties became more broadly based, more representative of emerging social sectors (especially the middle classes, the peasants, and the workers), and more program-matic. Having been excluded from power for most of their existence, they had a limited record of electoral competition, very little interparty violence, and, in contrast with Colombia, a long period of cooperation and alliances in underground mobilization and organization. These features of the parties and party system would work in their favor when they finally attempted to create a viable, enduring democratic regime.

Colombia and Venezuela thus differed markedly in terms of the origins, nature, and formative experience of their political parties. While the Colombian parties were elitist, patronage oriented, and internally mobilized, Venezuela's parties were more modern, programmatic, mass based, and externally mobilized. This had consequences for the relationship they established with their constituencies: the Colombian parties represented a broad social coalition dominated by elite, especially landed interests; the Venezuelan parties came to represent the socially and politically excluded, not only the middle sectors but also the workers and peasants.

There was also a clear divergence in the patterns of competition, conflict, and cooperation among the parties, stemming in part from their relationship with the state and the incumbent regime. Colombia's long electoral history stands alongside a long history of violence and civil strife between the parties. In contrast, the Venezuelan parties had a very short history of electoral competition (1945–48) and an almost negligible history of confrontation.

The complex and intertwined history of these two states and parties explains to a great extent the regime evolution of Colombia and Venezuela before and after their respective transitions to democracy. The older, stronger, patronage-oriented parties in Colombia go a long way toward explaining the long record of elections in that country, the absence of open military interventions in politics, and the overall stability of the system of elite representation. Their historical tendency toward fragmentation and intra- as well as interparty conflict, however, explains the relatively frequent episodes of political polarization and violence, including the regime breakdown of 1949[60]—and the ensuing violence. In contrast, the more programmatic and representative parties that emerged in Venezuela in the 1930s and 1940s had a contradictory impact on regime change: while at the beginning they elicited a strong reaction from the incumbent elites (as in the 1948 coup), in the longer run their capacity to provide adequate representation for a variety of constituencies turned them into the pillars of a long-lasting democratic regime.

The nature of these parties, as well as their established patterns of competition and conflict, also had an impact on the pacts that were signed in the late 1950s. At the time of their transitions, Colombia and Venezuela had two different party systems faced with different problems. In the Venezuelan case, I argue, there were two major challenges: on the one hand, Venezuela's parties needed to achieve enough consensus among them to be able to finally secure an effective transfer of power from the military; on the other, they needed to come to an agreement on the rules for limiting future competition between them, taming AD's majoritarian temptations, and creating trust among the remaining parties. As I discuss in the next chapter, the pacts achieved during 1958 clearly responded to these challenges. In Colombia the negotiation entailed overcoming a century-old history of violent confrontation and turning long-standing enemies into potential partners. Because the animosity between the two parties was so deeply ingrained, I argue in the next chapter, the guarantees offered by the pacts had to be even stronger in the Colombian case. To put it in game theoretical terms, whereas the Venezuelan pact was meant to solve a coordination problem among the various parties, the Colombian pact faced a taller order: it had to shift the entire game from a situation in which actors were rationally inclined not to cooperate to a structure of incentives that encouraged cooperation.[61]

The Political Foundations of Democratic Rule

I have focused here on the influence of two crucial sets of political institutions, the state and political parties, and argued that differences in the timing and sequence of their emergence and formation are crucial to explaining the divergent political trajectories of Colombia and Venezuela in the twentieth century. Even before the emergence of oil, some political differences had already surfaced in the last quarter of the nineteenth century: the secular weakness of the Colombian state and the protracted antagonism between the traditional Liberal and Conservative

Parties clearly set this case apart from Venezuela, where the disappearance of the nineteenth-century Liberal-Conservative cleavage gave way to a strong centralized state in the early twentieth century.

While the centralization of state power occurred relatively late (at the turn of the twentieth century) in both Colombia and Venezuela, differences in two crucial areas were shown to affect their subsequent political development: the timing of state consolidation in relation to the emergence of political parties and the main vehicle through which the state asserted its control over the territory and population. Whereas in Colombia the traditional parties, which had strong links to regional elites, predated the central state and thus became the main vehicles for state formation, in Venezuela the basic tasks of state consolidation were accomplished by military elites. Venezuela's military caudillos and, later, national army achieved greater success than Colombia's state makers in achieving a monopoly on violence throughout the territory and concentrating power at the center. This relative success, combined with the availability from the 1920s onward of abundant oil revenues that spurred bureaucratization, endowed Venezuela's civilian elites at the time of the democratic transition in the late 1950s with a strong and resourceful, potentially "usable," state apparatus. In contrast, the Colombian state remained weak and unable to broadcast power throughout the territory, which, in the long run, hindered the stabilization of a viable democratic regime.

I have characterized Colombia's parties as elitist and patronage oriented, with a long history of interparty warfare, extending back to their genesis in the mid-nineteenth century. In contrast, Venezuela's parties were shown to be more modern, representative, and programmatic. Emerging in the 1930s with no ties to the nineteenth-century oligarchic parties, they had incentives (as "outsiders") to mobilize mass support on the basis of programmatic appeals in order to gain access to the state. They also had a negligible history of violent confrontation; instead, incumbent authoritarian elites served as their common enemy, spurring them to build multiparty alliances to attain political power. Just as historical patterns of state formation in Colombia were, in the long run, less favorable for democracy than in Venezuela, the features of Colombia's parties and party system were less promising than Venezuela's for the creation of an inclusive and competitive regime.

In turn, the nature of these parties, as well as their historical patterns of conflict and cooperation, was to have a visible impact on the pacts signed in the 1950s (the topic of the next chapter). The more representative Venezuelan parties made for pacts that were not only politically but also socially more inclusionary. By contrast, the elitist, patronage-oriented parties in Colombia created pacts that were much less representative of societal interests and demands. Similarly, the historical patterns of conflict and cooperation among the parties would have an impact on the very content of the pacts. One of the central issues of the negotiation during the 1950s transitions in these two countries was the creation of mechanisms to change and overcome previous patterns of party interaction, which had led to the breakdown of previous democratic regimes: while the Venezuelan parties agreed on a more flexible set of mechanisms to tame competition and promote coordination, the Colombian pacts grew heavy with rigid restrictions meant to effect a radical change in the nature of the political game between the parties.

Part II

RETHINKING PACTED TRANSITIONS AND THEIR LEGACIES

> We must beware of that history which still simmers with the passions of contemporaries who felt it, described it, lived it, to the rhythm of their brief lives, lives as brief as are our own. It has the dimensions of their anger, their dreams, and their illusions.
>
> —Fernand Braudel, *On History*

CHAPTER THREE

Reading Pacts as Political Blueprints

The Institutional Legacies of Pacted Transitions

Colombia and Venezuela have usually been grouped together as successful, pacted transitions. As with other cases such as Spain and Uruguay, the pacted mode of their transitions has been closely linked to their success.[1] The transitions literature usually refers to these cases as belonging to a clearly delineated category with clearly specified consequences. However, a closer look at a handful of these so-called pacted transitions (Colombia, Venezuela, Spain, Brazil, Chile, and Uruguay, to note just a few) yields a simple yet compelling conclusion: not all pacted transitions are created equal. Instead, I argue that we need to break down the type "pacted transition" into subtypes in order to make sense of the variation in cases. In addition, we need to look deeper into the pacts themselves: who participated and the stipulations contained in the agreements are crucial variables in their long-term consequences.

Every democracy is "pacted" in the sense that underlying every democratic regime there is always some sort of implicit or explicit settlement among contenders for power (Rustow 1970). The term *pacted democracy*, however, has been reserved in the literature for those cases in which at the origins of the democratic regime there lies an explicit negotiation between contending elites regarding the architecture and distribution of political power that usually leaves clearly recognizable traces, for example, a written pact or certain legal and/or constitutional provisions.[2] When speaking of pacted democracies, one should restrict the universe of cases to those in which democracy originates as a result of explicit and deliberately negotiated agreements concerning institutional design,[3] thereby excluding those instances in which the gradual convergence of elites, in part the unintended outcome of structural changes, takes place over a long period, with no apparent or explicit agreement between them.

As more cases were added to the list of democratic transitions in the last quarter of the twentieth century, typologies proliferated in the effort to make sense of the diversity of paths toward democracy. Conceptual distinctions between types have become ever more subtle and complex. O'Donnell and Schmitter (1986) initially emphasized the differences between "pacted transitions" and transitions "by regime collapse." According to Schmitter's definition (1994: 65), a pacted transition is that in which "elites from the previous autocracy and its opposition reach a stalemate and find themselves compelled to respect each other's interests."[4] Pacted transitions, however, come in a variety of forms—a point often overlooked by theorists of regime change. In Colombia and Venezuela, for example, negotiations took place mainly and predominantly among democratic contenders, after the authoritarian regime had been weakened by the dictator's departure. As a consequence, the presence and relative weight of the incumbent military in the negotiations was significantly reduced.[5]

Mainwaring (1992) has proposed to distinguish between "transitions through transaction" and "transitions through extrication." The typology does not hinge so much on who initiates the transition as on the degree of control exerted by the authoritarian incumbents throughout the transition process. In a transition through transaction the incumbent authoritarian elite not only initiates the process of liberalization but also remains a decisive actor throughout the transition. In a transition through extrication the authoritarian government is weakened but not as thoroughly as in a transition by defeat and thus is able to negotiate crucial features of the transition, such as retroactive protection for abuses of power and violations of human rights (Mainwaring 1992: 323).

The distinction between the two subtypes has important implications in terms of the pacts that are signed and their effects on subsequent regime evolution: while the transition through transaction entails the now-classic pacts between the soft-liners (in the regime) and the moderates (among the opposition),[6] in transitions through extrication the balance of power between the regime and the opposition tilts in favor of the latter; indeed, much of the initiative during the transition process shifts to the leaders of the opposition, leaving the authoritarian elites in a secondary position. In a transition through transaction, because the leaders of the authoritarian regime retain a relatively high degree of power, guarantees are extended to the outgoing regime elites and especially to the military, usually in the form of military pacts. In transitions through extrication political pacts become more prominent, since these require first and foremost that opposition leaders achieve a degree of unity among themselves. In these cases pacts with the military, though crucial in securing the final transfer of power, are often implicit rather than explicit and take second place to the political pacts between the diverse forces making up the pro-democratic opposition. Ultimately, it is in the political pacts where the blueprint for the new institutional arrangement first emerges and takes form.

Table 3.1 shows the main contrast between transitions via regime defeat or collapse and pacted transitions while also capturing the important distinction, proposed by Mainwaring (1992), between transitions through extrication and transitions through transaction.[7] Colombia and Venezuela clearly belong to the subtype "transition through extrication": their transitions happened once the military regime had been substantially weakened after the dictators' flight, giving way to the creation of a provisional junta that initiated the liberalization process and later stepped down, yielding power to an elected civilian government. During the junta period, several pacts (implicit as well as explicit) were struck between the opposition and the military regarding their status after the transition, but neither the juntas nor the military-as-institution had the power to direct the course of the transition. In both cases it was the coalition of the opposition parties that dominated the stage between the downfall of the dictators and the inauguration of civilian regimes.

Table 3.1. Modes of Transition to Democracy

Transitions through *Regime Defeat/Collapse*	*PACTED TRANSITIONS*	
Costa Rica 1948	Transitions	Transitions
Greece 1974	through Extrication	through Transaction
Portugal 1975		
Argentina 1982–83	Colombia 1957–58	Brazil 1974–82
	Venezuela 1958–59	Spain 1975–78
		Ecuador 1979–80
		Uruguay 1984–85
		Chile 1989–90
		El Salvador 1992
		Guatemala 1996

Most of these typologies rest on the assumption that the process of regime change (or the mode of transition) exerts a powerful influence on the character and future evolution of the emerging democracies. Many authors have thus derived a series of effects and post-transition trajectories from the pacted transitions type, as these allegedly lead to relatively stable but otherwise quite limited, restricted, or conservative democracies.[8] Deriving outcomes automatically from the transition mode is, however, fraught with dangers. Different paths toward democracy certainly have an impact on further democratic evolution. However, as time goes by, the limited predictive capacity of the mode of transition becomes rather obvious: while cases such as Colombia and Brazil throw into question the presumably more stable and smooth progress of pacted democracies, cases such as Spain, Uruguay, and Venezuela cripple the argument about the conservative bias presumably present in this type of transition. Finally, cases such as Costa Rica and Portugal challenge predictions of instability commonly associated with transitions based on mass mobilization.

It is probably wise to reexamine the assumption that pact making leads to more stable, though conservative, democratic regimes. The evidence presented in this book throws into question a series of assumptions about the consequences of pacted transitions: as exemplified by Colombia and Venezuela, the outcomes can be quite different. As discussed in the first part of this book, many of the effects that we have long attributed to the mode of transition may be, instead, the outcome of historical continuities, including the state's (in)ability to control its territory and population, or patterns of party interaction with the state, society, and other parties. They could also be related to newly found problems and challenges or, alternatively, with "missed opportunities" as the democratic process unfolds.[9]

Despite this warning against the strong version of the mode of transition hypothesis, there is no doubt that a careful analysis of the new institutional realities created by the transition process continues to be warranted and can provide insights into the subsequent process of democratic evolution. Transitions are interesting not only as examples of situations of high uncertainty and undetermined political change but also as crucial episodes of institutional change and (re)design. It would be difficult to ignore the central importance of foundational pacts that set out to redesign the very architecture of a political system. Foundational political pacts act as political blueprints: they fix institutional patterns and thus give rise to more permanent institutions.

Pacts have been the subject of great controversy in the literature on democratization: although initially there seemed to be widespread consensus on the desirability of pacts as positive mechanisms that can render democracy both feasible and stable, a negative perception of pacts gradually gained ground and settled in. Unfortunately, as with many other aspects of these episodes of regime transformation, there is a dearth of conclusive findings about whether pacts are beneficial or dysfunctional for democratization. Despite opinions in favor of and against pacts as desirable means to build a democracy, little empirical research has been done on pacts and their impact on post-transition politics.[10] My research, based on two crucial examples of pacted democracy, Colombia and Venezuela, has sought a better understanding of pacts and their long-term impact. I take issue with both the positive and the negative assessments of pacts. Based on this research, I argue that pacts are not, by definition, either beneficial or dysfunctional for democracy. Instead of attributing an a priori positive or negative impact to them, I claim that whether pacts succeed or fail to establish the basis for a solid democratic regime depends on three key variables: (1) the number and range of actors who participate in their crafting (degree of inclusion/exclusion); (2) the nature and scope of the restrictions contained therein; and (3) the duration and degree of entrenchment of those restrictions (i.e., the flexibility or rigidity of the provisions contained in the pacts).

Initially scholars were cautiously positive about the desirability of pacts as necessary to certain transitions. Huntington (1984: 193), for example, underscored the importance of elite negotiations to the stability of the democratic regimes: "Democratic regimes that have lasted have seldom, if ever, been instituted by mass popular actions. . . . [Democratic] institutions come into existence through negotiations and compromises among political elites calculating their own interests and desires." That pacts endow democracies with healthy doses of stability was by and large the opinion held by scholars in the 1980s (O'Donnell and Schmitter 1986; Stepan 1986). Some saw pacts as the necessary price to pay for democratization in situations where, in the face of unbearable challenges (with uncertain outcomes and almost certain costs), party leaders have an incentive to come to terms with their opponents. Others make a much stronger case for pacts: in this view, pacts or elite settlements hold the key to democratic consolidation by promoting and cementing elite unity (Burton, Gunter, and Higley 1992).

On the opposite side of this debate, pacts have been harshly criticized on several counts. While some have stressed their elitist and undemocratic nature, others have pointed to their costs; most see them as leading to conservative socioeconomic outcomes, while some argue instead that they bequeath "birth defects" to the democracies that they help create. The first and most often repeated claim is that pacts are contrary to democracy, since they are elitist and undemocratic by nature. In much of the democratization literature, pacts have been characterized as exclusionary, elitist, basically undemocratic means to reach democratic outcomes.[11] That pacts are made by elites is a point that needs no further arguing: only elites, especially political elites, can engage in the process of bargaining and negotiation leading to pacts. However, that they are made by elites does not automatically render them "elitist," as in the claim that they only favor the interest of a certain group of (rich and powerful) people to the detriment of larger sectors of society. Neither does it render them undemocratic. Both claims—that pacts are beneficial only to the elites and that they are detrimental to democracy—need to be investigated and established empirically. This is by far the weakest of all arguments directed against pacts: what matters is not whether or not they are signed by elites but how those elites are chosen, whom they represent, and what they end up agreeing on. The democratic or undemocratic nature of pacts cannot be decided by theoretical fiat but rather by probing deeper into the process of negotiation, by interrogating the elites, their motives, and their capacity for representation as well as by analyzing the institutional outcome of their negotiations.

According to some scholars, "pacted democracies" imply a tradeoff between stability and socioeconomic reforms that leads to conservative socioeconomic policies.[12] Karl (1986: 198), for example, argued that "a democracy by pact can institutionalize a conservative bias into the polity, creating a new status quo which can block further progress toward political, social, and economic democracy." To the extent that pacts protect the interests of elites so as to stop them from using the military to impede the transition, they allegedly have an inherent conservative bias that goes against the inclusion of subaltern classes, thus guaranteeing the stability though not the quality of the emerging democracy.[13]

Despite their widespread acceptance, these early predictions have not been borne out by reality: three decades later it would be hard to argue that Spain's democratic consolidation has been hampered by its pacted nature, any more than Portugal's democracy has been propelled by its revolutionary origins;[14] or to argue, conversely, that Argentina has faced less severe obstacles in terms of advancing social or economic democracy than its neighbors Brazil and Chile, whose fledgling democracies would have carried pacts' indelible traces. Except for the outstanding and somehow exceptional case of Costa Rica,[15] predictions based on the (pacted vs. nonpacted) mode of transition have been increasingly contradicted by the existing evidence: not because pacted democracies have turned out to be more "progressive," but rather because nonpacted democracies turned out to be no less conservative than pacted ones. Perhaps all democracies, because of the guarantees that they confer to certain interests (e.g., business elites) have an inherent conservative bias. On the other hand, a case such as Spain—a pacted democracy where the incumbent elite preserved a high degree of control over the transition—serves as a warning to those making apocalyptic predictions about pacts. In the past twenty-five years, not despite pacts but thanks to them, Spain has managed to modernize and grow economically and to create a solid and vibrant democracy (see Encarnación 2005). Pacts, as the Spanish case evidently shows, do not preclude socioeconomic change.[16]

Finally, some of the most critical assessments of pacted democracies have focused on the institutional legacies or "traces" they leave behind.[17] In the stronger version of this argument, regimes that result from a pacted transition are seen as having emerged with birth defects. Karl (1990) and Hagopian (1990), for example, have argued that pacts have the ability to "freeze" democracy, acting as a source of political continuity that somehow weighs perversely on the prospects of democratic evolution. There is "abundant evidence from those countries with pacted democracies," contends Hagopian (1990: 151), "that the political system itself and not just the policy agenda may be compromised by elite-pact making." Elites secure their requirements through negotiation, thereby effectively impeding the ability of democracies to evolve and extend themselves. In Hagopian's (1996a: 22–23) words, "democratization is often slowed or stopped in regimes spawned by political pacts negotiated with traditional and authoritarian elites."[18]

In the case of Brazil, Hagopian (1990) has argued that political pacts compromised democracy because they strengthened and helped perpetuate some of the most authoritarian (or simply nondemocratic) features of the political landscape. The political pacts that crystallized during this country's protracted transition to democracy served to reinforce a powerful military with a substantial presence in domestic politics, as well as the power of traditional elites and their clientelistic practices. On closer inspection, however, the degree of influence attributed by Hagopian to the pacts becomes problematic; rather than the pacts, most of the evidence she presents points in a different direction—that is, to the persistent impact of certain historical institutional legacies (the weight of the military, the power of traditional, landed elites and their clientelistic modes of political mobilization) that exerted a continuous influence despite the transformations introduced by the transition. If anything, pacts should be portrayed as the consequence and reflection of those historical realities rather than the ultimate source of the political obstacles impeding democratic consolidation.[19]

In an effort to lend clarity to the actual impact of transitional pacts, I have strived to differentiate the restrictions inherited from the old patterns of doing politics and the new restrictions introduced by the pacts. I also acknowledge that pacts can be changed, transformed, and renegotiated as the democratic process unfolds. Pacts do not condemn democratic politics to the endless reenactment of past patterns and practices, or to the unmitigated dominance of the military and authoritarian traditional elites. My argument is rather that while addressing some of the problems of the past (e.g., political polarization in Venezuela and interparty warfare in Colombia) some—but by no means all—pacts may create new restrictions and therefore sow the seeds for unexpected future problems. I therefore take issue with the blanket accusation that all pacts have similarly negative consequences. Whether a pact may be conducive to democratic development or whether it may become a birth defect is not a matter of definitional fiat but of empirical investigation. Ultimately, the role pacts play in future political outcomes depend on three of their basic features: (1) the degrees of inclusion or exclusion with regard to its signatories; (2) the nature and scope of the restrictions they impose on the future development of the political game; and (3) the duration and degree of institutional entrenchment of these same restrictions (or degree of flexibility of the institutional arrangements installed by the pacts). Distinguishing among different types of pacts remains a crucial task to be accomplished. Only by doing so will it be possible to understand the conditions under which some pacts contribute positively to the installation of democracy while others become a liability in the path toward democratic development.

Comparing Colombia's and Venezuela's Pacted Transitions

By the mid-1950s Colombia and Venezuela were both under military rule. At the end of that decade the two dictators were overthrown almost simultaneously—in June 1957 in Colombia and in January 1958 in Venezuela—following street demonstrations that opened the way to a transition process that led to the inauguration of elected civilian governments a year later. There is widespread agreement that Colombia and Venezuela had similar kinds of transitions in the late 1950s: in both cases political pacts were signed among the leaders of opposition parties that provided assurances that none would be excluded from power and also promised economic actors and the church that their interests would be respected. In consequence, they have been portrayed as successful, pacted transitions from above.

Because of their timing, they both belong to what Huntington (1991b) has called the "second wave" of democratization, which took place between 1945 and 1962. This means that they occurred not only at the same time but also under the same set of international conditions. Factors such as the postwar expansion of the international economic system, the increasingly important role of the United States in Latin America, and the tensions introduced by the Cold War and the Cuban Revolution affected these two transition processes in a relatively similar way.[20]

The trajectory or sequence of events followed in the two cases was also strikingly similar. First, there was a rapprochement between the previously divided opposition parties, which then formed a loose opposition alliance. Second, a critical turning point was triggered by the attempt on the part of the two dictators to perpetuate their personal grip on power. Former key allies of the authoritarian regime (such as the church and business leaders) joined the opposition coalition in demonstrations and protests provoked by the succession crisis. Third, during this brief "popular upsurge,"[21] diverse groups in civil society mobilized under the leadership of the parties: students, clergy, women, businesspeople, and workers. In both cases the antiregime demonstrations were mostly urban, more elitist than popular, and evidently led by political parties.[22] Fourth, after the urban uprisings, a crucial, defining event occurred: the armed forces denied their support to the troubled dictators, thus prompting them to flee their respective countries. Fifth, a provisional junta was immediately appointed that took control of the government, promising a prompt devolution of power to civilians through elections. The sixth phase, which took place under the provisional junta's rule, encompassed a complex and multidimensional process of negotiation and pact crafting, among the opposition forces and also between them and the military-as-institution, in order to secure the return to a civilian government. Seventh and finally, the provisional juntas convoked elections, which were free and relatively competitive.[23] As a result of those elections a new civilian president, elected through universal, direct, and secret vote was sworn into office.

The entire process took approximately two years in each case. The transition in Colombia lasted twenty-five months, from July 1956 to August 1958. The transition in Venezuela lasted eighteen months, from August 1957 to February 1959. They were both brief transitions, especially when contrasted with the Brazilian transition, which lasted more than a decade. Duration in time is an important variable. As Hartlyn (1998: 103) has rightly noted, "The longer the time span [of a transition,] the more the likelihood that different characteristics and interactive effects, including actions by mass actors as well as elite ones, become important." In the cases of Colombia and Venezuela, there is no difference in terms of the duration of their respective transitions that could account for differences in their outcomes.

Finally, as noted above, both transitions have been classified as pacted transitions, that is, transitions from authoritarian rule to democracy in which pacts among elites played a crucial role in effecting the final transfer of power as well as in defining the institutional features of the subsequent regime. In the two cases pacts were essentially political, with party elites playing the main roles throughout the negotiation, as opposed to transitions in which military pacts or economic pacts occupy center stage. They were elite-led transitions from above, as opposed to transitions from below, either of a reformist or a revolutionary nature. These two pacted transitions, carried out during the second wave of democratization, were not only simultaneous and brief but also "successful"—at least in the sense that they led to the installation of elected civilian presidents while avoiding a regression to the previous authoritarian regime or the installation of some other, modified version of authoritarianism.[24]

And yet the aftermath of these two transitions was very different: whereas Venezuela rapidly became an inclusionary, competitive regime, in Colombia a limited democracy survived for decades, unable to expand beyond its originally confining conditions. Why? After considering these two cases, it is difficult to avoid the conclusion that the pacted mode of their transitions does not hold the key to their later evolution. What then? In the pages that follow I examine these two transition processes in detail, seeking to document the most revealing differences and points of departure between them in an effort to uncover the potential sources of divergence. A closer look at these two cases is warranted by the fact that these two pacted transitions have been an important source of empirical evidence for scholars writing about pacts. Both those who have seen pacts and pacted democracies in a negative light (e.g., Karl, Hagopian) and those who attribute mostly positive effects to them (O'Donnell, Schmitter, Stepan, Peeler, and, more recently, Encarnación) have built their arguments on the basis of empirical evidence coming from Colombia and Venezuela. By lumping them together, I argue, they have missed the analytical purchase offered by their contrasting experiences.

"The Twilight of the Tyrants": The Formation of the Opposing Coalition and the Fall of the Dictators (1956–1958)

The first phase of the transition process[25] began in Colombia on July 24, 1956, when the heads of the Liberal and Conservative Parties signed the Declaración de Benidorm, in which they agreed to work together to end the dictatorship.[26] It ended on May 10, 1957, the day Gustavo Rojas Pinilla fell and was forced to flee the country. In Venezuela the opening date is August 1957, when the first "Manifiesto" was issued by the opposing Junta Patriótica, composed of the URD, the PCV, AD, and COPEI (see Plaza 1978). The transition's first phase closed with the fall of Marcos Pérez Jiménez on January 23, 1958.

In both Colombia and Venezuela the transition began with the convergence of previously divided parties in an opposition coalition. This fact, rather than loss of legitimacy, is central to any explanation of these regimes' downfall. Although it is clear that losing the support of key actors such as the church hierarchy or the business community was damaging for their long-term continuity, the two authoritarian regimes could have continued had it not been for the organization and mobilization of a strong coalition of the opposition that succeeded in presenting itself as a viable alternative. In the absence of legitimacy, the threat of force can keep acquiescence going; ultimately, "what matters for the stability of any regime is not the legitimacy of this particular system of domination but the presence or absence of preferable alternatives" (Przeworski 1986: 51–52).[27]

Neither of these two was a transition by collapse or a transition initiated by the military government itself. They were both, instead, transitions through extrication, where the authoritarian government is weakened but remains able to negotiate crucial features of the transition (e.g., retroactive protection for abuses of power) (see Mainwaring 1992: 323). Since most of the transitions' pace and direction depends on the initiative and capacity for coalition building among the opposing parties, events happening on the opposition side of the game deserve special attention.

Colombia and Venezuela beautifully illustrate Rustow's (1970: 355) assertion that "what concludes the preparatory phase is a deliberate decision on the part of political leaders to accept the existence of diversity in unity and, to that end, to institutionalize some crucial aspect of democratic procedure." This acceptance came with the Declaración de Benidorm in Colombia and with the first Manifesto of the Junta Patriótica in Venezuela. These two documents signaled the rapprochement of parties and party factions, which had been bitterly divided up until that moment. The most striking case is the agreement between the Liberal and Conservative Parties in Colombia after a decade of full-blown interparty warfare known as La Violencia,[28] especially because it included the radical right-wing Laureanista faction from the Conservative Party. In the case of Venezuela, it was also significant that AD joined with its former adversaries, the PCV, URD, and COPEI, in the struggle against Pérez Jiménez. In both cases this process of rapprochement can be understood as the result of a political learning process, whereby the party leaders, after harsh years of violence and exclusion, repression or exile, learned the values of negotiation, tolerance, and compromise.[29] In both cases—perhaps more markedly in Colombia—it was the lessons from years of entrenched and violent conflict that finally led to the democratic breakthrough.

Even though this rapprochement had been going on for some time, in both cases there was a key event that galvanized the opposition and finally opened the first cracks in the authoritarian regime, thus forcing even some members of the incumbent regime to join the opposition. This catalyst was the declaration on the part of the dictators that they intended to remain in power for a longer period than initially expected. In Colombia, in October 1956, Rojas Pinilla announced his intention to change the composition of the National Constituent Assembly (ANAC) by appointing twenty-five new members of his own choosing. A few months later, in January 1957, his minister of war, General Gabriel París, announced the "irrevocable" decision on the part of the armed forces to support General Rojas Pinilla for another four-year presidential term starting in 1958. By then the Conservative Party faction that had been Rojas Pinilla's main civilian ally split from the governing coalition and joined the opposition. Together with the Liberal Party, the Ospinistas signed the Pacto de Marzo (Pact of March) in 1957,[30] confirming that there was basic agreement among all opposition forces on the need to unite against their common enemy, the dictator. The Pacto de Marzo sealed the coalition, which included all the existing party factions in Colombia.

In November 1957 elections were scheduled in Venezuela according to the constitution drafted by the dictatorship in 1953. Instead, General Pérez Jiménez decided to convoke a plebiscite designed to ratify and prolong his mandate. He even altered the constitution to give voting rights to foreigners who had been residing in the country for at least two years. This latter move, coupled with the attempt to perpetuate his rule, outraged most Venezuelans, including the armed forces. Fraudulent and manipulated elections took place in December 1957, with a majority vote in favor of Pérez Jiménez. Two weeks later, however, the Maracay garrison, an important nucleus of military power in Venezuela, took up arms against the government.[31] Although the rebellion was put down, the breakdown of unity in the armed forces and public awareness of the growing cracks in the regime gave way, a few weeks later, to the popular upheaval that led to Pérez Jiménez's flight from the country.

The attempts on the part of both dictators to remain in power and the electoral fraud designed to give a democratic aura to their incumbency led to crises that ended up uniting the opposition forces. These developments also gave key social forces a reason to join the political parties, which were already on the opposition side of the political divide. The final blow, however, was the military's decision to abandon the dictator at a critical moment. The withdrawal of the armed forces' support was the key factor in the downfall of both dictatorships. Had they decided to stay and use force against the mobilized population, the dictators could have stayed for at least some additional time. Instead the military decided to allow the mobilization and street demonstrations to proceed without repression. In doing so they finally tipped the balance in favor of the opposition. This decision was a result of divisions in the armed forces. Internal contradictions arose out of the contrast between the interests and values of the military-as-institution and the personal ambitions and interests of the dictators and their immediate circle of personal friends and collaborators.[32] Not every division in an authoritarian regime leads to a democratic transition, however. Those who break away from the government may resist liberalization and may even want to escalate repression, thus deepening the authoritarian nature of the regime. In both Colombia and Venezuela part of the opposition from within the authoritarian establishment stemmed from the personal ambitions of some higher-ranking officers who aspired to succeed the incumbent dictator. The point has been made before: authoritarian regime breakdown is not enough; it also takes a strong democratic opposition to build a democratic regime (see Stepan 1993).

The next crucial factor in the transition sequence was the construction of a strong coalition of the opposition. As soon as the military revealed signs of being either unable or unwilling to repress the opposition, as in Colombia, or when they showed open signs of discontent, as in the Maracay uprising in Venezuela, the scene was set for popular uprisings. These came in May 1957 in Colombia and in January 1958 in Venezuela. The increasing power of the opposition coalition, its potential for mobilization, the massive participation in street demonstrations, the breadth of the social groups included in the mobilizations, and, finally, the production strikes organized by the employers themselves served in both cases to show the strength of the opposition to the military-as-institution and to signal how costly it would be to back up the dictatorship by force.

As mentioned above, there is no transition until some feasible alternative to the existing regime appears on the political horizon. Such an alternative was offered in Colombia and Venezuela by the parties who had begun organizing the opposition campaign well before the popular uprisings took place. Faced with lack of support from the military and the coalescing of a broad social and political opposition front, both Rojas Pinilla and Pérez Jiménez realized the loss of crucial social, political, and institutional support for their regimes and fled.

The Provisional Juntas Period: Liberalization and the Crafting of the Pacts (1957–1959)

The second phase of the transition started with the installation, in both countries, of provisional junta governments. These provisional juntas could decide either to launch a liberalization process or to reverse the liberalization trends set in motion by the dictators' flight.[33] The decision to continue with a process of liberalization or reverse it depended mainly on the armed forces' perception of the risks and dangers faced by the military qua institution if it were to continue in power; that is, it hinged on a calculation of costs and benefits on the part of the junta. On the other hand, the decision to go beyond the liberalization phase into a democratization process depended mainly on the ability of the political parties to present the junta with an alternative arrangement that would guarantee the return to political competition while avoiding the risks of polarization and violence.[34]

This was the most complex and difficult phase of the negotiation among the parties: once the common enemy (i.e., the dictator) disappeared from the scene contradictions surfaced among the opposition parties, which previously had been united in the effort to topple the dictatorship. The "liberalization under a junta" phase ended when a basic agreement was struck between the parties on how to share power (Colombia) or how to tame competition (Venezuela). The stage was then set for the holding of elections and the transfer of power from the junta to the first elected civilian government. In Colombia this phase began on May 10, 1957, and ended on August 7, 1958, with the inauguration of President Alberto Lleras Camargo (Liberal). In Venezuela it began on January 23, 1958, and ended on February 13, 1959, with the inauguration of President Rómulo Betancourt (AD).

Liberalization is the term that best describes the political process under the provisional juntas: a gradual move to less censorship of the media, greater freedom to organize, the introduction of legal guarantees for individual rights, the release of political prisoners, the return of political exiles, and increasing toleration of political opposition. This phase was characterized in both countries by ceaseless—sometimes invisible or clandestine—bargaining and negotiation among leaders, successive accords and divisions, mini-crises, reconciliations, and the like. Negotiations typically involved the classical democratic dilemmas of dissent versus consensus, unity versus competition, harmony versus conflict, coalition making versus the need for an active opposition.

One interesting distinction between Colombia and Venezuela is the composition of the juntas that came to power. When Rojas Pinilla fled Bogotá on May 10, 1957, he left behind an all-military junta composed of five high-ranking officers whom he himself chose from his closest collaborators. These officers had held high positions in the Rojas Pinilla government (some of them with their own personal ambitions), indicating a high degree of continuity with the previous regime.[35]

Eight months later Pérez Jiménez fled Venezuela, and two members of the provisional junta that took power, Generals Casanova and Romero, both intended to continue the dictatorship.[36] The party coalition in the opposition then declared, through the Junta Patriótica, that they would not call off the street demonstrations and popular mobilization taking place until these two generals were removed from the provisional junta. Casanova and Romero resigned two days later and were replaced by two civilians, a clear example of how the continuing pressure of a mobilized society is a key to widening and deepening the democratization process (Collier 1999; Collier and Mahoney 1999). The mixed civil-military composition of the Venezuelan junta indicates that there was a greater risk of the military continuing in power in that country, with a sector of the military—represented by Casanova and Romero—vying for this option. It also shows that a strong mobilization and a strong stand on the part of the democratic opposition were key to offset this possibility. Finally, it confirms that there were some independent civilian "notables" who could be co-opted to serve on the junta as a guarantee of neutrality for the coming election. By contrast, in Colombia there were no national-level leaders who could claim to be "neutral" enough (in partisan terms) to impartially oversee the coming elections. Thus the composition of the junta was completely dominated by the military, even though the first cabinet of the junta's government was bipartisan.

In both cases the juntas made a decision to devolve power to the civilian opposition relatively quickly. There were, however, some attempts to reverse that process through military putsches and failed coup d'états by discontented sectors of the military. In Colombia there was an attempted coup against the military junta on May 2, 1958, just two days before the presidential election was scheduled to take place. In Venezuela there were two attempts, one on July 23, 1958, and another on September 7, 1958, both during the second phase of the transition. All the attempts were successfully overcome by the juntas, which could count on the loyalty of the majority of the armed forces. To some extent, as in Spain in 1981 (see Maravall and Santamaría 1986), these failed attempts to reinstall the military served to show that the institution of the armed forces was serious in its intention to leave power and helped to solidify public confidence in the armed forces' loyalty to the emerging democratic solution.

Finally, whereas the "military moment" (the final extrication of the military from power) was more difficult in Venezuela, it was the "political moment" (agreement among the opposition parties) that was most difficult in Colombia. The Colombian military was not as strong as that in Venezuela and did not have a long history of political intervention as the Venezuelan armed forces had. It was, instead, the parties that had a long history of interparty warfare to overcome. They feared each other more than they feared the military institution itself. In Colombia this second phase was destabilized much more often by the threats of party leaders to leave the negotiation table than by the military's threat of an authoritarian reversal. In particular, the deep division within the Conservative Party (between the radical Laureanistas and the moderate Ospinistas) made the political negotiation in Colombia much more problematic than removing the military from power. As a result, the pact-making process in this country was more difficult and staggered, with new conditions arising at every turn in the negotiation process. Concomitantly, the restrictions included in the pacts grew stronger and more rigid as the process went along.[37]

Types of Pacts, Signatories, and Contents

Many people have the mistaken impression that transitions occur instantaneously, almost like magic, after a pact has been agreed on and signed by political leaders who seem to have it all planned far in advance. As suggested by Tilly (1994: 1), "Recent theorists have accelerated the tempo so that at times the transition to democracy looks almost instantaneous: put the pact in gear, and go." In reality, pacts are the result of protracted negotiations, long chains of multiple, difficult, and interlocking agreements, each leading on to the next, often in unexpected directions. The Venezuelan Pact of Punto Fijo (1958), for example, makes explicit reference to "long and detailed conversations" between the party leaders before they reached the agreement that was made public.[38] The Colombian pacts, as well, were the products of multiple conversations between Alberto Lleras (Liberal) and Laureano Gómez (Conservative) initially in Spain and later in Bogotá. Mariano Ospina, leader of a Conservative faction opposed to Gómez, was included at a later stage, in March 1958.[39] Colombia's long chain of party agreements started with the Declaration of Benidorm (July 1956) and ended with congressional approval of the Acto Legislativo N° 1 of 1959,[40] a constitutional amendment mandating party alternation in the presidency. In Venezuela the pact-making chain started with the Manifiesto of the Junta Patriótica (August 1957) and ended with the new Constitution approved by Congress in 1961.[41]

Rather than a single event, foundational pacts are actually "a series of accords that are interlocking and dependent upon each other" (Karl and Schmitter 1991: 281). Depending on the importance and relative strength of the different players in the process, pacted transitions may require different types of pacts: political pacts are required when leaders of the authoritarian regime retain a degree of power that requires the opposition leaders to seek unity among themselves; military pacts are usually required as extensions of guarantees to the military before their exit from power. However, pacted transitions do not necessarily include an explicit, formal agreement between the military and civilians on the conditions for establishing civilian rule; that typically depends on the strength of the military-as-government vis-à-vis the opposition and, thus, on the character assumed by the provisional government. Finally, to ensure support or at least not active resistance from economically dominant groups in society, opposition leaders often seek to provide assurances, in the form of socioeconomic pacts, that radical redistributive programs will not be enacted (see Mainwaring 1992; Hartlyn 1998).

As shown in table 3.2, in Venezuela there were explicit political pacts with specific clauses addressing military issues and a separate socioeconomic pact. By contrast, in Colombia most of the pacts were of a political nature. A military pact was implicit in the text of the Colombian Plebiscite ratifying the previous party pacts, but there was no socioeconomic pact or Programa Mínimo de Gobierno (Minimum Program of Government) such as the one agreed on by the Venezuelan political parties. In addition, in both cases there were (implicit or explicit) agreements with the Catholic Church.

Differences in the types of agreements stem from differences in the main tasks facing the opposition at the moment they are crafted. Colombia was just emerging from a bloody partisan political conflict, a situation that merited a party-centered, predominantly political pact. Much more important than the military question, in this case, was the need to curb the political appetites of both traditional parties and their propensity to exclude each other by force. In Venezuela, on the other hand, the military question was much more prominent: competition for state control (and the attendant distribution of income from oil) was fierce not only among political parties but also between civilian and military elites. The Venezuelan transition thus required pacts that had a military dimension (granting civilian elites full control of the state in exchange for a handsome share of the state's resources and relative autonomy for the military) as well as a political one (to regulate competition among political parties) and a socioeconomic one (to preclude certain forms of radical reform while dictating the basic rules for distribution of state resources).

In Colombia the main objective was to put an end to the civil war that had consumed a decade and to overcome a century-long pattern of interparty violence by agreeing to share power between the two major parties and thus avoid the threat of widespread conflict. There were, however, implicit or tacit pacts between the outgoing military-as-

Table 3.2. Comparing Pacts in Colombia and Venezuela

Types of Pacts	Colombia	Venezuela
Political	- Pact of Benidorm (7/24/1956) - Pact of March (3/1957) - Pact of Sitges (7/1957) - Pact of San Carlos (11/1957) - Plebiscite (12/1957) - Alternation Amendment (9/15/1959)	- Manifesto of the Junta Patriótica (8/1957) - Pact of New York (12/1957) - Pact of Punto Fijo (10/31/58) - Declaration of Principles and Minimum Program of Government (12/6/1958) - Constitution of 1961
Military	Implicit in - Plebiscite (12/1957)	- Minimum Program of Government (12/1958)
Socioeconomic	Implicit in - Plebiscite Art. 11 (education)	- Workers-Employers Agreement (4/24/1958) - Minimum Program of Government (12/1958)
with the Catholic Church	Implicit in - Pact of March (3/1957) - Plebiscite (12/1957)	- Minimum Program of Government (12/1958) - Agreement between Venezuela and the Holy See (3/6/64)

institution and the leaders of the civilian opposition regarding the former's privileges and prerogatives, as well as agreed-on silences (or gag rules), especially concerning the institutions' role during the brief period of dictatorial rule.[42] In Venezuela a more explicit pact with the military was necessary, since the military had been and remained a powerful institution in that country. The mixed civilian-military provisional junta had already indicated a more protracted and difficult negotiation between civilians and military officers. An entire section of the Programa Mínimo de Gobierno was dedicated to military prerogatives and civil-military relations.[43]

In both Colombia and Venezuela there was an implicit negotiation with the church, which in Venezuela crystallized in a more formal agreement in 1964.[44] Although the Catholic Church has historically been more powerful and influential in Colombia than in Venezuela,[45] in the late 1950s it remained very influential in both countries. It had been a major force behind the installation of the authoritarian regimes. After changing its position vis-à-vis the dictatorship, it then provided shelter and support for the civilian opposition during the confrontation with the dictatorship, finally becoming a crucial actor encouraging and mobilizing popular protest during the urban uprisings in the two countries.[46] In addition, the main parties in each country, AD in Venezuela and the Liberal Party in Colombia, had a history of ideological and institutional confrontation with the Catholic Church, in particular, on the competing roles of state and church in politics and society, especially in the realm of education. Both parties were protagonists during the transition and had high probabilities of coming back to power (as eventually happened in both countries); therefore, an agreement with the Catholic Church seemed essential to guarantee the stability of the emerging regime.

Social contracts or socioeconomic pacts are usually signed by state agencies, business associations, and organized labor regarding property and labor rights, market arrangements, and the distribution of benefits. The presence or absence of socioeconomic pacts not only speaks to the relative power of different actors at the transition's critical juncture; it also has important consequences for the institutionalization of rights of representation and bargaining mechanisms. That a pact of this kind was signed in Venezuela and not in Colombia illustrates the extent to which the economy was a matter of contention between the signatory parties in the former.[47] Given the strategic role of the state as the holder of oil-based revenues, control of state resources and economic policy making have historically been crucial components of political contention in Venezuela. In Colombia, by contrast, the existence of a stronger and more autonomous private sector vis-à-vis a resource-poor state, coupled with a historically much lower degree of state intervention, has prevented a strong linkage between economics and politics.[48]

The presence of a socioeconomic pact in Venezuela and its absence in Colombia also speak to the strength of the working-class movement and its links with the existing political parties in the former case and its weakness in the latter. Because Venezuela had a strong labor movement that was strategically linked with the oil industry, labor was a crucial actor in the Venezuelan transition. Labor's connections with AD helped guarantee workers' acquiescence to the pacts. In turn, the socioeconomic pact and the Programa Mínimo de Gobierno offered crucial guarantees to business interests, whose opposition to AD's radical social and economic policies during the Trienio has been considered a crucial factor in the emergence of the authoritarian regime in 1948.

In Colombia, by contrast, the labor movement was historically weaker and further debilitated by a wave of repression and deliberate division promoted by the parties since the mid-1940s (see Archila 1991). Workers had also been courted by the outgoing military regime during its attempts to create a state-sponsored, Peronist-like workers' union. They were thus utterly divided during the process of regime change, with some sectors supporting the dictatorship until the end (see Urán 1983; Galvis and Donadio 1988). Moreover, Colombia's business associations were historically linked to the parties in a way that guaranteed that their interests would be preserved if any of these two parties or a coalition came to power.[49] In sum, while Venezuela witnessed a more encompassing negotiation with a wider array of actors and pacts, the Colombian negotiation process, clearly dominated by the Liberal and Conservative Parties, remained more strictly confined to the political realm.

The "Bargaining Cartel" and the Costs of Exclusion

To be successful, pacts do not need to include everybody. They must, however, include all relevant actors, that is, those with the capacity to stop or reverse the transition process. Since pacts are negotiated compromises in which contending forces extend assurances not to threaten each other, "they are only successful when they include all potentially threatening interests" (Karl and Schmitter 1991: 281). Whether pacts are beneficial or harmful for democracy depends, in part, on the constitution of what Encarnación (2005: 184) has called "the bargaining cartel." In particular, the diversity of actors included in pact making, as well as their ties to social organizations, determine not only "the scope of the political bargains embedded in the pacts and the effects they will have on the prospects for effective democratization" (Encarnación 2005: 184) but also whether the new democracy will be able to effectively manage the tensions, dangers, and dilemmas implicit in a pact.[50]

Who was included and who was excluded from the Colombian and Venezuelan pacts? In both cases political parties and their leaders were the protagonists of the transition processes, from beginning to end: in opposing the dictatorships, in mobilizing society, in controlling and channeling the popular uprisings of May 1957 and January 1958, and especially during the pact-making phase. Parties were crucial players, enacting various roles simultaneously: they aggregated grievances and made them public, they mobilized the opposition to the dictatorship and channeled demands for democratization, and, finally, they negotiated the shape of the new institutional arrangement.

In Venezuela the coalition of the opposition included a wider array of actors: in addition to the three main parties, AD, URD, and COPEI,[51] the socioeconomic pact was signed by two crucially important social organizations, FEDECAMARAS, an umbrella organization representing the main business associations in the country, and the Comité Sindical Unificado, which represented the main labor organizations. In Colombia the main and only actors involved in the negotiation were the leadership of the Liberal and Conservative Parties and only implicitly the military and the Catholic Church.

Differences between the two cases are not reduced to the number and diversity of signatory parties or the degree of inclusiveness of the bargaining cartel, though; they are also related to differences in the types of parties involved in the transition, the nature of their ties with society, and their capacity to represent diverse social sectors and organizations. Although both Colombia and Venezuela had elite-driven pacted transitions, led by political parties with the support of the church hierarchy and entrepreneurial groups, the participation of organized social sectors (including business and workers' groups but also the peasants) was much more significant in Venezuela than in Colombia. With the exception of the upheavals in Cali, the uprising against Rojas Pinilla came basically from the middle and upper classes in Colombian society. Once the pacts were crafted between the parties, the resulting institutional arrangement (which contained the main points of the agreement between the parties)

Table 3.3. Colombia: National Plebiscite, December 1, 1957

Vote	Number of Votes	Percentage
Yes	4,169,294	94.8
No	206,864	4.7
Blank	20,738	0.47
Void	197	0.004
Total	4,397,090	100.00

Source: Data from Corte Electoral Nacional, in Cámara de Representantes 1959: 45.

was ratified and enshrined in the constitution via a plebiscite held on December 1, 1957. As shown in table 3.3 the new institutional arrangement was ratified by an overwhelming majority (94.8 percent) of the electorate, in an electoral mobilization without precedent in that country.[52]

In Venezuela the pacts gained legitimacy and popular acceptance thanks to a relationship characterized by more organic ties between the parties (especially AD) and society (especially the workers' and peasant federations, CTV and FCV). The difference between these two cases in terms of the origins and nature of their parties, as well as their relationship with diverse social sectors, elaborated in chapter 2, turned out to be crucial: whereas Colombia's "clientelistic" parties in Colombia resorted to electoral mobilization to ratify their pacts, the "radical populist" parties of Venezuela relied instead on their stronger links to organized sectors of society, especially organized labor and an organized albeit shrinking peasantry.[53]

One crucial difference is that whereas Venezuela was coming out of a harsh dictatorship, Colombia was overcoming a long decade of bloodshed and interparty warfare (i.e., La Violencia), which explains why various social actors—especially the peasantry—were so disorganized and incapable of negotiating their participation in the pacts. Beyond that circumstance, the history of party emergence and building is quite illuminating: as detailed in chapter 2, while the Venezuelan parties, especially AD, had since the beginning acted as radical populist vehicles for the incorporation of both peasants and workers, in close alliance with the emerging urban middle sectors, in Colombia the parties remained under the control of urban middle and upper classes, which remained closely tied to the landowning elites. In contrast to Venezuela, in Colombia it was the outgoing dictator, Rojas Pinilla, who had tried to incorporate sectors of the organized working class as well as the urban underclass by means of a populist discourse and movement (see Urán 1983; Palacios 1999).

As a consequence of the nature of its political parties and of their links with wider sectors of the population, the Venezuelan pacts were not only more inclusive but also more representative—in the sense that they were signed by parties who had closer and more organic ties with society, especially with the popular sectors, oil workers and peasants included. In Colombia, by contrast, the signatory parties were more elitist and relied more heavily on electoral mobilization, a fact evidenced in the way in which they sought ratification of their agreements: the Plebiscite of December 1957. The way in which parties reflected, translated, and represented (or not) underlying long-term social cleavages and conflicts present in their societies was certainly bound to have an impact on the outcome of negotiations between party leaders.

Despite these differences, an important political exclusion was common to these two transitions: the Communist Party of Colombia (PCC) and the Communist Party of Venezuela (PCV). The exclusion of the Communists occurred in part because their presence, in the context of the Cold War, would have caused the withdrawal of support from some key actors, including the church, the military, the business community, and the United States,[54] all of which were crucial to the stability of the emerging regime. In the case of the Communist Parties, it was not their inclusion but their exclusion that became crucial to guaranteeing the transition.

Alberto Lleras and Rómulo Betancourt, two important pact makers who were to become the first elected post-transition presidents in Colombia and Venezuela, respectively, were both strongly anti-Communist, and both made their intention to exclude the Communists from the pacts clear from the outset. Both leaders were trying to garner support from conservative sectors (their political adversaries, the U.S. government, the armed forces, the church, and the business community). Furthermore, excluding the Communist Parties was part of a party-building strategy. AD and the Liberal Party were both situated to the center-left of the political spectrum, and their main electoral competitor, as well as in the process of mobilizing and controlling social organizations (the labor and student movements), was the left, usually dominated by the Communists. The decision to exclude them was therefore a strategic move within a larger struggle for ideological and organizational hegemony between AD and the Liberal Party, on the one hand, and the Communist Parties in Venezuela and Colombia, on the other.[55]

Lleras and Betancourt may have succeeded in occupying the center-left, but the costs of this strategy were undoubtedly high. These costs were to be measured not only in terms of the emergence of guerrilla warfare and the expansion of political violence but also in terms of the conservatization of these two once-progressive parties—a shift to the right that became apparent in the following decades—and the ensuing internal divisions they both suffered.[56] This was especially true for AD; to gain power and retain it, AD had to sacrifice its radical program of the 1940s and become a much more moderate, social democratic party. This ideological shift also implied sacrificing part of its constituency: the more radicalized, left-wing students and party cadres formed the backbone of the dissident wings that split from AD in the following years. Excluding the PCV and shifting to the right during the transition proved harder for AD: the two parties had been close allies and collaborators during the struggle against Pérez Jiménez. The PCV had been part of the Junta Patriótica and had also participated in drafting its famous Manifesto. However, it became increasingly isolated and was finally excluded from the pact-making process, which then became controlled by three leaders and their parties: Rómulo Betancourt (AD), Jóvito Villalba (URD), and Rafael Caldera (COPEI).

The costs and consequences of excluding the Communists were greater in Venezuela; at some point it even looked as if they might outweigh the purported gains. The PCV was more powerful than its counterpart in Colombia, in terms of its ties with the labor movement and the student movement, and it had played an active role in the struggle against the dictatorship.[57] Just as the Venezuelan transition was coming to its end, Fidel Castro entered triumphantly into Havana, presenting not only Cubans but also all Latin Americans with the possibility of a viable revolution in the Third World. The Cuban Revolution further radicalized the left in Venezuela—not only the PCV but also the most militant faction of AD, thus throwing a deep wedge within the moderate and the radicals sectors of the party. The year 1959 was one of growing separation between AD and its radical following: a socialist revolution on Cuban soil was happening at the same time that Betancourt was hoping to convince his fellow countrymen that a socialist revolution was impossible in Venezuela. In the eyes of the most radical segments of the party, Castro's triumph belied Betancourt's claims. The Cuban Revolution had a powerful effect on these radical sectors.[58] Having been excluded from the pacts and with the example of the Cuban Revolution around the corner just when the first competitive elections were taking place in Venezuela, the Communists decided to take up arms against the nascent democracy. By the early 1960s they had established one of the largest guerrilla movements in Latin America.[59] The Communists were joined in their guerrilla struggles by a radical sector of the student movement and the youth wing of AD (Movimiento Independiente Revolucionario [MIR]), which had grown increasingly disenchanted by the party's shift to the center, its moderate stance, and its willingness to negotiate with the church, the military, and the business sector—as well as by a fraction of the URD.

The Colombian Communists were not as significant, in electoral strength or their support base.[60] They lacked a significant electoral following and had no influence on the urban mass movements that contributed to the downfall of the dictatorship. The PCC had become a predominantly rural-based party, with active presence in some regions where they had been and remained influential since the 1930s (e.g., the coffee-growing regions on the Cordillera Oriental) and beyond the agricultural frontier where they migrated due to the repression carried out by the authoritarian governments of Gómez and Rojas Pinilla during the 1950s. When the bipartisan pacts were negotiated the PCC had no power to oppose them, even though the pacts excluded them more radically than did the Venezuelan ones: the Colombian pacts not only excluded the Communists from the pact-making process itself, but they also prevented them from participating in elections and having access to any office (elected or appointed) for the next sixteen years.

In 1957 the PCC showed an ambiguous but mostly positive reaction to the transition's founding plebiscite. There was even an attempt to participate in the electoral arena through the Movimiento Revolucionario Liberal (MRL). When these efforts came under attack in 1963–64 and once the military decided to occupy its zones of influence (the municipalities of Marquetalia, El Pato, and Guayabero), the PCC decided to take up arms again and founded a full-fledged guerrilla movement, the Fuerzas Armadas Revolucionarias de Colombia (FARC), which still exists today.[61] Because the PCC was weaker than the PCV, its exclusion had less immediate impact on the new democratic regime. It took more time and more repression on the part of the Colombian regime to turn the PCC into a disloyal opposition, in spite of the fact that their exclusion from the original pacts and the subsequent shaping of the political arena was evidently harsher in Colombia than in Venezuela. In any case, exclusions such as the one operated against Communist Parties in Colombia and Venezuela in the late 1950s imply, from the start, an obstacle to the expansion of the political arena and the construction of a loyal opposition.

Having said that, it is also important to recognize that there are different degrees of exclusion. Parties can be excluded from just one round of the political game, as occurred in Venezuela, where the PCV was excluded from the negotiations leading to the pacts but was subsequently permitted to participate in elections. Or they can be excluded for longer periods, as happened in Colombia, where neither the PCC nor any other party different from the Liberal and Conservative Parties were to compete or have access to office for four consecutive presidential terms, or sixteen years. Finally, actors can be excluded indefinitely from all subsequent phases of the game, as when parties are banned. The costs of exclusion can therefore be higher or lower, depending on the degree of exclusion and the previous strength of the excluded party.

In all cases, however, pacts draw a boundary between those inside the game of "legal politics"—even if they are adversaries, insiders are still partners in the same game—and "outsiders," those who are excluded and who can become enemies, by their own decision or by the incumbents' decision. This alienating consequence of pacts is crucial, since those left outside do not feel the obligation to behave according to the rules established in the pacts that marginalized and excluded them.[62] In short, by excluding certain actors—unless some mechanism is worked out to eventually expand the political arena and provide for the gradual inclusion of those initially excluded—pacts can create the conditions for the emergence of disloyal oppositions and ensuing regime instability. It is therefore by virtue of the exclusion of certain actors, not by their inherent nature, that pacts can be inimical to democracy.

The Content of Pacts: Scope, Degree, and Duration of Restrictions

The range of inclusion or exclusion accorded in pacts, the nature of the parties included, and their capacity for representation are crucial factors but not the only ones affecting the outcomes of pacted transitions. Despite their similar outlook, a careful reading of the Colombian and Venezuelan pacts yields some crucial differences regarding their stipulations.[63] A key difference is to be found at the level of the specific institutional mechanisms and restrictions imposed on the subsequent political process.

Pacts are about introducing a series of limitations, restrictions, and mutual guarantees into what otherwise would be a more fluid—but perhaps also more contentious—interaction between political players.[64] Now, these limits or restrictions may apply to the realm of participation and restrict the franchise, or they may apply to the realm of competition and restrict the opportunities for contestation. Finally, they may affect the level of uncertainty by reducing the range of possible substantive outcomes of the political process, that is, policies. They may also vary according to their degree (relatively soft or strong) and duration (short, long, or unlimited periods). Their duration, in turn is related to the degree of institutional entrenchment accorded to them by the signatories: some accords remain informal "conversations among gentlemen"; others are formally enshrined in laws and constitutions. While the Venezuelan pacts were more open, flexible, and forward-looking, aimed fundamentally at building trust among competing actors, the Colombian pacts were more restrictive, rigid, and backward-looking, aimed at conferring veto powers on the two main actors involved, the Liberal and Conservative Parties, and built on the basis of their mutual distrust.

None of the Colombian or Venezuelan pacts restricted the participatory dimension of democracy.[65] On the contrary, the franchise was expanded in the Colombian case, to include women during the Plebiscite of December 1957 for the first time in its long electoral history.[66] In that electoral contest Colombia crossed the threshold of universal suffrage by including all adults twenty-one years and older. In Venezuela universal suffrage for adults over eighteen, which had been introduced in the 1947 Constitution, was reestablished in the 1958 elections.

On the other hand, in both cases the pacts restricted competition. Nevertheless, the restrictions imposed on this dimension of the democratic regime were quite different in terms of their scope, degree, and duration. First, regarding electoral discrimination against "outsiders" to the pact, though both pacts excluded the Communist Parties, the Venezuelan pacts did not prevent the PCV from taking part in elections. By contrast, the Colombian pacts not only excluded the Communists but also all other third parties (aside from the Liberals and the Conservatives) from participation in elections for a period of sixteen years.

Regarding competition among "insiders" to the pact, the Venezuelan pacts foresaw only one coalition government (which included the three pacting parties), which would last five years or one presidential term. The clause was meant to guarantee that whoever was elected president would not use power to build a single-party government to the exclusion of all others. The mechanism designed to ensure this was a multiparty executive cabinet, in which no single party could predominate or seek exclusive rule. That restriction notwithstanding, the outcome of the electoral process was to remain open and uncertain, with the three candidates (AD's Betancourt, COPEI's Caldera, and URD's Larrazábal) participating in the same conditions. The main purpose of the pact was to tame AD's majoritarian intentions and build a minimum level of trust that would ensure the holding of elections and the forming of a coalition that could last at least for the first presidential period. In a sense, then, the Venezuelan pacts truly amounted to a "conversation among gentlemen."[67]

The 1958 elections in Venezuela actually determined who was to govern, and the uncertainty of electoral outcomes was respected. In fact, the second clause in the Pact of Punto Fijo[68] gave Venezuelans assurance that "the electoral process and the public powers arising therefrom will respond to the democratic norm of effective freedom to vote."[69] The pacts, then, were not meant to reduce the uncertainty of outcomes but rather to guarantee that the electoral process "will not only avoid the breakdown of the unitary front, but rather will strengthen it through the extension of the political truce, the depersonalization of the debate, the eradication of interparty violence and the definition of rules that will facilitate the formation of a government and deliberative bodies in a way that both may group, with equity, all sectors from Venezuelan society interested in the stability of the Republic" (112).

On the basis of these general principles, the parties expressed their agreement on three main issues, the first of which was that "elections will determine responsibility in the exercise of public power during the constitutional period 1959–1964." Each signatory party was committed to unite their forces in the event the electoral process was disrupted by force or its results altered ex post facto, an event defined as "a crime against the fatherland" (Pact of Punto Fijo, in López Maya, Gómez Calcaño, and Maingón 1989: 112). The pact makes explicit reference to the possibility of a coup: "Every single political organization has the obligation to act in defense of constitutional authority in case a coup d'etat is attempted or carried out" (12).[70] According to the pact, this "patriotic commitment" would remain in force for a period of five years (the first presidential term) and was not to be forsaken even if "the circumstances of autonomy which [the political] organizations have reserved for themselves may have put any of them in a position of legal and democratic opposition to the government" (12). Stated in the introduction to the pact and then highlighted in this paragraph, the autonomy of political parties and organizations, from each other as well as from the government, was a key aspect of the Venezuelan pacts. Despite their drive toward unity in order to complete the democratic transition, the parties were not meant to merge into a single party; rather, the possibility of an open, legal, and loyal opposition was recognized and accepted from the start.

The second compromise among the three Venezuelan parties included the main restriction imposed by the pact on the political game: a "government of national unity." Even though electoral outcomes would be respected, "the fate of the Venezuelan democracy and the stability of the rule of law among us require us to turn the defensive popular unity into a unitary government at least for as long as the factors that threaten the Republican experiment which was initiated on January 23, would last" (12). As much as this clause was meant to tame competition among political forces and "to avoid a systematic opposition that would debilitate the democratic movement," it was mainly aimed at AD; thus it explicitly stated that "none of the signatory organizations aspires to nor accepts hegemony in the executive cabinet, in which all the national political currents and independent sectors of the country must be represented" (112).[71] These restrictions applied only to the formation of the executive cabinet, and no specific distribution of power was fixed before the electoral results were known. Eventually, and confirming the flexibility of the pacts, when in 1962 one of the members of the coalition government (URD) left his post the coalition government continued, albeit with fewer participants.

Third, "in order to facilitate cooperation among political organizations during the electoral process and their collaboration in the constitutional government, the signatory parties agree to participate in said process supporting a common minimum program." This program, the Programa Mínimo de Gobierno (MPG), was written separately, signed by the three parties on December 6, 1958, and considered an appendix to the Pact of Punto Fijo.[72] Consisting of three pages, it defined the main general guidelines for policy making in the areas of political action and public administration, the economy, mining and petroleum-related issues, social and labor issues, education, the armed forces, immigration, and foreign affairs.

The MPG confirmed a central role for the state in economic development. While recognizing the need for participation of the private sector and foreign investment, the program explicitly stated, "The characteristics of the economic and fiscal structure of Venezuela give the state a predominant role in fomenting national wealth" (116), a central tenet that would only be reinforced by the oil bonanza of the 1970s. The state would make use of its resources through a variety of instruments to promote and protect private investment. Overall, it would reorganize and widen the scope of its direct participation in petrochemicals as well as in the iron and steel industries. The MPG reaffirmed public ownership of mineral resources as a sign of the nation's sovereignty, declared that everything related to the petroleum industry would be considered of public interest, and vowed to obtain greater and more effective control of all related activities. It also insisted on the need to refine a significant amount of oil and iron ore in Venezuelan territory, to create the National Petroleum Corporation, and a petroleum fleet, as well as any other organization necessary to get "Venezuela to begin working its oil directly" (117). If the abundance of oil resources had already made Venezuela a major oil exporter, the MPG served to ratify that the country's economic fate would become pegged to its oil wealth and that the state would directly control the country's main source of wealth.

The idea of elaborating a long-term, integral, national development plan, so much in vogue those days in all of Latin America, also found a place in the MPG. Apart from a vague mention of the need to reform and modernize the tax system, the MPG alluded to the need for significant agrarian reform as a tool for transforming the country's economy, endowing peasants with land and the resources to till them, and confronting "the rural problem in all its aspects: economic, social, technical, cultural, etc." (117). Other social policies were mentioned in vague terms.[73] However, when it came to labor rights, the MPG was much more explicit. Among the issues to be addressed by the next government were the following: defending workers and protecting the freedom to form unions and the unions themselves; fighting unemployment; reforming the labor code in order to modernize the regulation of worker-employer relations; implementing a family salary; and reorganizing the social security system. In addition, the MPG mentioned the need to promote education at all levels, to eradicate illiteracy, and to put education under the direct control of the state (118).

Under the section devoted to the armed forces, the MPG briefly described what had been up to that time implicit agreements between the civilian leaders and outgoing military elites: the armed forces were to receive the necessary resources for the "technical improvement and modernization of the different forces that compose the armed institution" and were offered a progressive improvement in the living standards of both officers and soldiers. The MPG dismissed the armed forces' role in the outgoing dictatorial regime and stated, "The merits and services of the men who form the armed institution will be recognized as well as their important cooperation in keeping public peace and as a guarantee of national progress." In return, the armed forces would agree to be defined as "a nonpolitical, obedient, and nondeliberating body." In order to reaffirm the principles on which the military was based, "institutional education" would be intensified across the board (118).

In a short statement referring to the church, the MPG declares the need to "normalize relations between church and state." Finally, in terms of the design of the institutional structure that would ensure the actual implementation of these policy guidelines, the MPG declares the parties' intention to write a democratic constitution which would reaffirm the principles of a representative regime and "include a bill of social and economic citizens' rights" (116). It emphasizes the need to defend the constitutional order and take strong measures against any antidemocratic activity. It proposes to eradicate any provisions that may go against public liberties while also proposing to grant greater autonomy to and strengthen the judiciary and legislative powers, as well as the municipal level of government.[74]

In addition to this list of good intentions, the MPG contained a set of limits that neither of the participating candidates could transgress in the event of being elected. To avoid the polarizing effects of open, competitive elections and to facilitate the tasks facing the first government, the parties signed this minimum agreement on policies in December 1958, a day before the election. The main objective of this agreement was to water down some of the most radical social and economic policies espoused by AD during its failed three-year rule (1945–48), especially its agrarian reform, education, and oil policies, and thus prevent polarizing discussions about potentially conflict-ridden issues. AD's agreement to thus limit the government's policy agenda was a crucial compromise that guaranteed the entrance into the pact of actors such as COPEI, the Catholic Church, and the business community; it is likely that without it these actors would have withdrawn their support for the new democratic experiment. It can be said that the MPG contained a built-in conservative bias. In the longer term, however, as democracy begins to take root and becomes institutionalized, agreements on substantive issues can be altered, removed, or overturned. Every democracy, whether explicitly pacted or not, entails concessions, guarantees, and compromises. The point is that the Venezuelan pacts of 1958 did not lock the Venezuelan political system into an irredeemably conservative path.

Since the MPG did not exclude the right of political organizations to defend causes not explicitly covered by it, an additional rule, agreed on in the Pact of Punto Fijo, encouraged moderation: "No unitary party will include in its particular program any points which may be contrary to the common ones in the minimum program, and in any event, public discussion on those issues which are not common will be kept within the limits of tolerance and mutual respect" (quoted in López Maya, Gómez Calcaño, and Maingón 1989: 112–13).

In closing the Pact of Punto Fijo, the signatory parties considered the factors that impeded the selection of a single candidate, the writing of a single list for deliberative bodies, or the formation of a single front ("frente único") on the basis of a single, integral program of government. The main reason argued was the existence of "natural contradictions between the parties" (113). The pact ended by reinstating the compatibility between the desired unity in the fight for democracy and the right of each party to present its own presidential candidates and its own lists of candidates for legislative seats. Thus, while aiming to tame it, the pacts preserved the competitive nature of elections in Venezuela.

The subsequent Declaration of Principles,[75] signed on December 6, 1958, on the eve of the election, by the three main presidential candidates, Rómulo Betancourt (AD), Wolfgang Larrazábal (URD, with the backing of the PCV), and Rafael Caldera (COPEI), reaffirmed the will of the parties and party leaders to respect the electoral outcome and to join all political forces in resisting any effort to overturn it by force. It also urged the elected president to form a government of "national unity" without party hegemony and with the representation of all political forces and independent sectors. In addition, it confirmed their intention to base their policy agenda on the MPG (signed on the same date). Finally, it insisted on the need to maintain and consolidate the political truce and the peaceful coexistence of all democratic organizations.

A commitment to moderation during the electoral process and in all political interactions more generally, a coalition cabinet during the first presidential term, and an agreement on the issues to be included in the first government's policy agenda—these were the main restrictions introduced into Venezuelan politics by the party pacts. As for their duration, apart from a brief mention of "the course of five years," the Pact of Punto

Fijo explicitly stated that it would endure "for as long as the factors threatening the democratic experiment persist," thus acknowledging the need to be flexible and adjust to a changing political environment. Political parties and leaders were called on to assess and decide if and when those factors had disappeared, but there was no fixed time duration agreed on beforehand. The architects of the pact were concerned about guaranteeing a spirit of conciliation and cooperation during the first presidential term, but there was no plan to extend these restrictions further.

The restrictions introduced by the Venezuelan pacts pale in comparison to their Colombian counterparts: viewed in a comparative light, the former were not only more limited in scope and more open in spirit but also more flexible, respectful of the uncertainty implied in democratic elections, and more capable of adapting to changes and variations as the political process unfolded. By contrast, the Colombian party pacts became increasingly rigid and restrictive as the negotiations proceeded. The first agreement between the two main party leaders, Lleras Camargo and Gómez, in Benidorm, Spain, called for the joint action of the parties to find ways to stop the interparty warfare and a rapid return to the constitutional order. One mechanism to attain the said objectives appears briefly mentioned in the pact: the creation of bipartisan coalition governments (with no specification of how many or for how long).[76] The next agreement, the Pact of March, which included the second most important faction of the Conservative Party (the Ospinistas), was a forceful response to the attempt on the part of the armed forces and the military government to perpetuate Rojas Pinilla's rule and legalize it through the manipulation of a handpicked legislature, the National Constituent Assembly. It insisted on the need to elect a series of coalition governments on an open-ended basis, until the restored institutions were solid enough and the conditions ripe for resuming the kind of party controversy and competition that are inherent to democracy. In addition, the Pact of March mentions for the first time the need to search for a constitutional formula that would guarantee the equitable sharing of power and alternation in the presidency between the two parties on a more permanent basis.[77] The parties proposed to return to the previous constitutional order and to do so via the traditional route: elections. To do so without risking a renewed cycle of interparty violence, the two parties agreed to present a single presidential candidate for the 1958 election. The Liberal Party acquiesced to supporting a Conservative candidate as a sign of its firm will to enter into a permanent coalition with the Conservatives.[78] Apart from this specific compromise, the signatories postponed the definition of the mechanisms that would constitutionally guarantee their more general aims and commitments.

In the Pact of Sitges, signed by Lleras Camargo and Gómez on July 20, 1957, the Liberal and Conservative leaders ratified their agreement on the need to restore the previous constitution, albeit with a few modifications intended to restrain competition between the parties: thus, the agreement on a single candidate for the first presidential election and the need to sustain a series of coalition governments. A duration of twelve years (or three presidential terms) was mentioned here for the first time. In addition, the pact extended the notion of equal power sharing between the parties beyond the executive cabinet to include the entire executive branch, including the regional and local levels of government: departmental governors as well as municipal mayors would have to be drawn from the two parties in equal proportions. It also mentioned the need to establish equilibrium between the parties in all deliberative bodies, including the national Congress, the departmental assemblies, and the municipal councils. Decisions in Congress would be taken by a qualified majority of 50 percent plus one. Finally, the pact included the novel idea of a plebiscite, designed to ratify and enshrine the proposed changes in the Constitution, in time for them to govern the upcoming elections.[79]

On October 4, 1957, the military junta issued Legislative Decree No. 247, which contained the full and final text of the party agreements, including the constitutional mechanisms to be approved by national plebiscite. In Article 1 the decree convoked a national plebiscite for December 1, 1957, in which all Colombian adults, male and female, twenty-one years and older, could approve or disapprove the constitutional amendments proposed by the party pacts. In its preamble the plebiscite made explicit recognition of the Catholic Church as a basis of national unity, and as such it was to be protected by all public powers (Legislative Decree No. 247, in Cámara de Representantes 1959: 42). Article 2 established equal power in the distribution of seats for all deliberative bodies: Congress, departmental assemblies, and municipal councils for a period of twelve years. Article 3 established a majority of two-thirds in order to approve any and all decisions emanating from any of these bodies.[80] Article 4 extended the norm of parity between the parties to the executive cabinet. In addition, the entire executive branch should be appointed following this parity agreement between the parties. Notwithstanding this rule, the article stated the possibility of appointing members from the armed forces to positions in the public administration.

Article 9 ambiguously fixed the date for the first elections to take place under the new system ("in the first semester of 1958")—thus leaving open the possibility of having either concurrent or nonconcurrent elections for president and Congress, a matter of significant contention between the parties, especially given the acute competition for power between the Laureanista and Ospinista factions within the Conservative Party. This issue was solved only days before the plebiscite, on November 22, 1957, through the Pact of San Carlos, which stipulated that congressional elections would take place in March, before the election for president scheduled for May 1958.[81] The idea was to let the majoritarian congressional faction select the Conservative candidate for the presidency.

Article 11 contains the only guideline in terms of social policy appearing in the pacts: "Starting on January 1, 1958, the National Government shall invest no less than ten percent (10 %) of the General Expenditure Budget on public education" (Cámara de Representantes 1959: 44). Article 12 extended the rule of parity to the judicial branch by stating that judges on the Supreme Court of Justice would be selected from the political parties "in the same proportion as they are represented in the Legislative Chambers" (44). Finally, Article 13 closed the door on future constitutional reform by extraordinary means, by granting the power to amend the constitution solely to Congress.

Just days after the plebiscite was approved by an overwhelming majority of close to 95 percent (see table 3.3), a crisis emerged concerning the selection of the union candidate. Given the impossibility of reaching an agreement between the deeply divided Conservative factions on a single candidate from that party—a controversy that occupied the party leaders from December 1957 to April 1958—Laureano Gómez finally threw his weight behind a Liberal candidate: Alberto Lleras Camargo, his coarchitect of the National Front pacts. This decision altered the arithmetic of the pacts: since the Liberal Party had acquiesced to supporting a Conservative candidate for the first term of a twelve-year sequence of coalition governments, it was necessary to grant a second period to the Conservative Party. With the Liberals electing the first president, the Conservatives would only have one presidential period down the line. The agreement to alternate the presidency was then extended to four presidential terms, or sixteen years, to ensure that both parties would have two periods and that the Conservative Party would get the last turn.[82]

The strong mutual guarantees included in the National Front pacts ensured that neither Liberals nor Conservatives would be excluded from power but also limited competition between them and blocked access to potential new parties. Party leaders agreed to complete parity in the three branches of government. Congress, departmental assemblies, municipal councils, and even the judiciary would automatically be half Liberal and half Conservative; cabinet posts, governorships, and mayorships would also be divided equally between the two parties. Furthermore, most legislation would require a two-thirds majority for approval. Finally, they agreed to alternation in the presidency from 1958 to 1974.

Beyond limiting participation and/or contestation, pacts can impose limits or even gag rules on the policy agenda, thereby reducing uncertainty regarding the substantive outcomes of the democratic process. This was the case with the MPG signed by the three competing candidates in the first Venezuelan election in 1958. In Colombia there was no substantive agreement between the parties to limit the policy agenda, except for a clause introduced in the plebiscite of 1957 that forced the government to spend at least 10 percent of the General Expenditure Budget in public education[83]—admittedly a progressive rather than conservative passage of the accords. What proved much more conservative were two procedural clauses that set strict limitations on the enactment of social, economic, or political reforms: the first was a qualified two-thirds majority to pass legislation at any and all levels (in all representative bodies). Article 3 of the Legislative Decree calling for the plebiscite stated that "for all legal effects the majority will be two-thirds of the votes; however, Congress may, through a law voted by two-thirds of the members of both chambers, decide on those issues for which an approval by simple majority will be enough, for periods of up to two years" (quoted in Cámara de Representantes 1959: 42–43). This procedural rule acted as a powerful barrier to any party imposing its own agenda without crafting a previous agreement on the issue with at least half of the opposing party. It also gave the most conservative factions within the two parties the equivalent of veto power on legislation.[84] Similarly, the pacts reinstituted a relatively strict amendment procedure: constitutional reforms could only be carried out by Congress, in two consecutive ordinary sessions, with the approval of two-thirds of both chambers.[85]

The increasingly restrictive nature of the Colombian pacts is indicative of the degree of distrust between the signatories and the need to build strong barriers against defection. The agreements became constitutionally entrenched: first through the plebiscite of December 1957 and then through the constitutional amendment introduced on September 15, 1959. Indeed, by virtue of the consociational guarantees granted to both parties, the National Front agreements "conspired to strip elections, the most sacred of liberal democracy's institutions, of most of their meaning" (Hagopian 1990: 150). While competition between the parties was nullified, all political competition was transferred inside the parties: a fierce competitive struggle ensued among the party factions for control of each party's share of the state apparatus. Simultaneously, the idea of a legitimate, viable opposition practically disappeared from both the institutional framework and public discourse: any opposition to the National Front agreement was considered disloyal and therefore harshly repressed. There was no place for dissent beyond the coalition government, except outside the system, which is exactly what happened. A disloyal opposition movement was engendered. Finally, as a result of the two-thirds majority rule as applied by a bipartisan congress, a legislative bias in favor of the status quo was practically guaranteed. This was certainly not a recipe for institutionalizing a full democracy. The uncertainty of electoral outcomes, together with the notions of competition and contestation—both defining characteristics of any democracy— became severely compromised in the Colombian pacts, which did not look like a conversation among gentlemen but rather a hard-won agreement between long-standing enemies.

The stipulations contained in the Colombian pacts thus differ from their Venezuelan counterparts in almost every respect, not only in terms of their content but also in terms of the time frame and the fact that they became constitutionally enshrined and locked into the constitution thanks to strict amendment rules. When viewed comparatively, there is no question that the Colombian pacts were much more rigid, inflexible, and restrictive than the Venezuelan ones. Table 3.4 summarizes the main restrictions introduced by the pacts in each of these cases. It clearly shows the wide gap that separates the strictures of the Colombian pacts from the lesser and more flexible restrictions introduced by the Venezuelan pacts. On the other hand, while the Venezuelan pacts included substantive limits on the policy agenda, the Colombian pacts included a procedural mechanism, the two-thirds majority required to pass legislation, which granted veto powers to the party factions, thus endowing them with the capacity to limit the system's capacity to enact reforms.

As time would show, the Colombian procedural mechanism proved much more difficult to change than any of the substantive limits on policy pacted in the Venezuelan case. In addition, the flexibility that became the hallmark of the Venezuelan agreements was expressed in the fact that they did not specify duration, stating only that the agreement between the parties would prevail for "as long as the factors threatening the democratic experiment persist." The spirit of Punto Fijo may have endured a long time, but the specific restrictions contemplated in the pacts did not last beyond the first presidential term. By contrast, the rigidity of the Colombian pacts was evident not only in their fixed duration but also in the fact that their provisions were permanently locked into a constitution that was difficult to change. In Venezuela the pacts remained as written agreements between the parties and then gradually evolved into a consensual constitution drafted by the elected Congress in 1961.

Venezuela's pacts were thus not only more inclusionary but also less restrictive and more flexible. They contained the political blueprint for an institutional arrangement that would be more open and adaptable, more forward-looking than its Colombian counterpart. More important, they preserved three crucial features of democracy: party competition, uncertainty of electoral outcomes, and the possibility of engendering a loyal opposition. By contrast, the Colombian pacts were premised on the exclusion from elections of the Communist Party or any other party besides the Liberals and Conservatives, the fixed parity between the parties in the Executive, Legislative, and Judicial branches of power, and the mandatory alternation of the presidency. The institutional arrangement created by the pacts and enshrined in the Constitution precluded the uncertainty of electoral outcomes, robbing elections (until 1974) of their raison d'etre. Even worse, the very notion of a legitimate opposition disappeared from the Colombian political landscape. As can be gleaned

Table 3.4. Restrictions Introduced by Pacts: Nature, Scope, Duration, and Entrenchment

	Venezuela	*Colombia*
Restrictions on Participation	No	No
Restrictions on Contestation		
Coalition Cabinet	Yes	Yes
Pre-fixed presidential alternation	No	Yes
Power sharing in Executive Branch*	No	Yes
Power sharing in the Legislature	No	Yes
Power sharing in the Judiciary	No	Yes
Electoral discrimination against third parties	No	Yes
Restrictions on Policy Making	Yes (substantive)	Yes (procedural)
Duration	5 years initially (no fixed duration)	16 years
Degree of Institutional Entrenchment	Gradually evolved into new constitution (1961)	Enshrined in constitution (via plebiscite and constitutional amendment)

* Beyond the cabinet.

from these two cases, not every political pact compromises the process of democratization in the same way. As I show in the following chapters, these variations made all the difference as these two processes of democratic development unfolded.

How do we account for the differences between these pacts? Again, a look back into history proves useful. As similar as their trajectories may seem, democratic transitions in Colombia and Venezuela yielded different institutional outcomes in part because they were designed by a different set of actors to confront and solve different problems. In Venezuela it was largely a matter of creating, almost from scratch, a representative, competitive, and democratic regime. Although the 1947 Constitution served as the blueprint for the new constitution drafted in 1961, the institutions contained in the former had worked for less than a year (December 1947–November 1948). The central problem to be solved by the pacts was prior to the implementation of a constitutional order: how to build trust among competitors for power. How to convince the players that the game is fair and will not be taken over by the most advantaged player in any specific round. In a nutshell, the Venezuelan dilemma was to create an inclusionary, self-reinforcing competitive process that would allow everyone to participate while preventing the winner from eventually excluding the losers. The central issue was to tame AD and thus create trust among those actors who had tried to participate in the first aborted attempt at democratizing Venezuela's political system in the mid-1940s. The lessons of the Trienio had been learned; now the parties wanted to give it a second try without the polarizing and catastrophic consequences of the Trienio experiment (see Corrales 2006b).

Venezuela's Pact of Punto Fijo was less concerned with the creation and consecration of formal institutional guarantees and restrictions. It was directed instead at the creation of "trust" among the players in the first competitive round, the first election, which would then be followed by the crafting of a new constitution by all those included in the game, a new set of rules to regulate further rounds of the same game. The challenge facing the Venezuelan elites at the moment of transition—that is, at the moment of institutional design—was thus how to create a competitive regime that gave all the significant actors a stake in the game and thus make it a self-reinforcing one.

The central issue in Colombia was not only one of distrust among the players or political forces involved but also one of open, violent confrontation between them. The Liberal and Conservative Parties were the protagonists of eight civil wars fought during the nineteenth century. A truce took hold after the War of a Thousand Days and lasted until the mid-1940s, with sporadic, short, and localized episodes of partisan violence emerging occasionally during this four-decade period. In the mid-1940s, however, that truce was broken, and the decade-long partisan confrontation known as La Violencia erupted nationwide. La Violencia was deeply rooted in the socioeconomic changes brought about by the country's development throughout the first three decades of the twentieth century, the reforms introduced by the Liberal Party during the 1930s and the Conservatives' reaction to them,[86] coupled with the tendency in these two parties to seize and monopolize power.[87] The spiral of partisan conflict not only caused a death toll calculated between 200,000 and 300,000 (of a population of almost 10 million), but it also caused the breakdown of Colombia's "oligarchic democracy" in 1949 (Wilde 1978, 1982).

After that breakdown, two attempts were made to install authoritarian regimes. The first was the attempt by President Laureano Gómez to approve through his handpicked Constitutional Assembly a new corporatist constitution modeled after Spain's Francoist charter. Once this attempt failed, General Gustavo Rojas Pinilla tried another type of authoritarian regime with a populist bent, less elaborated in a constitutional formula, following in the footsteps of Perón and his attempt to create a populist movement supported by the mobilized urban poor and working classes. These attempts failed. They also failed to put an end to the violent confrontation between the parties.

By 1957 the parties had two tasks at hand. The most immediate one was to put an end to military rule and restore control of the state to the civilian elite. The second and most demanding one was to put an end to the seemingly endless cycle of political violence (including its latest round, started in 1946) which they had contributed to fueling for over a century. Putting an end to interparty violence not only meant demobilizing their partisan followers but also, and above all, creating the conditions under which neither of the parties would be able to create party hegemony. This was a necessary condition not only to close the immediately preceding decade of violence but also and most important to eliminate the causes of partisan violence from reappearing in the future, once and for all. Indeed, the only way to understand why the Colombian agreements reached such rigid and restrictive terms is to understand that through them the parties attempted to break and change a pattern of interparty relations that was already deeply ingrained. The difficulties of reaching such demanding compromises were compounded, moreover, by the fact that the Conservative Party was deeply divided at the moment of the negotiation and that one of its factions, the Laureanistas, had an immense veto power over the negotiations due to the active role it had played in promoting partisan violence during the preceding decade. In sum, the Colombian pacts were more backward-looking, concerned more with past experience than with the future and intended to close a century of partisan confrontation rather than to open a new cycle of regime change.[88] By contrast, the Venezuelan pacts were forward-looking; they were more concerned about the future, the creation of new institutions, and the generation of trust in the aftermath of a previous experience whose failure had left bitter memories and lessons to keep.

Similar Pacted Transitions with Divergent Institutional Legacies

This chapter addresses the crucial puzzle of why democratic regimes in Colombia and Venezuela evolved quite differently in the post-transition period despite the countries' seemingly identical "pacted transitions": whereas Venezuela attained relatively rapid institutionalization of democratic rules and practices, Colombia remained entangled by difficulties and obstacles to democratic progress. These divergent outcomes, despite striking similarities in their transition processes, throw into question the "mode of transition hypothesis." I have challenged a common interpretation of democratization whereby much of what transpires after a transition to democracy owes its dynamics (whether negative or positive) to favorable or unfavorable conditions established by the mode in which the transition happened. The present investigation shows that the generic modality of transition does not have as much impact as it was previously believed. Instead, it is crucial to consider the specific traits encapsulated in the term *mode of transition,* or, in other words, to unpack the different sets of factors that are usually bundled together in this concept. The different evolution and combinations of elements bundled together under this umbrella term can help us understand why different modes of transition may not necessarily have opposing effects and why similar paths toward democracy (as in the cases of Colombia and Venezuela) may not lead to the same outcomes.

Though critical of the mode of transition hypothesis, I have not wholly dismissed its explanatory potential for this critical period of political change. Instead, I have identified more precisely other factors and mechanisms—often obscured under the umbrella term *mode of transition*—at play in processes of regime change that may exert a lasting impact on political development. Democratic institutions are built through negotiations among contending elites, which at times are made explicit in written pacts. In this sense, "pacted" transitions present an analytical advantage over other types of transitions, because the pacts constitute clear blueprints of the institutional arrangements being put in place by elite agreements; they delineate with great precision the institutional architecture being created during the transition process. Through a comparative analysis of the Colombian and Venezuelan pacts I have arrived at the conclusion that the most significant difference between them lay not in the overall mode of transition but rather in the pacts themselves and the institutional legacies they left behind. Three issues emerged as crucial in this regard: first, the degree of inclusion/exclusion characterizing the pact-making coalition; second, the nature and scope of the restrictions imposed on the democratic game by the institutional arrangement installed as a consequence of the pacts; and third, the duration and degree of entrenchment of the pact's stipulations in the course of political interaction.

As applied to the cases at hand, this conceptual reformulation yields a compelling account of the contrast between the two cases: Venezuela's pacts, aimed fundamentally at building trust among competing actors, were not only more inclusionary but also less restrictive and more flexible. They contained the political blueprint for an institutional arrangement that would be more open, adaptable, and forward-looking than its Colombian counterpart. More important, they preserved three crucial features of democracy, including uncertainty of electoral outcomes, party competition, and the possibility of building a loyal opposition. In contrast, the Colombian pacts, aimed at conferring veto powers on the two main actors involved and built on the basis of their mutual distrust, were much more exclusionary, restrictive, and inflexible. These institutional outcomes had negative implications for the evolution of democracy in Colombia.

There are, indeed, different types of pacts. Some, as in Spain and Venezuela, are able to operate a break with the past—a radical shift in regime type and in the everyday practice of politics. Others, as in Colombia and Brazil, are much less able to do so, ensuring a greater degree of continuity, sometimes even helping to entrench traditional practices and institutions that are problematic for the institutionalization of a full democracy. If Brazil and Colombia retained features limiting democracy because of their elite-driven pacted democracies, in Spain and Venezuela democracy evolved thanks to and because of political pacts. These critical variations have not been captured in the literature on pacts, neither by those who have applauded them nor by those who have criticized them.[89]

The evidence collected throughout my research has led me to reconsider earlier views of political pacts and to a more nuanced and contingent appraisal of their impact. Pacts are crucial turning points because of their capacity to change the institutional design and thus alter the previous regime trajectory or path. By (re)defining the rules of the game, pacts have the capacity to limit uncertainty, to shape a priori the probabilities of future outcomes, and to give each of the signatories the guarantees they require to enter the game. The importance of pacts, then, lies in their function as institutional blueprints as well as in their distributional effects.[90] This may lead to positive outcomes, such as stability. Pacts reduce uncertainty. This is why pacted transitions are typically less openended in some of their political and institutional implications than are nonpacted ones. This is not necessarily a negative side effect: limiting uncertainty may be a necessary condition for democratization. In some cases, pacts are not only desirable but also absolutely necessary to establish the ground rules for a successful transition from authoritarianism to democracy. In effect, some societies (such as Colombia in the 1950s and perhaps again today) must pay the price of pact making in order to put an end to civil war and manage a peaceful transition to democracy. On the other hand, pacts are not only about "constraints"; they are also about creating "opportunities."[91] As the Venezuelan transition shows, through pacts political elites may establish new modes and expectations of behavior and create new institutional rules that may, in turn, generate long-lasting patterns of democratic interaction.

Another characteristic inherent to all pacts and pact making is that they are by nature elitist processes, designed to exclude and to confer guarantees to some but not all. Only elites can engage in pact making; but this fact does not automatically render them "undemocratic." Their "democraticness" depends on who is included or excluded in the pacts, as well as on their contents—that is, the nature, scope, and duration of the restrictions created by them. While Spain and Venezuela attest to the possibility of rapid democratic institutionalization thanks to pacts, Colombia and Brazil attest to the difficulties encountered by pacted democracies. Again, the clue does not lie in the "pacted" mode of the transition but rather in some more specific features pertinent to the pacts, including the range of actors who participated in them and the very nature of the things pacted. As I have argued throughout this chapter, differences in the nature and scope of restrictions as well as their duration and degrees of entrenchment have a lasting impact on the subsequent political process.

Pacts, I claim, are much more than just a conservative scheme to maintain the status quo. In some cases they may be absolutely necessary in order to guarantee the successful completion of a transition process and provide some degree of stability to a fledgling democracy. Now all pacts imply a price. However, as the cases of Colombia and Venezuela demonstrate, some pacts may turn out to be much more costly than others, in terms of the exclusions and the restrictions they impose on the subsequent political processes and how those exclusions and restrictions constrict democratic development. My comparison of Venezuela and Colombia has abundantly made this point: both were pacted transitions; both involved pacts among the opposition parties in order to make a viable transfer of power from a weakened military regime to a coalition of former competitors. However, differences in the actors involved as well as in the nature and scope of the restrictions created by each one of these pacts made a great difference in terms of their impact on the longer-term evolution of these two democratic regimes.

In closing this chapter, it is perhaps time to warn against assigning all the responsibility of future developments to pacts. Pacts do not determine, once and for all, every future outcome of the political process. Pacts can be renegotiated and changed, as the recent constitutional reforms in both Colombia and Venezuela show.[92] Some of the restrictive features of pacts can be eliminated, or its duration shortened, while others may be extended, having a more durable impact on the regime's workings. The eventual modification of previous pacts should not, however, lead us to the optimistic conclusion that everything can be changed for the better. Some changes, reforms, and renegotiations can be made in order to reiterate, prolong, and even reinforce the restrictions of the original pact. The conclusion, however, remains the same: once in place, as long as the regime is in some significant sense democratic—meaning that despite its restrictions and limitations it still permits some significant degree of competition and uncertainty of outcomes—the institutional legacies of pacts can be changed by the ongoing interaction among actors engaged in the political process. Whether restrictions are lifted and the pact made more inclusive or whether more restrictions to the open-ended game of democracy are instituted, thus limiting democracy even further, depends largely on the constellation of forces present at any given time.

That is to say that not all the variation in Colombia's and Venezuela's democratization processes can be attributed to these pacts. Pacts have a specific institutional weight, but they do not explain everything. Again, democratization is best conceived as an ongoing struggle among actors who seek to preserve, modify, or radically change the institutional legacies from the transition.[93] As we shall see in the chapters that follow, much of the struggle that ensued after these democratic transitions consisted precisely of political battles to maintain, modify, or drastically change the institutional legacies put in place by the original pacts. The range of options available to political actors is determined by long-term structural and institutional factors on the one hand and the institutional legacies inherited from the transition on the other. None of them, however, precludes the transformations that may come from the continuously contingent nature of political outcomes. While rejecting structural determinism, the theoretical framework proposed here is also inimical to institutional determinism. My analysis of what transpired in the decades after 1958 in Colombia and Venezuela is framed by the long-term structural and institutional factors analyzed before, as well as by the institutional legacies of the transitions. And still it leaves room for the fluid nature of politics.[94]

Part III

THE STRUGGLE FOR DEMOCRATIC INSTITUTIONALIZATION

> Democratization is a dynamic process that always remains
> incomplete and perpetually runs the risk of reversal.
> —Charles Tilly, *Democracy*

CHAPTER FOUR

Subduing the Challengers

Disarming, Subordinating, and Incorporating
Contenders on the Right and the Left

This book is built on the conviction that democratization is better conceived as an ongoing process—a continuum rather than a dichotomy—that admits intermediate stages, advances as well as setbacks. Instead of relying on the dichotomous notion of democratic consolidation, it conceives democratic institutionalization as a contentious process whereby different sets of democratic institutions may become resilient and self-sustaining. Democratic institutionalization is a multilayered process, occurring simultaneously in different arenas or dimensions that interact, sometimes reinforcing each other, sometimes neutralizing or even reversing previous achievements. It consists, to a great extent, "of eliminating the institutions, procedures and expectations that are incompatible with the minimal workings of a democratic regime" (Valenzuela 1992: 70), thereby permitting the beneficial ones to develop further. The process involves a struggle between those who benefit from and those who lose due to these formal and informal institutional arrangements and hence "unfolds through precedent-setting political confrontations that alter or revalidate the institutional and procedural environment in its perverse or beneficent aspects" (71). Such struggles do not take place in a political vacuum, however, but within the limits imposed by the historical and institutional context, inherited from the preauthoritarian period, the authoritarian experience, and the transition process.

This chapter and the next trace the post-transition development of democracy in Colombia and Venezuela as contentious, multifaceted institutionalization processes that depended on the interaction between political actors and their strategies, on the one hand, and a set of constraints and opportunities fixed by both historical continuities and by the legacies from the transition pacts, on the other. Fresh out of their respective transitions, Colombia and Venezuela faced a series of crucial challenges. One of the most significant was the elimination of political violence—that is, the elimination or neutralization of armed challengers coming from the right or the left and their successful incorporation into the polity. In return, the newly incorporated political parties or movements needed to accept and adapt to the constraints and opportunities offered by the democratic rules of the game. Thus one of the greatest challenges faced by these two fledging democracies was the formation of a party system in which a legitimate opposition could become a viable enterprise, a process that is taken up more fully in the next chapter. This process included the (re)legalization of previously banned parties and the inclusion of the opposition from both ends of the political spectrum into the legal political arena. Faced with a set of common challenges, the two countries confronted them in different ways, with different degrees of success. These differences, in turn, had an impact on their ensuing democratic trajectories: whereas Venezuela turned out to be a surprising case of rapid democratization, Colombia's democracy remained stunted by a series of shortcomings inherited both from its past and its transition process. Both cases, however, suffered from limitations to the full development of democracy that eventually led to their decay, a process analyzed in the last chapter of this book.

The process of democratic institutionalization analyzed below involves three overlapping and interlocking processes; for each one of them, long-term historical structural-institutional factors combined with the immediate institutional legacies from the transition to shape the set of opportunities and constraints faced by actors. I call the first process "the taming of the shrew," whereby the Colombian and Venezuelan governments in the late 1950s and early 1960s defeated military conspiracies aimed at reinstalling authoritarian rule and tried to subordinate the military and assert civilian supremacy. The second process, which I call "a farewell to arms," relates to confronting and defusing the challenge of armed contenders from the left.[1] This involves eliminating political violence on the part of actors beyond the state and monopolizing the use of force in the hands of the state's own coercive apparatus.

The Taming of the Shrew: Subordinating the Military and Asserting Civilian Supremacy

Controlling the military is a critical dimension of any democratization process: the armed forces command a society's means of coercion and therefore have the capacity to overturn the game board at any time during a democratic transition.[2] Subordinating the military and making them accountable to civilian authority are also essential to achieving two fundamental dimensions of democracy: protecting civil rights and liberties while ensuring accountability. Only in a political system where those who control coercion are clearly and unambiguously subordinated to the dictates of the elected civilian government and bound by the limits imposed by the rule of law can we truly speak of the effective protection of citizens' rights and liberties. On the other hand, if accountability means that elected officials should be responsible to the citizenry for their actions, it also means that the power to make decisions should be clearly vested in their hands and that no other person, group, or institution above and beyond them should have the power to dictate, veto, or overturn the decisions they make.[3]

The goal of subordinating the military involves confronting and offsetting military challenges to democratic continuity, as well as establishing and affirming civilian supremacy (Agüero 1995b). While the first task may be a difficult one, the second involves a more protracted effort. The long-term assertion of civilian supremacy consists of eliminating any "reserved domains" of policy-making authority.[4] Once the civilian elected authorities can make decisions in all policy areas—including defense and internal security—without having to admit either de jure or de facto supervision, tutelage, or imposition from the armed forces, one can say that civilian supremacy has been achieved and a major feature of democracy secured.

I first explore Colombia's and Venezuela's efforts to eliminate the military's threat of toppling the newly installed democratic regimes through rebellions and coups. I also investigate the process whereby the civilian elites tried to assert supremacy over the military, which obviously goes beyond merely preventing military coups.[5] I find that in both cases civilian authorities made successful efforts to defeat military coups in the late 1950s and into the 1960s. By the mid-1960s military coups were already fading from the collective imagination as plausible avenues to power—signaling an important milestone in the process of democratization, especially in Venezuela where the military had historically played a much more prominent political role than in Colombia.[6] In both cases, however, military autonomy,[7] together with a series of institutional prerogatives, was the price civilian elites had to pay to send the military back to the barracks.

Staving Off the Threat of a Countercoup

As is usually the case with transitions from authoritarianism to democracy, the most urgent task regarding the military entails the need to confront and offset any attempts to reinstall military rule. Colombia and Venezuela, in the 1950s and 1960s, were no exceptions. Tables 4.1 and 4.2 show the most important civil-military conflicts that took place during the transition and the first few years of democratic rule in both countries. Although in both cases civilian elites were faced with numerous countercoup threats, a comparison of the tables suffices to show that the threat of a military coup and thus of an authoritarian regression was much stronger in Venezuela than in Colombia.

Table 4.1, which summarizes the main conflicts in Colombia, shows five of these attempts: the first happened during the junta period (1957–58) just before the founding elections, the next two happened under the first civilian government (1958–62), and the last two happened in the mid- and late 1960s. Compared to Venezuela, conflicts in Colombia were fewer in number and more dispersed in time. The last two were more an occasion to show civilian control of the military rather than a direct, real threat of military insubordination (see Pizarro 1988; Leal 1994; and Dávila 1998).

Table 4.1. Colombia: Main Civil-Military Conflicts, 1958–1969

Date/Type of Event	Forces Involved, Motives, and Outcome
May 2, 1958 / Attempted coup	Battalion No. 1 (Military Police) backed by pro–Rojas Pinilla conservative civilians. Against military junta and the National Front candidate. The army opposed the attempt. The rebels surrendered, and the military junta recovered full control.
December 3, 1958 / Conspiracy	General Rojas Pinilla, retired officers, and former officials of dictatorial regime. The government revealed a conspiracy backed by those forces against the National Front regime. State of siege declared and lasts two months. Rojas Pinilla and civilian allies detained.
October 11, 1961 / Rebellion	"The Lieutenants Rebellion." A company of the army, Grupo Mecanizado de Reconocimiento, led by Lieutenants Escobar and Cendales, planned to ignite a rebellion starting in the eastern plains. The army reacted in favor of the constitutional government. The rebels surrendered, and Escobar was killed. State of siege (in force in some regions) extended to the entire territory. Decrees prohibited public meetings and controlled mass media.
January 27, 1965 / Rumors of military coup	Gen. Alberto Ruiz Novoa, minister of war (1962–65). Rumors of military coup of a "reformist" kind, to be conducted by Ruiz Novoa with backing of labor federations. Ruiz Novoa is removed by President Valencia and replaced with General Rebeiz Pizarro.
March 1969 / Civil-military disagreement	Gen. Guillermo Pinzon Caicedo, army commander. Pinzon writes an article in the army's journal protesting civilian interference in matters of military spending. President Lleras Restrepo strips Pinzon of his appointment as army commander.

Sources: Pizarro 1988; Valencia Tovar 1992; Leal 1994; Dávila 1998; *Revista Javeriana,* 1958–70; interview with General (ret.) Alvaro Valencia Tovar, Bogotá, May 24, 1996.

Table 4.2 shows that in Venezuela there were nine major attempts during the first four years after the fall of Pérez Jiménez to overthrow either the provisional junta or the newly elected civilian government, the last seven of which happened during the Betancourt administration

Table 4.2. Venezuela: Main Civil-Military Conflicts, 1958–1962

Date	Forces Involved, Motives, and Outcome
July 22, 1958	Minister of defense and army. General Castro León, minister of defense, attempts a removal of AD and PCV members from the cabinet, state governors, and other state dependencies in order to reestablish full control over the junta by the military. The provisional junta rejects Castro Leon's demands.
September 7, 1958	Municipal Police School, Military Engineering Service. Attempted coup d'etat by Moncada Mendoza. Unveiled and defeated by the provisional junta.
January 11, 1960	Anti-AD military and civilians.
May 5, 1960	Garrisons in Táchira, Mérida, and Trujillo.
July 26, 1960	Air force, with backing from URD.
January 1962	Battalion No. 1 of the Marine Corps, with backing from PCV.
February 1962	Marine Corps, "Motoblindado," National Guard.
May 4, 1962	Marine Corps, National Guard, MIR-PCV. The "Carupanazo," an infantry battalion in Carúpano, rises against the government. An uprising with military overtones. PCV and MIR supported. Confrontation lasted two days. Garrison surrendered. PCV and MIR banned by presidential decree.
June 2, 1962	Marine Corps, National Guard, Army-Air Force; PCV-MIR. The "Porteñazo." Naval Base in Puerto Cabello rebels and takes control of city. Armed confrontation, including guerrillas and rebel armed forces, against army. Hundreds dead and wounded during two days of armed confrontation. Loyal troops regain control of the city and put down the uprising.

Sources: Burggraaff 1972; España 1987: 564–65; López Maya, Gómez Calcaño, and Maingón 1989: 124, Appendix 5.

(1959–64). Whereas the first half of these rebellions came from the right—that is, from sectors within the military who wanted to return to a military dictatorship—the second half had the support of political parties of the left—the PCV, URD, and MIR. Still, all of them, whether launched from the right or from the left, indicated a sustained effort on the part of the military to regain direct control of the Venezuelan state. Nevertheless, by the end of the first post-transition government (1959–64) the threat of an authoritarian regression via a successful military coup had been practically eliminated in Venezuela.

While Colombia and Venezuela were both fairly successful in sending the military back to the barracks, in Venezuela this occurred practically for the first time since independence.[8] Explaining the two countries' success, as well as the difficulties encountered and the costs incurred in the process of subordinating the military, illustrates the interplay between historical continuities, institutional arrangements, and political agency.

One outstanding difference between Colombia and Venezuela is the historical role of the military in domestic politics. As was noted earlier, while Venezuela had an almost uninterrupted record of military rule since the beginning of the twentieth century,[9] during the same period Colombia experienced a very brief military government (1953–57), which was installed and controlled by the political parties. The Colombian military did not have a tradition of direct intervention and control over the state as the Venezuelan military did. Moreover, the degree of military involvement in the previous authoritarian regime was much higher in Venezuela than in Colombia. Thus the task of subordinating the military and asserting civilian supremacy was especially demanding for the Venezuelan civilian elite.

In Colombia, despite the fact that the provisional junta that took power after Rojas Pinilla's flight was entirely made up of men in uniform, the junta rapidly and emphatically declared its will to call elections and transfer power to an elected government.[10] This is not to say that the Colombian military was totally exempt from temptations leading to the re-installation of military rule, as the attempted coup against the provisional junta in May 1958 shows. However, the episode made quite clear that the majority of the troops and, even more important, the leadership of the armed forces did not favor a new intervention of the military in politics. In fact, much as in Uruguay in the 1980s (see Stepan 1988: 116), the transition was seen both by the military and by the civilian elites as a case of "restoration" of the status quo ante in terms of civil-military relations. With only slight modifications, the civil-military model that prevailed before the breakdown of democracy in 1949 was seen by both as an appropriate model.

By contrast, in Venezuela after the fall of Pérez Jiménez, the pro-democratic coalition was forced to stage an additional series of street demonstrations against the all-military junta to make sure that it would not become a permanent government of the armed forces. The original junta was the product of a negotiation among the different branches of the military without any participation by the civilian opposition. In addition to one representative from each branch, it included two hardliners (Colonel Casanova from the army and Colonel Romero from the air force) who seemed intent on preserving the military government, only without Pérez Jiménez. Junior officers who had started the rebellion against Pérez Jiménez joined the Junta Patriótica (the civilian opposition coalition) in a daylong protest against the original all-military junta. Using mobilization in the streets as their main weapon, the parties and the junior officers achieved the goal of forcing the two colonels out, replacing them with two civilians, Blas Lamberti and Eugenio Mendoza, and thus forming a mixed civil-military junta.[11] In short, additional political and military pressure from the parties, from mobilized groups in society, and from the junior officers was needed in Venezuela to convince the outgoing military to leave power once and for all. This was the first struggle for military subordination in Venezuela but by no means the last. The Provisional Junta government, especially President Larrazábal, played a crucial role in offsetting many other rebellions and insubordinations, including the attempted coup of September 1958.

In sum, both the historical record and the initial conditions facing the civilian elites at the beginning of the process of subordination seemed much more difficult in Venezuela than in Colombia. In Venezuela there was not only a historical tradition of supremacy of the military but also a higher degree of military involvement in the outgoing authoritarian regime. Accordingly, the Venezuelan military had a higher degree of influence on the transition process: they were crucial in the first phase (overthrowing the dictatorship) and tried to maintain their control during the second phase (when they selected the first all-military provisional junta). It took a greater degree of mobilization and pressure by political parties and groups in civil society to wrest power from the military and gain enough leverage to guarantee the successful completion of the transition process.

Not surprisingly, the different historical weights of the armed forces in the two countries came to be reflected in the pacts: whereas in Colombia there was only a brief mention of the armed forces in the National Front pacts,[12] the Venezuelan pacts included a whole section on policies vis-à-vis the military.[13] In other words, differences in the written pacts regarding the thorny issue of the armed forces' role in politics were clearly a result of differences in each country's previous institutional history. In both cases the military was granted permanent representation in the executive cabinet through the presence of the highest military officer as minister of war (later, minister of defense). In addition, the Venezuelan pacts (in particular, the Programa Mínimo de Gobierno) contained a list of specific provisions: the branches of the military would be modernized and technically enhanced; the signatories recognized the merits and services rendered by the armed forces as well as their role in maintaining public peace and fostering progress; the living conditions of officers and soldiers would be progressively improved; and, finally, military service would be compulsory for all male Venezuelans regardless of social class. In the same paragraph the signatories circumscribed the role of the armed forces so as to leave no doubt about their apolitical nature: "The Armed Forces form an apolitical, obedient and nondeliberative body, and in order to reassert the principles on which they are based institutional education of all its cadres will be intensified."[14]

In both cases the unity of the civilian elites in support of democracy was crucial. Elite unity, achieved in the struggle against the dictatorship and consolidated through the respective party pacts, empowered them vis-à-vis the military, which remained divided. In both cases the military-as-institution opposed the continued rule of the military-as-government. This division was skillfully used by party elites, who finally achieved a successful transfer of power from the armed forces. In exchange they

granted the military some privileges, protective measures, and prerogatives in the party pacts.

Establishing and Sustaining Civilian Control of the Military

Once the new democratically elected governments were in place in
the two countries, there was still a long way to go before the subordination of the military was an accomplished fact. The appeasement of the
military and the neutralization of any threat of a coup d'etat required
strong leadership and a great deal of political maneuvering on the part of
the two presidents, Lleras Camargo (Colombia) and Betancourt (Venezuela).[15] As became painfully evident to these and subsequent democratic governments, subordinating the military and asserting civilian
authority entails a much more difficult and protracted process than just
offsetting the threat of a countercoup, as it implies the permanent re-
moval of the military from routine involvement in domestic politics.
This process has two dimensions: one concerns the gradual reduction of
military contestation against the policies of the new civilian government;
the second concerns the reduction of military institutional prerogatives
(Stepan 1988: 68).

    In terms of reducing military contestation, three difficult issues ap-
pear high on the policy agenda: human rights violations; the organizational mission, structure, and control of the military; and the military
budget. Unlike most democratization processes during the 1980s and
1990s, the issue of trials and legal reprisals for human rights abuses was
not a contested one on the transition agenda of either Venezuela or Colombia in the late 1950s. In the case of Venezuela, there were purges but
no trials. Moreover, rather than insert any terms of retaliation or retribu-
tion against military wrongdoing in the pacts, there were instead words
of praise and recognition of the role the armed forces had played in Venezuela's history. The Programa Mínimo de Gobierno, signed by the party
leaders in 1958, explicitly stated its "recognition of the merits and services of the men who make up the armed forces and of their important
collaboration in the maintenance of public peace and as guarantors of
national progress."[16]

    In Colombia the civilian leadership decided to place all the blame
on the person of Rojas Pinilla and exempt the military qua institution

from any responsibility for what had happened. It is quite telling, in this regard, that at some point in the process the democratic coalition changed its name from Frente Civil (Civil Front) to Frente Nacional (National Front) to signify that it was not only or exclusively a coalition of civilians against military rule but rather a coalition of all (including the military) against the person of the dictator, Rojas Pinilla.[17] This strategy was consciously pursued throughout the negotiation process between the parties in every declaration or document through which the pacts were crafted.[18] The same strategy was finally and most obviously deployed at the beginning of the Lleras Camargo government when the parties decided to subject Rojas Pinilla to a public trial before Congress. After a trial of four months the political elites declared the former dictator guilty of corruption and indignity in the exercise of the presidency.[19] The line was clearly drawn between those who supported Rojas Pinilla (who were seen as disloyal to the historical tradition of the Colombian armed forces) and those deemed loyal to the constitutional regime and to the traditional parties.

In terms of the organizational mission, structure, and control of the military, there were significant changes in Venezuela but very little that changed in Colombia. In both cases the armed forces were deeply divided about the authoritarian experience, which was widely viewed as damaging to the institution. In Venezuela the main dividing line ran through the different branches of the armed forces, pitting the navy and the air force against the traditionally more powerful army. In this case a reorganization of the armed forces granting more autonomy to the navy and the air force vis-à-vis the army and direct consultation between the president and the commander of each branch were crucial to guarantee the loyalty of the navy and air force—while also ensuring the authority of the chief executive over the commanders of each branch of the military. Two other organizational changes within the Venezuelan armed forces prevented the formation of a stable and unified military command that could coordinate actions against the civilian government: a mandatory rule limiting service to a maximum of thirty years and rapid rotation of the military among posts.[20] In terms of internal organization, the civilian elite in Venezuela clearly decided on a policy of "divide and rule" to tame the military.

By contrast, in the case of Colombia no major internal reorganization of the armed forces or purges took place during those years. On the contrary, previous organizational changes introduced during the dictatorship were preserved, such as the nationalization of the police and its placement, along with the other three branches of the armed forces, under the jurisdiction of the Ministry of Defense.[21] A major difference between the two cases, then, was that while the Venezuelan civilian elite was forced to introduce major reforms in the organization of the armed forces and play skillfully the "divide and rule" game, the Colombian civilian elites had an easier task at hand: instead of a major restructuring of the armed forces, they simply isolated and punished the dictator and exempted the rest of the institution from any responsibility.

There was a second important difference in the approach taken by the civilian elite vis-à-vis the armed forces. In Colombia, because the politicization of the armed forces (especially the police) had been a major cause of the "partial collapse of the state" (Oquist 1978) and the escalation of violence in the 1940s and 1950s, a major effort was made by the civilian elite to depoliticize the police and the armed forces and turn them into a neutral body in terms of party loyalties and affiliation. The famous speech delivered by President-elect Alberto Lleras Camargo before the military officials in the Teatro Patria in 1958 just after his election was clear in this respect:[22] as much as the civilians would not allow the military to intervene in political affairs, the military could expect civilian authorities to abstain from interfering in military affairs. This approach to civil-military relations had one major intended effect, in addition to a few unintended ones. The major intended effect was the gradual and almost complete depoliticization of the Colombian armed forces in terms of party affiliation and identity. In fact, one of the major accomplishments of the National Front is that the military became subordinated to civilian rule but this time not on account of particular party affiliations. Instead, its subordination was based progressively on loyalty to the idea of shared bipartisan rule. However, this depoliticization had another, more problematic side. First, it allowed for greater autonomy of the armed forces than would be desirable within a democratic regime. Second, it allowed the armed forces to acquire and reproduce a doctrine of their own, the national security ideology, which was influenced by a combination of the military doctrines of Brazil and the Southern Cone as well as the anticommunist counterinsurgency strategy of the United States.[23]

Meanwhile, the Venezuelan political parties took a completely different approach to civil-military relations. Rather than adopt a position of noninterference in military affairs, they attempted and succeeded in politicizing the military along party lines. Although the Programa Mínimo de Gobierno and, later, the 1961 Constitution (Article 132) expressly demanded that the military abstain from political involvement, the two main parties in Venezuela actively pursued a policy of rapprochement with the institution in an effort to establish fluid channels of communication with them. Though this had the intended result of "civilianizing" the military, it also produced the perverse effect of politicizing it, in particular, politicizing the procedures through which military promotions and rotations were decided.[24] The politicization of the promotions process would later be cited as one of the motives for the 1992 military rebellion.[25]

The gradual adoption of the national security ideology in both countries was certainly aided by the emergence and persistence of a military threat in the domestic arena: the revolutionary guerrillas who emerged in the mid-1960s. The proliferation of revolutionary guerrilla *focos* (groups) and movements in Colombia and Venezuela during the 1960s was a key element in the struggle for the subordination of the military. On the one hand, it helped to forge an alliance between the incumbent regime and the military against a common enemy, the leftist insurgency, thus placing the military squarely on the side of the civilian governments. On the other hand, it provided a much-needed justification for the redefinition of military doctrine, mission, and strategies. This was especially true in Venezuela, whose military had to undergo a major transformation of its role in society and politics and, most important, a deep transformation of its own perception of that role.

For a few years, in both countries, guerrilla warfare provided the cement for a closer relationship between the newly elected governments and the military, as well as a way to redefine the military's mission, doctrine, and strategies away from direct control of the state. The Venezuelan army was rapidly turned into a counterinsurgency army as it became endowed with the type of weapons and equipment needed for this type of internal warfare.[26] While it endured, the struggle against the revolutionary guerrillas was skillfully used by the Venezuelan civilian leadership to introduce a major reorientation in the function of the military. The guerrillas were mainly portrayed as agents of foreign (basically Cuban) intervention in Venezuelan domestic politics. The war against them was seen as a war against a foreign enemy, not against fellow Venezuelans. It must also be remembered that the Venezuelan guerrillas were easily and promptly defeated mainly due to their lack of social bases, which did not extend much beyond the intellectual elite, disaffected party cadres, and the radicalized student movement.[27] These factors contributed to minimizing the scars left in society as well as in the military corps by internal warfare and to the rapid rebuilding of a degree of trust in civil-military relations. None of this has been possible in Colombia, where the original guerrilla groups became a "chronic insurgency" (Pizarro 1996a) and internal strife has endured for over four decades.

In Venezuela, after the guerrillas were finally defeated and the counterinsurgency effort was over, the armed forces were again rapidly reoriented toward external defense, in part through the skillful political use of unresolved border conflicts with Colombia and Guyana, the threat of Brazilian gold miners penetrating the southern Amazon border, and the prospect of an eventual conflict with Cuba in the Caribbean.[28] From the early 1970s until the late 1980s, the Venezuelan armed forces remained oriented outward, with their doctrine, mission, strategy, and equipment geared to the possibility of external conflict. As a consequence, they played no role in the containment of public disorders or internal threats.[29]

Finally, in terms of military budget, figures 4.1 and 4.2 show changes in military expenditure and the size of the armed forces in Colombia and Venezuela after their respective democratic transitions. Unlike recent democratic transitions, where a drastic cut in military spending and personnel is usually part of the agenda, in Colombia and Venezuela there seems to have been a gradual increase in military spending as well as a steady increase in the number of military personnel over the years. In terms of military expenditures as a percentage of GDP, the increases introduced by the military regime became more or less permanent in both cases throughout the 1960s. Starting in 1970 there was a steady decline in the case of Colombia, with expenditure levels reaching their lowest point (0.8 percent of GDP) in 1977. After that, as figure 4.1 clearly shows, there was a dramatic hike throughout the 1980s, followed by a stabilization at about 2 percent of GDP. In Venezuela a sharp increase in the second half of the 1970s coincides with the oil boom. In the 1980s, coinciding with the steep fall in oil prices, there was a dramatic decline (from almost 3.5 percent to 2 percent between 1982 and 1985), which was also at the root of the discontent that began to stir among the second-tier officers precisely at that same time. Yet in both cases military expenditure sits comfortably between 1 and 2 percent of GDP, and in no case was there a visible deterioration of the military budget after the transition to democracy.

In terms of personnel, Colombia more than tripled the size of its military forces during the first decade of democratic rule (Ruhl 1980: 187), while Venezuela, growing at a slower pace, almost doubled its number of personnel in the same period (Bigler 1981: 95). As a result, the twin issues of the size of the armed forces and the military budget never became a major bone of contention between civilians and the military. Rather, the military in both countries was rewarded with increases in both fronts from the democratic transition onward.

Figure 4.1. Military Expenditures in Colombia and Venezuela (as percent of GDP)

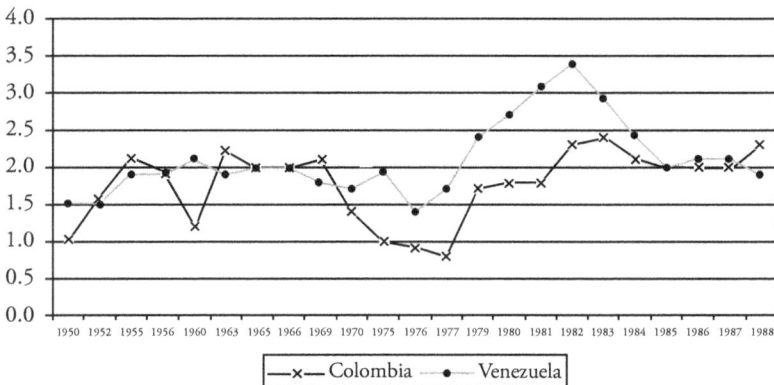

Sources: For 1952, 1956, 1960, 1963, 1966, 1969: SIPRI Yearbook 1973. For 1950, 1955, 1960, 1965, 1975, 1976, 1977, 1978: SIPRI Yearbook 1980. For 1979–88, SIPRI Yearbook 1990. For 1990+: SIPRI Yearbook 2000.

Figure 4.2. Armed Forces Personnel in Colombia and Venezuela (in 1000s)

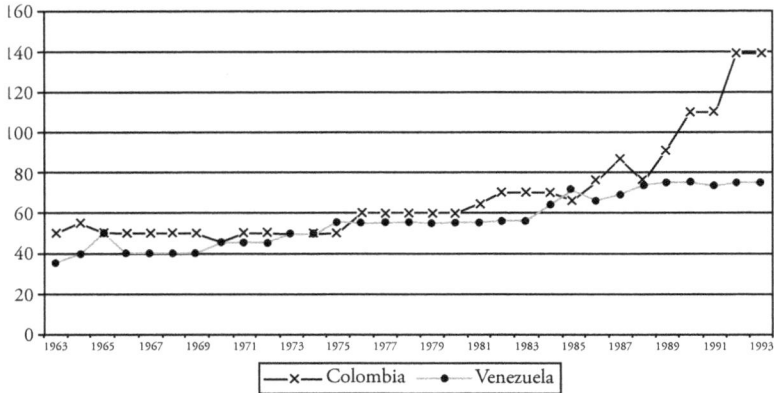

Sources: For 1963–72: ACDA World Expenditures and Arms Trade 1963–1973. For 1973–82: ACDA World Military Expenditures and Arms Transfers (ICPSR 6516), Online Data Set for 1973–83. For 1983–93: ACDA World Military Expenditures and Arms Transfers (ICPSR 8532) Online Data Set 1983–93.

Though material improvements and increases in the budget and size of the armed forces were part of an implicit deal between civilian elites and the military, an explanation of subordination based exclusively on material gains is overly simplistic and at best incomplete. Instead, I argue, an explicit recognition of their political role, an increased degree of autonomy vis-à-vis civilian authorities, and the granting of special prerogatives were probably as or more important in a multipronged strategy to appease and subordinate the military in both cases.

Subordination with Autonomy and Institutional Prerogatives

Unlike other more recent Latin American transitions, dealing with the military in Colombia and Venezuela was made easier by the fact that the armed forces were divided and their intervention in politics totally discredited by the time civilian elites took power. Still, during the first few years after the transition, the military in both countries preserved the capacity to threaten the continuity of the democratic regime and extract concessions in exchange for security. The ability of the civilian leadership to maintain the support of crucial actors (Congress, the church, the parties) at critical moments, plus the perceived failure of the previous authoritarian regime, finally tipped the balance toward military subordination. They kept enough influence to guarantee that the military qua institution would not have to pay any cost or acknowledge any responsibility for previous wrongdoing. In addition, they obtained material benefits, gained participation in the cabinet, retained the ability to control their own affairs free from civilian interference, retained a constitutional role that went beyond its responsibility for national defense,[30] and obtained a high degree of autonomy in key policy-making areas.

Given the complexity of some issues related to military strategy, combat arms, and techniques, asserting civilian supremacy means reaching a delicate balance whereby while securing indisputable civilian control in terms of the formulation of military policy, the military still enjoys enough institutional autonomy for the efficient pursuit of its mission.[31] To achieve a situation in which civilian supremacy becomes deeply institutionalized, while granting the military discretionary decision-making authority and reserved zones of expertise and action, a process of expansion of civilian prerogatives and an increasing contraction of military prerogatives needs to take place (Stepan 1988).

In both Colombia and Venezuela, however, civilian elites fell quite short of achieving this best case scenario; while avoiding military insubordination, they remained stuck in a gray area where significant military autonomy and prerogatives were granted to the armed forces. Between the late 1950s and the late 1980s there was little progress in terms of enhancing the prerogatives of the civilian elites in the defense sector, with little in the way of transferring effective authority over defense policy from the general staff to the civilian elite in either the Ministry of Defense or Congress. In both cases, throughout the period in question, the post of minister of defense was occupied by an active duty military officer.[32] In both countries, even though the legislature and the Ministry of Finance may have had a say in terms of allocating the military's budget, there was very little monitoring on the part of either the minister, Congress, the political parties, or civil organizations after the resources were granted. In general, civilians had a very limited role in shaping the patterns of military expenditure and investment. With very little in the way of oversight capacity, this lack of monitoring allowed for a gradual expansion of military autonomy over the years. Finally, in both countries the military was granted wide discretion in terms of judging their own through military tribunals, which guaranteed an elevated degree of protection if not outright impunity—especially in the Colombian case. In sum, then, though military subordination and the elimination of tutelary powers were part of a virtuous institutionalization cycle in both countries, the failure to assert full civilian supremacy and the persistence of substantial military autonomy in some crucial reserved domains of policy making was at best a serious limitation for democratic institutionalization and at worst a perverse element that undermined the workings of these two democratic regimes. The final outcome in both cases was subordination with autonomy and relatively high institutional prerogatives.

This parallel notwithstanding, the degree of autonomy and the number of prerogatives granted to the Colombian military remained higher and expanded beyond those of Venezuela. Colombia's civilian elite openly abdicated their responsibility in terms of formulating and implementing policy in the areas of defense and security, therefore granting the military key reserved domains in these policy-making areas, which the armed forces were happy to expand in the context of an ongoing counterinsurgency war. Due to the persistence of an armed conflict with leftist guerrillas, military autonomy in Colombia has consistently expanded, including in the strategic arena of internal security. In that specific policy arena, the Colombian armed forces have certainly had more power and influence than their Venezuelan counterparts. Such power does not translate, necessarily, into deliberate attempts to control the central government but rather is exercised through capturing and preserving crucially important reserved domains in the areas of internal security and public order, in addition to maintaining control over the internal management and organization of their forces, the allocation of the military budget, the jurisdiction of military criminal justice, and immunity regarding gross violations of human rights, leading to a clearly undemocratic degree of impunity.

By contrast, in Venezuela after 1958 political elites took important steps toward reducing the "unbounded autonomy" characteristic of mili-

tary dictatorships (Cruz and Diamint 1998: 116) by introducing important reforms in military organization, as well as attempting to shape
career patterns through the use of civilian-controlled promotion and re-
tirement policies. As a result of these policies, as well as a relatively
prompt resolution of the confrontation with leftist guerrillas, they managed a significant redefinition of the military's mission (see Bigler 1981;
Agüero 1995a). Once the guerrillas were defeated in the late 1960s, the
armed forces were quickly reoriented to their classic function, external
defense, and equipped and trained in order to accomplish the typical
tasks of a conventional war at the borders (against either Colombia,
Guyana, Brazil, or, eventually, in the Caribbean) and kept from intervening in the management of domestic affairs. The Venezuelan military
kept two reserved domains. The first was related to "their own internal
functioning and development [and] the second to external borders' policy. . . . This is what was granted to the armed forces in exchange for their
support within the framework of Punto Fijo."[33] The military in Venezuela did indeed preserve a high degree of autonomy in the area of external defense policy making and in matters of budget allocation and
internal organization; however, its autonomy was less pronounced than
that enjoyed by its Colombian counterpart.

Figure 4.3 shows the two countries' divergent trajectories in terms of
civil-military relations: starting in the late 1950s and into the mid- to
late 1960s, both Colombia and Venezuela were successful at reducing
military contestation. In exchange for military support, however, civilian
elites in both countries agreed to grant substantial prerogatives to their
armed forces. In Colombia, until 1991, those prerogatives were gradually consolidated and extended to include the crucial domain of internal
security and public order. Without attempting to gain direct control over
the government, the Colombian armed forces nonetheless secured a high
degree of control over their own affairs, as well as over the areas of external defense and internal security, plus a clearly undemocratic degree of
impunity from any accountability in regard to violations of human rights
during the course of the internal war. A major effort to assert civilian authority over the military began in the early 1990s simultaneously with
the drafting of a new constitution. In 1991 President Cesar Gaviria
(1990–94) appointed Rafael Pardo Rueda as the first civilian minister

of defense in almost four decades while also empowering a series of civilian staffed agencies (including the Department of National Planning [DNP]) with decision making in certain policy realms that had until then been considered one of the military's reserved domains.[34] In Venezuela, by contrast, fewer prerogatives were granted throughout the democratic period. However, a serious reversal in 1992, when levels of military contestation rose again, showed that the process had been incomplete and its outcomes were quite fragile. After the two attempted coups of 1992, especially since the arrival of Hugo Chávez to the presidency (1999), the military has secured an ever-increasing role in government as well as an expanding level of military prerogatives.

From the 1960s to the late 1980s Venezuela made great progress in subordinating the military and asserting civilian authority, especially with regard to decision making in the realm of internal order—albeit not entirely successful in terms of the military's capacity to decide on matters

Figure 4.3. Contestation, Prerogatives, and Civil-Military Relations: Post-transition Evolution in Colombia and Venezuela

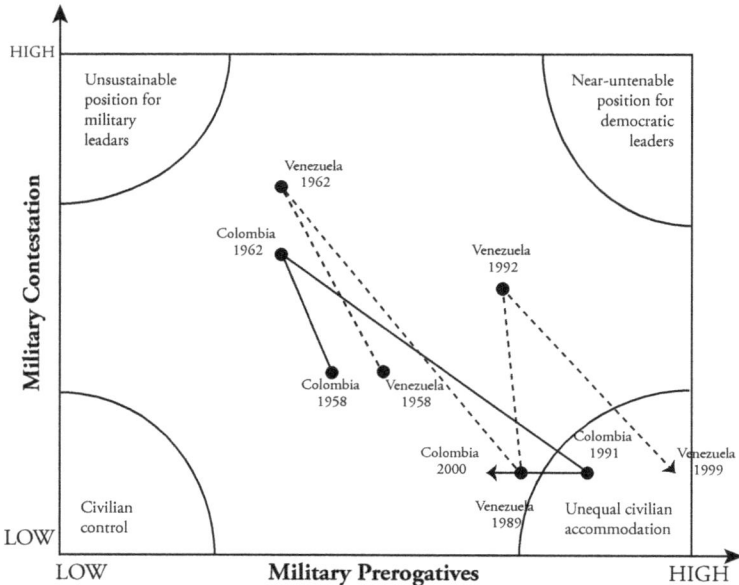

Source: Based on Stepan 1988: 122, fig. 7.3.

of external defense. This was due to the positive coincidence of three related factors: the defeat of the armed insurgency in the late 1960s and the effective reincorporation of the armed rebels into politics in the early 1970s; the subsequent reorientation of the armed forces' mission toward external defense; and the effective subordination of the military to Congress, through a combination of institutional design and the skillful co-optation of the military high command by party elites. Unfortunately, this process of subordination saw a major reversal with two attempted coups in the early 1990s, with dire consequences for Venezuela's democracy. Since the attempted coups in 1992, though the levels of contestation have decreased significantly, the level of military prerogatives has only increased over time.

Colombia's trajectory was different, yet not entirely favorable to democracy either. The consolidation of the National Front regime gave rise to a situation in which, despite being formally subordinated to the civilian authorities, the military kept a significant degree of autonomy and a series of institutional prerogatives, especially in the realms of internal security and defense policy, which became increasingly strategic as the internal conflict continued to rage for more than four decades. Unlike the Venezuelan elites, the Colombian politicians did not attempt an active co-optation of the military high command: much to the contrary, in their efforts to depoliticize the armed forces, they explicitly rejected any efforts to incorporate the armed forces politically. This opened up the space for an increasingly independent stance on the part of the armed forces vis-à-vis domestic matters, which did not lead to open interventions in domestic politics but rather to increasing levels of autonomy on the part of the military institution vis-à-vis the civilian elite. In a country ravaged by violence, decision making on internal order and security has an obvious strategic importance and has remained a critical reserved domain for the military, with visibly negative impacts on human rights, the rule of law, and accountability—all crucial dimensions of democracy.

In Colombia the military developed and expanded its autonomy, a high profile within the state apparatus, and, since the early 1980s, became increasingly linked with a network of right-wing paramilitary militias in the rural areas, an alliance that makes them partly responsible for the country's gruesome record of human rights violations.[35] Colombia's democracy has suffered the detrimental consequences of this legacy: it engendered a political elite that has lacked the knowledge, the capacity, and sometimes even the interest to handle issues of defense and security,[36] thus also lacking the capacity to control the military. In a country in a permanent state of internal war, this has had disastrous consequences for human rights as well as for the formulation of a democratic defense and security policy.[37]

Since the mid-1980s, in part linked with the peace negotiations with the guerrillas initiated by President Belisario Betancur (1982–86), there has been a sustained effort on the part of the civilian elites to retake control of the issue of internal order. In the early 1990s the government of Cesar Gaviria launched a conscious effort to reduce military autonomy and prerogatives and to place control of the military in the hands of a civilian elite newly trained in matters of security and defense (Dávila 1998; Deas 1999). This, together with the protracted negotiations with the guerrillas (1982–2002) and the attempt to clamp down on human right abuses committed by the armed forces, has led to staunch resistance by the military, which in part explains the emergence and proliferation of the right-wing militias (or paramilitary groups, as Colombians prefer to call them). In the final balance, while there are some commendable advances in this regard—the appointment of a civilian minister of defense since 1991, the introduction of serious restrictions on the president's emergency powers in the new Constitution of 1991, a deep restructuring of the police in 1993, and an increased capacity on the part of the civilian elite and some state agencies to formulate and implement a more "civilianized" security policy—the battle is far from being won: alongside an abysmal human rights record promoted by a judicial structure that guarantees almost complete impunity, the Colombian military continues to have a powerful veto on matters of internal security.[38]

By contrast, in Venezuela, where the military had wielded power almost without interruption since independence, its return to the barracks was most remarkable. Their withdrawal from power was also more complete than in the Colombian case: they reoriented their professional role toward external defense more rapidly, and their influence in the domestic arena withered away more quickly. Venezuela thus achieved a rather swift and extraordinary subordination of the military. And yet the full assertion of civilian authority remained an unfulfilled promise in both cases. In terms of civil-military relations, the Venezuelan elite went further than the Colombian one in promoting a redefinition of the military's mission, organization, strategy, and self-perception. With the cooperation of Congress, the executive branch under President Betancourt enacted some important military reforms. The parties in Venezuela made a particularly strong effort to penetrate and establish closer links to the military. By contrast, the Colombian political elite left the military largely on its own and declined to take any initiative regarding military affairs. While this may have had the positive effect of depoliticizing the armed forces, it also granted them an enormous amount of autonomy vis-à-vis civilian authority. One of the most powerful events shaping this new military role and self-perception was the Cuban Revolution and the emergence of guerrilla groups all over Latin America during the 1960s. While the Venezuelan elite used the struggle against the guerrillas to begin a thorough process of reorientation of the military's role, the same event gave rise to a long and deep involvement of the Colombian military in domestic politics.

Despite a greater degree of civilian control, over the years the Venezuelan military carved for itself a larger space for action and a higher degree of autonomy. It managed to remain "somewhat protected from outside public control by developing, with the compliance of party elites, a buffer zone that deters the prompt investigation of irregularities, excesses in the use of force, or outright corruption" (Agüero 1990: 267).[39] Unlike Colombia in the 1990s, there was no parallel effort on the part of the civilian elite to reduce military prerogatives. Instead, they learned to take the support of the military for granted. However, the implicit understanding underpinning the stability of civil-military relations in Venezuela was upset as a consequence of the generalized turmoil of the Venezuelan polity since the late 1980s. In 1992, thirty years after the military uprising of 1962, there were two attempted coups d'etat. The crisis of the late 1980s, especially the traumatic events of "el Caracazo," dislodged the seemingly stable relationship between the civilian authorities and the military.

The violent urban riots known as el Caracazo that took place on February 27 and 28, 1989, are widely regarded as a watershed in recent

Venezuelan history.[40] They sounded the alarms about the crisis of the parties and party system and the generally poor state of democratic representation; also, for the first time in more than three decades, the military was called to play an independent role as an enforcement agency during an episode of intense urban turmoil, a role the military deeply resented. The combination of the socioeconomic crisis leading to el Caracazo, together with the mismanagement of the situation by the national government, opened up the opportunity for the violent expression of a dissident group within the military that had been hatching since the early 1980s: the Movimiento Bolivariano Revolucionario 200 (MBR 200). The young military officers of MBR 200 were behind the first coup on February 4, 1992. However, rather than an alliance of the military with the propertied classes, the rebellion signaled a violent reaction on the part of a younger military generation to the overall crisis of Venezuelan society.[41] This conspiratorial nucleus within the Venezuelan armed forces notwithstanding, the main impetus for the failed coups of 1992 came rather from exogenous factors: it was not the military's attempt to reenter politics but the general crisis of the political system, especially the parties' inability to respond to the challenges that had become so painfully obvious in the events of February 1989, that prompted the military to intervene. This was not a typical Latin American coup d'etat; it was rather the classic "praetorian moment" (Huntington 1968). It was the crisis of the political parties, the absence of party mediation of social conflict, that opened up the space for the reemergence of the military in Venezuelan politics.

For a while, after that brief praetorian moment in 1992, Venezuela's society seemed to side with the established political elites and give them a new (and last) opportunity to steer away from troubled waters, introduce reforms, and find a new equilibrium that would save Venezuela from returning to a past dominated by the military in politics. Unfortunately, the failure of the traditional parties to find that new equilibrium opened up the space for the emergence of a political outsider, Lt. Col. Hugo Chávez, whose arrival to the presidency opened up the gates for increased participation of the military in politics, which was later enshrined in the new Constitution of 1999. Unfortunately, as Stepan (1988) warned two decades ago, "Brumarian moments" can easily turn into "praetorian decades." Despite the fact that the coups of 1992 failed, later developments in Venezuela seem to confirm Stepan's dire predictions: with the ascent to power of the former coup plotter, the military has regained a level of participation in Venezuelan politics that they have not had since the late 1950s. In his first two years in office Chávez appointed high-ranking military officers to head the Ministries of Interior, Infrastructure, Justice, and Defense and to the presidencies of PDVSA (the state-owned oil company), CITGO (its retail distributor for the North American market), and the Corporación Venezolana de Guayana (CVG). In addition to the military's overwhelming presence in the cabinet, most social assistance programs have been carried out by the military (Corrales 2002, 2006a; Trinkunas 2002). This increased participation of the military in Venezuela's domestic politics should not be interpreted solely as a consequence of Chávez's attempt to militarize politics; it is also a consequence of the lack of political intermediation, on the pro-Chávez as well as on the anti-Chávez sides of the political divide. Lacking a party to organize his following and support his government's agenda, Chávez initially relied on the military. In sum, it is the dramatic reduction in the capacity of the parties to represent Venezuelan society and to exercise civilian control over the military that explains the breakdown of the civil-military pact that characterized the three decades since 1958 and the reemergence of a long tradition of military involvement in politics in that country. As with many other aspects of its democracy, since the late 1980s Venezuela has witnessed a clear reversal from the advances achieved between 1958 and 1988 in terms of the subordination of the military and the assertion of civilian authority.

A Farewell to Arms? Defeating and Incorporating Armed Challengers on the Left

The two fledging democracies had to confront yet a second armed contender: the revolutionary guerrilla groups. In this regard the contrast between the two cases is even more stark: whereas the Venezuelan guerrillas were promptly defeated and then incorporated into the realm of constitutional politics, the Colombian state is still fighting a war against some of the armed contenders that emerged in the early 1960s. This divergence is in part explained by structural and historical factors: the existence of a significant peasant population and the persistence of a dramatically skewed land distribution pattern in Colombia are part of the answer. In addition, I argue that political factors such as the strength of the state, the parties' capacity to penetrate and represent the rural population, and, finally, the role of leadership and strategic decision making are also an important part of the explanation.

In the early 1960s Colombia and Venezuela, together with most other countries in Latin America, witnessed the surfacing of armed challengers on the left. It happened more or less at the same time: in 1961 in Colombia,[42] in 1962 in Venezuela.[43] These groups emerged only a few years after the inauguration of the civilian democratic governments in both cases and, most important, shortly after the Cuban Revolution. Many have argued that the emergence of these guerrilla groups was a direct and almost mechanical consequence of the "closed" character of the emerging democratic regime and the exclusion of the left—more specifically, the exclusion of the Communist Parties[44]—from the transition pacts. Upon closer scrutiny, however, one finds that initially both the Communist Party of Venezuela and the Communist Party of Colombia acquiesced to the pacts and even participated actively in political life once the first democratic government had been elected under the conditions agreed to. The PCV participated in the founding elections (1958), as well as in the drafting of the new constitution in 1961, until the party was banned in 1962. For its part, the PCC issued a communiqué on December 7, 1959, in which, despite some skepticism regarding the class orientation of the new government, they acknowledged the triumph of the party coalition against the dictatorship, endorsed the alliance with the democratic sectors, recognized the legitimacy of the new government, and vowed to support it against any "reactionary coup attempt."[45] In both cases the relegalization of the Communist Parties and the opening of political opportunities associated with the return to democratic rule was a powerful incentive to accept the conditions imposed by the pacts. Another powerful incentive came from the international sphere: the acceptance of a "peaceful road to socialism" by the international Communist movement and a certain opening within the USSR since the mid-1950s under Khrushchev seemed to favor a less confrontational stance vis-à-vis "bourgeois" democracies.

A few years later, however, both parties came to reconsider their positions regarding democracy. In the pages that follow I trace the evolution of the (mainly Communist) left in Colombia and Venezuela during the years immediately following the transition to democracy. This includes a brief exploration of the various factors accounting for the decision to take up arms against the two democratic regimes. My main goal is to account for the divergent outcomes in these two cases, by exploring the degree to which structural conditions and historical legacies on the one hand and the restrictions and exclusions imposed by the transition pacts on the other explain the successful resolution of the guerrilla question in Venezuela, as opposed to the failure to do so in Colombia.

Venezuela

The PCV was excluded from the pacts of New York and Punto Fijo, the Declaration of Principles, and the Minimum Program of Government—but it was not excluded from electoral competition altogether.[46] In fact, the PCV participated, openly and legally, in the 1958 presidential and legislative elections. During the first presidential contest, in 1958, the PCV backed the candidacy of Admiral Wolfang Larrazábal, candidate of URD and president of the Provisional Junta Government. With the support of both URD and PCV, Larrazábal obtained 903,479 votes (34.6 percent of total votes), coming in second after the elected president, Rómulo Betancourt, who obtained 1,284,092 votes, or 49.2 percent of the total (Kornblith and Levine 1995: 49). In the 1958 legislative elections the PCV garnered 160,791 votes (6.23 percent of total votes), which granted it two seats in the Senate and seven seats in the Lower Chamber (Kornblith and Levine 1995: 49–52). "Back then," Teodoro Petkoff said, "the Communists were not aggressive for fear of a coup or retaliation on the part of the military. . . . During the entire year 1958 the PCV's policy was to allow democratic stabilization of the country."[47]

The two elected senators and seven chamber deputies from the PCV participated in the drafting of the new constitution for Venezuela, which was approved by Congress on January 23, 1961 (Kornblith 1989b). By

1962, however, the PCV openly declared that it was in favor of armed struggle against the regime and joined the Movimiento de Izquierda Revolucionaria in an effort to create and reproduce guerrilla focos all over Venezuela.[48] In May 1962, after two failed coups d'etat promoted by the left, the government banned the PCV and MIR from legal political action by presidential decree. Armed confrontation had begun, and it would last until the end of the decade.

The Venezuelan guerrilla movement, however, had a very short life span. Its first major defeat happened soon after it was established, when the military uprisings of Carúpano and Puerto Cabello failed, giving way to a major wave of repression.[49] Furthermore, the elections in 1963 proved a major political defeat for the armed left, when the strategy of boycotting the elections backfired. Despite a nationwide call for electoral abstention as a sign of protest, Venezuelans voted massively in that election: 3,107,563 of 3,369,986 (or 92.2 percent) of registered voters showed up at the polls on election day. The abstention rate was 7.8 percent.[50] After this political debacle the Venezuelan guerrillas took a radical turn and decided to move from the cities to the countryside, where they suffered a series of military defeats. In 1965 the leadership of the PCV was already considering the possibility of giving up the armed struggle. In 1966 the PCV officially declared an end to guerrilla warfare and expelled a group of militants who opposed any proposal leading to a truce, negotiation, or rolling back of guerrilla warfare. This group, led by Douglas Bravo, continued to take part in armed conflict under the name Partido Revolucionario Venezolano (PRV).[51] MIR followed the PCV's lead and decided to abandon its support for armed struggle in 1967. A small minority remained armed into the 1970s, divided into three small groups: the Movimiento Bandera Roja (MBR), the Organización de Revolucionarios (OR), and the Liga Socialista (LS) (Martínez 1980: 328). By 1968 the guerrilla movement had become completely marginalized and had no political significance in Venezuela.

The PCV and MIR decided to give up armed struggle before military defeat had been officially acknowledged and before any negotiation had yet taken place between the guerrillas and the government. In recognition of this, in 1968, the Leoni government instructed the Supreme Electoral Council to allow the official registration of a new party, Unión para Avanzar (UPA), knowing that it would function as a vehicle for the participation in elections of the outlawed PCV. In an interview Gustavo Machado, a leader of the PCV, said, "When we got out of San Carlos we created the UPA, which was an indirect form of the Party. The government knew that the Communist Party was behind UPA. Nevertheless, it decided to legalize us, and we evidently did a good electoral campaign."[52] This gesture on the part of the government opened the doors for the final reinsertion into politics of the Venezuelan guerillas. UPA participated in the 1968 elections and obtained a little over 100,000 votes. A return to electoral participation "led the party to begin a process of recovery of the disaster suffered during the armed struggle, to reach out to the masses," said Guillermo García Ponce, another leader of the PCV.[53] Finally, in the view of Petkoff, the elections of 1968 played a crucial role as a bridge for the guerrilla's reinsertion into legal politics: "The [Leoni] government created a bridge. . . . [I]t legalized the UPA and turned a blind eye to the fact that this was the very same Communist Party. . . . That is the most important antecedent of what Caldera did later, with a lot more audacity." What Rafael Caldera did was to understand that the PCV's policy was not deceitful, "that there truly was a real shift in the party's policy, that the armed movement was completely defeated, and that, under those conditions, one had to stimulate those factors that could lead toward a liquidation of armed struggle within the left."[54]

Caldera, founder and candidate of COPEI, won the 1968 presidential election. In early 1969, right after his inauguration, President Caldera announced his pacification policy and appointed the Pacification Commission. His measures were prompt and effective: the leaders of the PCV, imprisoned since the early 1960s, were freed a month after Caldera's inauguration. The PCV, which had been banned since 1962, was legalized again. Amnesty was granted to those who had participated in the armed struggle. No counteroffer was demanded from the guerrillas; with the exception of the radical faction under Bravo, the PCV had already dismantled its armed apparatus. MIR remained outlawed until 1971. It was granted legal recognition in 1972, before the general elections of 1973. By late 1973 even the most radical guerrilla factions had decided to enter a unilateral truce.[55]

In this case there was no formal negotiation between the insurgents and the incumbent regime of the type recently observed in Colombia (1982–2002), El Salvador (1991–92), or Guatemala (1994–96). The government simply created the conditions under which the former guerrillas could take active part in the legal political process—granting amnesty to political prisoners as well as legal recognition to the outlawed parties. Besides a few significant gestures to welcome back the prodigal sons, no major concessions were granted; nor were political, social, or economic reforms enacted in order to lure the Venezuelan guerrillas into the legal political struggle. A series of specific conditions paved the way for a prompt and successful resolution of guerrilla warfare in that country. In the first place, the Venezuela of the 1960s had somehow solved its agrarian question, not necessarily by way of an agrarian reform, but rather by way of rapid urbanization linked to the oil industry and the growth of the service sector. In addition, the remaining peasant population had been politically mobilized and organized by AD since the 1940s, a strategy that left no political space available for the penetration and consolidation of the radical left. Under such conditions the probability of consolidating a successful armed challenge was close to nil, and the guerrillas suffered a rapid political and military defeat.

By 1968 the guerrillas' defeat was undeniable, but their successful reinsertion was also a consequence of the fact that by then both leftist parties (the PCV and MIR) had made the decision to dismantle their armed apparatus and reenter the game of democratic politics. All they needed was an open door. For the regime, the costs of toleration were low because the guerrillas had been isolated politically and militarily. For the guerrillas, the costs of reincorporation were lowered by the legalization of their parties and the existence of an electoral system favorable to the inclusion of small parties (see Shugart 1992).

In winter 1970 the PCV became divided. In January 1971 the Communist Youth and most Communist former guerrillas formed the Movimiento al Socialismo (MAS). The experience of the emergence and incorporation of MAS into Venezuelan politics is of great interest not only because of its doctrinal and organizational innovations (see Ellner 1988) but also because of its success as an experiment of guerrilla reincorporation into democratic politics, a test case in the study of post-guerrilla politics.[56] With its participation in the elections of 1973 and a respectable electoral showing,[57] the left demonstrated that playing according to the rules was not only possible but politically profitable as well. These elections closed the circle of armed insurgencies in Venezuela. By the end of the Caldera administration, in 1974, confrontation between the guerrillas and the state was definitely over. This meant that the Venezuelan state could finally and successfully claim a complete monopoly over the means of coercion, a goal never quite accomplished by its Colombian counterpart.

Colombia

Although the Colombian government has also confronted guerilla movements of different kinds and stripes since the early 1960s, it has been unable to eliminate its armed contenders and incorporate all those involved in the armed struggle into the realm of institutionalized politics. Despite efforts at peace negotiations spanning more than two decades (1982–2002), guerrilla warfare persists today. Two groups formed in the mid-1960s, the Ejército de Liberación Nacional (ELN) and the Fuerzas Armadas Revolucionarias de Colombia (FARC), grew steadily over the years and covered a sizable range of national territory (see Leal 2003; LeGrand 2003). These armed challengers on the left remain as a living testament to the fact that some significant sectors of the population still believe in other means, different from elections, to establish and change governments. To paraphrase Linz and Stepan's (1996a) famous dictum, in Colombia democracy has not yet become "the only game in town."

The Colombian Communist Party at first adopted an ambiguous position concerning the bipartisan pacts crafted between 1956 and 1957. It favored the return to civilian rule and the party's relegalization, but it was concerned that the traditional parties had excluded the PCC from all negotiations leading to the reestablishment of democracy. More than anything else, it was concerned that according to the conditions included in the National Front pacts, the PCC—and any other party besides the Liberal and Conservative ones—was to be excluded from electoral politics for the next sixteen years. It thus decided to call for a blank vote in the plebiscite of December 1, 1957, which ratified the party accords.[58] The results were, however, extremely poor: 20,738 votes (or less than half a percent) were counted as blank (see table 3.3).

The PCC had been hard hit by years of repression during the Conservative governments of Ospina (1946–50) and Gómez (1950–53), as well as during the military dictatorship (1953–57).[59] Massive urban repression and the deactivation of the labor movement—engineered by the two traditional parties since the late 1940s in reaction to the pro-labor reforms of the 1930s[60]—had since turned the PCC into a predominantly rural party, with its bases of support concentrated mainly in areas of recent settlement controlled by the PCC since the 1930s, where they declared a strategy of "self-defense of the masses."[61] These peasant communities organized by the PCC had taken up arms in self-defense during the conservative dictatorship of Laureano Gómez, had laid them down without giving them up during the "pacification" of Rojas Pinilla, and had taken them up again after the military government decided to strike back against the Communists in 1955 during the "Villarica war."[62] By the time of the transition from authoritarian to civilian rule, the rural-based Communist groups laid down their arms again and gave the civilian government their support, if only for a few years.

They eventually participated in electoral politics, not on their own, but through an alliance with a dissident faction of the Liberal Party, the MRL, which purported to represent those on the left who felt excluded from the National Front.[63] A peasant leader, who was widely recognized as belonging to the Communist Party, Juan de la Cruz Varela, was elected among others in a MRL list to the Chamber of Representatives in 1960. This was certainly not the same as participating in their own right (as the PCV could do), but there were still some open cracks in the regime through which the opposition on the left could squeeze. However, by 1964 the most conservative faction within the Conservative Party, the Laureanistas, decided to call for a major military operation against the so-called independent republics—that is, the areas under the control of the Communist Party—with the argument that they were creating an untenable situation of dual sovereignty.[64] The government, which was a coalition government by design, depended on keeping all or most of the party factions together in order to build working majorities in Congress. It thus yielded to the Conservatives' demand for a military strategy to deal with these peasant communities, which resulted in "Operation Marquetalia" and others that followed in the municipalities of El Pato, Riochiquito, and Guayabero against the Communist strongholds, provoking in turn a major reaction and exodus of the peasant communities beyond the agricultural frontier into the eastern plains, where the FARC would be formally founded two years later, in 1966 (see Pizarro 1991b).

The exclusion of the PCC by the traditional parties was certainly worse than that suffered by the PCV. However, it took a combination of political exclusion and open military repression to finally drive the Colombian Communists to form a guerrilla movement. And yet the PCC never openly declared war against the establishment, as the PCV did in 1962 (Ellner 1988: 43–44). It decided instead on a strategy of "combining all forms of struggle"[65]—an ambiguous mixture of electoral participation and armed confrontation—which had nefarious consequences both for the emerging democratic regime and for the left itself.[66] Since 1957 the PCC has never been outlawed, but from 1958 to 1972 it could not participate openly, in its own right, in the electoral arena. By the same token, as in a mirror image, the PCC has never made an open call to take up arms against the regime, but it has nonetheless clandestinely sponsored the existence of an armed branch of the party, the FARC, thus playing the role of a semiloyal opposition.[67] The dramatic result of this "combination of all the forms of struggle" is that the FARC grew steadily stronger, until it became in the 1980s the leading force, swallowing the legal PCC and subjecting its members to the spiral of violence it contributed to creating.

The Radicalization of the Left

Beyond the formal exclusion enacted by the party pacts, the dynamics of the coalition governments worked to marginalize and radicalize them even further. In both Colombia and Venezuela during the first few years after the transition, polarization was the order of the day. The governments of Betancourt (Venezuela) and Lleras Camargo (Colombia) were forced to attempt a difficult balancing act between the demands of their more radical constituencies (workers and students) and the demands of their newly gained allies on the right (the church, the conservative parties, business, and the military). Despite their previous reputation as progressive or even radical populist, AD and the Liberal Party were forced to make major concessions to their conservative partners. These concessions were not only political but also substantive, in terms of refraining from introducing major social and economic policy reform. In the early 1960s the two countries suffered severe economic recessions. The effects of these economic crises combined with the austerity measures taken in both cases resulted in an increased social mobilization, especially in the urban areas, whose protagonists were organized workers and university students. In a climate of growing polarization the right perceived this mobilization as dangerous and pressed for harsher measures against the leaders. At the same time the two elected governments were trying to implement the effective subordination of the armed forces, a task that involved defining a new mission for them: containing social mobilization and repressing internal disorders became part of this new mission, especially in the Colombian case. In this context the radicalization of some sectors in the parties was inevitable: the youth wings of both parties, Juventud Adeca and Juventudes MRL, rejected the compromises made by the leadership of their parties and opted for armed rebellion, thus forming the MIR in Venezuela and in the case of MRL joining the pro-Cuban ELN.

A number of international factors also influenced the decision made by the Communist leadership and other groups to take up arms against the democratic regimes in Colombia and Venezuela in the first half of the 1960s. The epoch-making influence of the Cuban Revolution was no doubt a major one.[68] As many have pointed out, the success of the Sierra Maestra rebels signaled not only the possibility of a Communist revolution in the developing world but also the actual possibility of a revolution in the western hemisphere, more particularly in Latin America, the backyard of the United States. Besides the Cuban Revolution, a broader flow of ideas and world events, such as the national liberation struggles in Africa and Asia, especially the Vietnam War, combined into a kind of zeitgeist that favored the option of taking up arms against incumbent regimes in much of the Third World.[69] The Cuban Revolution was not by any means the only event associated with this zeitgeist, but for Latin America it was by far the most consequential one. It drastically changed the available cultural repertoire of collective action (Tilly 1978) in the region. Starting on January 1, 1959, political democracy was no longer considered a blessing but a curse by the Latin American left.[70]

The Cuban experience also served to question the "peaceful road to socialism" proposed by the international Communist movement and drove a wedge into the Communist Parties of the world. Gradually, the orthodox wing of the Communist movement started to loose its firm grip on the left in Latin America (Ellner 1988: 15). New groups sprang from this questioning of the Communist orthodoxy, many of them opting for armed struggle. Paradoxically, the Communist Parties in many countries—and the PCV and PCC were no exceptions—ended up opting for armed rebellion in part out of fear of losing out to their more daring competitors on the left. In Venezuela there was MIR, a splinter group from AD formed in 1960 by the radicalized youth wing in the party, which ignited the guerrilla movement in 1962. In Colombia the decision to found the FARC in 1966 had to do in part with the fact that there already existed a number of guerrilla *foquista* experiments, most notably the ELN, which emerged in 1965 with a clear pro-Cuban orientation. In 1967 the Maoist wing of the Communist movement founded the Ejército Popular de Liberación (EPL). Finally, in 1973, a new group emerged, the pioneer of the so-called second generation of guerrilla movements in Colombia: the Movimiento 19 de Abril (M-19).[71]

Similar as these two experiences may seem, what really sets Colombia and Venezuela apart in this respect is not the early implantation of guerrilla focos in the 1960s but rather the fact that the Colombian guerrillas became consolidated, persisting today, while they rapidly failed in Venezuela, giving way to the emergence of a loyal opposition on the left and its successful incorporation into the political system.

Explaining Divergence: The Role of Historical Continuities
One factor favoring the implantation and consolidation of a rural guerrilla movement in Colombia and explaining the failure of such an experiment in Venezuela has to do with the size and relative weight of the peasantry. While Colombia in the mid-1960s still had half of its population in the countryside, in Venezuela the peasantry was quickly disappearing as a result of rapid urbanization (see fig. 1.3). The Venezuelan guerrillas, like many other guerrilla movements that sprang up across the continent in the 1960s, were mostly made up of students, professors, urban professionals, and intellectuals. In the words of Venezuela's former

President Ramon J. Velásquez, "The guerrilla experience in Venezuela was an intellectual experiment rather than a political event . . . ; guerrillas are made out of peasants and workers, but here it was just a university experiment."[72] For a guerrilla movement to implant itself, consolidate, and grow, it needs to establish a social base of support. This was never accomplished by the Venezuelan guerrilla groups; they remained a mainly urban, middle-class affair.

By contrast, in Colombia stronger links developed between the guerrillas and the population, due in part to the fact that a significant proportion of the population (over 50 percent) remained in the countryside. However, it is not just the existence of a large number of peasants but the persistence of a wide range of rural conflicts and their lack of resolution that fueled rebellion among the peasantry. The guerrilla movement was most successful, initially, in those areas where there was an old tradition of social and political struggle against landowners and the state.[73] Another reason the Colombian guerrillas managed to spread and consolidate in large parts of the country is a tradition of using violence as part of the repertoire of collective action. Most of the Colombian revolutionary guerrillas in the 1960s were born and took root in the same regions ravaged during La Violencia in the immediately preceding decade. They built on a tradition of violence as an accepted means of political struggle and action, a tradition that is totally absent in Venezuela.[74]

There is also the role played by political institutions such as the state and the parties. The Venezuelan state not only had the capacity to monopolize the use of violence but also had a greater capacity for distribution of resources among the population. In this sense the oil rent accruing to the state was a factor that facilitated the reincorporation of the guerrillas, thus helping to promote at least an instrumental attachment to the democratic rules of the game. While the role played by oil in the advent of democracy may be a subject of dispute,[75] that played by the oil rent as facilitator of democratic stability, in that it helps alleviate distributive conflicts, is a matter of agreement among students of Venezuelan politics.[76] By contrast, the Colombian state was not only weaker to begin with but also had suffered a "partial collapse" (Oquist 1978) during the previous decade, in part as a consequence of La Violencia. With a weak state just recovering from a decade of havoc, its military and police force in serious disarray, and its judicial apparatus on the verge of ruin, it should come as no surprise that the challenge from armed revolutionaries could spring up and take root more easily. In addition, the Colombian state has historically been fiscally poor, a condition that only changed slowly during the National Front.[77] In the Colombian case the state lacked the resources to distribute and offset the appeal of the guerrillas' offers to a deprived peasant population.

Finally there is the role played by the political parties. The Venezuelan parties, especially AD, had a strong following among the peasant population. The peasant leagues and the Federación de Campesinos de Venezuela were the creation of AD in its initial stages and remained a strong base of support until the mid- to late 1950s, when Venezuela became predominantly urban. Thus since the 1940s AD and later COPEI had built a strong and lasting alliance with the peasantry that acted as a bulwark against the penetration of radical discourse and guerrilla tactics in the 1960s. The parties, especially AD, provided a channel for the articulation of peasant demands as well as an institutional vehicle for their representation in the political arena.[78] With strong organizational links forged between the FCV and AD and the mediation between the FCV and the state provided by the presence of AD in the government, there was no political space in Venezuela for revolutionary vanguards or anti-system organizations to tap into the peasants' grievances and demands and thus garner support for extrainstitutional activity. By contrast, the proliferation of rural guerrillas in Colombia is witness to the failure of the traditional parties to fulfill the functions of interest articulation and representation of the peasantry. There was thus a much wider space available for the penetration of revolutionary discourse among a population that was barely under the control of the two traditional parties, a population in need of representation in a political arena in which the only mechanisms for incorporation thus far had been either civil war or clientelism.

The Exclusionary Nature of the Pacts: How Much Does It Explain?

The exclusion of the Communist Parties from the party pacts in both countries partially accounts for the radicalization of the Communists, as well as the fringe sectors of the signatory parties (MIR and

MRL). Exclusion from the party agreements is obviously one of the main factors that produced a strong reaction against these two fledging regimes and the emergence of armed challengers on the left. The Venezuelan pacts, however, while excluding the PCV from the coalition cabinet, allowed for its electoral participation. The PCV decided to join in the armed struggle against the regime for reasons that go beyond its initial exclusion from the pacts, electoral discrimination not being one of them. Rather, that the regime provided the possibility for open and legal representation of the left in political society partially accounts for the failure of the armed experiment. Shugart (1992: 130) has captured well this apparent paradox in the Venezuelan regime: "Because of the pact that accompanied the reestablishment of democracy in 1958, the regime had a certain exclusionary character, a factor without which the decision of some elites to opt for guerrilla warfare would have been less likely. But the regime against which the guerrillas were fighting was indeed democratic and rather favorable to minority parties." When the guerrillas called for abstention in the 1963 Venezuelan elections, the population responded by voting massively. They clearly said no to arms and yes to the possibilities opened up by peaceful electoral competition. A higher degree of political inclusion in Venezuela than in Colombia produced wider acceptance of the pacts and the political regime by political actors, thus leaving little space available for revolutionary alternatives.

By contrast, in Colombia the left was prevented from participating as an independent political force in every election from 1958 to 1974. Armed challengers thus became, to a certain extent, the representatives of a left that was denied open and fair access to political society. A decade and a half after the transition a legal civilian left clearly predominated in Venezuela over those who claimed the need for armed rebellion. It was completely the opposite in Colombia, where only a small fraction of the left, in particular, the Movimiento Obrero Independiente Revolucionario (MOIR), favored the possibility of competing peacefully for a place in the political scene. By the mid-1970s these small groups had definitely lost the struggle against the armed groups for dominance within the left.

The openness and flexibility of the Venezuelan pacts—as opposed to the closed and rigid character of the Colombian ones—also made a difference at the moment of reincorporation of the guerrillas. The Venezuelan electoral system used a closed-list proportional representation system, which had a very low barrier for the inclusion of small parties (a party could get a seat in the Chamber of Deputies with as little as 0.55 percent of the nationwide vote), and an impartial board for conducting and overseeing elections.[79] Its closed-list system meant that parties would compete on the basis of party platforms, unlike systems like the Colombian one in which candidates within parties were forced to compete with one another. The Colombian electoral system not only excluded any competition from the left but also promoted intraparty competition, thus forcing individual candidates to deliver "pork" funds to followers in exchange for votes and reinforcing a long tradition of political clientelism. Venezuela's closed-list electoral system, together with the low barriers to new parties, allowed for the representation of new alternatives, including the former rebels, "without needing prior access to budgetary largesse" (Shugart 1992: 130). As a result, the Venezuelan rules of the game favored an easier and more rapid incorporation of the armed challengers into the political arena, whereas the Colombian rules of the game by definition prevented any political force distinct from the multiple factions belonging to the two traditional parties from participating in legal politics. In the latter case, there were no incentives to reenter the game—at least until 1974 when the formal restrictions imposed by the pacts were lifted.

The institutional arrangement forged during the transition thus plays a double role: it is an incentive for the decision to take arms against the regime, and it is an incentive (or disincentive) to lay down arms and reenter legal politics. The institutional incentives present in the Venezuelan institutional framework made the reincorporation of the guerrillas as relevant electoral actors into the system possible, whereas the institutional features of the Colombian regime precluded such a path for the Colombian guerrillas.

Confronting the Challenge: The Role of Actors and Strategic Action

In addition to the historical and institutional factors contributing to the success or failure of the armed guerrillas in Colombia and Venezuela, there were differences in the decisions made by political actors at certain critical junctures. President Caldera (COPEI), who was elected in late

1968, moved swiftly to grant amnesty to the guerrillas and legal recognition to the PCV and MIR. Under Caldera, previously banned leftist parties were legalized and guerrillas successfully incorporated into the democratic process. Presiding over the first noncoalition government in Venezuela's democratic experiment, Caldera actively promoted the reincorporation of the radical left and the widening of political society in Venezuela as a way to widen his own government's support. It is also significant that the deal granting amnesty was made after the alternation in executive power from AD to COPEI, thus allowing the rebels to deal with a party other than that from which they had split years before (Shugart 1992). As Hartlyn (1998: 115) has written, "Targeted government expenditures facilitated by oil revenues, effective assurances regarding the physical integrity of former guerrilla leaders, and widespread legitimacy for democratic institutions in the country all facilitated the process."

In Colombia the first two post-transition governments—Lleras Camargo (1958–62) and Guillermo León Valencia (1962–66)—dealt with the remaining groups from the period of La Violencia, a phenomenon called "bandolerismo" (banditry), until it was successfully overcome in the mid-1960s. After winning the war against the bandits, the civilian leadership did not take an active role in confronting the guerrilla challenge. They gradually delegated all power to decide on matters of internal security and public order to the armed forces, which, in the absence of a political strategy from the civilian leadership, confronted the problem exclusively by using force.[80]

On the other hand, in Venezuela there was the clear decision on the part of the armed left to lay down arms and take up the challenge of entering the political game with all its opportunities but also its risks and costs. In Colombia, on the contrary, the guerrillas did not make that decision until the early 1990s—and then only some of them. In the late 1960s a couple of military defeats plus the experience of the new European left had made some groups aware of the limits of the armed experience. Some of them criticized the guerrillas and made an effort to engage in electoral politics.[81] However, the apparent official fraud committed against the former dictator and candidate of the populist ANAPO, Rojas Pinilla, in the 1970 elections, plus the violent overthrow of President

Salvador Allende in 1973 in Chile, had the combined effect of marginal-izing these small critical groups and strengthening the most radical pro–armed struggle groups. In the early 1970s a new leftist group emerged that criticized the Communist Party and the orthodox paradigms of the left, claiming to have a new, fresher approach to politics, directly related to the national experience and not dictated by foreign doctrine. This group, M-19, was not, however, ready to give up armed struggle as a means to its ends. Those critical of the armed experience remained fewer in numbers and marginal, while those who preferred arms became the dominant force within the Colombian left.[82]

In Venezuela the guerrillas were defeated and the armed left made a conscious decision to step within the legal borders separating bounded conflict from open confrontation. It thus is not only a matter of the re-gime opening its doors to the opposition; it also takes a decision on the part of the opposition to lay down its arms and enter into the space of democratic politics. Once a major group has made the decision to enter into institutionalized politics, this decision has a demonstration effect on other armed challengers: after the PCV made that decision, MIR fol-lowed suit. With the entrance of the former guerrillas into electoral poli-tics, a cycle was closed in Venezuela: by the early 1970s all the former armed challengers—from the right and from the left—had been drawn into the rules of the game. The reincorporation of the guerrillas also had a positive feedback effect on the attitudes of the military, thus taking away the justification to intervene in domestic politics. Thereafter, a vir-tuous cycle ensued in which the previous consensus on the democratic regime became broader, the party system strengthened, and a revaluation of democracy by an important set of political actors emerged. In Vene-zuela, after the 1973 elections, given the participation of MAS and MIR, democracy certainly became "the only game in town."

By contrast, Colombia has suffered from a protracted insurgency (Chernick 1988; Pizarro 1996a) that has contributed to a vicious circle that permanently undermines the working of democracy in that country. The state's inability to defeat the armed challengers, combined with the latter's decision to persist in their armed struggle, even without a chance of winning, has produced a gradual strengthening of the authoritarian tendencies of some actors inside and outside the game of democratic politics (including the military). An almost permanent state of siege, an increasing militarization of state and society, a gruesome record of human rights violations on the part of the state forces, and the emergence of violent right-wing militias (the so-called paramilitary groups) are just some of the signs of this perverse pattern of institutionalization.

In sum, while a common characteristic of post–Cuban Revolution Latin America is the emergence of radical revolutionary groups and guerrilla movements, there are interesting variations in the degree to which these armed experiments managed to take root or were defeated, giving rise, in some cases, to loyal oppositions on the left. Colombia and Venezuela offer important examples.

I have used the explanatory factors proposed in this book, historical continuities and institutional legacies, to explain the divergent experience with guerrilla politics in these two countries. Some structural factors, such as the existence (in Colombia) versus the absence (in Venezuela) of a significant peasant population and the availability, in the Venezuelan case, of state resources that could lure certain groups into participating in legal politics, may help to explain the short duration and rapid decline of the guerrilla experiment in Venezuela. Nevertheless, political factors such as the capacity of the state to control its territory and population and the capacity on the part of the parties to organize and represent disaffected sectors of the population seem equally relevant.

I have also briefly referred to the role of agents (whether individuals or organizations) and the decisions they make at certain critical junctures. While the PCV was quick to recognize its defeat and quickly decided to put an end to the armed experiment and give electoral politics a chance, until the 1990s the Colombian guerrillas, especially the Communist FARC and the ELN, threw away every opportunity for negotiation.[83] My point here is simply to reassert the role of agency, thus reminding us that armed contention is a decision made by actors and organizations conscious of their choices and capable of following up on their decisions. Equally important, the decision to move away from armed struggle into the realm of institutionalized electoral competition takes agents and organizations willing to make that strategic shift and follow it through.

The context in which these decisions are made is, of course, strongly determined by the institutional architecture in which these actors interact. In the Venezuelan case, despite the initial exclusion of the PCV from the pacts, the flexibility and openness of the political regime designed by the pact makers of 1958 set the stage for a successful reincorporation of the radical left after 1968. In Colombia, by contrast, the rigidities introduced by the pact, coupled by their duration, only added incentives to an insurgency that also had strong structural and historical roots on which to thrive. As a result, while Venezuela could claim to have eliminated all armed challengers on the left and the right by the third presidential term after its transition, in Colombia the guerrilla groups that took up arms in the early 1960s have grown stronger with time, thus perpetuating an armed conflict that has done enormous harm to that country's democratization process.

Defeating armed contenders and opening a proper place for their participation in the democratic game are both crucial to achieving what for many is the hallmark of a settled, institutionalized democracy: the creation of a loyal opposition.[84] The subordination of the military and incorporation of the left, together with the building of a representative and competitive party system (taken up in chapter 5) are thus at the very center of the institutionalization process whereby democracy takes hold.

Limiting the Use of Force: A Sine Qua Non in a Democratic Polity

This chapter explored an interrelated set of challenges faced by Colombia and Venezuela's fledging democracies; both relate to the fundamental task of eliminating political violence within the polity and monopolizing coercion in the hands of the state. I first addressed the challenge of defeating military conspiracies to reestablish authoritarian rule and asserting civilian control of the military in terms of policy-making prerogatives, then went on to consider the task of defeating guerrilla insurgencies and successfully incorporating them into the realm of legal politics.

Indeed, subduing, disarming, subordinating, and incorporating those actors bent on using violence as an avenue to political power remain key tasks of any democratic regime. Despite facing challenges similar to those of its neighbor, Colombia, Venezuela achieved a much faster resolution of the issue of eliminating the use of violence in the polity and gaining state monopoly over coercion. Nevertheless, as with so many aspects of Venezuela's democracy, the 1980s witnessed a severe deterioration of civil-military relations, leading to the failed coups of 1992. More recently, an upsurge in urban crime has turned Caracas into one of the most violent cities in the hemisphere. Although this phenomenon does not indicate the emergence of political armed contenders, it certainly reveals the continued erosion of the Venezuelan state's capacity to monopolize coercion and guarantee peaceful interaction within its jurisdiction.

CHAPTER FIVE

Institutionalizing Inclusion and Contestation

The Making of a Democratic Political Society

Democracy is obviously more than elections. But without open, free, fair, and truly competitive elections, there can be no democracy. Elections are, for good reason, at the very heart of democracy. This chapter takes a look at some of the institutions essential to making elections work: political parties, party systems, and electoral rules. Taken together, these institutions form a political society—namely, "that arena in which the polity specifically arranges itself to contest the legitimate right to exercise control over public power and the state apparatus" (Linz and Stepan 1996a: 8).[1] A focus on political society provides an excellent vantage point to observe the factors at work in the evolution of a democratic regime.

Comparing Party Systems in Colombia and Venezuela

In his classic work on parties and party systems, Giovanni Sartori (1976) proposed a typology based on two criteria: the number of relevant parties and their degree of ideological polarization. Using these two variables as the main criteria for comparison, Colombia and Venezuela can be seen as very similar cases: from the late 1950s to the late 1980s both were considered stable, ideologically centripetal, two-party systems, with Colombia being the closest to a two-party system and Venezuela a little further from that score.[2] In terms of polarization Venezuela's party system was rated moderately high—having a somewhat greater ideological spread between its relevant parties—while Colombia was classified as moderately low. Both were seen, nevertheless, as lying close to the middle of the spectrum, or having limited polarization (see Mainwaring and Scully 1995: 31). The most important difference in this regard was the existence in Venezuela of a "relevant" party on the left (first URD, then MAS, and later La Causa Radical [LCR]) that was a viable political contender even if it was unable to win the presidency.

In 1995 Mainwaring and Scully proposed the notion of party system institutionalization as a useful conceptual tool for comparing Latin American party systems. "The number of relevant parties competing and the intensity of ideological polarization are still relevant," they noted, "but are more useful once the extent of institutionalization of a party system is determined" (6). They argued that parties and party systems have far-reaching consequences for the performance and viability of Latin American democracies and proposed four dimensions whose variation affects the overall degree of institutionalization. These dimensions are the regularity of interparty competition, the depth and stability of parties' roots in society, the degree of acceptance of parties and elections as legitimate institutions determining who governs, and the stability of the parties' internal rules and structures (1). According to these four measures, both Colombia and Venezuela were classified as institutionalized competitive party systems.

The two countries scored high on most of these dimensions: patterns of party competition were deemed quite stable in Colombia and moderately so in Venezuela (7), as evidenced by relatively low levels of electoral volatility. Colombia and Venezuela, together with Uruguay, appeared at the lower end of the Latin American scale based on an aggregate indicator that combined volatility for both legislative and presidential elections. Colombia had a mean volatility of 9.7 percent, Venezuela 18.8 percent.[3] Equally significant, Mainwaring and Scully showed that parties had won the allegiance of many citizens in Colombia and Venezuela, as well as in Uruguay, Costa Rica, Chile, and Argentina, as evidenced in the low difference between presidential and legislative votes, in survey data (11), and in the qualitative information presented elsewhere in their volume. Interestingly, they found an important difference between these two cases with regard to their second criterion, the parties' roots in society: while the Venezuelan parties had stronger connections with organized interests in society (including trade unions, peasant and student groups, teachers organizations, neighborhood associations, and professional societies), which they had helped organize and within which they kept an active presence, this was not the case in Colombia; in that country, in the authors' words, "the linkages between parties and social organizations are weaker than in the other, more stable, democratic party systems" (13). Still, their emphasis on the stability of parties' roots in society downplayed the nature of these roots. I come back to this crucial difference later in this chapter.

On the third dimension of party system institutionalization—the extent to which citizens and organized interests perceive parties and elections as the legitimate route to power—Mainwaring and Scully argued that despite the absence of reliable and comparable survey data covering the entire period, in these two cases (together with Costa Rica, Chile, and Uruguay) parties had indeed been central and that the major actors had by and large accepted a major role for elections in determining who governs (14). Finally, according to their fourth criterion, the authors were very confident in their assessment that party organizations in Venezuela, Costa Rica, Chile, Uruguay, Mexico, and Paraguay were among the strongest and most institutionalized in Latin America (16). By this, they meant that "political elites are loyal to their parties and party discipline in the legislature is reasonably solid. Parties are well organized, and although they are centralized, they have a presence at the local and national levels" (16). By contrast, party organizations were deemed somewhat weaker in Colombia and Argentina. In the case of Colombia, intense factionalism, the fact that party factions could draw up their own set of candidates and print their own ballots, and the gradual loss of organizational control were seen as manifestations of an erosion of party organizations in the preceding decades. Despite Colombia's shortcomings, though, neither Colombia nor Venezuela was seen as having the extreme degrees of personalism and atomization that characterizes what they called "inchoate" party systems (examples of which were Brazil, Peru, Ecuador, and Bolivia).

After adding the scores for the four criteria used to classify party systems, Colombia and Venezuela ended up at the higher end of the scale, each with an aggregate score of 10.5 of a possible 12 points.[4] Ranking high on all criteria, Colombia and Venezuela clearly fit their "institutionalized party systems" category. Parties had been and continued to be central actors in Venezuela's democracy since 1958, Mainwaring and Scully concluded. They were institutionalized, disciplined, and centralized. They controlled candidate selection and were the central actors in electoral campaigns. Furthermore, parties maintained strong links with organized groups in society, and most citizens identified with the parties and voted consistently for them (17). If anything, they noted, parties in Venezuela could be seen as "too strong, disciplined and centralized"—leading to political reforms from the mid-1980s on. Colombia, on the other hand, had one of the oldest and stablest democratic party systems in Latin America, formed by the traditional nineteenth-century parties. Party identities were found to be strong, despite the limited ideological and policy distance between the two parties. Their internal organization, however, was found to be less cohesive or centralized than that of Venezuelan parties: indeed, party factions were found to play a central role in presenting candidates and organizing campaigns, as well in garnering the allegiance of voters over and above the party label (18). While the authors saw no signs of the impending collapse of the Venezuelan party system, they warned about serious erosion in the Colombian case (21).

Mainwaring and Scully put forth a compelling argument about the importance of party system institutionalization for the stability and quality of democracy. Nevertheless, by focusing mainly on the negative implications and perils of weak party system institutionalization, they overlooked the ways in which highly institutionalized party systems can contribute to the erosion and outright decay of democracy. This is precisely the case with Colombia and Venezuela: despite having highly institutionalized party systems, some of the features of these systems and of the individual parties became central factors in the crises they have experienced since the late 1980s.[5]

Let us now turn to the evolution of these two party systems in the three decades following the transitional pacts. I argue that we should focus on how their divergent histories, their varying modes of organization, and their links to both state and society led to fundamental differences in their institutionalization process.

Venezuela

Political parties were at the center of the democratic regime that emerged in Venezuela in the late 1950s. In the two decades since the death of Juan Vicente Gómez, parties mobilized and expressed the multiple social interests emerging from economic, social, and political change, thus becoming the primary agents for channeling political conflict in that country. Party leaders were the main architects of the transition to democracy in 1958, and party organizations remained a crucial part of the political landscape until the mid-1990s.[6] That these parties became weakened to the point of collapse and virtual disappearance from the electoral scene goes a long way toward explaining the recent crisis of Venezuela's democracy.

For over half a century all successful parties in Venezuela followed the pattern established by Acción Democrática. Venezuelan parties were conceived and built as highly cohesive, disciplined, and vertically integrated organizations, with powerful links between local, regional, and national structures. Despite their active links with and representation of an array of social classes and organizations, control remained in the hands of a strong centralized leadership (Kornblith and Levine 1995: 41).

These parties did not emerge overnight, and neither were their patterns of interparty competition established by constitutional fiat. As documented in chapter 2, the parties emerged in Venezuela in the second half of the 1930s, after the death of Gómez. By the late 1950s, when democracy was established, there were four parties that could be considered relevant and legitimate contenders for power: AD, COPEI, URD, and the PCV.[7] In the early years of Venezuela's democracy, its party system had the potential to become a multiparty system.

The founding elections in 1958 showed that AD's overwhelming majorities (see table 2.1) were a thing of the past. Nevertheless, AD retained a comfortable dominant position within the emergent party system (with close to 50 percent of the vote), followed by a coalition of URD and the PCV on the left, which captured a third of the vote, and then by COPEI, which garnered 16 percent of the vote. In 1958 URD was among the three largest parties in Venezuela, having played a key role in the opposition to Pérez Jiménez. URD was also a vital coalition partner during the first two AD governments (1958–63 and 1963–69). However, due mainly to its founder's personalistic control (Kornblith and Levine 1995: 47), URD's party organization declined steadily after 1958 and disappeared by the late 1970s (see declining shares of the vote for URD in tables 5.1. and 5.2).

In the 1963 elections AD suffered a significant decrease of its electoral support (from 49 to 32 percent), in part as a result of a series of damaging splits (in 1960 and in 1962) that cut deeply into the party's organization. COPEI managed to capture only a slim part (4 percent) of that change. The left remained strong but went to the polls divided into two separate camps, URD and Fuerza Democrática Popular (FDP), which together obtained 28 percent of the vote; there was also an emerging small party on the right of the political spectrum: Uslar Pietri's Frente Democrático Nacional (FDN). Despite winning the first two presidential contests (1958 and 1963), effective competition—both from the left and from COPEI—kept AD from falling again into the majoritarian temptation that had led to the demise of the Trienio experiment. In 1968, with the left mostly fighting outside the confines of the political system, a splinter movement, Movimiento Electoral del Pueblo (MEP), undermined AD's dominance and gave COPEI's candidate, Rafael Caldera, the presidency with a small plurality of less than 30 percent. From then on, COPEI became the second most important party in Venezuela. The year 1968 also marks the last time in which personalistic electoral vehicles played a significant role in Venezuelan elections.[8]

After 1968 the political game changed considerably: party system fragmentation was overcome, and a system dominated by two-party competition emerged. AD and COPEI rose to joint dominance while URD and the PCV practically disappeared. From 1973 to 1993 a growing number of small parties on the left (of which the most important was MAS) were able to survive and grow, though they were never able to

Table 5.1. Presidential Elections in Venezuela, 1958–2006

Year	Party –Candidate (%)
1958	**AD – Betancourt (49.2)**
	URD/PCV - Larrazábal (34.6)
	COPEI – Caldera (16.2)
1963	**AD – Leoni (32.8)**
	COPEI – Caldera (20.2)
	URD - Villalba (18.9)
	IPFN - Uslar (16.1)
	FDP - Larrazábal (9.4)
1968	**COPEI – Caldera (29.1)**
	AD – Barrios (28.2)
	URD-FND-FDP – Burelli (22.2)
	MEP – Prieto (19.3)
1973	**AD – Pérez (48.7)**
	COPEI – Fernández (36.7)
	MEP – Paz (5.1)
	MAS – Rangel (4.3)
	URD – Villalba (3.1)
1978	**COPEI – Herrera (46.6)**
	AD – Piñerúa (43.3)
	MAS – Rangel (5.2)
	MEP – Prieto (1.1)
1983	**AD – Lusinchi (58.4)**
	COPEI – Caldera (33.5)
	MAS – Petkoff (3.5)
	MEP – Rangel (3.4)
1988	**AD – Pérez (52.9)**
	COPEI – Fernández (40.4)
	MAS-MIR – Petkoff (2.7)
	URD – Villalba (0.8)
1993	**CONVERGENCIA+ – Caldera (30.5)**
	AD – Fermín (23.6)
	COPEI – Alvarez Paz (22.7)
	LCR – Velásquez (22.0)
1998	**MVR+ – Chávez (56.2)**
	PRVZL/AD/COPEI+ – Salas Romer (40.0)
	IRENE+ – Saez (2.82)
2000	**MVR+ – Chávez (59.8)**
	LCR+ – Arias (37.5)
	EN – Fermín (2.7)
2006	**MVR+ – Chávez (62.84)**
	Coalition+ – Rosales (36.9)

Sources: For 1958–88: Kornblith and Levine 1995: 49, table 2.1. For 1993: López-Maya and Meléndez 2007: 287–90. For 1998–2006: Consejo Nacional Electoral, www.cne.gov/ve/elecciones (accessed June 3, 2009).

+ = In coalition with other parties.

break the hold of the two dominant parties on Venezuela's electoral politics. Thus a two-and-a-half-party system was born.

Venezuela's party system was not fixed *ex ante* by institutional design: it became a two-party system only gradually, after years of fragmentation, dispersion, and electoral volatility. Unlike their Colombian counterparts, the Venezuelan pacts were committed to respecting the outcome of free and fair elections. The agreement was to respect electoral outcomes, to ensure interparty consultation, and to share political responsibility (and patronage) through the vehicle of a coalition government. During the first two presidential terms (1959–69), even though AD's partners changed, coalition rule remained constant as a general orientation.[9] Explicit coalition rule ended when COPEI formed a single-party government in 1969. Nevertheless, over the next two decades party cooperation would remain a defining feature of the system.

In February 1969 power was effectively transferred for the first time from AD to COPEI's newly elected president, thus obtaining one of the most critical markers of democratic development: the successful and peaceful transfer of power from a losing incumbent party to the opposition. As Przeworski (1991: 10) remarked, "It is only when there are parties that lose and when losing is neither a social disgrace nor a crime that democracy flourishes." The peaceful and effective transfer of power from one party to another indicates that trust in democratic procedures has taken root in political practice. In this case AD showed confidence that, following those same democratic procedures, it could eventually come back to power, and thus it was willing to step down if only temporarily.

During the 1973 elections it became evident that the Venezuelan system was becoming a two-party system with a dominant role for AD and COPEI in all elections. Power was peacefully transferred once again in 1974, this time from COPEI back to AD, when its candidate, Carlos Andrés Pérez, won the 1973 presidential elections. Alternation between these two parties happened peacefully again in 1978 and 1983.[10] This was no minor achievement in a country that had had little experience with party competition or alternation in power.

A second remarkable feature of the Venezuelan party system is that from its inception it allowed the existence of and accommodated a third party on the left, first URD and then MAS. Although before 1998 no leftist party had been able to win the presidency, there was always space for political opposition to emerge, compete in elections, and play a significant role in Venezuelan politics. Table 5.2 summarizes electoral outcomes for legislative elections in Venezuela from 1958, highlighting the electoral fortunes of the parties on the left before the advent to power of Hugo Chávez.

From 1958 to 1993 presidential elections in Venezuela were decided by a plurality of the vote, and a bicameral legislature was elected on the basis of proportional representation with closed and blocked party lists, electing legislators in multimember districts using a D'Hont allocation formula (see Shugart 1992; Coppedge 1994a; Kornblith and Levine 1995: 50; Molina and Perez-Baralt 1996).[11] Given that lists were drawn by the party elites and that all elections were held on the same date (until

Table 5.2. Venezuela: Legislative Elections, 1958–2000

	Percentage of Seats in Lower Chamber									
Year	*1958*	*1963*	*1968*	*1973*	*1978*	*1983*	*1988*	*1993*	*1998*	*2000*
AD	54.9	37.1	30.8	51.0	44.2	56.5	48.5	27.4	30.0	19.4
COPEI	14.3	21.4	27.6	32.0	42.2	30.0	33.5	26.4	12.8	3.0
URD	25.6	16.3	8.4	2.5	1.5	1.5	1.0	0.5		
PCV	5.3			1.0	0.5	1.5	0.5		1.0	3.0
MIR					2.0	1.0				
MEP			11.7	4.0	2.0	1.5	1.0	0.5	0.5	
MAS				4.5	5.5	5.0	9.0*	11.9	11.8	10.9
LCR							1.5	19.9	3.0	1.8
CN								12.9	2.5	2.4
MVR									17.2	48.5
PRVZL									9.8	4.8
PPT									5.4	1.8
PJ										1.8

*MAS-MIR coalition.

Sources: For 1958–78: Kornblith and Levine 1995: 52, table 2.4. For 1983–2000: Payne, Zovatto G., and Mateo Díaz 2006: Appendix 3, "Venezuela–Composición Cámara Baja."

1979), this electoral system favored highly centralized, vertically integrated parties and promoted legislators' disciplined behavior as they were controlled by tightly knit party elites, the infamous *cogollos*.[12] Over time the party system's fragmentation was overcome by the electoral success and gradual consolidation of AD and COPEI as the two dominant party organizations. For more than three decades AD was the biggest party in both houses of Congress, while COPEI gradually rose to a consistent second place. The rest of the seats were held by parties and movements that rarely survived for more than two electoral periods, with the exceptions of the leftist URD and MAS.

During the first decade and a half after the transition, the two would-be dominant parties in Venezuela, AD and COPEI, shared power with URD. This third reformist party became a crucial partner in the coalition government after early 1959. According to the pacted rules of the game, forming part of a coalition government was optional, not compulsory, for the parties. Thus URD was able to leave the coalition government in 1961 after opposing the Betancourt administration's position in favor of excluding Cuba from the Organization of American States. This was another key moment in the process of democratic institutionalization in Venezuela: it opened up the possibility of exercising a loyal opposition against some government policies and even against the government itself while endorsing the basic rules of the game. With its decision to leave the governing coalition while still backing the democratic regime, URD inaugurated the existence of a "loyal opposition" (Linz 1978) in that country.

During the 1960s URD alternated between the roles of coalition partner and opposition party and then began to fade away electorally; by 1973 its share of the vote was less than 5 percent. The space left by URD was to be occupied by a new party, created in January 1971, when the division of the PCV led to the creation of the socialist party MAS (see Ellner 1988). MAS committed itself from the beginning to mass organization and electoral politics and became the only competitor to AD and COPEI able to survive and grow for more than two decades.[13] During the first three elections after it was established (1973, 1978, and 1983) MAS garnered a consistent even if minority share (around 6 percent) of the vote. In the late 1980s it gained strength due to a combination of political decentralization and electoral reforms, coupled with the steady decline of the two traditional parties. By 1993 it became a partner of Convergencia Nacional (CN), a coalition of smaller parties, in a coalition government under the presidency of Rafael Caldera. In the late 1990s, however, its fortunes became tied to the fate of the two older parties as a wave of antiparty sentiment swept through Venezuelan society. Ultimately, it became divided over the new political phenomenon epitomized in the rise of Hugo Chávez to the presidency, with some sectors supporting Chávez and others, led by its founder and most visible leader, Teodoro Petkoff, deciding to mount one of the most vocal and articulate sources of opposition to the current president and his political project.[14]

Despite what we see today as the many flaws and shortcomings of the Venezuelan parties and party system, there is no denying that for over three decades Venezuela had a representative and competitive party system. After 1958 barriers to participation were dropped and active political involvement was encouraged. Voting became obligatory for all Venezuelan adults, and election turnouts were consistently high (above 75 percent) during the first three decades of electoral competition until they started to decline, quite dramatically, from 1988 on (see fig. 5.1).[15]

Figure 5.1. Turnout in Legislative Elections: Colombia and Venezuela Compared (Total Votes as Share of Voting Age Population)

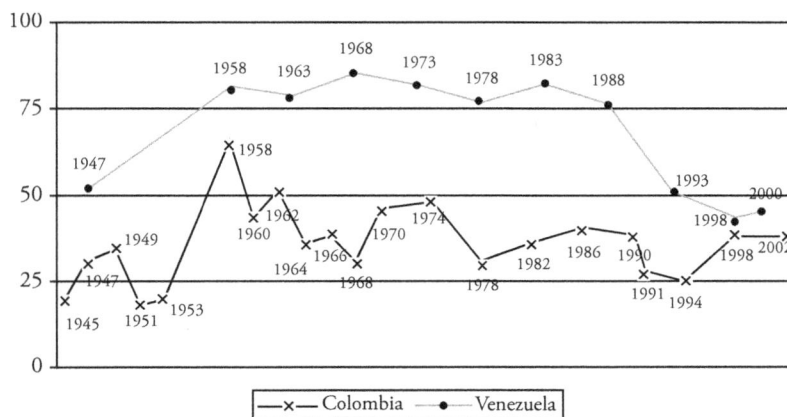

Source: Data from International IDEA, Voter Turnout Website, www.idea.int/vt/index.cfm (accessed 2007).

Note: The number beside each data point is the corresponding year of election.

During that same period, the major political parties maintained a vigorous institutional life, actively seeking to organize the country's growing electorate and maintaining a strong presence in labor, peasant, student, and professional associations.

From its inception until major transformations rocked the party scene in 1993, the Venezuelan party system evolved into a two-and-a-half party system, as a result of the political process. The shape of the party system was not, however, dictated by the pacts. On the other hand, despite the dominance of AD and COPEI as the main parties, the system was always able to accommodate one or more opposition parties from the left of the political spectrum. Thus, unlike Colombia, two major features of democracy—toleration of political opposition and alternation of contenders for power through elections—were preserved in Venezuela. This was the case until 1993, when the economic and political crisis came to be reflected in a major dislocation of the party system. Electoral volatility became extreme between 1993 and 1998, and the party system entered a period of flux and uncertainty. Since 1998 there has been a major collapse and recomposition of the party system, apparently toward a "dominant party system" centered on the Movimiento Quinta República (MVR; now the Partido Socialista Unido de Venezuela [PSUV]). I come back to the reasons for the collapse and subsequent realignment of the Venezuelan party system and its consequences in the final section of this chapter and in chapter 6.

Colombia

As discussed earlier, the traditional Liberal and Conservative Parties have existed throughout Colombia's political history as an independent nation, endowing the country with a degree of continuity that is lacking in most other Latin American nations. Their resilience and endurance, however, should not deceive us: under their astonishing capacity to maintain control of the electoral arena lie two poorly disciplined and increasingly fragmented party organizations. As the strong affective ties of yesteryear began to fade (most notably, after the National Front pacts) larger and larger portions of the electorate have withdrawn from political participation altogether or sought new, extrainstitutional, sometimes violent channels of representation. It is nonetheless remarkable that despite decades of political crisis and an apparent realignments in recent elections,[16] Colombia's party system retained the contours of a stable two-party system. Indeed, as argued by Ron Archer (1995), Colombia's traditional Liberal and Conservative Parties have withstood every signifi-cant challenge and thus perceiving them as weak, failed, or irrelevant is clearly a mistake. They have, instead, "combined great electoral and af-fective strength with weak organizational and representational capaci-ties" (Archer 1995: 170).

Before 1958 alternation of power between the two major parties was usually accompanied by major episodes of violence. One way to deal with this systemic tendency was to form coalition governments made up of the moderate wings of the two parties, but these coalitions often proved fragile and temporary. In 1949, after the last and most dramatic of these episodes of violent interparty competition, Colombia's oligar-chic democracy collapsed, giving way to a decade of authoritarian ex-periments (first led by civilians and then by the military) and a renewed cycle of nationwide killings and unremitting violence—La Violencia—between 1948 and 1958. Party leaders identified the main cause for this tragic pattern in Colombian politics and finally came to agree on a long-lasting solution: the attempt to achieve hegemony would be replaced with a formula to share power between the two parties. Such was the main thrust of the National Front pacts.[17]

Chapter 3 discussed the details of the National Front pacts and their central features. Suffice it to recall here that the pacts established a "constitutional coalition government," in Archer's (1995: 177) felicitous words. The three branches of power were equally divided between the two parties; and the presidency alternated between the two parties for four consecutive elections, or sixteen years. In addition, all legislation needed a two-thirds vote to be approved, thus ensuring support from the majority of both parties. These institutional innovations, aimed at cur-tailing competition between the parties, proved to have profound and long-lasting impact on these two political organizations and their pat-terns of interaction. Indeed, there was a drastic reduction in partisan conflict over the next decades. However, this transformation did not come without a few unexpected costs: growing congressional deadlock, declining partisan identification, increasing abstention, and a growing extralegal opposition. As figure 5.1 shows, after 1958 and to a great extent as a consequence of the party pacts, electoral participation declined steadily, as did the parties' "affective, organizational, and representational capacities" (Archer 1995: 178; see also fig. 5.1).

During the National Front years, Liberals and Conservatives alternated in the presidency three times (1962, 1966, and 1970). It was not the uncertain outcome of elections that produced this alternation but the certain outcome of pacts previously enshrined in the constitution. The first openly competitive election leading to a democratic alternation in power happened in 1974 when the last conservative president of the National Front period, Misael Pastrana, handed over power to the elected liberal candidate, Alfonso López Michelsen (table 5.3). However, a constitutional amendment approved in 1968 compelled the winning party to share power with the second major party, and thus the López Michelsen government (1974–78) and its successors (until 1986) were coalition governments.

With regard to legislative elections, the even distribution of seats between the two parties (regardless of electoral outcomes) effectively shifted the locus of competition from between the parties to within them. Table 5.4 shows the discrepancy between the share of the votes obtained by each party and the actual percentage of seats allocated to each—with a systematic bias in favor of the Conservative Party. Table 5.5 shows the increasing fragmentation of the traditional Liberal and Conservative Parties and the proliferation of factions within them. These factions competed against each other for a share of their party's fixed portion (50 percent) of the seats in electoral contests at all levels (Congress, departmental assemblies, and municipal councils). As these two tables illustrate quite clearly, the two parties grew increasingly fragmented as competition between newly emerging elites led to the formation of competing party lists. With the advent of the National Front, the capacity of the old party elites (the so-called *jefes naturales*) to keep competing factions under control and bring coherence and unity to the parties declined.[18] After reaching a peak in 1958, as elections became relatively meaningless competitions between regional and subregional elites within the same party, turnout declined consistently (see fig. 5.1). Simultaneously, the executive's task of creating governing coalitions became increasingly difficult.

Table 5.3. Presidential Elections in Colombia, 1958–2006

Year	Party – Candidate (%)
1958	**PL/FN – Lleras Camargo (79.9)** PC – Leyva (19.8)
1962	**PC/FN – Valencia (62.1)** MRL – López Michelsen (25.9) PC – Leyva (11.7)
1966	**PL/FN – Lleras Restrepo (71.4)** ANAPO – Jaramillo Giraldo (28.0)
1970	**PC/FN – Pastrana Borrero (40.3)** ANAPO – Rojas Pinilla (38.8) PC – Betancur (11.7) PC – Sourdis (8.3)
1974	**PL – López Michelsen (56.2)** PC – Gómez Hurtado (31.4) ANAPO – Rojas de Moreno (9.4) UNO - Echeverri (2.6)
1978	**PL – Turbay Ayala (49.3)** PC – Betancur (46.4) Left* – Pernía (2.0)
1982	**PC – Betancur (47)** PL – López Michelsen (41.0) NL – Galán (11.0)
1986	**PL – Barco (58.2)** PC – Gómez Hurtado (36) UP – Pardo Leal (4.6)
1990	**PL – Gaviria (47.8)** MSN – Gómez Hurtado (23.7) M-19 – Navarro (12.4) PSC - Lloreda (12.1)
1994	**PL – Samper (51.0)** PC(NFD) – Pastrana Arango (48.9) M-19** – Navarro (3.8)
1998	**PC – Pastrana Arango (51.9)** PL – Serpa (48.1) MSC**– Sanín (27)
2002	**PRIMERO COLOMBIA – Uribe (53)** PL – Serpa (31.8) FSP+ – Garzón (6.1) MOV. SI COL – Sanín (5.8)
2006	**PRIMERO COLOMBIA – Uribe (62.3)** PDA – Gaviria Díaz (22) PL – Serpa (11.8)

Sources: For 1958–78: Archer 1995: 192, table 6.6; Hartlyn 1994: 325, table 9.3. For 1982–90: Dávila 2002: 115–16, tables 7 and 8. For 1994–98: Payne, Zovatto G., and Mateo Díaz 2006: Appendix 3, "Colombia: Elecciones Presidenciales"; for 2002–6, Registraduría Nacional del Estado Civil, www.registraduria.gov.co/ (accessed June 3, 2009).

* A coalition of diverse parties of the left.
** First round of the presidential election only.

Table 5.4. Colombia: Legislative Elections (Lower Chamber), 1958–2002 (% Share of Vote by Party)

	PL*	MRL	NL	PC*	ANAPO	Left**	Other
1958	57.8			42.2			
1960	44.2	13.9		41.7			
1962	35.1	19.5		41.8	3.8		
1964	33.5	16.9		35.5	13.7		
1966	39.4	12.6		29.8	17.8		
1968	47.7	2.2		33.7	16.1		
1970	36.0	0.9		27.2	35.5		
1974	55.6			32.0	9.0	3.1	
1978	55.2			39.4		4.3	1.1
1982	56.4			40.3		2.0	1.3
1986	47.8		6.6	37.1		2.0	6.4
1990	59.2			33.3	0.01	0.35	7.2
1991	50.6			25.6		12.2	11.5
1994	56.2			26.7	0.14	4.1	12.9
1998	48.2			20.6	0.03	2.7	28.0
2002	31.6		0.8	13.7	0.24	2.0	51.6

Sources: 1958–74: Percentages calculated on the basis of data from the Registraduría Nacional del Estado Civil. 1978–2002: Payne, Zovatto G., and Mateo Díaz 2006: Appendix 3, "Colombia: Elecciones Cámara Baja."

*Figures for both the Liberal (PL) and Conservative (PC) Parties include share of votes for all the factions within the party.
**Includes votes for different parties and coalitions on the left.

The constitutional arrangement of power sharing, with its elimi-nation of competition between the parties, ended up creating a bizarre party system in Colombia during the period from 1958 until 1974. As Hartlyn (1998) has noted, Colombia's party system during the National Front simultaneously displayed the characteristics of a one-party, a two-party, and a multiparty system. Because presidents had to come from one of the two traditional parties, bipartisan agreement was mandatory. The elected president then headed a bipartisan government that appeared to be made up of a single party. Within each party, however, different fac-

Table 5.5. Party Fragmentation in Colombia, 1958–2002
(Number of Party Lists Registered for Congressional Elections)

Year	Senate	House
1958	67	83
1960	-	113
1962	97	143
1964	-	192
1966	147	215
1968	-	221
1970	206	316
1974*	176	253
1978	210	308
1982	225	343
1986	202	330
1990	213	351
1994	251	628
1998	319	692
2002	321	883

Source: Pizarro 2006: 84, table 3.1.

*Until 1970 members of the House were elected every two years. Starting in 1970 elections for the House and the Senate are scheduled to coincide on the same date every four years.

tions emerged. Since important pieces of legislation required two-thirds majority for passage, extensive negotiation on the part of the president with what appeared to be "a squabbling multi-party system" was required (Hartlyn 1998: 113).

Thus behind the facade of Colombia's highly institutionalized two-party system there lay a collection of undisciplined party factions that seemed closer to the kind of fragmentation observed in Mainwaring and Scully's (1995) "inchoate" party systems. As a consequence, since 1958 Colombia has experienced the kind of policy paralysis and conflicts between the executive and legislative branches that are typical of systems in which presidents cannot count on their own parties for support (see Linz and Valenzuela 1994b; Mainwaring and Shugart 1997; Corrales 2002). Colombia's party system in fact functioned like a weakly institutionalized one, with multiple party factions hindering the operation of the legislature, the building of coalitions, and the necessary negotiations for democratic governance. It thus replicated the difficult combination noted by Mainwaring between extreme multipartism and presidentialism.[19] The low levels of organizational coherence and high levels of fragmentation of the component units—the parties—belied many of the virtues attributed to the institutionalization of its party system.

To make things worse, from 1958 to 1974, according to the pacts, only the Liberal and Conservative Parties were allowed to compete in national, regional, and local elections.[20] Even though some dissident factions represented those sectors opposed to the National Front (Leyva's faction in the Conservative Party, the MRL in the Liberal Party, and the populist movement ANAPO, disguised as a bipartisan opposition front), the system did not provide legal space for organizing an open and viable loyal opposition. Yet, as is widely accepted, for democracy to take root and thrive, "what matters above all is the creation of a loyal opposition; that is, an opposition which refuses to entertain plans to change the system and to exterminate its rivals—thereby of course ensuring its own safety" (Hall 1993: 272). The handicaps of the National Front system did not stop with this inability to allow the creation and accommodation of an opposition party outside the dominant two-party system. The pacts also eliminated the possibility of a loyal opposition emerging within the boundaries of the system, thus inviting conflict against it.

Institutionalized party systems are supposed to allow for the expression and channeling of conflict in ways that do not overwhelm the political system. They can also help control and contain conflict by directing it toward electoral and legislative channels. The way in which the Colombian party system was created, however, produced the opposite outcome. By virtue of the electoral distortions and outright political discrimination implied by its restrictive stipulations, a new line of cleavage between the included and the excluded was created, which in turn became a permanent source of political conflict and violence. Some party systems "have dampened conflict by deliberately seeking *not* to express social cleavages or political demands, but rather to constrain partici-

pation, often through clientelism. They have thus invited the sort of reaction from society that institutionalized party systems are presumably
intended to avert" (Hartlyn 1996a: 176). One of the most damaging legacies of the National Front was the spawning of a number of guerrilla
movements that thrived on the political exclusion imposed by the party
agreements. Up until this day, Colombia continues to struggle with the
dire effects of this legacy. The elimination of genuinely free party competition had disastrous effects on the dimensions of participation, accountability, and contestation in Colombia's democracy. Above all, it
had disastrous consequences for the formation and institutionalization
of a competitive and representative political society. In striking contrast
to Venezuela, the Colombian party system remained a rather confined
two-party system, enshrined as such in the constitution, with competition severely restricted to the detriment of those who were not represented by the two main parties. The elimination of compulsory presidential alternation in 1974 returned competition to the presidential
contest, and congressional races also took on renewed meaning, leading
to the spike in electoral participation shown in figure 5.1. However, the
informal remnants of the National Front lasted until 1986 when a Liberal candidate, Virgilio Barco, won the presidency by a significant margin, thus effectively shutting the Conservatives out of the cabinet and
other high-level positions. Finally, the Constitution of 1991 did away
with the remaining institutional traces of the National Front pacts.

The remarkable continuity of the party system's main features from
1974 to 1991 offers a good example of the path-dependent evolution of
political institutions. For over three decades, beneath the surface of a
relatively concentrated party system, Colombia hid the reality of a fierce
interfactional competition that for all intents and purposes worked in
a multiparty fashion. Only during presidential elections did the system
function as a two-party system. And even then, during the National
Front period, because of the mandatory coalition between the two parties, Colombia resembled a hegemonic party system.[21]

With the gradual loss of party control over candidate selection and
campaign finances that occurred after the formal end of the National
Front period, plus a series of electoral reforms instituted from the 1980s

on, the fragmentation of the Colombian party system reached unprece-
dented proportions (see table 5.5). In 1999 Valenzuela and colleagues
(1999: 237) labeled the electoral system in Colombia the "most personalistic" in the world (see also Pizarro and Bejarano 2007). As the Colombian case shows, the methods for counting "effective" parties tend to
obscure the reality that, given certain forms of internal organization (in
this case a highly decentralized and loose federation of regional and local
party groups) and a certain set of electoral incentives (a semiproportional, closed-faction-list electoral system, which tended to reward party
factionalism),[22] the existence of a two-party system may be no more than
a mirage. In reality, throughout these years the Colombian party system
was much more fragmented and its parties much more factional and disorganized than conventional measures on the "effective number of parties" will tell.

Over the years, Colombia's two traditional parties, especially the Liberal Party, have managed to accommodate diverse ideological factions
under the same tent. However, they were increasingly pushed toward the
center-right by a combination of the regime's restrictions and the increasingly radical response on the left. As the ideological distance between the
two parties became greatly diminished, the division between the two traditional parties and the left became a chasm. Thus a new polarization
emerged in the political system that was not visible to those focusing
solely at the "established" or legally recognized party system: the new polarization of Colombian politics was expressed rather by a virulent form
of confrontation (rather than competition) between those "inside" the
legal game of politics and those "outside" it, namely, the many guerrilla
groups that formed during the 1960s and 1970s. Again, the seeming stability and lack of ideological polarization of the Colombian bipartisan
system was to a great extent a delusion created by a particular combination of the dynamics between the actors on the ground and the formal
rules of the game that framed their interaction.

Exploring the Contrast

Two crucial differences separate the party systems that emerged in
Colombia and Venezuela after their democratic transitions. The first is
the capacity of the Venezuelan party system to tolerate and accommo-

date an opposition party on the left. In Colombia that possibility was simply barred from 1958 to 1974 and then between 1974 and 1991 any effort to organize a democratic left suffered greatly under the combined effect of the radicalization of the armed left and the repression exercised by the state in combination with the extraparliamentary right (the so-called paramilitary groups). In Venezuela an active opposition from the left, represented first by the PCV and URD and then by MAS and other smaller parties, was tolerated and accommodated from the beginning of the democratic regime. Secondly, in Colombia there was a two-party system by design, with extremely harsh measures against nontraditional parties; in Venezuela, by contrast, the party system was from the start more inclusionary and representative of the different interests and ideological leanings present in society, and it was also more genuinely competitive: alternation occurred regularly between the two main parties as a result of shifting electoral majorities. By contrast, in Colombia, although there was regular alternation in power between the two parties, this was a constitutionally mandated provision enshrined in a party pact, not a result of uncertain electoral outcomes.

Both party systems were equally well established and institutionalized in the period under consideration. However, they exhibited different patterns of party institutionalization: whereas the Colombian parties remained lax federations of regional, local, and personalistic factions, Venezuela's parties became highly centralized, hierarchical, vertically integrated organizations, within which the party directorates, or cogollos, had unlimited power over their respective parties.[23] It was in great part due to this rigidity that these parties were unable to weather the wave of antiparty sentiment that took hold among the Venezuelan public after the 1989 social explosion known as el Caracazo and the subsequent dramatic unraveling of Venezuela's democracy. They emerged extremely weakened in the 1993 elections and finally succumbed to an outsider and his supporters in the 1998 elections.

What this contrast seems to suggest is that in addition to focusing on the institutionalization of the party system, as proposed by Mainwaring and Scully (1995), we ought to reconsider the parties' history, organization, degree of internal coherence, and capacity to adapt to exogenous change. As discussed in chapter 2, the parties that developed in

Colombia and Venezuela were historically very different. They thus contributed to the formation of two different types of party systems: although both were bipartisan, relatively well institutionalized, and low in terms of ideological polarization, they were in fact quite distinct in terms of their degrees of internal fragmentation (very fragmented in Colombia vs. extremely coherent in Venezuela) and their internal authority structure (more decentralized in Colombia's case vs. completely centralized in Venezuela's). This was in part the result of the incentives provided by the electoral systems.

In both cases legislative elections were based on a proportional representation (PR) system. However, whereas Venezuela had a closed party list with a D'Hondt formula for distributing seats, in Colombia the proportionality of the system was tempered by the exclusion of contenders beyond the Liberals and Conservatives while permitting party factions to present their own lists; this is why it has been labeled a "semiproportional faction list" electoral system. Colombia also differed in that it used the Hare formula to distribute seats (see Wills Otero and Pérez-Liñán 2005: 68, 77). In the end, these features had a divergent impact on the countries' capacity to adapt to the dramatically changed political circumstances in the late 1980s and 1990s. Ironically, the more decentralized, more fragmented, and undisciplined parties of Colombia were better able to adapt to the changing circumstances (and to the reforms introduced by the Constituent Assembly in 1991) than the Venezuelan ones. By contrast, the highly successful, highly centralized Venezuelan political parties succumbed to dramatic changes in the Venezuelan political landscape and have disappeared almost entirely from the electoral scene since 1998.

The contrast between the evolution of these party systems during the three decades after the transition to democracy is also relevant for this discussion. In Colombia, rather than actively seeking to mobilize and organize the electorate after La Violencia, the political parties sought to demobilize the country's population—a fact evident in the dismal electoral turnout, which has historically hovered below a mediocre 50 percent of the eligible population (see fig. 5.1). Even though the 1957 pacts mandated coalition rule for sixteen years, it lasted for an additional twelve years, and the spirit of "cohabitation" has survived over time.[24] Despite guaranteeing decades of governmental stability, the rigidity of the pacts between the two traditional parties allowed a simmering sense of political exclusion to fuel guerrilla warfare that persists today. Meanwhile, attempts to open space for a legitimate, institutionalized, and legal opposition have become stalemated by the enduring political violence that has raged in the country for the past four decades.

Meanwhile, not all was well in Venezuela. Serious problems lurked behind what looked like a highly institutionalized party system. Recent developments notwithstanding, it is clear that the Venezuelan party system became more inclusionary, representative, and competitive than the Colombian party system ever was. In what follows I explain the divergent post-transition evolution of these two party systems on the basis of the two central variables highlighted in this study: historical continuities from the past and institutional legacies inherited from the transition period.

Explaining Divergence: The Role of Historical Continuities

One of the major differences between Colombia and Venezuela has to do with the historical evolution of their political parties and party systems (see chap. 2). I have argued that the timing of the emergence of partisan organizations and its relation to the process of state consolidation had a strong impact on the type and nature of the parties that took part in the democratization process in both countries. In terms of their origins, one of the main differences between the Colombian and Venezuelan parties was the timing of their emergence. While the Colombian parties emerged in the mid-nineteenth century, the Venezuelan parties emerged during the second half of the 1930s. In the early twentieth century, while traditional, elitist, oligarchic parties continued to dominate the state in Colombia, it was the state (mainly the army) that dominated all other organizations in Venezuelan society, as the traditional parties, Liberal and Conservative had already disappeared. The new parties that emerged after Gómez's death in 1935 kept no ties to the traditional oligarchic parties of the nineteenth century. Nor was the population in Venezuela tied to those older partisan identities. There was thus plenty of available political space to build a qualitatively different type of party organization, more modern regarding their internal structure, more representative of social cleavages, more closely tied to the new groups emerging from Venezuela's rapid social transformation.

Whereas the Colombian parties were the main and only actors controlling access to and exercising political power since the 1850s, the Venezuelan parties (mainly AD) had only had a short opportunity to exercise state control: the Trienio period (1945–48). They were fledging organizations compared to other institutions in Venezuela, such as the state and especially the army. By contrast, the traditional Liberal and Conservative Parties were used to holding sway over Colombian politics undisturbed. In part due to the weakness of the state and in part due to the agrarian configuration of Colombian society, the Colombian parties of "notables" were the most important institutions of social and political control up until the late 1950s.

The timing of the parties' emergence had strong implications for the extent to which parties could become the representatives of societal cleavages. In Venezuela, with a strong state preceding the formation of the parties, these tended to become the institutional representation of social cleavages. Instead, in Colombia, with a weak state (built in part by the parties themselves and totally subordinated to them), the parties became "engines of authority-legitimation" (Nettl 1968), and the articulation of interests and/or cleavages in party terms was largely inhibited.

When the Liberal and Conservative Parties in Colombia emerged in the mid-nineteenth century they were expressions of cleavages that divided the elites along religious and regional lines and differing worldviews. Though these divisive issues eventually disappeared, the party identities remained, strengthened by a combination of electoral mobilization and the violent history of interparty competition and conflict. In the end the two parties ended up forming two different political identities with strong emotional appeal but not necessarily tied to socioeconomic cleavages.

By contrast, the political and social configuration of Venezuela was favorable to the emergence of parties that were not the natural representatives of the oligarchy and that had a higher stake in incorporating and representing the excluded. Indeed, one of the most important political effects of the oil-induced decline of agriculture in Venezuela was the elimination of a rural base of support (a strong landed elite) for a conservative political party that could shift the political spectrum to the right (Karl 1986: 200). The "populist radical" parties of Venezuela (Collier and Collier 1991) became instead the builders of a pro-democracy coalition of the new urban middle sectors, the organized working class, and the mobilized peasantry.

Completing this contrast is the fact that even though the parties in Venezuela had experienced competition, conflicts, and divisions, there was never the kind of widespread violence between their leaders or rank and file that one finds in Colombia's history. Violent repression under Pérez Jiménez made their partisan activities more costly, risky, and difficult. By the same token, however, state repression and illegalization acted as catalysts for a new era of cooperation between the parties. In 1958 political parties in Venezuela were faced with the dual challenge of securing enough consensus among them so as to be able to oppose the military and guarantee an effective transfer of power while at the same time coming to an agreement on the rules for limiting future competition between them. The pacts achieved during 1958 came as a response to these challenges: they guaranteed that future competition would be maintained within agreed-on boundaries in order to avoid polarization and eventual democratic breakdown.

By contrast, the history of interparty relations in Colombia is plagued by conflict and violence. A long record of electoral competition stands beside a parallel history of party warfare. Many authors have emphasized the recurrent use of coalitions between the traditional parties as the defining feature of the Colombian party system and political process. However, one should not lose sight of the fact that such a tendency coexisted with its contrary, a tendency toward building hegemonic governments with the complete exclusion of the other party. This tendency toward conflict implies an obstacle to the institutionalization of a loyal opposition and the consolidation of democratic competition. The extreme levels of antagonism reached by the partisan division in Colombia hindered the creation of a common terrain on which relations between political adversaries could be established within an agreed-on normative framework. Instead, the two parties framed their relation as one of mutual exclusion, behaving essentially like enemies. The absence of a common terrain prevented the emergence and toleration of an opposition party with all its prerogatives, legal and political. The existence and legitimacy of the opposition came to depend almost entirely on the benevolence of the incumbent party or its need to share power and disappeared automatically as soon as this party foresaw the opportunity to gain absolute control of the state apparatus. Amid this convulsive alternation between moments of exclusion and moments of coalition, it was impossible to build a robust set of rules providing for the institutionalization of a legitimate political opposition, as was the case in Venezuela.

Coming from such different histories, these two bipartisan systems were formed by quite different parties: by the late 1950s the Colombian parties were still parties of notables, while the Venezuelan ones were more mass-based, populist parties. While the Colombian parties were a hundred years old, the Venezuelan ones dated to only a couple of decades earlier. In organizational terms, while the Colombian Liberals and Conservatives were in some sense inchoate federations of local and regionally based party fractions (see González 1997a), the Venezuelan major parties, AD and COPEI, were highly centralized, hierarchical, and disciplined organizations (Coppedge 1994a). This variation in internal organization may be attributable in part to the striking difference in their formative experiences: whereas the Colombian parties have always functioned in an environment that allowed some competition and contestation (even if violence also has always been a feature of that environment), the Venezuelan parties grew in a repressive environment. Many of their internal features and practices draw from their early experience as clandestine political organizations. In addition, and in part as a result of the relationship with their respective states, while the Venezuelan parties managed to represent and mobilize major social cleavages (at least until the early 1980s), the Colombian parties remained effective electoral machines lacking the capacity to represent social divisions and conflicts. Finally, while the pre–National Front Colombian bipartisan system was frequently on the verge of collapse due to its centrifugal tendencies and its tradition of interparty confrontation, the Venezuelan parties had come out of the experience of the Trienio and the repressive dictatorship that followed with a strong incentive for cooperation, which meant that a centripetal tendency was at least emerging by the late 1950s.

Institutional Legacies of the Transitions

Some of the characteristic features of the parties and party systems in Colombia and Venezuela disappeared during the post-transition process. Party leaders in both countries underwent a fruitful learning process (Bermeo 1992) during the dictatorship years and came out of it with a clear view of where the main institutional problems lay and how to overcome them. As a consequence, some institutions were expressly designed in the pacts to overcome political bottlenecks. The results of these efforts were, however, decidedly mixed.

The Colombian National Front, for example, produced a series of positive effects that one would be hard pressed to ignore: it significantly lowered the intensity of interparty competition, thereby dramatically reducing the levels of interparty violence. As a result, at the beginning of the 1960s La Violencia came to an end. Also, as a consequence of the forced alternation of the parties in power, the party leaders and rank and file as well as the electorate learned to share power with their lifelong "enemies"; instead of eliminating each other, they could become adversaries within a framework of mutually accepted rules. Due more to its unexpected consequences than to conscious institutional design, the system also opened up space for the opposition within its borders: given the internal fragmentation of parties, some party factions (Leyva within the Conservatives, the MRL within the Liberal Party, and the ANAPO disguised alternatively as ANAPO-liberal and ANAPO-conservadora), stealthily played the role of opposition to the National Front majoritarian coalition. Finally, the National Front agreements restored the basic trappings of a democratic regime in Colombia: Congress was reopened in 1958, a decade after its closure by Ospina; the president-appointed Constituent Assembly was replaced by an independent judiciary; elections resumed; and executive power was devolved from the military to the civilian elite.

In Venezuela the pacts served well the goal of taming AD and restoring a measure of trust among the parties, which could make competition viable albeit under some restrictive conditions. As agreed to in the pacts, the first two post-transition governments in Venezuela were coalitions. The flexibility of the pacts permitted, however, the gradual emergence and consolidation of a viable and legitimate opposition in the Venezuelan system. It thus gradually evolved into a two-and-a-half-party system, with two dominant parties at the center and a legitimate opposition on the left.

These accomplishments notwithstanding, however, some of the provisions on party competition contained in the pacts, in particular, those related to elections,[25] deepened some of the perverse elements already present in these parties and party systems while also producing some new negative, even if unintended, effects. The restrictions on party competition put in place by the National Front agreement had a series of unintended effects that compromised Colombia's democracy until further changes were introduced in 1991. By exacerbating the competition among party factions it aggravated the tendency to party fragmentation. As a consequence of the power-sharing formula (whereby each party would gain access to 50 percent of all state offices regardless of electoral outcomes) the system became semiproportional rather than fully proportional. Competition within the system's boundaries in Colombia became synonymous with competition inside the parties and not between them. This fragmentation, in turn, worsened two other deeply rooted features of Colombia's party system: its centrifugal tendencies and the parties' undisciplined behavior. In addition, by restricting competition the institutional arrangement had a negative impact on electoral participation. As shown in figure 5.1, abstention rates grew ceaselessly during the National Front period, decreasing only in 1974 when some measure of credible competition was restored to the system. Finally, by excluding and discriminating against all but the Liberal and Conservative Parties, the rules of the game pushed the nonbipartisan opposition beyond the confines of the system.

To add to this long list of perverse effects, two institutional features of the National Front agreement—namely, compulsory coalition governments and a qualified (two-thirds) majority for approving legislation—aggravated the dilemmas posed by presidential systems, especially the tendency to generate deadlocks between the president and Congress.[26] The executive, which was usually a minority government, was routinely forced to negotiate with each party faction in Congress. Party factions, in turn, acquired enormous leverage and veto power because of the qualified two-thirds majority required to pass legislation. The enormous clout that this system gave to small party factions was an additional incentive that fed on an old tradition of internal divisions and fragmentation within the party organizations.

The need to confront this tendency to deadlock produced two additional perverse reactions: the granting of legislative powers to the president by Congress or, in the absence of this, the declaration of an almost permanent state of siege that allowed the president to circumvent Congress via legislation by decree.[27] Both mechanisms, legislative powers and emergency decree power, were a solution to deadlock but contributed to strengthening the executive branch at the expense of Congress—with an obvious perverse effect on the process of democratization. Indeed, during the National Front years many constitutional norms were suspended de facto by a quasi-permanent state of siege (see Gallón 1979; Dávila 1998). In addition, decision making progressively shifted from the parliamentary arena to the more circumscribed arena of executive power. The more Congress lost decision-making power, the less important it became for the electorate as an arena for effective representation of interests. As a consequence, the gulf between political and civil society grew wider and deeper. Congress increasingly assumed a new role as impediment to presidential initiatives; while this veto power can serve as a check on executive power, the Colombian Congress became instead an arena where control and/or support for the president could be negotiated on a case-by-case basis.[28]

The more the parties and Congress lost their roles as vehicles to channel and represent the people's demands and grievances, the more political society became divorced from civil society. The elimination of competition between the elites, formalized through the mechanisms of parity and alternation, meant that they had no need to compete for mass support and thus no need to be responsive to the people's demands. The members of such an altered political society (i.e., the party cadres and representatives in Congress) became more autonomous from the electorate; since they would still get access to half the seats in Congress no matter how they behaved or how many votes they received, they could afford to be disconnected from their constituencies and become increasingly inward oriented, primarily attuned to their own interests and conflicts as a political class. Thus they became increasingly distanced from the interests and demands of significant sectors of Colombian society.

The crisis generated by La Violencia and the tradition of violent confrontation that characterized the interparty struggle in Colombia had caused the parties to introduce strong restrictions in the pacts. However, by making them so restrictive and by closing the door to the pacts' adaptation to changing social and political conditions, they also created new sources of opposition to the system. The Colombian pacts were made to reconfirm and perpetuate the bipartisan nature of the party system and did not include provisions that would eventually permit a widening of political society to accommodate other actors, either new or formerly excluded. As a result, the existence of an open, legal, vibrant opposition was rendered virtually impossible.

The previous history of party formation and interparty relations combined with the institutional legacies of the transition produced several perverse effects that prevented the Colombian party system from evolving in a competitive and inclusionary direction, one of which was the lack of uncertainty when it came to electoral outcomes (see Przeworski 1988). It also almost completely banned competition between different political alternatives while simultaneously promoting a damaging tendency toward internal division and harsh competition among the parties' own factions. In addition, it did not allow for a loyal opposition to emerge within the system but, on the contrary, fostered the growth of an extrainstitutional violent opposition. Finally, the parties that formed part of this tightly closed system gradually lost the capacity to represent major social cleavages.

The combination of historical evolution and the specific institutionalization pattern in Venezuela. Although the Venezuelan party system also came to be dominated by two parties, there was an important difference: in this case bipartisanship was not imposed by the institutional agreements made at the time of the transition but rather came as the unexpected by-product of the accords, the specific features contained in the electoral system, and the historical characteristics of the parties.[29]

When contrasted with the Colombian case, several aspects of the evolution of the parties and the party system in Venezuela (from 1958 to

1993) stand out. First, since 1958 uncertainty of outcomes has been a major feature of the electoral process in Venezuela. Second, the limits imposed on competition were not only fewer and less restrictive in the Venezuelan case but also lasted for just one presidential term. Starting with the 1963 elections, there were no formal limitations on the scope or content of that competition, except that it had to be conducted within the democratic rules of the game. A major turning point in the process of institutionalizing competition came in 1968 when the candidate of the major opposition party, COPEI, was elected president. Third, from its inception the system allowed the existence and electoral participation of other parties different from those who made up the foundational coalition. The institutionalization of contestation and opposition were confirmed not only by COPEI's electoral victory in 1968 but also by the continued presence and significant turnout for parties on the left such as URD (between 1958 and 1973) and MAS (after 1973). That the Venezuelan regime permitted the existence of an institutionalized opposition may have also contributed to the ideological coherence and programmatic identities of the parties, a key to survival in a competitive system. Fourth, at least until the late 1980s the two main center parties plus the small leftist party in the Venezuelan system could claim to represent major sectors of Venezuelan society.

However, and this turned out to be their major Achilles' heel, they became too successful as party organizations. Added to their already centralized, hierarchical, and vertical nature, these parties became victims of Michels's "iron law of oligarchy" (1968), thus becoming increasingly bureaucratic and overinstitutionalized.[30] In a fateful turn of luck, the institutionalization of Venezuela's party system coincided in time with the unexpected tenfold increase in state revenues from the early 1970s oil boom. This turned the parties even more into machines for the allocation of patronage and clientelistic favors and multiplied the incentives for corruption.[31] The increasing recourse to particularistic practices and the blatant acts of corruption that came to light during the economic crisis of the early 1980s added to their excessive centralization and internal vertical control and finally produced a rift between the parties and Venezuelan society that became evident during the tragic episode of el Caracazo.[32]

In short, I argue that between 1958 and the late 1980s Venezuela went further than Colombia in institutionalizing a competitive and representative political society. It not only managed to create and sustain uncertainty of outcomes,but also permitted open and regular competition between diverse parties. Moreover, the most consequential difference in the behavior of these two party systems lies in their ability (Venezuela) or inability (Colombia) to promote the emergence and tolerate the existence of a legal, legitimate, vibrant political opposition. Finally—though it can be argued that a serious representation problem had been incubating in Venezuela—up until the early 1980s the party system in that country was able to represent rather fairly the society's diverse interests.

And yet, as shown by recent evidence, "since the early 1980s, the very role of political parties, and more precisely, of parties of the kind that dominate the Venezuelan scene, has come under increasing criticism and direct challenges" (Kornblith and Levine 1995: 38). These two party systems harbored a series of problems and shortcomings. We now turn to the different reasons they became, in the 1990s, a central piece of these two countries' political decay.

Party System Decay and the Crisis of Political Representation

Paradoxically, the very parties that contributed to the stability of democracy in Colombia and Venezuela for more than three decades are now seen as a central factor in the crises currently besieging these two democracies. What went wrong?

The degree of party fragmentation has increased significantly in both cases over the past two decades. In Colombia, which had an intensely factionalized two-party system to begin with, changes in the electoral system (especially those instituted during the Constitutional Assembly of 1991) and the gradual weakening of the two traditional parties have contributed to proliferation of newer and smaller parties and movements.[33] It may still be too soon to declare the end of bipartisan hegemony in Colombia, but there is no escaping the conclusion that the two traditional parties no longer have a monopoly over political representation.

The system seems to be coming to terms with what used to be an extrainstitutional polarization. With President Uribe and his followers, including the Conservative Party and important factions within the Liberal Party, aggregating votes on the right and the reorganization of the democratic left around the Polo Democrático Alternativo (PDA)—despite the persistence of two guerrilla groups that are still active—the ideological divide seems at last to have found expression in the realm of legal politics in Colombia. Some say that the system is more polarized now than it was two or three decades ago. The fact is that the party system has become a more accurate mirror of the existing polarization within Colombian society—and in that sense, a more representative one.

In Venezuela, on the contrary, rather than a gradual adaptation of the party system to new realities on the ground, what we have seen is the sudden decay and eventual collapse of the party system, resulting in large part from the discrediting of the traditional parties, AD and COPEI, and the constant tinkering with electoral reforms.[34] It is difficult to predict whether the new Venezuelan party system, which has been slowly emerging since 1999, will eventually gel as a hegemonic, a two-party, or a multiparty system. Electoral volatility remains high, the political situation in a constant state of flux. However, it seems safe to say that the once-stable, cohesive, centripetal two-party system has disappeared, leaving in its wake an immense vacuum of representation that has been filled mainly by the charismatic current president, Hugo Chávez and his Movimiento Quinta República (MVR, now the Partido Socialista Unido de Venezuela [PSUV]).[35] So far, the opposition has encountered enormous difficulties putting together a united front, despite efforts to overcome their dispersion and deep divisions.[36] The apparent electoral dominance of Chávez and his movement should not, however, be mistaken for an absence of political polarization in Venezuela. Much to the contrary, if anything has changed in Venezuela in the past decade it is the emergence and solidification of a new and deep political cleavage that reflects the socioeconomic divisions present in Venezuelan society but goes much further: it draws a line between those who felt included and those who felt excluded by the previous political regime and model of development; it incorporates issues of racial, ethnic, and cultural difference; and, finally, it revolves mainly around the mercurial and deeply polarizing figure of President Chávez.

Much has changed in these two countries in the past two decades. While according to Mainwaring and Scully's measure Colombia and Venezuela had low levels of electoral volatility, over the years both have moved up that scale. In both cases electoral volatility doubled; however, it achieved worrisome levels in Venezuela while it remained within acceptable limits in Colombia. While Venezuela has become clustered with Bolivia, Brazil, Ecuador, Guatemala, and Peru, which exhibit high (and extremely high) levels of electoral volatility, Colombia has remained a case of moderate electoral volatility. As tables 5.6 and 5.7 show, both countries surpassed the Latin American average volatility index (= 25). While Colombia remained within average limits until the presidential election of 2002, Venezuela clearly surpassed that mark since 1993.

In Venezuela, prior to the 1990s, patterns of electoral competition were among the most stable in the region. However, the decline in the appeal and mobilization capability of the two major political parties, coupled with constant changes in the electoral system, resulted in a surge

Table 5.6. Electoral Volatility in Colombia, 1978–2002

Period	Volatility Index*
1978–82	9.8
1982–86	22.0
1986–90	37.5
1990–94	34.6
1994–98	26.3
1998–2002	59.5
Average	31.6

Source: Roncagliolo and Meléndez 2007: Appendix 1, p. 392; p. 399, table 3.

*Measures electoral volatility following Pedersen's methodology (see Mainwaring and Scully 1995) by taking into account those parties that obtained at least 3 percent of valid votes in presidential elections.

Table 5.7. Electoral Volatility in Venezuela, 1978–2000

Period	*Volatility Index**
1978–83	14.9
1983–88	8.6
1988–93	49.7
1993–98	57.5
1998–2002	40.5
Average	34.2

Source: Roncagliolo and Meléndez 2007: Appendix 1, p. 392; p. 401, table 9.

* Measures electoral volatility following Pedersen's methodology (see Mainwaring and Scully 1995) by taking into account those parties that obtained at least 3 percent of valid votes in presidential elections.

in electoral volatility and the emergence of an extraordinary large number of parties and movements. The first and most dramatic change happened in 1993 when the presidency did not go to either AD or COPEI but was instead won by a coalition of smaller parties, Convergencia Nacional. In Colombia changes in the electoral system (introduced by the 1991 Constituent Assembly) and growing fragmentation of the two traditional party systems also contributed to a significant, albeit less dramatic, increase in volatility.

A similar trend is observable when one compares the fate of the parties over time in these two countries. While in Venezuela AD and COPEI suffered a combined loss of 64 percent in the share of legislative seats under their control between 1978 and 2000,[37] the Colombian Liberal and Conservative Parties, together, suffered a decline of over 50 percent.[38] Despite the centrality of parties for democratic politics, they consistently fail to win the allegiance of a significant portion of the population in both countries: close to 60 percent of the respondents to a Latinobarometro survey in 1996 and 1997 said that they did "not feel close" to any party.[39] In contrast to the previous democratic periods, when we could safely assume that the traditional parties in both countries had deep roots in society, the more recent period since the late 1980s has been marked by a steep decline in societal support for these parties.

In terms of the parties' legitimacy and the level of agreement among social and political actors on the importance of parties and elections in determining who governs, the scene definitely looks more troubled now than in the 1970s, when one could safely assume that most actors accepted parties and elections as the only legitimate avenue to power. Already in 1995 Mainwaring and Scully added a caveat to their conclusions on Colombia and Venezuela: in these countries, they said, "the major political actors accept that elections determine who governs, though such acceptance has diminished in Venezuela, in light of the failed coup in 1992, and possibly in Colombia" (1995: 14). In Venezuela, despite all the recent turmoil, elections are still regarded as the key to access power; however, political parties have suffered a bruising defeat, especially the traditional parties, AD and COPEI. In Colombia, on the other hand, while elections may have gained some terrain vis-à-vis those who thought of revolutionary warfare as a legitimate avenue to power, parties are still very much regarded as corrupt, self-serving organizations. According to table 5.8, which shows levels of confidence in parties, Colombia scores well below the Latin American average (18.9 percent), which is already quite low by comparative standards. Despite a surge of confidence in the years since the election of Hugo Chávez, Venezuela surpasses the Latin American average by only one percentage point. In terms of their confidence in elections, as shown in table 5.9, both countries score well below the Latin American average (44.8 percent), with Colombia showing a greater discrediting of elections as the main avenue to gain power. As Payne and colleagues (2002: 138) note, "Regardless of whether such perceptions reflect real deficiencies, they certainly impair the ability of representative institutions to assume their full roles in the democratic process, and may deprive governments and political parties of the legitimacy necessary to govern effectively."[40]

Along with the erosion of the public image of parties has come a steep decay in party organizations. The fragmentation, personalism, and proclivity to populism that used to characterize a few party systems on the continent have now become much more extended in recent decades. Parties have become less disciplined, party switching has become commonplace in the region, and parties tend to have fewer resources and a

Table 5.8. Confidence in Parties, 1996–2004 (%)

Country/Year	1996–97	1998–2000	2001–2	2003–4	1996–2004
Colombia	16.1	16.1	11.2	14.9	14.6
Venezuela	16.1	19.3	24.6	17.8	19.4
Latin America average	24.5	18.7	16.5	14.2	18.5

Source: Payne, Zovatto G., and Mateo Díaz 2006: 178, table 6.4, based on data from Latinobarometro 1996–2004.

Note: Table shows the percentage of respondents who expressed that they had "a lot" or "some" confidence in political parties.

Table 5.9. Confidence in Elections, 1996–2000 (%)*

Country/Year	1996	1997	1998	1999–2000	Average 1996–2000
Colombia	15.3	13.1	22.6	28.4	19.8
Venezuela	8.2	11.9	27.8	67.0	28.7
LA average**	45.4	40.2	42.8	50.4	44.8

Source: Payne, Zovatto G., and Mateo Díaz 2006: 179, table 6.5, based on data from Latinobarometro 1996–2000.

Note: The question was not included in the Latinobarometro survey between 2001 and 2004.

* Shows the percentage of respondents who perceive that elections are conducted fairly.

** Latin American average.

limited organizational presence between elections and at the local level. Of the two cases that concern us here, Venezuela has seen the most dramatic decline in terms of the parties' internal organization. In Colombia there has been a more gradual erosion in terms of party organization, discipline, and control, as well as a rapid increase in party factionalism in part as a result of changes in the electoral system since 1991. In both cases, however, the personalization of politics has gained space, displacing institutionalized parties from the scene, and propelling strong personalities such as Uribe and Chávez to center stage.

Institutionalizing Inclusion and Contestation

Colombia and Venezuela managed to build relatively well institutionalized party systems in the first three decades after their transitions to democracy. However, by the end of the century their party systems had weakened, had become much more fragmented, and had much more diffuse bases of social support. Again, superficial comparisons can lead to error: while the former conclusion may be true, it is equally important to note in what ways and to what degrees the two cases varied. A central premise of this chapter is that lumping the two cases together, as is commonly done in the literature on party systems, prevents a useful understanding of their evolution and ability to adapt to political crises by obscuring significant differences between the two.

Often classified as stable, well-institutionalized two-party systems with very low degrees of ideological polarization, Colombia and Venezuela's party systems in fact demonstrate divergent histories, modes of organization, and links to state and society. In both cases the apparent high degree of institutionalization concealed deep-seated problems: extreme party fragmentation and fierce interfactional competition in Colombia and the stiffening of party hierarchies and the inability to adapt in Venezuela. These features had important implications for the party systems' capacity to adjust to changing circumstances, leading to the political crises of the late 1980s and 1990s.

In addition, the lack of representation of the left within the parameters of the legally recognized party system simply threw the deep ideological cleavage among Colombians outside the boundaries of the system, thus creating the opportunity for the production and reproduction of an armed insurgency on the left. While in Venezuela, despite the accommodation of a host of small parties on the left, the party system lost the ability to follow and adapt to significant social transformations and emerging social cleavages, in particular, the division between the winners and the losers in the prevailing model of economic development and their representatives within the existing political system.

Paradoxically, Venezuela's more representative and competitive party system fared worse than the less representative Colombian system in the political crisis of recent decades. Speaking generally about the decay of parties across the world, Diamond and Gunther (2001: xv) have noted that the historical model of the centralized, hierarchical, mass-based party has been waning across the world, with only religious fundamentalist parties still keeping to the model. Most parties seem to have evolved in the opposite direction—that is, "toward leaner, more organizationally 'thin' structures that perform a limited set of functions, focused principally around elections" (xv). This description roughly coincides with most descriptions of Colombia's traditional parties, which were "tied together by clientelistic relationships, with weakly articulated organizations and minimal programmatic content" (Dix 1967: 89).

Kenneth M. Roberts (2003: 45) has concluded that "the most electorally stable party systems in Latin America during the 1980s and 1990s were not those boasting strong mass-based party organizations, . . . but rather those rooted in nineteenth-century oligarchic forms of domination." Paradoxically, then, recent general trends seem to favor the kind of parties that emerged and took root in Colombia: lax, highly decentralized organizations functioning mainly on the basis of informal mechanisms of negotiation and bargaining. What used to be considered a liability may instead be considered part of the explanation of why, despite all their problems and limitations, they have managed to persist over time. Despite their ups and downs, the traditional Liberal and Conservative Parties continue to provide a thread of continuity to Colombian politics that has been absent from Venezuela's political history. In the latter case, the parties that emerged in the 1930s had virtually ceased to exist at the turn of the twenty-first century, thus inaugurating a new dramatic episode of discontinuity in Venezuela's political life. Yet support for both systems has eroded since the 1980s. By the end of the twentieth century, the fragmentation, personalism, and proclivity to populism characteristic until then of a few party systems in the region had spread to both countries.

CHAPTER SIX

From Exceptions to Rules?

A Tale of Two Unhappy Democracies

Unlike so many of their neighbors who fell victim to the wave of authoritarianism that gripped Latin America in the 1960s and 1970s, Colombia and Venezuela boasted a tradition of democratic stability that began in 1958 and lasted for more than three decades. As Hagopian and Mainwaring (2005: 12) have written, "In 1978, at the start of the third wave of democratization in Latin America, they were, along with Costa Rica, the only democracies in Latin America." By the late 1980s, however, Colombia and Venezuela were showing signs of erosion and decay. After decades of being bracketed together as cases of stable and rather successful democratic development, Colombia and Venezuela are being grouped together again, this time on account of their political crises. In 2005 Hagopian and Mainwaring included the two countries, with Peru (the sole case of an outright democratic breakdown in the region), in the set of cases where democracy had experienced serious setbacks. Even more, these two authors contend that the unraveling of Venezuela's once-stable democracy is "the most disheartening political development of the past decade in Latin America" (12).

Though Colombia has never been a model democracy, its political stability, coupled with its moderate but healthy economic performance, set it apart from most of its neighbors for decades. From the mid- to late 1980s, however, the country was rocked by heightened levels of violence that seemed to threaten the foundations of its political system. The last decade of the twentieth century began in bloodshed: three presidential candidates were assassinated during the 1990 election campaign. Instead of decreasing, the levels of violence in the country had grown worse since the mid-1980s: new armed actors—drug traffickers, paramilitary groups,[1] and death squads—were added to the original contenders (i.e., the state's armed forces and various guerrilla groups), thus engendering a multipolar dynamic that grew in spiral fashion. All political parties and forces have been affected, but the democratic left, the various demobilized guerrilla groups, and the leadership of popular social movements have taken the heaviest toll. Representatives of the "establishment" have not escaped the use of force by their adversaries either: hundreds of judges and police officers, several former cabinet ministers, an attorney general, and many local, regional, and national party leaders also were victims of the 1990s bloodshed.

Violence, however, was not the only problem that confronted Colombia's troubled democracy. Voter abstention continued to grow, and the two traditional parties, although historically fragmented, became atomized beyond recognition. Meanwhile, drug traffickers infiltrated politics in all its electoral and nonelectoral forms to the point of jeopardizing the stability of the regime—a dramatic example of which was their involvement in the 1994 presidential campaign. In fact, drug trafficking organizations have undermined key state institutions such as the judiciary, the army, and the police as well as penetrated significant sectors of the economy and society. The reformist efforts launched since the mid-1980s (the numerous peace negotiations with the guerrillas and the new Constitution of 1991) did not succeed in thwarting the advance of one of the worst crises the Colombian political system has ever confronted.

While war raged in Colombia, by contrast, Venezuela seemed completely at peace. While most of Latin America was under military dictatorship, Venezuela held peaceful, competitive elections every five years, with the opposition often replacing the party in power. Finally while hyperinflation, high unemployment, and irresponsible economic management were the norm in most of Latin America, the oil-fueled Venezuelan economy seemed immune to the economic catastrophes that beset its neighbors. In 1989 the idyllic picture of Venezuela changed forever.

The decade between 1989 and 1999 saw several failed attempts at economic restructuring, a major urban uprising, repeated military coup attempts, the impeachment and jailing of an elected president, the collapse of the party system, the rise to power of a former coup plotter, and the complete overhaul of the country's institutional framework. Underlying these convulsive events was a combination of complex causes. A steady decline in the prices of Venezuela's major export and source of revenue, oil, resulted in a dramatic impoverishment of the population. AD and COPEI, the two political parties that had played a major role in building and sustaining Venezuela's democracy, were unable to step up to the situation: incapable of reforming their rigid organizations to respond to social and economic decline and blinded by their previous success and unrestricted access to the state's abundant coffers, they became overwhelmed by the demands of a resentful electorate and practically disappeared from the scene in the last election of the twentieth century. The Venezuelan state, aggrandized by the oil windfall of the 1970s, became increasingly centralized and corrupt, as well as incapable of reforming either itself or the economy on which it had thrived since the 1920s. In short, the two pillars that sustained Venezuela's successful democratic experience since 1958—the state and the party system—foundered as the century drew to a close. In the vacuum created by this political cataclysm, a new set of political elites emerged, bringing in their wake a new set of rules of the game. The Constitution of 1999 symbolizes the replacement of the old party coalition by a new one whose focal point is President Hugo Chávez, with a diverse array of leftist parties, the military, and the disorganized urban poor as his most important bases of support. Judging from its rhetoric, this new coalition seems staunchly committed to social equality; by the same measure, however, it seems much less committed to the cause of liberal democracy.

Larry Diamond (1996: 62) provides an apt synthesis of these twin processes in the 1990s: "Venezuela and Colombia, second only to Costa Rica in the number of years of continuous democracy, slipped into semi-democratic status amid growing signs of institutional decay and popular alienation." How did these crises originate? Are they the by-product of factors exogenous to the regimes, that is, the fall in the price of oil or the expansion of drug trafficking? Or are they instead intrinsically related to the original design and historical configuration of the regimes themselves? Are these contemporary crises an outcome of previous political development, or are they the unexpected result of new challenges and unforeseen dilemmas? In the pages that follow I draw on the arguments advanced in this book to throw light on this critical period of democratic decay in Colombia and Venezuela. Countering a tendency to cluster them together, I claim that there are significant differences in the causes and the outcomes of these twin crises.

The Gradual Erosion and Uncertain Recovery of Democracy in Colombia

Between 1958 and 1991 Colombia's democracy was often classified as a "restricted" or "controlled" democracy.[2] References to its limited nature have more recently been replaced in the literature with descriptions of this democracy as "besieged" (Archer 1995) or "under assault" (Kline 1995).[3] The shift in semantics is revealing: Colombia's democracy indeed remains limited by a series of constraints that merit the continued use of qualifiers, but as I have argued elsewhere (Bejarano and Pizarro 2005), any characterizations of the current political regime must take note of fundamental changes that have occurred since the mid-1980s, most notably the drafting of a new constitution in 1991. While previous language emphasized internal or endogenous limits on the political regime, Archer's (1995) term *besieged* rightly captures the role of exogenous factors that make it difficult for democracy to function adequately. Until 1991 democracy's limitations resulted from restrictions on political competition introduced in 1958 by the National Front pacts. Since the new constitution was introduced, however, its limitations are better understood as being rooted in factors external to the regime's institutional design: the erosion of the state, the expansion of violence, and the rise of powerful extrainstitutional actors who constrain the democratic playing field.

Any effort to classify Colombia's political regime confronts a series of paradoxes. Elections are held on a regular basis, but candidates and elected officers are also regularly assassinated. The press is free from state censorship, but journalists and academics are systematically murdered. Electoral authorities recognize a growing number of political parties, and minorities have increasing participation in representative bodies, and the new constitution and the law explicitly address the opposition's rights and responsibilities; simultaneously the killings of opposition leaders have multiplied. For a century and a half control of the state has been in civilian hands, except for a few brief (and exceptional) periods. Nevertheless, the military has retained a high degree of autonomy in matters of internal public order, as well as a series of prerogatives that place it above civilian control. The state claims that it alone can exercise legitimate use of force while at the same time admitting its inability to contain one of the world's highest murder rates. Can this legitimately be called a democracy?

In my view it would be a misinterpretation to cross the border that separates democracies from nondemocracies and classify Colombia as an authoritarian regime. Instead, I propose to use the three-part classification proposed by Mainwaring, Brinks, and Pérez-Liñán (2001), which provides a useful borderline type in which to locate cases such as Colombia. Based on quantitative indicators, Mainwaring (1999a) and Altman and Pérez-Liñán (2002) show no hesitation in classifying Colombia as a semidemocracy since 1958,[4] with the exception of a short democratic period between 1974 and 1990 (see also Mainwaring and Pérez-Liñán 2005). These authors carefully describe and quantify important changes in political regimes that are generally classified as democratic. Yet, in addition to dating and describing processes of change, we also need to understand their nature. In the Colombian case it seems worthwhile to note that the nature of the limits imposed on democracy has changed from one semidemocratic period to another.[5] While the first period (1958–74) was characterized by restrictions on competition resulting from the National Front pacts, restrictions during the second period (post-1991) are related to the Colombian state's inability to guarantee basic civil rights and liberties. Thus rather than unify in a single measure the multiple dimensions that are critical to democracy, it seems best to consider them separately. In this way we will be better equipped to understand the nature of threats to, and limitations on, democratic regimes and to compare their variation across cases as well as time.[6]

Among the alternative subtypes analyzed by Collier and Levitsky (1997), that of "illiberal" democracy is the one most able to capture the situation of Colombian democracy up until 2002. It alludes to the absence of a state capable of guaranteeing a constitutional order—or the rule of law that makes the liberal dimension of modern democracy possible.[7] Colombia's regime is a democracy whose faults are not to be located only at the level of the typical dimensions of polyarchy (i.e., participation and opposition, following Dahl 1971) but whose main failure is related to the precarious nature of the rule of law. The state of Colombia's democracy can be conceived as a game being played simultaneously on two fields. On the one hand, there is an electoral field, where the rules of the democratic game are largely respected among legally recognized political actors; on the other, there is an extrainstitutional field, where the rules of war rather than the rules of democracy apply, including the accumulation of instruments of force such as men, territory, and arms. The electoral game is in a way "suspended" over a field of extrainstitutional forces, which have a powerful impact on its outcome. This impact comes not only from the interconnections between institutional and extrainstitutional actors but also from the fact that the space available for the electoral game depends on the expansion or contraction of the space designated for the second game: war. This is why the "besieged democracy" metaphor seems especially apt to describe Colombia's political regime.

As this case illustrates well, the holding of competitive and fraud-free elections in which the whole adult population has the right to participate is not always accompanied by the other essential attributes of democracy.[8] Colombia has fulfilled the first attribute of any democracy (universal suffrage) since the 1957 plebiscite, when women exercised the right to vote for the first time. The second attribute, which deals with the quality of the electoral process, suffered serious restrictions between 1958 and 1974, especially with regard to political competition. Since the National Front pacts not only excluded third parties but also limited competition between the two dominant parties (Liberal and Conservative), the regime at the time has been correctly described as semicompetitive, restricted, or limited. The situation between 1974 and 1986 is difficult to define with any precision, since most of the formal restrictions were gradually lifted after the National Front period ended. A constitutional reform passed in 1968 lifted the formal restrictions on competition at the local level starting in 1970. Most of the restrictions limiting competition in congressional and presidential elections were eliminated in 1974. The rule requiring partisan parity (power sharing) in the executive branch was formally extended until 1978 and practiced informally thereafter for eight more years, until 1986. Finally, the rule requiring party parity in judicial branch appointments remained in place until 1991. Despite this staggered dismantling of the National Front accords, many informal restrictions remained—an inescapable legacy of the formal limits placed on the democratic playing field. However, an era of political reform began under President Betancur (1982–86): the Basic Statute of Political Parties (Law 58) was passed in 1985; and municipal reforms and the popular election of mayors were approved by Congress in 1986. From 1986 on (with the decision on the part of President Barco's government to put together an exclusively Liberal administration and the Conservatives' attendant decision to act as an opposition party), the last of the remaining restrictions related to the composition of the executive branch fell away. Delegates to the 1991 Constituent Assembly legalized this situation, and the new constitution finally eliminated all vestiges of the National Front pacts.[9]

Simultaneous to these political reforms, between 1989 and 1994 successful negotiations took place with five guerrilla movements: the April 19 Movement, the Revolutionary Workers' Party, the Quintín Lame Armed Movement, the Socialist Renovation Current, and the Popular Liberation Army.[10] As a result of these negotiations, some four thousand former combatants were reincorporated into civilian life (Palacios 2000: 362). Consequently, from the beginning of the 1990s we can speak of the existence in Colombia of a democracy that unambiguously meets the first two requirements of any contemporary definition of democracy: broad participation and free competition. From the early 1990s on it would be inaccurate to classify this regime as some subtype of authoritarianism. It seems best, instead, to classify it as a subtype, even if still "diminished," of democracy (Collier and Levitsky 1997).

These advances notwithstanding, Colombia has not been able to achieve a robust, resilient democracy. Despite efforts to incorporate armed rebels and to broaden its institutional framework, the regime deteriorated after the mid-1980s. Yet the nature of democracy's erosion during the most recent period is fundamentally different from that experienced by the regime during the period that began with the National Front. The causes of the current situation are found primarily in the state's inability to effectively guarantee civil rights and liberties. A cursory look at the country's gruesome human rights record shows ample evidence of the state's growing inability to protect its citizens' lives, rights, and freedoms. In Colombia in the late 1990s nearly fourteen persons were victims of sociopolitical violence on average every day. Of these, "more than eight were victims of extrajudicial executions and political homicides; close to one was forcibly disappeared; there was one homicide every two days committed against socially marginal persons; and more than four people died in combat each day" (Comisión Colombiana de Juristas 2000: 9). In the second half of the 1990s the annual average number of homicides reached approximately 26,000. During the same period, more than 7,000 people were kidnapped. Since 1995 approximately 1.6 million people have been forcibly displaced.[11]

Despite its gruesome human rights record, Colombia's regime does not deserve the adjectives commonly reserved for facade democracies—in which the military holds the real power over civilian puppets—such as "guarded" or "tutelary" democracy. As discussed in chapter 4, mainly because of the history of state and party formation in the nineteenth century, the Colombian military has not occupied the political center stage since independence. Yet even though the military has not obstructed the civilian government's ability to govern, since 1958 it has had an ample degree of autonomy and an increasing number of prerogatives. Specifically, the Colombian military has enjoyed a great deal of latitude in defining policies for external defense and internal security, both of which have become critical given the country's protracted internal conflict. Rather than apply the term *tutelary democracy* to the Colombian case, I would rather highlight the military's prerogatives (Stepan 1988) and reserved domains (Valenzuela 1992) as perverse elements that compromise the quality of Colombia's democracy. These prerogatives and reserved domains grew steadily as the internal war expanded and the military's involvement in antidrug efforts increased.[12]

In the final balance, since the mid- to late 1980s two contradictory tendencies have been at work simultaneously in Colombia: on the one hand, a tendency toward greater democratization, with the elimination of prior restrictions and the broadening of the space for political participation and competition; and on the other, a tendency toward deterioration of the indicators of "civility," of respect and protection of basic citizens' rights and liberties,[13] and civilian control of the military. The latter factors do, of course, have a negative impact on the components of participation and competition typical in any democracy. Neither competition nor participation can be complete in a context of widespread armed conflict, as is the case in Colombia. Although election fraud does not appear to be massive or widespread, distortions in the electoral process—especially at the local and regional levels—are very serious. Since the end of the 1980s, and especially since the first popular election of mayors (1988), local and regional elections have been increasingly subject to limitations on competition resulting from the actions of different types of armed actors who seek to capture and control territory and population. In many municipalities control of the local power structures is in the hands of armed actors rather than in those of political parties. In fact, the struggle for control among armed actors has greatly diminished the space for democratic political competition, especially at the local and regional levels. Numerous regional and local government officials have been assassinated following their election.[14] Simultaneously, the electorate's ability to vote "freely" (i.e., free from fear and/or coercion) has also decreased as the areas controlled by one armed actor or another have expanded—and above all, where armed actors compete bitterly for the control of territory and people. Without a doubt violence has distorted the participatory and competitive dimensions of Colombia's democracy, both before and after elections.

It is difficult to pinpoint an exact date or specific event that marked the beginning of this contradictory process of democratic erosion. Unlike Venezuela, where el Caracazo in 1989 and the two failed military coups in 1992 unambiguously mark the onset of the political crisis, Colombia's democracy has witnessed a process of gradual erosion rather than a sudden breakdown.[15] After years of a precarious stability, a severe decline began in the mid- to late 1980s, although some prefer to date its origins to 1989–90.[16] Without discounting the multifaceted nature of the Colombian conundrum, in what follows I use the framework proposed in this book to offer an explanation that focuses mainly on its political-institutional dimensions, in particular, on the restrictions and recent transformations of the political regime installed in 1958, as well as on the persistent weakness of the state.

From its beginnings in 1958, critics decried the bipartisan institutional arrangement of the National Front as antidemocratic. Many diagnoses of Colombia's democratic crisis and armed conflict were based on the argument of a "restricted democracy," which, while formally democratic, was stifled by the legacies of a series of exclusionary formal institutions and informal practices (such as clientelism, patronage, and other types of "particularism").[17] Inherited from the National Front, these restricted free competition and gave traditional parties a near-monopoly on political life, closing off any possibility for the emergence and consolidation of a democratic leftist opposition. The proposals for reform that proliferated during the 1980s (many of which grew out of peace negotiations with the guerrillas) had their roots in this diagnosis, which also served as the cornerstone of the constitution-making process of 1991. A central objective of the 1991 Constitution was therefore to dismantle the restrictions on Colombian democracy once and for all.

From the mid-1980s to 1991 the rules of the political game were fundamentally transformed, allowing an opening in the channels of access to power that led to a broader representation of society in the state. All formal restrictions on democratic competition were abolished with the 1991 Constitution, allowing for the emergence of an extremely proportional electoral system that imposed almost no institutional barriers to entry. The opening of the channels of political representation (including political decentralization at the local and regional levels) at a time when the two-party system was showing signs of exhaustion was one positive effect of the 1991 constitutional reform. The extreme atomization of political representation was an important negative effect. The overall result of reforms has been decidedly mixed (see Bejarano 2002). Today it would be difficult to argue that formal institutional restrictions on the political regime continue to be the main source of the problems in Colombia's democracy. It would also be unconvincing to maintain that informal rules of the game or specific political practices, such as clientelism, undermine the regime's democratic character. Evidently, such practices and their frequency affect the "quality" of democracy. Yet, undesirable as they are, the mere existence of particularistic practices does not prohibit the possibility of classifying the Colombian political regime as democratic.[18]

The main element related to the regime's institutional design that helps explain its recent crisis is no longer associated with its "restrictions" but instead with the dramatic opening that began in the 1980s and culminated in 1991. This time the pendulum seems to have swung too far in the opposite direction: the "logic of incorporation" pervading this wave of reforms led to the design of an extremely lax electoral system[19] that produced enormous disorganization among parties (both new and traditional) as well as in the system of political representation (see Pizarro 2006; Pizarro and Bejarano 2007). Some could argue, correctly, that Colombian parties have always lacked organization and discipline and that their tendency toward dispersion and fragmentation is nothing new. That caveat notwithstanding, the institutional reforms that have taken place since 1985—especially those related to the electoral system, the election of mayors and governors, and the statute on parties[20]—sharpened these historical tendencies among Colombian parties by creating additional incentives for fragmentation and atomization. These incentives became so strong that they also led the new political parties and movements in this direction.[21]

This situation gave rise to an attenuated (and highly atomized) two-party system, accompanied by a motley collection of smaller parties (which were also highly fragmented). This disarray of the parties and the party system had an enormously negative impact on effective governance, given the absence of minimal party discipline at the various levels of political representation (Congress, departmental legislatures, municipal councils) and the relative autonomy of each of the many dozens of "electoral micro-enterprises" that captured the country's space for political representation. Until the 2003 reform that tried to correct this negative trend (see García and Hoskin 2006), party-based lists and party-appointed candidates had practically disappeared in Colombia. This atomization generated enormous obstacles to coordination between the executive and legislative branches, making the task of governing all the more difficult. It impeded the formation of both a stable government coalition and a coherent opposition with the capacity to offer a credible alternative.

The democratic reforms of the 1980s and 1990s had additional perverse effects on the state and democracy in Colombia (see Bejarano 2002). Decentralization weakened the central government while devolving power to actors who control regional and local governments, among them, in some regions, the very rivals of the state, guerrillas and drug traffickers. In part because of the transfer of resources from the center to the periphery mandated by the 1991 Constitution, the fiscal deficit seriously deepened. The executive branch also saw its power diminish vis-à-vis Congress and the courts after 1991. While desirable and convenient from a democratic point of view, these reforms have nevertheless added new hurdles and difficulties to the central state as it attempts to recover and affirm its authority throughout the territory. In a different context, perhaps, such effects could be considered the necessary price to pay for the political opening operated since the mid-1980s. Nevertheless, at times when the drug traffickers, the paramilitary groups, and the revolutionary guerrillas intensified their siege of Colombia's democratic institutions, some of these reforms contributed instead to the latter's erosion and decay. Colombia thus serves as an illustration of the paradoxical situation in which efforts to strengthen democracy can instead contribute to its erosion.

The multiple problems besieging Colombia's democracy are not only located in the most visible dimension of its political regime but also at its foundations, the place where every democracy finds indispensable support—that of a state that effectively protects the citizens' basic civil rights and liberties. In Colombia these rights and liberties are violated daily by each and every one of the armed actors engaged in the ongoing conflict—including agents of that very same state. The common cause of these violations is the loss of the Colombian state's coercive and normative capacities, that is, the erosion and sometimes even collapse of those state organizations that must guarantee the effective exercise of full citizenship throughout the nation's territory.

The consolidation of a central state in Colombia was a slow and difficult accomplishment, due to the combination of a daunting geography, a weak, outwardly oriented economy with a very small domestic market, and a precarious national identity fractured by deep regional and party cleavages. Its traditional weakness took a downward turn in the last two decades of the twentieth century, reaching a point of "partial collapse" in the late 1980s and the beginning of the 1990s (see Bejarano and Pizarro 2004, 2005). One of the most dramatic indicators of state decay is the number of homicides. In 1960, when La Violencia came to an end, Colombia still had the highest rate of nonaccidental deaths in the world (see Oquist 1978: 11). Around the mid-1960s the homicide rate decreased, reaching an annual level of about 20 homicides per 100,000 inhabitants. It remained relatively stable at that point until the beginning of the 1980s.[22] Since the mid-1980s the homicide rate experienced a dramatic increase, reaching a new peak of about 80 homicides per 100,000 inhabitants in 1991. Since that time it has decreased slightly.[23]

By the mid-twentieth century the intraparty warfare known as La Violencia brought about a serious decay and crisis of the state's authority and capacity, which Oquist (1978) labeled the first "partial collapse" of the Colombian state. The National Front period witnessed a slow and selective process of state reconstruction (Bejarano and Segura 1996). In the 1980s severe erosion occurred again as the result of two main factors: a divided elite and the emergence of powerful competitors, to the left and to the right, financed by the rents accruing from the drug trade. Elite divisions contributed to the erosion of the state "from within,"[24] while the expansion and consolidation of its competitors meant a gradual erosion "from outside." Both trends contributed to a spiral of state decay that led to a major contraction of the state's capacity to "broadcast its power" (Herbst 2000) throughout the national territory and society.

This partial collapse of the state can be read as having two meanings: geographic and functional.[25] In geographic terms, *partial* refers to the fact that the central state is unable to extend its reach throughout the territory, in particular, to the peripheral zones beyond the agricultural frontier. The Colombian state has never been able to broadcast its power throughout the entire territory. This is a fact widely recognized and documented by geographers, historians, and sociologists, especially those who have devoted their studies to the *zonas de colonización,* or regions of recent settlement. But it is also a fact that this capacity shrank in the last two decades of the twentieth century, as a result of the capacity of rival armed organizations, the guerrillas and the paramilitaries, to occupy and control ever-increasing portions of the national territory. The problem therefore is not only that the Colombian state historically failed to control the territory under its jurisdiction but also that its capacity to do so increasingly "contracted" from the mid-1980s on. Since the mid-nineteenth century the Colombian state partially compensated for its weakness by exercising indirect control at the local and regional levels through the traditional parties. For this very reason, the weakening of these two parties and of their organizational capacity added one more dimension to the Colombian state's loss of control over the country. In some regions the state delegated the fulfillment of basic functions to right-wing organizations such as the Auto-Defensas Unidas de Colombia (AUC), thus clearly abdicating its power in their favor.[26] In other areas the state's control was seriously challenged by rival armed organizations, the guerrillas, as in the zones where coca growing has expanded since the early 1980s (the lowlands east of the Andean range, including the Orinoco and the Amazon basins). This geographic contraction of the Colombian state happened in tandem with the growth and expansion of the state's organized rivals, who were successful at challenging the state's control over an increasing portion of the territory under its formal control and jurisdiction.

In a functional sense, the collapse of the Colombian state is also "partial" in that while some state organizations (i.e., the bureaucracy, the technocracy, the representative bodies) retain a certain coherence and capacity for action, some other crucial state agencies (most notably those in charge of security and justice) have become increasingly unable to fulfill their functions and deliver the services that are expected of them or have increasingly deviated from their constitutional functions (e.g., the armed forces).

Adding to this already complex situation, the 1980s witnessed the expansion of a market for illegal drugs in the West, especially in the United States, and the increasing role of Colombian entrepreneurs in these transnational drug circuits. Drug trafficking certainly plays an important role in the Colombian crisis but not in and of itself, as a phenomenon exogenous to politics, but rather precisely on account of its multiple economic, social, and political ramifications, in particular, its impact on the process of state erosion and decay. The criminal organizations linked to the drug business have had devastating consequences for society and politics in Colombia (see Camacho 1988 and 1996; López 1998; López-Restrepo and Camacho-Guizado 2003). On the one hand, the drug traffickerse have sought to translate their enormous fortunes into political influence, gaining access to political decision making via multiple paths—including creating personal electoral vehicles, openly participating in the traditional political parties, financing electoral campaigns[27]—and wielding a disproportionate degree of influence in local politics. On the other hand, in order to combat the U.S.-backed anti-narcotics policies implemented by the state, the narcotraffickers have resorted to all kinds of means, from bribery and corruption all the way to death threats, assassination of state officials (prison guards, policemen, judges, magistrates, military officers, cabinet ministers, and national politicians), and the use of large-scale terrorism.

Besides its direct impact on the state, the rents produced by the drug trade have fed all armed actors in Colombia. Private militias guarding the narcotraffickers, paramilitary groups, and even the guerrillas have all based their expansion on the resources extracted from the drug business. The 1980s and 1990s boom in the drug trade changed the magnitude of the armed conflict in Colombia. Thanks to the impact of drug trafficking the state has seen its capacity diminish not only in absolute terms—as a result of corruption and the threat and use of force—but also in relative terms, as the rents accruing from drugs allowed its rivals to expand their reach and their operational capacities while the state was losing its own. In addition, since the beginning of the 1980s the U.S. antidrug policies in the Andean region have contributed to the deterioration of state authority in Colombia. This policy, aimed at cutting off the supply of drugs from South America, has limited the autonomy of the Andean states and made it impossible for them to design alternative strategies for combating the production and trade of narcotics. Perhaps the most perverse effect of the policy, in the Colombian case, has been the increasing militarization of the fight against drugs (involving first the police and now the army). This militarization has put additional pressure on the state to increase the resources, prerogatives, and hardware available to the military to the detriment of support for other key branches of government such as the judiciary.[28] Imbalances within the state have become deeper as a result.

As the central state loses its monopoly of coercion and becomes, as a consequence, less able to offer protection to the citizenry, alternative suppliers of protection come onto the scene. The "partial collapse" of the Colombian state and the strategic location of Colombia in the international narcotics trade have cleared the way for the emergence and expansion of many different political entities, including all kinds of "warlords," "coercive entrepreneurs," and "aspiring state-makers" (Bejarano and Pizarro 2004): despite two decades of peace negotiations two guerrilla groups still remain active, the FARC and the ELN; at the other extreme of the ideological spectrum, myriad right-wing groups came to be united under a single umbrella organization identified as the AUC. As the capacity of the Colombian state to monopolize power dwindled in the late 1980s, the size of these illegal forces increased. Both the guerrillas and the paramilitaries expanded enormously after the early 1980s, but the latter seemed to grow at a faster pace. The expansion of these two groups throughout the 1980s and 1990s was associated with their access to the rents accruing from the drug trade. Their political influence has gone beyond their territorial strongholds and extends throughout the national territory by way of capturing or otherwise influencing the structures and relations of power at the local level. Of a total of Colombia's 1,092 municipalities, at least 600 have been targeted "politically" by one group or the other (Forero 2000), causing much of the ongoing violence. In these municipalities the guerrillas and/or the paramilitaries give open or tacit approval to candidates, force some to withdraw, and assassinate others.

The state's diminished control over the means of coercion also has a negative impact on its capacity to deliver justice. Impunity is yet another face of state weakness and failure (Méndez 1999a: 20). It goes hand in hand with the other phenomena included here as symptoms of the state's erosion and "partial" collapse. Levels of criminality skyrocket when the state is unable to prevent or contain them. Criminal organizations charged with taking justice into their own hands tend to mushroom. In Juan Méndez's words:

Private armies and vigilante squads complicate the matter of assigning responsibility. It is not always clear that their actions are conducted under color of authority, or even that they are officially
tolerated, although in certain regions evidence to that effect is not
lacking. Yet, even if no policy exists of encouraging these actions,
their existence and growth demonstrate a signal weakness in the
ability of the state to keep peace and maintain order. (1999: 21)

From the late 1970s to the late 1990s the Colombian homicide rate
more than quadrupled. The influence of the main armed organizations
increased in a parallel fashion. During the same period the criminal system's capacity to investigate homicides was reduced to one-fifth of its
previous level (Rubio 1999: 214–15). The weakness of state institutions
in protecting citizens from potential abuses of their rights—combined
with the state's inability to punish the guilty and provide effective mechanisms for conflict resolution—is one of the biggest threats to democracy in Colombia as well as in the rest of Latin America. This lack of
capacity on the part of the judiciary affects a crucial dimension of any
democratic state, the rule of law, whose erosion threatens the very foundations of democratic rule. A state that claims to be democratic not only
claims a monopoly on violence in society but also and more important
claims that this monopoly is a necessary condition for effectively guaranteeing the rights and freedoms of the citizens under its jurisdiction.
However, the state's inability to provide protection and justice limits
the democratic regime's performance and belies its promise to deliver
greater equality and freedom, effective representation, and universal participation.

At the turn of the twenty-first century, a steep decline in the economy
coupled with a deepening political crisis and a widespread "negotiation
fatigue" (Arnson and Whitfield 2005) prompted a significant majority of
the Colombian electorate to vote for Alvaro Uribe Vélez, a dissident member of the Liberal Party running on a platform emphasizing the need to
restore security. His election by a clear majority during the first round of
presidential elections in 2002 amounted to a plebiscite against the failed
attempts to negotiate with a powerful recalcitrant guerrilla group, the
FARC, during the previous presidential term of Andrés Pastrana. The
Uribe government rapidly embarked on an effort to strengthen the mili-

tary's capacity to combat the guerrillas, funded by an increased fiscal effort within Colombia but also, and fundamentally, by a dramatic increase in military aid provided by the United States since 2000 under "Plan Colombia."[29] Beginning in 2003, he also embarked on an extremely controversial negotiation process with the paramilitary groups, which failed to produce the complete dismantling of these criminal organizations.

In May 2006 President Uribe was reelected with 62 percent (7,363,297) of the votes in the first round, 40 points ahead of Carlos Gaviria of the leftist PDA. A solid majority of Colombians favored the president's reelection mainly because between 2002 and 2006 Uribe's heavy-handed policies delivered a speedy recovery of most security indicators: the number of killings and kidnappings dropped significantly; attacks from both guerrillas and paramilitaries against small rural hamlets also declined; and, for the first time in decades, Colombians felt free to travel out of the cities thanks to the strong presence of the armed forces along the country's main roads and highways.[30] Simultaneously, in part due to this renewed sense of internal security but also due to higher international prices for commodities, the economy witnessed a steady recovery from the low point of the late 1990s, when the country suffered from the worst economic recession in a century.

Uribe was the first president reelected for a second term in more than a century in Colombia, as immediate reelection was banned at the beginning of the early twentieth century. That he got away with amending the constitution to favor his own reelection is a measure of the political power he managed to marshal. But it did not stop there: during the March 2006 congressional elections four parties that supported his reelection (the traditional Conservative Party plus three newly created, pro-Uribe parties: el Partido de la U, Cambio Radical, and the Movimiento Alas/Equipo Colombia) obtained comfortable majorities in both chambers of Congress. A former Liberal, Uribe also astutely used a divide-and-conquer strategy vis-à-vis his old party comrades, with dire consequences for the latter: historically a dominant party in the Colombian political landscape, the Liberal Party garnered a dismal 12 percent in the 2006 presidential contest, a distant third from the victor, lagging far behind the PDA, a new party of the left that became the main source of opposition to Uribe's government.

During his second presidential term (2006–2010) Uribe delivered more of the same: a tough stand against the FARC, a softer hand for the paramilitary armies—with whom he had negotiated since 2003—and a close relationship with the United States in matters related to drugs, security, and free trade. The strategy, however, suffered from two fundamental problems: the first obvious blind spot was the belief that strengthening the state's coercive power was enough; while increasing the size of the armed forces was obviously necessary to win the fight against the FARC and having a police presence in every municipality contributed greatly to lowering the overall levels of criminal violence, Uribe's approach suffered from a particular blindness to the fact that a democratic state needs to elicit voluntary consent as much as it relies on imposed obedience. To gain its subjects' hearts and souls, the Colombian state also needs to build roads, hospitals, and schools, deliver prompt and fair justice, hire more doctors and teachers, provide a measure of social justice, and protect its citizens across all regions and sectors of society.

The second problem is related to the negotiation with paramilitary forces. Here the government took a big gamble: by arguing that this was a significant step toward ending Colombia's conflict, Uribe opened the door wide for the social, legal, and political reincorporation of myriad regional private armies—mostly financed with drug moneys—who committed some of the most atrocious war crimes during the past two decades in Colombia. Faced with the dilemma between peace and justice, Uribe's government placed its bet on peace, to the detriment of justice. However, given the enormous social, political, and economic clout accumulated in the hands of the paramilitary commanders, the president's gamble might end up producing a tragic outcome: by legalizing their fortunes and their political presence throughout the country, Uribe may have sacrificed both justice and the prospects for a long-term, sustainable peace.

Clearly, the reconstruction of the state is the sine qua non for recovering and consolidating Colombia's political democracy (Bejarano 1994). Nevertheless, as difficult as it may sound, these two tasks must be carried out not sequentially but simultaneously. A strategy that puts the accent on state rebuilding without simultaneously paying due attention to the fate of justice and democracy can easily lead down the path to an authoritarian reconstruction of state power. The goal is to rebuild authority without authoritarianism: a difficult balancing act that Mr. Uribe was not entirely able to pull off.

The Slow Death of Democracy in Venezuela

The two attempted coups by the Venezuelan military in 1992 (the first, on February 4, was led by then–Lieutenant Colonel Hugo Chávez) may have come as a surprise to those of us looking at the country from a distance. Venezuelan analysts, however, were not entirely surprised: at least since the mid-1980s many of them had been warning about the signs of democratic erosion (see, e.g., Naím and Piñango 1984; Romero 1986; Ramos Jiménez 1987; Rey 1987; Guevara 1989). Indeed, the very creation of the Presidential Commission for the Reform of the State (COPRE) in 1984 signaled a keen awareness on the part of the political elites of the shortcomings of Venezuela's political system. At that point, however, nobody knew how deep and protracted the crisis would be; neither was it obvious that its aftermath would lead Venezuela in the direction it has taken since 1998. In other words, while we can retrospectively account for the crisis of Venezuela's democracy, the magnitude, evolution, and outcome of that crisis were by no means predetermined or entirely predictable. We therefore need to recognize an important role for the perceptions, decisions, and strategic (mis)calculations of the key actors involved, as well as a role, however minimal, for political *fortuna*.[31]

Some date the beginning of the Venezuelan crisis to February 18, 1983, when Venezuela's currency, the bolívar, suffered a traumatic devaluation caused by massive capital flight and the fall in the international prices of oil (Kornblith 1998: 22). That "Black Friday" (as the date is remembered by Venezuelans) symbolized the end of the nation's prosperity: for the next two decades the country suffered a protracted crisis of its economy, society, and political system. The fall in oil prices was not only steep but also sustained: except for a brief recovery in 1991 (a consequence of the Gulf War), the international price of oil declined steadily for almost two decades. According to Moisés Naím (2001: 21), "In 1974, oil contributed $1,540 per person to the national treasury and represented more than 80 percent of total government revenues; 20 years later, the figure had dropped to $200 per person and accounted for less than 40 percent of total fiscal revenues." Meanwhile, of course, Venezuela's population continued to grow, at an average annual rate of 2.5 percent, between 1981 and 1990.[32] The combination of a persistent decline in oil income and population growth, in addition to the continued failure to develop other productive activities, led in the 1990s to a deep crisis of Venezuela's structural foundations—a situation that has only been masked, but not solved, by a dramatic increase in oil prices since 2003. Its most painful manifestation has been the dramatic impoverishment of the Venezuelan population. In 1982, 32 percent of Venezuelans lived in poverty. This number went up to 53 percent in 1989, and by 2001 it had reached 68 percent.[33] Unemployment has hovered around 15 percent, and almost half the jobs are in the informal economy. Equally problematic, however, was the decline in the Venezuelan state's sources of revenue, a fact that further weakened its already strained capacity to respond to an overextended list of obligations and increasing social expectations.

Despite simplistic explanations of Venezuela's crisis that attribute the country's economic decline and gradual impoverishment to corruption and graft, these are dictated instead by the structural dynamics of declining international prices and population growth in an oil-dependent economy and society.[34] Rather than simple corruption, what underlies Venezuela's economic woes is the secular and probably irreversible decline not only in the price but also in the strategic importance of the one commodity, oil, that provided the structural foundations of Venezuela's economy and society throughout the twentieth century. As I have argued earlier, however, economic factors do not translate mechanically into political outcomes. For even if the fate of oil revenue figures prominently in any explanation of Venezuela's contemporary crisis, it was political factors—the ways in which the state and the political parties confronted this dire economic situation—that led to the fateful events of the late 1980s and early 1990s and finally to the denouement that began with the election of President Chávez in 1998.

The turning point came on February 27 and 28, 1989, with el Caracazo, a massive urban uprising that started in Caracas and spread through other major cities in protest against the package of stabilization and

structural adjustment measures taken by the government of Carlos Andrés Pérez in accordance with IMF recommendations. In part a reaction
against a generalized sense of economic deprivation but mostly due to
the frustrated promises of a return to prosperity during Pérez's second
term (1989–93), el Caracazo sounded the alarm about the impending
crisis.[35] The events of February 1989 marked a turning point in recent
Venezuelan history. Most Venezuelans still cite them as the symbolic
starting date of the current crisis. Susana Rotker (2000: 217–18) has
written, "On February 27, 1989, the tenuous thread that held the social
fabric together—the Rousseaunian contract binding citizens who are
conscious of their rights and above all of their duties vis-à-vis their
community—began to unravel. Even though countries do not change
overnight, it is without a doubt that that day marked a before and an
after for the entire [Venezuelan] society."[36]

El Caracazo and its violent aftermath (hundreds if not thousands of
casualties resulting from confrontations between the urban poor and the
armed forces) signaled the decay of the two pillars of Venezuela's democracy: the state and the political parties. The spontaneous and uncon-
trolled nature of the popular riots and the lack of leadership patent
during those two days pointed to the loss of connections between the
parties and Venezuelan society, in particular, their inability to channel
much less control, the demands of an impoverished and angry population. On the other hand, the collapse of police capabilities and the need
to use an ill-prepared armed force in the containment of social turbu-
lence pointed to the increasing weakness of the Venezuelan state. In the
1980s Venezuela had an average rate of 10 homicides per 100,000 inhabitants, similar to that of the United States and much lower than that
of Colombia. In 1989, the year of el Caracazo, the homicide rate increased to 13.5 deaths per 100,000 inhabitants. A new spike was visible
in 1992, the year of the coups: 16.3 violent deaths per 100,000 inhabitants. Since then it has continued to soar, reaching a rate of 50.96 deaths
per 100,000 inhabitants in 2003.[37] This has placed Venezuela, together
with Colombia, among the most violent countries in the world.

Throughout the twentieth century the Venezuelan state was certainly more coherent and had achieved a higher degree of control over
the means of coercion than its Colombian counterpart. Over the years,

however, and contrary to its appearance as a strong and resourceful state, it grew increasingly weak, burdened, and less effective in great part due to its dependence on oil revenues. The continued reliance on oil prevented it from entering into the positive-sum bargain that links states and societies through taxation of productive activities; neither did it provide the incentives for recruiting a meritocratic bureaucracy. These shortcomings notwithstanding, in part because of its mythical qualities as a "magical state" (see Coronil 1997), social demands and expectations kept growing, overloading the state with expanded public functions. Despite the seeming autonomy from social classes afforded by the oil rents, the Venezuelan state became increasingly tangled in a web of rent-seeking groups and special interests spawned by the economic policies of the 1970s and 1980s. Since the 1980s the steady decline of the oil income had produced chronic fiscal deficits.[38] At the end of that decade the Venezuelan state may have still looked rich and powerful, but the socioeconomic crisis epitomized by el Caracazo revealed a poorly staffed, overburdened, and corrupted state that was increasingly unable to perform its basic functions or sustain even a limited version of the rule of law. By the end of the twentieth century it had come to resemble its Colombian counterpart in many ways.

After the Caracazo and its violent aftermath, the Pérez government had trouble surviving the turbulent waters of the economic crisis, the growing antigovernment mobilization, and the discrediting of the political parties. And the rigidities typically associated with presidential systems added fuel to the precipitation of the crisis. From February 1989 to early 1993 Venezuelans struggled to find a formula to remove the head of the executive branch from office.[39] On February 4, 1992, the continuity of the regime was seriously threatened again: an insurrection of middle rank officials led by Lieutenant Colonel Hugo Chávez tried to seize power by means of a military coup. The coup failed, but it sent a strong message to Venezuelans as well as to the international community: Venezuelan democracy had been on the verge of a "sudden death."[40] That all political parties without exception and the majority of the armed forces declared their loyalty to the democratic system temporarily saved the country from succumbing to this military revolt. Pérez's government, however, entered an irreversible crisis. Given his reluctance to resign and the continued rise in street demonstrations throughout the year, some upper rank military officers believed the time was ripe for a successful coup. This second attempt came on November 27, 1992. On this occasion the military mobilization was even greater, involving the navy and the air force as well as the army. By this time there was no doubt that democracy in Venezuela was undergoing the worst crisis since its foundation in 1958 and risked its own disappearance.[41]

Given the lack of mechanisms by which to put an end to Pérez's government in an institutional fashion and the inability of political parties to offer viable solutions to the crisis, Venezuela was thrown into a "praetorian" situation (Huntington 1968), which prompted sectors of the military to step into the political arena for the first time in more than thirty years. The intervention of the military was prompted by the crisis of political intermediation and representation (see chap. 4). The lack of credibility of the parties was in some sense compensated by the enormous credibility enjoyed by the military among the Venezuelan population. The two attempted coups of 1992 signaled at best a serious reversal in terms of the subordination of the military and at worst the beginning of a new pattern of civil-military relations in which the military not only has gained in autonomy and expanded prerogatives but also has returned to exercising a degree of influence in domestic politics that is clearly inimical to democracy.

Between November 1992 and May 1993 the political impasse deepened as the ill-reputed president became the focus of Venezuela's polarized politics. Pérez's refusal to acknowledge his part in the tragedy and resign induced many to predict the inevitable fall of the democratic regime. In the final hour, however, the Supreme Court of Justice found grounds to accuse him of misuse of funds from the "secret consignment" of the presidency. Congress accepted the charges and after an impeachment trial replaced him with a member from his own party, Ramon J. Velásquez, as interim president. The transition government managed to survive during the nine months of its fragile existence and presided over a peaceful electoral contest in December 1993,[42] in which the historical leader of the Social Christian party, COPEI, and founder of Venezuela's democracy, Rafael Caldera, was elected president.

In 1993 it seemed as though the country had run full circle. Some thought that the worst part of the political crisis had been surmounted, as the regime appeared to have entered into a "re-equilibration" phase.[43] But in reality many things had changed. Among these, and most important, was the party system. Caldera was not elected by his party but by a last-minute coalition of numerous small parties (Convergencia Nacional), including a dissident faction of his original party. The other historic pillar of Venezuelan democracy, AD, suffered a crushing defeat while a relatively unknown leftist party, Causa Radical, reached an outstanding place amid a rapidly changing political party scenario (see López Maya 1994, 1997). After Caldera's second administration (1994–99) the party system fragmented even further. The leading parties were defeated in the 1998 presidential election and have been completely repudiated in every election since, including the elections to choose the delegates to the Constitutional Assembly of 1999. As documented in chapter 5, a cursory look at the electoral results since 1993 suffices to show the debacle of Venezuela's traditional parties, as well as the immense fragmentation and volatility of the emerging political organizations (see tables 5.1, 5.2).

Velásquez's interim government (May 1993–February 1994) and Caldera's second presidential term (1994–99) represent the traditional parties' last-ditch attempt to recover control of the political situation while keeping democracy afloat. Ultimately, they failed. To some extent the avoidance of a sudden regime breakdown was the result of the political reforms enacted since the mid-1980s, in particular, decentralization (see López and Lander 1996; Penfold-Becerra 1999). On the other hand, even if it is true that the sudden death of democracy was avoided, it would not be an exaggeration to characterize the recent evolution of the political regime in Venezuela as the slow death of democracy.[44] This has become evident since the landslide election of Hugo Chávez.[45] By late 1998, when Chávez was elected president, the dismantling of the party system was almost complete. Venezuelans voted unequivocally for an end to the "partidocracia"—the traditional two-party system—that was already on its last legs when Caldera won the presidential election in 1993. By rejecting the parties and electing Chávez, they took a big leap into the unknown.

Nevertheless, the collapse of the party system and the disappearance of Venezuela's traditional parties did not happen overnight; neither were they entirely President Chávez's making. In fact, as Naím (2001: 18) has argued, "Chávez's ascendancy owes more to the long-term dilution of the political power once held by Acción Democrática and COPEI." Beyond the frontal attack led by Chávez against the institutions of the ancien régime, the traditional parties owe their demise to the inability of their leadership to anticipate, react, and adapt to the changes in Venezuela's economy and society—and even to the institutional changes (such as decentralization and the various electoral reforms enacted since the late 1980s) that they themselves contributed to designing (see Penfold-Becerra 2001; Bejarano 2002). Why were these parties so utterly incapable of responding and adapting to these changes? The response to this question is related in part to their internal structure and to their relations with society: both AD and COPEI became powerful, disciplined, and hierarchical organizations with very little room for generational renewal in their leadership or feedback from the electorate. They also cultivated a tendency to monopolize the electoral process, to dominate the legislative process, and to penetrate all sorts of civil organizations.[46] As Coppedge (1994a: 158–59) has argued, "The pervasive penetration of society by parties and the extreme centralization of authority within parties in Venezuela became, over a period of three decades, a net disadvantage for stability"—and, I would add, for themselves.

In a sense, then, the Venezuelan parties were victims of their own success, a textbook illustration of the costs of Michels's "iron law of oligarchy" (1968) and the perils of overinstitutionalization. In addition, of course, their continued access to inflated public funds and their reliance on oil income and state patronage made them unaware of the changes that were literally sweeping the floor below their feet. The separation between party and state that gave rise to the radical populist mobilization tactics of AD in the 1940s became blurred over the years, especially after the oil boom of the 1970s. Venezuelan parties, as I have argued in chapter 2, emerged not only after but also in strong opposition to the Venezuelan state created and controlled by Juan Vicente Gómez and his military successors. By the 1990s, however, the two parties had become so tightly wedded to the state and dependent on its largesse that it was no longer feasible to disentangle and differentiate the former from the latter.

Such perverse fusion, of course, is in part responsible for the existence of an inefficient and poorly staffed bureaucracy and a corrupt and partisan judiciary. As in Colombia, the dominance of the parties over the state prevented serious reform of the civil service, as well as the effective functioning and strengthening of the court system, thus perpetuating the typically Latin American and highly problematic "politicized state" (Chalmers 1977). In Venezuela the politicization of the state included the military; in addition, the parties politicized every organization in civil society (students, workers, peasants, professional and neighborhood associations) to an extreme level (see Crisp 2000). Unlike Colombia, where part of the National Front settlement was to demobilize society and depoliticize the state after a decade of civil war, Venezuela's parties' efforts to mobilize every sector of Venezuelan society ended up producing the undesirable effect of an excessive penetration of state and society by two highly centralized parties. As oil revenues dwindled, the parties found themselves not only with less money to distribute but also with a dire socioeconomic situation that they were not used to confronting, in their hands a bloated state that had grown as big as it was ineffective. Worst of all, they confronted a disgruntled population that they no longer understood, whose angry demands they no longer channeled much less controlled. When the crisis hit the decline of state and parties went hand in hand, and with it, the inevitable erosion of Venezuela's democracy.

Between 1988 and 1998 the two political parties that had been building Venezuelan democracy lost almost all their influence, giving way to a proliferation of parties and movements that have not yet gelled into a new, stable party system. Since 1998 the predominant political actor has been President Chávez and his Movimiento Quinta República, which so far has shown no signs of turning into a conventional political organization but has rather remained as a vehicle for mass mobilization directed from the top down by its charismatic leader.[47] Circulating around it there are myriad smaller parties and movements on the left. The opposition has so far been unable to build any semblance of a unified political organization, a party or a movement. Thus Venezuela went from a situation of high concentration of power in the hands of two highly centralized, vertically structured party organizations to the opposite: the weakening and virtual disappearance of the institutions of representation, especially of political parties, the extreme fragmentation and volatility of the party system, and a political vacuum that, since 1999, has been filled by the deeply polarizing figure of Hugo Chávez. Since his election in 1998, and especially since the drafting of the new constitution in 1999, Chávez has been hard at work building a new sociopolitical coalition that will enable him to bring about a radical displacement of the established social, economic, and political elites. The 1999 Constituent Assembly turned into an excellent vehicle to build such a coalition. In the process Venezuela's democracy took a fatal blow.

The issue of reforming the constitution was put on the table on February 4, 1992, when Lieutenant Colonel Chávez, together with a group of young military comrades calling themselves the Movimiento Bolivariano Revolucionario 200, attempted to overthrow President Pérez via a military coup. Their manifesto did not blame the institutions contained in the 1961 Constitution as much as the actors (in particular, the parties and the political elites) who created it and thrived in that institutional environment for the problems of Venezuela. Nevertheless, and even though they explicitly argued that they had risen to defend the constitution, the manifesto ended by calling for a constituent assembly "which will define through a new Magna Carta the model of society toward which Venezuela should orient itself."[48]

In 1998 Chávez, coup maker turned presidential candidate, raised the banner of constitutional reform once again.[49] During his campaign he argued that Venezuela needed a constituent assembly in order to radically transform the state and political regime, what he calls "refundar la república." Many analysts have insisted that there was no constitutional crisis in Venezuela in the late 1990s and that there was no pressing institutional need to reform the 1961 Constitution (see Coppedge 2003: 177). Despite this, Chávez was elected on December 6, 1998, with 56.2 percent of the vote and a clear mandate to overhaul Venezuela's political architecture. Chávez's calls to a "refounding of the republic" were read as a promise for a radical transformation of the political, social, and economic order. Socially, the new republic would end all discrimination, do away with the social dominance of the elites, and incorporate the destitute Venezuelan masses as citizens with all rights and privileges. Politically, the new order would eliminate the old parties deemed corrupt and authoritarian while creating a new, participatory version of democracy, conceived as popular sovereignty rather than as a liberal, constitutional, democratic regime.[50] The Constituent Assembly was seen as the vehicle for building this new majority, a coalition against the old social and political elites, especially the party elites. With the support of the military, President Chávez managed to build a pro-reform coalition of outsiders together with some old leftist parties—such as the PCV, MEP, and PPT[51]—most of which had remained on the margins of the party system dominated by AD and COPEI between 1958 and 1993.

By 1999 the traditional parties had completely lost their capacity to mobilize the electorate and compete against Chávez's powerful coalition. Organized labor (CTV) as well as the business federation (FEDECAMARAS) were also on the losing side of the political divide, given their close relationship to the party establishment. Very few social organizations had survived the parties' debacle. For all Chávez's inclusionary and participatory rhetoric, his coalition relied mostly on the military and a collection of small radical leftist parties rather than on civil organizations.[52] Meanwhile, social organizations and groups were left with no meaningful participation in the process, besides a minor role as "cheering crowds."[53]

On February 2, 1999, Chavez was sworn in as the new president of Venezuela with his hand on what he called the "moribund" Constitution of 1961. The day of his inauguration he issued a decree calling for a referendum to decide on the election of a constituent assembly. On April 25, 1999, the referendum took place: more than 80 percent of the voters approved the convening of a national constituent assembly as well as the electoral system for choosing delegates.[54] Elections for the Constituent Assembly were held on July 25, 1999, using a version of the mixed-member proportional system designed by Chávez and his direct entourage.[55] The assembly would be formed by 131 delegates: 24 would be elected in a single national district (of magnitude 24); 104 would be elected in 24 regional districts (of different magnitudes), which coincided with the territorial divisions, that is, with the 23 states and the Federal District of Caracas. In addition, the president had the right to appoint three delegates as representatives of the indigenous communities. Candidates could choose whether to run on a party ticket, on a social movement ticket, or as independents. Voters were allowed to cast as many votes as there were seats to be filled in each district, and the candidates (not the parties) with the largest pluralities were elected.[56] The majoritarian tendencies inherent in the electoral system combined with the campaign tactics used by Chávez and his followers,[57] as well as the disorganization and dispersion of the opposition,[58] led to the overrepresentation of the pro-Chávez alliance in the assembly. Having obtained 65 percent of the votes, the pro-government coalition occupied 93 percent of the seats in the assembly. By contrast, the opposition, with more than 34 percent of the votes obtained only 4.6 percent of the seats in the assembly.

Unlike the Colombian experience of 1991, the Venezuelan Constituent Assembly of 1999 was dominated by the overwhelming presence of a pro-government coalition, the Polo Patriótico, "an ad hoc, last-minute mélange of small, marginal parties of the left and the military sector, with support from defecting factions of some traditional parties" (Corrales 2002: 299). This led to an assembly that was tightly controlled by the government and biased against the opposition. It is little wonder that such an assembly produced an extreme version of delegative democracy that fits only too well the type described by O'Donnell (1994a: 59–60) in which "the president is taken to be the embodiment of the nation and the main custodian and definer of its interests. . . . After the election voters/delegators are expected to become passive but cheering audiences of what the president does."

While the Colombian constitution-making process yielded a more representative assembly and a more balanced constitution, a majority-dominated assembly in Venezuela produced instead an institutional arrangement so heavily biased toward presidential domination that it has endangered democracy in Venezuela more than it has helped its reequilibration after the crisis. The constitution of 1999 concentrates enormous powers in the hands of the president who can, among other things, legislate by decree, convene all sorts of plebiscites and referenda, dissolve the national assembly, and promote the military top command without legislative approval. The president's term was extended from five to six years, and immediate reelection was introduced.[59] The checks on executive power were severely weakened, Congress was reduced from two chambers to one (thus crippling the representation of the regions at the national level), a strong centralization trend was reintroduced, and the notion of political parties, especially opposition parties, completely disappeared.[60] Together with the enormous political capital that Chávez has managed to sustain in election after election since 1998,[61] the "crowding out of the opposition" (Corrales and Penfold 2007) accomplished by the institutional architecture enshrined in 1999 certainly amounts to a radical change in Venezuela's regime. Corrales and Penfold (2007: 100) have termed it Venezuela's "transition toward authoritarianism." Others have already classified Venezuela as a case of "competitive authoritarianism" (Levitsky and Way 2002; Corrales 2006a). Regardless of the specific label used to describe Venezuela's form of government under Chávez, there is no doubt that, as a result of a protracted process of democratic erosion and decay, especially the changes introduced in the past decade, Venezuela has gotten closer and closer to crossing the threshold that separates democracies from nondemocratic regimes.

Contrasting Patterns of Decay in South America's Oldest Democracies

The main purpose of this book has been to chart and explain the divergent post-pact regime trajectories of Colombia and Venezuela through the 1960s, 1970s, and 1980s. Yet it could not have concluded without a consideration (albeit brief) of the recent crises in these two South American democracies. For over the past two decades, even as the rest of the continent (re)democratized—more or less successfully—serious crises developed in these two long-standing democracies. Colombia evolved from a "restricted" democracy to an increasingly "besieged" one, with a weak state incapable of eliminating guerrilla violence while penetrated by drug traffickers and illegal paramilitary armies. In turn, Venezuela shifted from a stable and relatively successful democracy to a severe crisis of representation, followed by a collapsed party system, and, with the emergence of Hugo Chávez, a gradual transition to authoritarianism. At the turn of the century, instead of being hailed as Latin America's most stable and enduring democracies, Colombia and Venezuela came to be regarded as deeply flawed, precarious democracies.

Similar as they may seem, these two crises had different origins and consequences. This chapter has endeavored to highlight divergence not only in the kinds of problems confronted by these two regimes during the past two decades but also in the ways in which political leaders have confronted and attempted to solve them, leading to quite dissimilar outcomes—not entirely happy in either case. Indeed, as stated in the introduction to this book, "every unhappy democracy is unhappy in its own way."

Some may argue that today's Colombia and Venezuela exemplify the almost "natural" decay that haunts pacted democracies as their elite pacts become exhausted with time. However, as discussed in chapter 3, Venezuela's political pacts of 1958 were never as formal, rigid, exclusionary, or restrictive as Colombia's. Also, they were never enshrined as a permanent feature of the political regime in the national constitution, as was the case in Colombia. It would thus be difficult to argue that in Venezuela the pacts had become straitjackets for the development and subsequent adaptation of the political regime to new social or economic conditions. On the contrary, the Venezuelan accords demonstrate that not all pacts necessarily act as a hindrance to democratic development and institutionalization; some can play a beneficial role, provided that they are not only open and inclusionary, allowing new players into the political game, but also flexible and capable of adapting to changing national and international circumstances.

Obviously, as time goes by and conditions change, pacts that give birth to a political regime and its "foundational myth" may become outdated. Certainly, the wide democratic consensus that existed in Venezuela in the late 1950s has not remained intact. However, more than the natural erosion of the foundational pacts, what seems to have eroded in Venezuela is the basic political institutions—the state and the political parties—that served as the foundations of its democratic regime over three decades.

If Venezuela's democracy had an advantage over Colombia's because of the way it handled civil-military relations, as well as on account of the diversity and vitality of its political society, the erosion of these two dimensions stand out as some of the most significant sources of its recent democratic decay. The reasons for such a reversal are not to be found solely in the fall of oil prices or the steady decline of that country's GDP per capita. In addition to those exogenous changes, it is the progressive decline of the Venezuelan central state, together with the deterioration and final collapse of its party system, that explains the severe crisis undergone by its democracy.

A key factor in explaining the erosion and decay of Venezuela's democracy is the collapse of its parties and party system. This relatively sudden collapse of the system of political intermediation has, in my view, very little to do with the transition pacts. Instead, it should be interpreted as the combined result of two strong, highly centralized party organizations with access to a wealthy rentier state dependent on income from oil exports. Rather than blame it on the pacts, Venezuela's democratic erosion can be attributed to the inability, on the part of the state and the political parties, to adequately respond to new problems and challenges. Thus, paradoxically, what proved to be an initially favorable setting for democracy in Venezuela over time turned into a problem to be reckoned with: the excessive centrality of the state and the party system and their extreme dependence on declining oil revenues.

By contrast, Colombia's democratic erosion is related, to a greater extent, to the restrictions inherited from the National Front pacts that crippled its democracy for over three decades. After the democratic opening offered by the 1991 constitutional reform, however, the sources of decay seem to have shifted: instead of restrictions on democratic participation and competition, the regime's shortcomings stem more clearly from the frailty of a state that, until now, has not been able to either eliminate or incorporate an armed opposition that grew over the years in part fueled by the trade in narcotics. Other rivals of the state, most notably, the paramilitary groups, have thrived in that same environment, thus further weakening the central state's capacity to monopolize coercion and sustain a democratic rule of law throughout the territory. In addition to its secular weakness, a combination of factors, including elite divisions, the strengthening of the state's rivals, and the impact of drug trafficking, conspired in the 1980s to cause a partial collapse of the Colombian state. Simultaneously, the parties lost political influence and became extremely fragmented, though they did not collapse in the same dramatic way as their Venezuelan counterparts. In a deeply fractionalized way, they do have a presence throughout the territory, especially in the rural areas where they still hold on to the regional and local structures of political power.

In sum, while in Colombia the nature of the transition and its institutional legacies seem to be more closely connected to its contemporary political problems, in Venezuela the nature of the transition and its institutional legacies seem to be less related to that country's contemporary predicament. In both cases long-term institutional factors such as the nature and attributes of their states and party systems are seen as consequential in explaining the dynamics of their recent democratic decay. The framework advanced throughout this book has thus provided a useful vantage point from which to observe and understand these twin crises and their aftermath. Again, rather than exclusively emphasize the role of structural factors (export of oil, coffee, or narcotics drugs) or pay undue attention to the comings and goings of their leaders, my account of the recent travails of democracy in Colombia and Venezuela has placed the accent on political-institutional factors such as the state, the parties and party systems, and the legacies of recent episodes of institutional change.

Conclusion

In the 1960s and 1970s Venezuela earned a reputation as one of the most stable democracies in Latin America. During its early years, it survived several coup attempts and guerrilla warfare as it continued to hold regular, free, and fair elections characterized by strong party competition. During those first three decades (1958–88), Venezuela was not only more democratic than most of its neighbors (save for Costa Rica) but also more democratic than it had been prior to 1958. As I have argued throughout this book, it was also more democratic than its neighbor, Colombia. In Colombia an equally stable democracy developed, but, by contrast with Venezuela, it was unable to defeat guerrilla insurgencies, it saw the autonomy and prerogatives of the military increase steadily over time, and, though elections were celebrated at regular intervals, competition was seriously dampened by restrictions and discrimination against third parties introduced since the transition.

This book offers the first systematic comparative analysis of the emergence and evolution of these two increasingly troubled South American democracies. Together with Costa Rica, Colombia and Venezuela emerged as the only countries where democracy survived against a regionwide collapse of democratic regimes in the 1960s and 1970s. Neither one fits easily within the conventional classifications that separate the more industrialized nations of Latin America (Mexico and the Southern Cone) from the less developed countries to the north (Central America and the Caribbean). They are considered part of the Andes, but they are not quite like their neighbors to the south, Ecuador, Peru, and Bolivia.

Many scholars have thus grouped Venezuela and Colombia as exceptional in the Latin American context, seeing them as similar cases of regime endurance, a situation commonly explained by the legacy of their seemingly successful "pacted" transitions. I have argued that this narrative is not only partial but also misleading—creating, for example, the sense that pacts alone have the power to forge and sustain durable democracies. My empirical findings show that these two cases are quite distinct. While pacts did in fact precede the founding of democracy in both Colombia and Venezuela, pacts alone do not explain the emergence and sustainability of democracy. The quality of the democracies that emerged from the 1950s transitions resulted from the content of the pacts as well as from the historical political institutions that existed prior and in fact helped shape that process. Indeed, Colombia and Venezuela were different prior to and subsequent to their simultaneous transitions to democracy. Historically divergent constellations of political institutions (rather than pact making alone) explain the types of democracies that emerged and endured in the second half of the twentieth century in these two South American nations.

My research is squarely grounded in the comparative historical institutional approach to political analysis. I have examined a number of approaches to understanding political change while privileging the influence of the historical development of political institutions, especially with regard to the timing, sequence, and patterns of their consolidation. Instead of taking either side in the debate between structures and agency as the main causal engine behind political outcomes, I chose to build on the notion of "structured contingency," coined by T. L. Karl in 1990, placing it at the center of my analysis of the democratization process in Colombia and Venezuela.

Part I throws into question the commonplace attempts to explain the differences between Colombia and Venezuela in terms of structural conditions—that is, as a result of oil-led development in Venezuela and coffee or drugs in the case of Colombia, arguing instead for the need to evaluate the impact of prior patterns of state formation and party systems on the process of democratization. I have argued for the hold of historical political institutions on the democracies that were forged at mid-twentieth century. But this book is more than a discussion of political history: it also engages contemporary debates on the consequences of following different paths toward democracy.

Part II takes issue with those accounts that have placed excessive emphasis on the mode of transition, particularly with those arguing that all "pacted democracies" follow a common, predictable trajectory. Whether political pacts exert a beneficial or a negative impact on the subsequent democratization process depends, to a great extent, on the specific contents of those pacts. As shown in chapter 3, the pacts' historical importance in terms of their impact on the extent and depth of democratization depends on three main factors: (1) the range of actors included in the pact; (2) the nature and scope of the restrictions imposed on subsequent political interactions; and (3) the degree to which these restrictions become entrenched in constitutional provisions.

The third and last part of the book shows how, from their simultaneous transitions onward, these two countries followed divergent democratic trajectories. Crucial actors such as the military, left-wing insurgents, and political parties behaved in strikingly different ways from one case to the next, responding both to a different set of historical legacies and to very different institutional arrangements inherited from the transition. Since the late 1980s, despite their long-hailed stability, these two democracies became increasingly troubled. A comparative analysis of these twin crises again reveals how, despite their simultaneity, the two are fundamentally different, owing to the previous divergent institutionalization patterns followed by each one of these two countries. While the recent crisis is more closely connected to the nature of the transition and tighter restrictions imposed by the Colombian pacts, Venezuela's demo-cratic crisis, dramatically illustrated by its party system collapse in 1998, had little to do with initial transition dynamics and pacts. Still, in both cases the erosion and decay of democratic politics are ultimately related to the erosion and decay of fundamental political institutions: the po-litical parties and the state.

By showing how the sequencing of state formation and party sys-tems shaped the quality of the democracies that were to emerge out of political pacts during the second half of the twentieth century, I have highlighted the crucial role of historical political institutions. This book will have served its purpose if it sheds some light on the puzzling conver-gence and divergence of regime trajectories and the quality of democratic politics in these two critical South American cases.

A decade or so ago, observers of Latin American politics were pre-dicting that the region's fledging democracies would follow one of two predictable paths: they would consolidate into fully effective liberal de-mocracies, or they would fail to consolidate and thus, either slowly or suddenly, fall back into some form of authoritarianism (Whitehead 1993; O'Donnell 1992; Schmitter 1994, 1995). Following that line of think-ing, Shugart (2005: 926) stated that "the very notion of a 'limited de-mocracy' being institutionalized is an oxymoron." Yet Colombia's and Venezuela's five decades of democratic development confront us with that very troubling possibility: though unable to develop the full package of attributes associated with liberal democracy, precarious, "unhappy" de-mocracies can actually become rather stabilized and endure—even if, ad-mittedly, they may also be vulnerable to erosion and decay.

By focusing on Colombia and Venezuela, where democratic institu-tions managed to endure for more than four decades, and by exploring the causes of their stability as well as their enduring shortcomings, this study seeks to contribute to an understanding of the conditions under which—short of full democratic consolidation and in the absence of an open authoritarian regression—precarious democracies may evolve and endure. Once considered enigmatic exceptions to Latin America's au-thoritarian swing, Colombia and Venezuela may now be regarded as po-tential models—both in their accomplishments and in their limitations—of the future of democracy in the region.

Given the astounding durability of Latin America's third wave democracies, it is perhaps safe to say that the regime change pendulum has stopped in the region. Nevertheless, for many countries the final station does not look like full democracy but rather an intermediate one, situated halfway between democracy and authoritarianism. We may not be witnessing a massive return to authoritarian politics in the region but rather an unsettling institutionalization of various precarious, unhappy democracies. Under the combined weight of weak states and party systems, and seemingly caught between economic stagnation and the deleterious impact of the boom-and-bust cycles of international commodity prices, many Latin American nations may have gotten stuck in the gray zone of semidemocratic politics.

NOTES

Introduction

1. Each year beginning in 1972 Freedom House has ranked all countries from 1 (the best score) to 7 on civil liberties and political rights. Political rights are conceived of as rights that enable people to participate freely in the political process and include the rights to vote, run for public office, and elect representatives. Civil liberties include the freedoms of expression and belief, associational and organizational rights, rule of law, and personal autonomy without interference from the state. Though they are not without their problems, Freedom House scores represent a reasonable measure, with the additional advantages of their ready availability and, unlike most governance variables, their usefulness for tracking changes over time (although they should not be considered fully comparable due to slight changes in methodology from one year to the next). See Mainwaring 1999a: 22, for an explanation of the growing use of Freedom House scores as a measure of democracy. For the purposes of figure 0.1, the scores in the two categories (political rights and civil liberties) were combined and rescaled to produce an index that ranges from 2 to 14, with higher values corresponding to a higher degree of freedom (a proxy for democracy).

2. The "most similar systems" design is a research strategy based on Mill's method of difference in which the researcher "brings together systems that are as similar as possible in as many features (properties) as possible, thus allowing a large number of variables to be ignored (under the assumption that they are equal)" (Sartori 1991: 250). See also Lijphart 1975.

3. That Tolstoy's famous phrase could be turned into a powerful research strategy was first suggested to me by Lisa Anderson. Later I found it deployed in Jared Diamond's *Guns, Germs and Steel* (1999), where it was labeled "the Anna Karenina principle."

4. Leo Tolstoy, *Anna Karenina* (New York: Norton, 1970), 1.

5. These four basic requirements build on the work of Robert Dahl (1971) and coincide with many contemporary definitions of liberal, representative, procedural democracy, including those of Schmitter and Karl (1993), Collier and Levitsky (1997), Mainwaring (1999a), and Mainwaring, Brinks, and Pérez-Liñán (2001).

6. With the development of the third wave of democracy in Latin America, especially because of its unexpected long duration, a number of labels have emerged to classify these unhappy or "diminished sub-types" of democracy (see Collier and Levistky 1997). Mainwaring has proposed the category "semi-democracy" to conceptualize them: "a semi-democratic government or restricted democracy refers to a civilian government elected under reasonably fair conditions, but with significant restrictions in participation, competition, and/or the observance of civil liberties" (1999a: 14). The problem with this concept is that it lumps all these variations together without offering a way to differentiate between them or their causes.

7. A pioneering volume on the topic is Mainwaring, O'Donnell, and Valenzuela 1992. Three major books added to this emerging literature on consolidation: Higley and Gunther 1992; Gunther, Diamandouros, and Puhle 1995; and Linz and Stepan 1996a. Two useful reviews of this literature are Ross-Schneider 1995 and Schedler 1998.

8. See O'Donnell's article "Illusions about Consolidation," *Journal of Democracy* 7, no. 2 (1996): 34–47; and the response by Gunther, Diamandouros, and Puhle, "O'Donnell's Illusions: a Rejoinder," *Journal of Democracy* 7, no. 4 (1996): 150–59. O'Donnell responded again in "Illusions and Conceptual Flaws," *Journal of Democracy* 7, no. 4 (1996): 159–67.

9. For the minimalists, democratic consolidation equals democratic survival. Once a transition is complete, a democratic regime's consolidation is indicated solely by the number of years it manages to survive, independently of the quality of its institutions or their performance. Some of this literature gives the impression that consolidation is a unilinear process, an easy progression from newborn to mature democracy where time is the only relevant variable. This simplistic thinking about democratic consolidation led some to classify Colombia and Venezuela as successful cases of democratic transition *and* consolidation. See Higley and Gunther 1992, especially the chapter by Peeler.

10. Including Higley and Gunther 1992; Gunther, Diamandouros, and Puhle 1995; and Linz and Stepan's exceedingly complex definition (1996a) as well as the extremely exacting one proposed by O'Donnell himself in 1992.

11. Ross-Schneider had anticipated this outcome when he wrote that "regime consolidation is a clumsy concept and needs to be disaggregated if not discarded" (1995: 216).

12. This was in part inspired by Putnam's book on the quality of democracy in Italy (1993). The topic has received a great deal of attention recently.

13. This is the main thrust of the UNDP's Report (2004), as well as of O'Donnell's recent contribution (2004).

14. For an eloquent example of this, see the article by Diamond and Morlino (2004) in which they define "quality of democracy" as having eight dimensions!

15. See Schmitter and Karl 1993. Understood in this sense, "institutionalization" closely resembles the idea of "success" of the democratic method as posed by Schumpeter (1950: 290). It also bears resemblance to the idea of "habituation" or "routinization" that characterizes the last phase of Rustow's (1970) democratization model.

16. There is also, of course, the possibility that a series of elements may lead to a cycle of perverse institutionalization that undermines the workings of democracy. According to Valenzuela the perverse elements that could become institutionalized, thus affecting democratic performance are (1) the existence of nondemocratically generated *tutelary powers;* (2) the existence of *reserved domains* of authority and policy making; (3) the existence of major discriminations in the electoral process; and (4) the conviction, on the part of significant political actors, that there are alternative means other than elections to constitute and substitute legitimate governments (Valenzuela 1992: 62–70). Processes of virtuous and perverse institutionalization may coexist in conflict, but consolidation is possible only under circumstances that permit the former to predominate over the latter.

17. Some historians would argue that the impact of the colonial experience varied within the Spanish empire, according to the degree of importance attached by the Crown to each of its component units. In our case, the Viceroyalty of Nueva Granada (present-day Colombia) would have been more important than the General Captaincy of Venezuela (present-day Venezuela), at least regarding its extractive and administrative functions. This observation notwithstanding, the most important distinction still holds between these two countries as objects of Spanish colonization, on the one hand, and the experience of other countries colonized by either the British, French, Belgians, or Dutch, on the other.

18. The figure of the strong personal caudillo was nevertheless much more important in the Venezuelan case than in Colombia. In the latter, personal caudillos gave way much more rapidly to the institutionalization of parties as the organized representatives of regional oligarchies. I come back to this crucial difference in chapter 2.

19. In Colombia "most of the population (60%) is classified as mestizo (mixed race), although there are significant minorities of both European (20%) and African origin (18%). Indigenous communities make up about 2% of the population" (Economist Intelligence Unit 2001: 7). In Venezuela "it is estimated that 67% of the population is mestizo (mixed race), 21% Caucasian, 10% black and 2% indigenous" (Economist Intelligence Unit 2001: 14). Despite the difficulties inherent in measuring ethnic populations, these figures are confirmed by the estimates presented in Yashar 2005. Colombia and Venezuela also differ from countries in the Southern Cone of Latin America, like Argentina and Uruguay, where the original indigenous populations were decimated, there

was little slave trade during the colonial period, and the resulting ethnic or racial composition of the population is thus more homogeneous.

20. While the relationship between the state and the Catholic Church has at times given ground to deep political controversies in both countries, there has not been a religious cleavage in either of them. There is, however, a difference in the degree of influence of the Catholic Church: it is much more pronounced in Colombia than in Venezuela. See Levine 1981.

21. Only very recently (in the past two or three decades), and coinciding with a continent-wide wave of ethnic mobilization, have the indigenous groups of Colombia mobilized and formed a series of important social and political organizations, with a clear ethnic basis. See Gros 1991; Van Cott 2005. Nothing similar happened in Venezuela until 1999, when three seats in the Constituent Assembly were allocated for representatives of the indigenous communities.

22. Both Rustow (1970) and Linz and Stepan (1996a) consider the recognition of one and only one political community as a crucial prerequisite for democracy to emerge and take root.

23. This way of labeling the difference between the two draws from Rueschemeyer, Stephens, and Stephens: "An agrarian society before or in the incipient stages of penetration by commercial market relations and industrialization is unlikely to gain or sustain a democratic form of government. Democracy by any definition is extremely rare in agrarian societies. . . . The typical forms of rule in agrarian societies are and have been autocracy and oligarchy" (1992: 2).

24. The Trienio cannot be considered a phase of "oligarchic" democracy. It was, instead, an experiment in radical democracy, both because of the way it came about (a military coup) and because of the sweeping political, social, and economic reforms enacted during such a brief period. The protagonists of the Trienio experiment attempted a definite and radical break with Venezuela's political past. Despite its failure, the Trienio left a blueprint that would influence the future design of the democratic regime. Important institutional legacies from the Trienio years were the Electoral Statute of 1946 and the Constitution of 1947. See Kornblith (1989b, 1991, 1992a). Basic information on the Trienio can be found in Gibson 1989. More detailed discussions of the period and its implications can be found in Betancourt 1969; Castro 1988; Stambouli 1980; and López Maya 1996.

25. See Wilde 1978, 1982. Solaún (1980) calls it a protodemocracy. On the role of regional rivalries in shaping the Colombian regime, see Ocampo 1987; Montenegro 2006.

26. A valuable exception is, of course, Collier and Collier, "Shaping the Political Arena" (1991). Collier and Collier not only include Colombia and Venezuela in their eight-case comparison but also emphasized their differences, thus prefiguring many of this book's arguments. Their main focus is on the differences between Venezuela's "radical populist" parties and Colombia's traditional ones—

in terms of the ways in which they incorporated labor in the first half of the twentieth century and their impact on subsequent regime trajectories. My arguments differ in that I have chosen a different set of critical junctures as the basis for comparing the two cases and take into account a range of variables. In addition to the parties and party system, I focus on the nature and strength of the central state, as well as on the legacies from the transition pacts, as key variables that explain divergent outcomes over time.

27. Neither Colombia nor Venezuela are included in Malloy and Seligson 1987 or in Mainwaring, O'Donnell, and Valenzuela 1992. The influential collection edited by O'Donnell, Schmitter, and Whitehead (1986), while including a chapter on Venezuela written by Terry Lynn Karl, ignored the Colombian case. Valuable exceptions to this pattern are Linz and Stepan 1978; and Diamond, Linz, and Lipset 1989, both of which include chapters dedicated to both Colombia and Venezuela. More recently, Hagopian and Mainwaring (2005) have also included the two cases in their valuable assessment of the third wave of democratization in Latin America.

28. For reasons having to do with Costa Rica's peculiar transition to democracy, I decided to focus on a paired comparison of Colombia and Venezuela's paradigmatic cases of pacted transition. I have no doubts, however, that a full appraisal of democracy in Latin America should take the Costa Rican experience fully into account.

29. See, e.g., Dix 1994, which includes both Colombia and Venezuela as "successful cases" coming out of the second wave. According to Dix, "Successes indicate polyarchies that have survived from the date of their inauguration . . . to the present" (94).

30. See also Karl 1990: 19 n. 25 for comments that are especially relevant to an understanding of the concept of structured contingency.

31. The new institutionalism as a novel approach in the social sciences first developed in economics. For an example, see North 1990. It has spread to other social sciences, including political science, where it has developed in two related although different variants: one is the rational choice approach, closer to neoinstitutional economics; the other is historical institutionalism, as developed by authors such as those included in the volume edited by Steinmo, Thelen, and Longstreth (1992). See also Hall and Taylor 1994; Thelen 2003. For an example of historical institutionalism as applied to Latin America, see Mahoney 2001.

32. Mahoney (2003) provides an excellent discussion of the contrast between these two theoretical approaches to the study of democracy and authoritarianism.

33. The notions of path-dependency and critical juncture used here closely follow those proposed by Collier and Collier (1991) and discussed by Mahoney (2001).

Chapter 1. Oil versus Coffee

1. It was only in 1925 that the value of Venezuelan oil exports surpassed that of coffee exports. Three years later oil exports were worth three times more than all Venezuelan exports combined (Bergquist 1986: 204).

2. As early as 1928 oil was generating 75 percent of Venezuela's export earnings; by 1936 that figure had climbed to 90 percent, where it remained for much of the twentieth century (Bergquist 1986b: 208). See additional data in Tugwell 1975; Valenilla 1975; Baptista and Mommer 1987; España 1989; and Karl 1997.

3. Bergquist (1986b), for example, seeks to explain the evolution and fate of the labor movement. Yet he also makes the broader claim that the export sector's structure and its impact on working-class formation and mobilization is a key to understanding the contemporary social and political histories of these two as well as other Latin American cases.

4. Although Karl begins by declaring that she conceives of the relationship between structure and statecraft as a dynamic one (1986: 196), she rapidly turns to an explanation of political change that is heavily biased in favor of structural variables, in this case the impact of oil. See also her article in the *Latin American Research Review* (1987), where she presents a very similar, if more nuanced, argument about Venezuela's democratization. She later wrote a highly influential book on the politics of oil exporting countries, *The Paradox of Plenty* (1997). In that book, however, the dependent variable shifts from political regime type to the choice of development path and its consequences, a choice that, according to Karl (1997: 16), is made narrower for leaders of countries with vast oil exporting capabilities. Karl's 1997 book is more useful in explaining why oil can lead to economic deterioration and political decay than in accounting for regime type or regime change. In fact, in the book regime type is controlled for by the variety of regimes included in her "most different cases" design rather than figure as an independent or dependent variable of any significant weight. I return to a discussion of her book's many useful insights and contributions to the debate on the politics of oil exporters in chapters 2 and 6.

5. Bergquist (1986b: 204) agrees: "The social forces generated by oil-based economic growth first undermined the legacy of the Gomez dictatorship, then set Venezuela on a path of liberal economic and democratic political development unique in Latin America."

6. In *The Paradox of Plenty* Karl's focus shifts from explaining regime outcomes to explaining policy outcomes in oil-producing countries. The argument put forth there seems far more accurate: the economic and political distortions introduced by the oil boom in the 1970s did great harm to Venezuela's economic and political stability.

7. The fifteen states most reliant on oil exports (where oil reliance is measured by the value of fuel-based exports divided by GDP) are, in descending order, Brunei, Kuwait, Bahrain, Nigeria, Democratic Republic of Congo, Angola, Yemen, Oman, Saudi Arabia, Qatar, Libya, Iraq, Algeria, Venezuela, and Syria (Ross 1999, 2001). Indonesia is another interesting (and recent) exception to this rule (see Karl 1997).

8. Ross (2001) further specified three causal mechanisms whereby oil exerts its antidemocratic influence: the "rentier effect," the "repression effect," and the "modernization effect."

9. It also seems clear that the recent crisis of democracy in Venezuela is associated not only with the decline in oil prices starting in the early 1980s, but rather with the perverse effects of the oil boom of the early 1970s on the state and the parties. See also Ross 2001 on the effects of the oil-exporting state on democracy and Karl 1997. This is an argument that I explore further in the last chapter of this book.

10. See, e.g., Abel 1987; Deas 1993; González 1997a; Hartlyn 1988; Oquist 1978; Posada-Carbó 2006; and Wilde 1978, 1982.

11. Data come from Thorp 1998: 347. See also Palacios 1983; Bergquist 1986b.

12. See Collier and Collier 1991, as well as the work of the Colombian social historian Mauricio Archila (1991).

13. For the case of Costa Rica, see Winson 1989; for Brazil, see Font 1990. Two interesting comparisons of the Central American cases are Williams 1994 and Paige 1997. For a comparison of Brazil and Colombia, see Bates 1997; for Colombia, see Palacios 1983.

14. This is the typical political economy argument for the emergence and sustainability of democracy in Costa Rica (see Winson 1989)

15. This comparison draws from Palacios and Safford 2002: 497.

16. Bergquist (1986b: 210, 267) provides the following data on employment in the oil industry: in 1938 it employed 22,496 workers, and "at its peak in 1948 it numbered about 55,000 blue- and white-collar workers, about three percent of the national work force."

17. My account obviously draws from Collier and Collier (1991) and their perception of the "radical populist" parties of Venezuela as key to understanding regime outcomes in that country.

18. Bergquist (1986b), for example, seems convinced that the struggle for democracy in Venezuela was spearheaded and waged first and foremost by the oil workers. "Venezuela . . . has registered the most impressive record of economic growth and maintenance of democratic political forms in our own time. The social element most maligned in the traditional historiography, the Venezuelan working class, contributed most to this contemporary outcome" (204).

Or, "In the twentieth century, the Venezuelan working class, spearheaded by workers in oil production, emerged as the prime mover behind and principal guarantor of the liberal economic and political order that has distinguished contemporary Venezuela's history from that of the majority of its Latin American neighbors" (205). Collier arrives at a more sobering conclusion: while attempting to remedy an excessive focus on elite actors in transition studies, she admits that in most cases the lower classes were hardly the engines of democratization. She settles for a middle ground that aims at the integration of class-based analysis with strategic and resource-based explanation of regime change. See Collier 1999.

19. On the Venezuelan working class, see Bergquist 1986b. On efforts by both the PCV and the AD to control it, see Ellner 1980.

20. In a related vein, Collier and Collier (1991) have distinguished modes of incorporation as "radical populist" in the Venezuelan case, by contrast with Colombia's electoral mobilization by traditional parties.

21. The argument in favor of an important role for the middle classes in the process of democratization is forcefully presented by Huber Stephens (1989: 300–305). It also finds abundant empirical confirmation in the volume by Rueschemeyer, Stephens, and Stephens (1992), though their argument tends to diminish the importance of the middle sectors in favor of the working classes.

22. In this respect my account differs slightly from that of Collier and Collier (1991), who attach enormous importance to the role of the working class in determining future political outcomes in the eight Latin American cases they consider. For a view on the importance of middle-class sectors that coincides with mine, see Levine and Crisp 1999. For the role of the middle sectors in democratizing coalitions, see also Yashar 1997.

Chapter 2. Beyond Oil and Coffee

1. The analysis presented in this book seeks to demonstrate that it is useful to locate strategic considerations in a macrohistorical context. Despite some tension between scholars who analyze the strategic choices of politicians (labeled rational choice) and those who study the historical development of political institutions (historical institutionalism), I see no fundamental incompatibility between these two approaches. See also Mahoney 2001.

2. See Huber Stephens 1989; Collier and Collier 1991; Mainwaring and Scully 1995; Mainwaring 1999.

3. See Chalmers 1977; Huber Stephens 1989; Collier and Collier 1991; Rueschemeyer, Stephens, and Stephens 1992; Cavarozzi 1991; O'Donnell 1994a; Linz and Stepan 1996a.

4. In his study of the importance of timing and sequence in individual cases of state formation, Centeno (2002: 264) concluded, "There are no absolute causal sequences to be found without appropriate attention paid to starting points." My purpose is precisely to pay attention to the initial circumstances and historical sequences through which political development occurred in the two cases under discussion.

5. This is the central theme of the volume edited by Evans, Rueschemeyer, and Skocpol (1985). See also Anderson 1986. I conceive the state as the permanent and differentiated ensemble of organizations (bureaucratic-administrative, legal, extractive, and coercive) located in a given territory, within which it exercises a monopoly on collectively binding decision making, backed by the monopolistic control of the means of coercion. Apart from the work of Max Weber, this definition draws heavily from the conceptual definitions offered by Mann (1984), Anderson (1986), and Hall and Ickenberry (1993). I understand state consolidation as the process whereby the organizations that make up the state become differentiated from society and acquire both the authority to rule over it and a monopoly on coercion. This process of state consolidation precedes, both temporally and functionally, the emergence of the state as a central actor in the economy or in the provision of public welfare. It is also crucial for the establishment and stabilization of democracy.

6. In his seminal article on democratization, Rustow (1970) identified national unity as the single most important background condition for the kind of elite settlements and institutionalized competition that he saw as forming the basis of democracy (350–51). While Rustow focused on citizens' perceptions and attitudes, Huber Stephens (1989: 340) emphasizes the state's effective control over national territory and population. The latter argument is the one I adopt in this chapter. It has also been recently echoed in Tilly's (2007) work on democracy.

7. For Latin America's relative lack of international wars and its impact on state formation, see Centeno 2002. For the impact of geography, demography, population density, and distribution on state formation, see Herbst's (2000) fascinating account of state making and consolidation in Africa. Regarding the relationship between state making and low population densities, it is interesting to note that Latin America, North Africa, and the areas of the former Soviet Union have population densities that are historically much closer to Africa than to Europe. See Herbst 2000: 16, table 1.1.

8. For a similar perception of the difficulties of state formation in Latin America, see Safford 1992; Adelman 2006.

9. See Bergquist 1986a; Huber Stephens 1989: 295; Palacios 1995; Palacios and Safford 2002.

10. See, e.g., Bergquist 1986a; Huber Stephens 1989; Rueschemeyer, Ste-

phens, and Stephens 1992. According to Rueschemeyer, Stephens, and Stephens (1992), the crucial event during this period was the switch to commercial agriculture. However, in some countries (e.g., Colombia and some in Central America) the transformation of agriculture was delayed and the institutional foundations of democracy were laid before the switch to commercial agriculture happened (López-Alves 2000: 42; Mahoney 2001).

11. See also Bergquist 1986a, 1986b. As I will further argue, despite its role in providing the Venezuelan state with additional income with which to solidify its hold on the national territory and population, oil came late in the process of state building in Venezuela and thus cannot be credited with being the main resource on which the state was built. In this sense my account departs from Karl (1997) as well as from Coronil's illuminating account of state formation in Venezuela, "The Magical State" (1997).

12. These are spelled out in López-Alves 2000: 47, table 1.4. Although I agree with the general thrust of the argument, López-Alves's interpretation is not without its problems. For one, it could be argued that searching for democracies in the last quarter of the nineteenth century in Latin America is rather anachronistic. For example, classifying Colombia's regime before 1936 as a "restrictive democracy" is problematic; I would argue that it should be classified as a competitive oligarchy or at best a protodemocracy. Most important, the argument lacks specification of the causal mechanisms linking state formation routes and their political regime outcomes.

13. I have emphasized the significance of this peculiarity of the Colombian case on several occasions. See Bejarano 1994; Bejarano and Pizarro 2004, 2005.

14. After the collapse of Gran Colombia (1830), the territory we now know as "Colombia" was 1,218,830 square kilometers. After the loss of Panama in 1903, the area was reduced to 1,141,748 square kilometers. Colombia's geography is made even more difficult due to the fact that its highly mountainous topography is located in the tropics. For additional evidence of the geographic challenges presented by Colombia's topography, see Palacios and Safford 2002: 15–34.

15. As quoted by Alfonso López Michelsen, in the preface to Deas 1993: 13. See also Deas's essay "Los problemas fiscales de Colombia durante el siglo XIX" (1993) and the argument in Deas 1999: 50 n. 38.

16. For good reason, as López-Alves (2000: 102) argues, the literature on state making in Colombia has concentrated on the last quarter of the nineteenth century, the period known as La Regeneración. Bergquist (1986a) and López-Alves (2000) provide interesting, though contrasting, interpretations of this most crucial period of Colombian political history. See also the opening chapter of Palacios 1995, "Colombia: entre la legitimidad y la violencia."

17. While some (e.g., Leal 1984) have seen class alliances as the key explanation for this occurrence, others (Safford 1977; Bushnell 1993; González 1997a) have disputed a class-based interpretation of the emergence and consolidation of parties in Colombia. López-Alves (2000) offers an account based on the regional elites' need for allies in the struggle to establish local and regional control. The parties were also, indeed, expressions of other social cleavages, most important, the one dividing those who supported a strong role for the church from those who opposed it.

18. "Both the Uruguayan and Colombian militaries lost political space vis-à-vis the political elite," says López-Alves (2000: 12). See also Fernán González 1989a for the importance of parties as state builders.

19. See López-Alves 2000: 119, table 3.2. This is also the number of civil wars and conflicts offered by Deas 1999: 20.

20. At the turn of the century, when total population was about four million, the approximate size of the military was 5,500; see López-Alves 2000: 138, table 3.3. "Partisan and penetrated by the parties, the central army never gained autonomy. . . . Until the 1880s, the army remained small and the military budget low and irregular" (López-Alves 2000: 137).

21. The point has been highlighted by Collier and Collier (1991) to distinguish the Colombian experience in labor incorporation from other cases in Latin America.

22. This point is stressed by Oquist (1978).

23. For a classic statement of the profound impact of colonial legacies, see Stein and Stein 1970; for a critique and recent revival of this debate, see Adelman 1999.

24. The argument draws from Centeno 2002: 156. However, one can see evidence of state building beginning already under Guzmán Blanco's long rule. See also Coronil 1997.

25. After the Federal War the Venezuelan Conservative Party ceased to exist.

26. The "Andinos" Centeno is referring to are the military elites who came from the Andean states (especially Táchira), which included Cipriano Castro, Juan Vicente Gómez, and Gómez's successors, Eleázar López Contreras (1935–41) and Isaías Medina Angarita (1941–45).

27. Ziems 1979 describes the basic components of military reforms undertaken by Gómez.

28. On the link between the oil industry and state consolidation, see also the celebrated work of Coronil (1997), who locates the origins of Venezuela's modern state almost exclusively within the political economy of oil during the Gómez dictatorship. Karl (1997) makes the same claim, by arguing that the oil industry not only coincided with but also fundamentally shaped the emergence of a central state in Venezuela (see esp. chap. 4, "The Making of a Petro-State").

29. See fig. 1.2. In the late 1920s government revenue derived directly from the oil industry was 10 percent of government income (Bergquist 1986a: 207). It was in 1928 that Venezuela became a major oil exporter. By then Gómez had been in power for twenty years.

30. The time gap between state consolidation and the emergence of the oil industry in Venezuela, plus the similarity in terms of the material basis of state power in Colombia and Venezuela lend additional support to my critique of the political economy approach presented in the previous chapter. They also echo Anderson's (1986: 23) contention that "state formation must be disengaged theoretically from the more general process of integration into the global economy, and the causal significance of the presence—or disappearance—of a bureaucratic territorial state for social structural and political organization must be examined independently."

31. Indeed, "the possibility of collecting revenue generated directly or indirectly by the mineral export sector gave the state greater potential autonomy from the local elites" (Huber Stephens 1989: 288).

32. For evidence of this process during Gómez's rule, see Kornblith and Quintana 1981.

33. A cursory comparison of the degree and frequency of violent episodes in the two countries during the twentieth century will suffice: whereas Colombia was plagued by violence, this was not the case in Venezuela. Unfortunately, reliable comparative data on violent crime for the first half of the twentieth century are not readily available.

34. This is Deas's (1999: 46–47 n. 34) rendering of Gómez's correspondence with his envoys in Colombia, derived from a reading of the *Boletín del Archivo Histórico de Miraflores*. Translation is mine.

35. Other accounts choose to privilege the role of social actors and movements in the transition to democracy. This book highlights instead the role of parties in opposing authoritarian rule and in crafting democratic institutions.

36. The programmatic mass party may have also practiced clientelism at the local level. "However, they also had a commitment to a distinctive program at the national level and they attempted to socialize their followers into a particular world view, something absent in the purely clientelistic parties" (Huber Stephens 1989: 305).

37. A claim that was later taken up by Shefter (1994) in his account of parties and the state in the United States.

38. Mainwaring (1999) makes a similar point about the impact of political elites and states on parties and party systems. My point is that beyond any intentional shaping of the party system state and parties shape and reshape each other from the beginning and that this relationship between state and parties explains some of the variation we see in cases such as Colombia and Venezuela.

39. "Incumbent elites might find it necessary to appeal for popular support to sustain their position if they are challenged by an externally mobilized party or if a deep cleavage develops within the governing class and one side undertakes to mobilize outside supporters in an effort to overwhelm the other" (Shefter 1994: 6).

40. Their formation began in the late 1920s and early 1930s, but they were fully acknowledged and legalized only in the 1940s. Acción Democrática (AD) was formally created in 1941; Comité Político Electoral Independiente (COPEI) and Unión Republicana Democrática (URD) were founded in 1946, during the Trienio. For the history of the Venezuelan parties, see Martz 1966; Luque 1986; Ellner 1988; and Kornblith and Levine 1995. Collier and Collier (1991) place these parties in comparative perspective.

41. Since the 1930s the Liberals gained greater presence in the urban areas due to the social transformations taking place and the party's strategy to mobilize and include the urban popular sectors (Palacios 1995). However, this cleavage was never severe enough to draw a clear line between an urban-only Liberal party and a rural-only Conservative party. Both parties had strong constituencies in both rural and urban areas.

42. See Abel 1987; Deas 1993; Oquist 1978; Bergquist 1986a; Sánchez and Meertens 1983.

43. On this, see the numerous works by Eduardo Posada-Carbó, especially *La nación soñada* (2006).

44. A chronology of the periodic coalitions that have taken place since the mid-nineteenth century can be found in Silva 1989.

45. Silva (1989) is the main proponent of such a view. While disagreeing with the application of the consociational model to the Colombian case, Leal (1984) also interprets the Frente Nacional experiment as the natural culmination of a tendency toward coalition among political elites, present since the nineteenth century. Lijphart's (1969) original idea of a "consociational democracy" was first used to describe the Colombian political system by Wilde (1978, 1982) and Dix (1980). It was later developed into a full discussion about the consociational features of the Colombian model by Hartlyn (1988).

46. It was in 1910 that an "oligarchic democracy" emerged in Colombia as a result of a series of constitutional reforms enacted by the bipartisan Constituent Assembly. See Wilde 1978, 1982.

47. One of the two parties totally abstained from going to the polls in each of the following presidential elections: in 1926 the Liberal Party abstained; in 1934, 1938, and 1942 the Conservative Party abstained; in 1949 the Liberal Party abstained.

48. For a historical account of the animosities that ignited the interparty civil war known as La Violencia, see Perea-Restrepo 1996.

49. On this generation's history and political impact, see Velásquez 1979; Acedo de Sucre and Nones Mendoza 1994. On Rómulo Betancourt and the emergence of Acción Democrática, see Carrera Damas 1994.

50. Many insist that the Venezuelan parties were built following a Leninist model. This is only true regarding internal organization, not their ideology or their relationship with their constituencies. It is true that given their clandestine and conspiratory nature they may have followed Lenin's technical advice on how to organize in order to take over state power, thus their vertical, hierarchical, very centralized nature. But regarding their ideology and the type of relationship they established with the urban and rural masses, they followed in the steps of other European and Latin American experiences with populism and mass-based parties. Interview with Juan Carlos Rey, a specialist in Venezuelan political history, Caracas, November 1995.

51. Quoted in Kornblith and Levine 1995: 40 n. 6.

52. A fine discussion of the way Rómulo Betancourt conceived, as early as 1931, the type of party needed in order to transform Venezuelan politics is in Carrera Damas 1994.

53. The qualification applies more neatly to AD than to the other parties. Huber Stephens (1989: 288) offers an explanation of the formation of Venezuelan parties on the basis of class alliances.

54. Such competition happened mainly between the older PCV (founded in 1931) and the emerging AD (founded in 1941) and concentrated first on the control of the organized workers (Ellner 1980).

55. At the end of the Trienio, there were some episodes of interparty violence. Rafael Caldera, COPEI's main leader, who had been appointed attorney general by the Provisional Junta in 1945, resigned in 1946 as a way to protest the abuses of the rank and file of AD, the government party. Allegedly AD was creating militia groups to defend the October Revolution from its enemies. The creation of civilian militias by AD was one of the reasons the military gave for their decision to step back in and put an end to the Trienio experience, to prevent a dangerous spiral of civilian violence. Nevertheless, the situation never went as far as Colombian interparty warfare, and whatever confrontation there was among party followers in Venezuela, it soon disappeared after the 1948 coup.

56. Interview with Edgardo Lander, a renowned Venezuelan intellectual and son of former AD leader, Luis Lander, who went into exile from 1948 to 1958. New York, September 1996.

57. On political learning, see Bermeo 1992.

58. The first expression of this coalition was the Junta Patriótica, which included the PCV. Later, on the exclusion of the PCV, it was made up of three parties, AD, COPEI, and URD.

59. On the lessons of the Trienio experience and the dictatorship, see also Levine 1973; Levine and Crisp 1999.

60. On the breakdown of democracy in Colombia, see Wilde 1980, 1982.

61. This reflection was inspired by Penfold-Becerra (2001), who follows the typology of pacts proposed by Przeworski (1992). While Penfold-Becerra argues that the Venezuelan pact was of the second type, I would argue that it was meant as a coordination mechanism rather than a radical alteration of the incentive structure. Proof of the above is the fact that the electoral rules adopted in 1958 were almost identical to those adopted in 1947 during the Trienio. See chapter 5 for more on this issue.

Chapter 3. Reading Pacts as Political Blueprints

1. See Stepan 1986: 65; Karl and Schmitter 1991: 277–81.

2. This is what Higley and Gunther (1992) have termed "elite settlements," as opposed to elite convergence: whereas the latter implies a gradual, incremental, maybe even unintended rapprochement among different factions of the elites, a settlement clearly entails a conscious action on the part of divided elites to attain a solution to their division through the design of mechanisms that allow for elite circulation or power sharing without threatening stability and national unity.

3. The universe of cases is arguably small but growing, with only a few cases in the postwar era (among them Colombia and Venezuela) and many more cases in the third wave (Spain, Brazil, Chile, Uruguay, Poland, Hungary). Cases have increased lately and include the peace settlements in Central America (Nicaragua, El Salvador, and Guatemala) and elsewhere (South Africa, Angola).

4. For similar statements, see also Karl 1990; Karl and Schmitter 1991.

5. Stepan (1986: 65) included both cases under a subtype of transition he called "party-pact" where "the oppositional forces play the major role in terminating the authoritarian regime and in setting . . . the framework for redemocratization."

6. As modeled by O'Donnell, Schmitter, and Whitehead in their now-classic "Tentative Conclusions about Uncertain Democracies" (1986).

7. The table excludes those cases where democracy was imposed by an external actor after a defeat in war, such as Germany or Japan, since those have been rather infrequent in Latin America, with the probable exception of Panama in 1989. The various subtypes are illustrated by listing a number of cases under each one, but this list is by no means exhaustive.

8. See O'Donnell and Schmitter 1986; Stepan 1986; Karl 1990; Karl and Schmitter 1991; Mainwaring 1992; Hagopian 1990, 1992.

9. Commenting on Brazil's and Argentina's similar evolutionary trajectories despite very dissimilar transition paths, Hartlyn (1998: 111) argues that "continuities from the past and urgent problems of the present, . . . more than institutional realities defined as a 'mode of transition,' appeared to be at least as important—and probably more important—in determining the evolution of democratic politics in these countries." On the topic of missed opportunities, see also Cavarozzi 1991.

10. With few exceptions, such as Hagopian 1990, 1996a; Munck and Skalnik Leff 1999; and more recently Sánchez 2003; Corrales 2005; Encarnación 2005.

11. See O'Donnell and Schmitter 1986: 38; Karl 1986, 1990; Karl and Schmitter 1991; Hagopian 1990. Przeworski (1992) also warns about the exclusionary character of pacts that can lead to "cartels of incumbents against contenders." See Levine 1988 for a rebuttal of such criticisms.

12. See Przeworski 1986, 1992; O'Donnell and Schmitter 1992; Levine 1988.

13. See Huber Stephens 1989: 322–23. By contrast, in the cases of transition by collapse, the likelihood of fuller, less restricted democracies appears greater because of the inability of the armed forces to impose its conditions on the subsequent civilian government as they exited from power. At the same time, the risks of authoritarian reversal were also greater in these cases since the military, forced to exit from power, could not count on any of the guarantees that pacted democracies typically provide the military-as-institution.

14. The contrast between the two cases is developed in Fishman 2002.

15. Due to its exceptional path toward democracy Costa Rica managed to carry out a series of reformist policies at the beginning of its democratic period (see Yashar 1997).

16. This short survey of cases seems to suggest that the presence or absence of substantial socioeconomic reform may depend on other factors, different from the mode of transition. Substantive pacts are difficult to enforce. So long as the structure for democratic participation and competition is in place, a democratic polity should provide the necessary room for debate and reform of specific clauses limiting the scope of socioeconomic reforms. Hagopian (1996a) admits this possibility in her latest analysis of Brazil's democratic evolution.

17. For this strand of argument, see Przeworski 1991: 98–99.

18. She cites Italy in 1876, Colombia, and Brazil as cases in point.

19. In a more nuanced presentation of her argument, in her 1996 book, Hagopian admits the possibility of positive change even in the most restricted settings. On the recent evolution of Brazilian democracy, see Weyland 2005.

20. The U.S. anticommunist campaigns, typical of the Cold War era, proved an important source of pressure toward exclusion of the left across Latin America throughout the period, especially after the Cuban Revolution in 1959.

21. To follow the terminology coined by O'Donnell and Schmitter 1986: 54.

22. The elitist character of this mobilization seems stronger in the Colombian case. Nevertheless, for both countries I found that the "popular upsurge" was neither as popular nor as spontaneous as the mythology that surrounds it, as well as the literature on democratization, would both affirm. In Venezuela there may have been a higher degree of popular participation given that the parties had stronger links with popular sectors such as the peasants and working class (grouped in the FCV and the CTV, respectively) than the parties in Colombia. In both cases, however, this "resurrection of civil society" or "popular upsurge" was organized and led, from beginning to end, by the political parties, who played a crucial role throughout the transition, including this mobilization phase. This seems to contradict the sequence posited by O'Donnell and Schmitter (1986) in their transition model, according to which there is first a resurrection of civil society, which culminates in a spontaneous popular upsurge. In their view it is only after that point, when elections are in sight, that parties become part of the political landscape and the action shifts from civil society to political society (48–58).

23. I do not say "fully competitive" since, as we shall see, the Colombian pacts imposed heavy restrictions on competition, thereby preventing the holding of truly open and competitive elections in that country from 1958 to 1974. The Venezuelan pacts also implied some restrictions on competition, at least during the first presidential term.

24. For a definition of a complete democratic transition, see Linz, Stepan, and Gunther 1995.

25. My expression "Twilight of the Tyrants" in the heading of this section is borrowed from *The Twilight of the Tyrants* (1959), by the journalist Tad Szulc.

26. For the complete Spanish transcription of the Declaration de Benidorm, see Cámara de Representantes 1959: 12–16.

27. Bermeo (1990: 368) reinforces this point by stating that "authoritarian regimes will not be transformed unless someone presents a 'preferable' and (to be more specific) 'feasible' alternative."

28. Colombian social scientists have produced a wealth of analyses on this dramatic episode of political violence. A valuable compilation of articles by influential scholars is Sánchez and Peñaranda 1986. Among those, perhaps the most important academic work on the topic has been produced by the historian Gonzalo Sánchez (1984, 1985, 1986). See especially his work with the anthropologist Donny Meertens, "Bandoleros, Gamonales y Campesinos," in Sánchez and Meertens 1983.

29. For an interpretation of the Venezuelan process based primarily on a political learning approach, see Levine 1973, 1978. Bermeo (1992) makes a strong case for a political learning approach.

30. The full transcript of this pact can be found in Cámara de Represent-antes 1959: 16–29.

31. See Plaza 1978; Stambouli 1980; López-Maya, Gómez Calcano, and Maingón 1989; and *Revista SIC* (January–March 1958).

32. From the 1952 elections onward, Pérez Jiménez concentrated power in his own hands and the regime became a more personalized military dictator-ship. It then started to distance itself from the military institution. Pérez Jiménez increasingly relied on his civilian advisers, Laureano Valenilla-Lanz and Pedro Estrada, and on the security apparatus, Seguridad Nacional (SN). The military resented the increasing autonomy of the SN. The SN even began to repress members of the army. This fact contributed to the alienation of the army's support for Pérez Jiménez. In Colombia the division among different military factions—stemming from the contradiction between the personal aspirations of the dictator and his closer allies on the one hand and the interests of the military qua institution on the other—was a key reason for the split. In addition, the military was wary of the dictator's effort to politicize the corps and use it as an instrument to build an autonomous political force. Rojas Pinilla's first attempt in this regard was Movimiento de Acción Nacional (MAN); he then tried to form the Tercera Fuerza (Third Force), beyond the bipartisan divide, which was to be a coalition of the armed forces and "the people." When former President Ospina resigned from the presidency of ANAC, the split between the military and its civilian allies became open and clear, and the Ospinistas then joined the opposition. This decision was provoked by the attempt on the part of Rojas Pi-nilla to perpetuate his personal rule for four more years. With political support for the regime waning and an increasingly strong opposition, the military be-came wary of supporting the government by force and finally abandoned the dictator.

33. As Linz, Stepan, and Gunther (1995) have argued, provisional gov-ernments can pose special problems for democratic transitions. If the provi-sional government quickly sets a date for elections and rules as a neutral care-taker, this can be a rapid and efficacious route toward democracy. However, if the provisional government claims that its actions in overthrowing the govern-ment give it a legitimate mandate to make fundamental changes (including postponing democratic elections), it can set into motion a dangerous dynamic placing the democratic transition at peril. They write, "The most dangerous course of action is the postponement of elections *sine die*" (87). On the potential problems of provisional governments, see also Shain and Linz 1992, 1995.

34. The difference between liberalization and democratization is spelled out in O'Donnell and Schmitter 1986.

35. The junta was headed by General Gabriel Paris (Rojas Pinilla's former minister of war) and composed of General Luis Ordóñez (former head of the Intelligence Service [SIC]), General Deogracias Fonseca (former commander

in chief of the police), Admiral Rubén Piedrahita (former minister of public works), and General Rafael Navas Pardo (former commander general of the army).

36. Interview with Juan Carlos Rey, Caracas, November 1995. See also Burggraaff 1972.

37. For a detailed description of the negotiation process, see Hartlyn 1988.

38. See Pact of Punto Fijo, originally published in *Documentos que hicieron historia* and reprinted in López Maya, Gómez Calcano, and Maingón 1989: 111–14.

39. These conversations are detailed in Vasquez Carrizosa 1969.

40. See the full transcription of all these documents in Cámara de Representantes 1959.

41. Regarding this Constitution and its relationship to the 1947 Constitution, see Kornblith 1989b, 1991. See also Corrales 2006b.

42. On the implicit agreements between the parties and the military in Colombia, see chapter 4; see also Leal 1994.

43. This issue is fully treated in chapter 4.

44. Called "Convenio entre Venezuela y la Santa Sede," signed on March 6, 1964. The complete document appears as Anexo N° 4 in López Maya, Gómez Calcaño, and Maingón 1989: 119–23.

45. For a comparison, see Levine 1981. On the Venezuelan church and its role during the transition, see Levine 1973. On the Colombian church, see Wilde 1980; Abel 1987; González 1989a, 1997b.

46. This was, indeed, a prelude to the role that the Catholic Church would play in later transition processes (in southern Europe, the Southern Cone, and Eastern Europe) during the third wave of democratization.

47. The pact, titled "Workers-Employers Agreement," was signed by the Venezuelan Federation of Chambers and Associations of Commerce and Production (Federación Venezolana de Cámaras y Asociaciones de Comercio y Producción) as representative of the business sector and the Unified Union Committee (Comité Sindical Unificado) as representative of organized labor, on April 24, 1958. Published in *El Nacional,* April 25, 1958, 1, and reprinted in López Maya, Gómez Calcaño, and Maingón 1989: 109–10.

48. This contrast is elaborated in chapter 1. See also Bates 1997.

49. In Colombia there was no explicit pact with the business groups. However, Bagley (1984) has argued that there was an implicit agreement whereby a project of rapid capitalist economic modernization would be implemented. On the role of the business sectors in democratic transitions, see Cardoso 1986; Kaufman and Haggard 1995. On interest representation in Colombia, see Bailey 1977. See also Hartlyn 1988, 1993.

50. In addition to Encarnación's emphasis on the inclusiveness of the pact-making coalition or cartel, I make a case for an emphasis on the contents of the pacts, as well as their duration and degree of institutional entrenchment, as relevant to explaining outcomes. I disagree, however, with Encarnación's reading of the evidence coming from Venezuela. That the Venezuelan "bargaining cartel" was much more inclusive and politically diverse than he acknowledges in his article (2005) will become readily apparent in the pages that follow.

51. Initially it even included the PCV. The party was subsequently marginalized and finally excluded from the negotiations. This issue is discussed further in chapter 4.

52. This was the first time women were allowed to vote in Colombia. The complete text of the plebiscite appears in Cámara de Representantes 1959: 45.

53. This contrast between the two cases, which emphasizes differences in the type of party organizations and their mobilization strategies, obviously draws from the contrast established by Collier and Collier (1991). Their pioneer volume is a forerunner of the comparison of Colombia and Venezuela, and many of my own arguments are indeed prefigured in that book.

54. Rather than attribute all exclusions to the pact makers, it is important to remember the antidemocratic influences emanating at the time from international factors: the ideological polarization entailed by Cold War and U.S. support for and training of the military. U.S. pressures induced many governments to outlaw Communist parties and thus to allow at best for restricted democracies, even in those cases where these parties played the role of a loyal opposition, abiding by the democratic rules of the game.

55. On the PCV, see Ellner 1980. On the PCC, see Medina 1980.

56. I elaborate on these and other effects of exclusion in chapters 4 and 5.

57. Ellner 1980; 1988; Blanco Muñoz 1980, 1981, 1982; Petkoff 1976, 1986, 1990; Caballero 1988.

58. Even though the Cuban Revolution had a significant demonstration effect all over Latin America, the closer relationship between Venezuela and the Caribbean basin made it especially salient for this country. Venezuela not only exerts a powerful regional influence in the Caribbean but also feels the effects of events in the region more strongly. It is worth noting, for example, that three weeks after the revolutionary triumph, on January 12, 1959, Fidel Castro was in Caracas, celebrating the "Venezuelan Revolution." Colombia, by contrast, is a much more Andean-oriented country. The fact that Bogotá, the political, economic, and administrative center, is situated high in the mountains, at the center of Colombia's large territory, explains some of this country's "Andean orientation" as opposed to Venezuela's "Caribbean orientation."

59. The emergence, development, and end of the guerrilla movement in Venezuela is discussed in chapter 4. See Ellner 1988. See also my interviews with

Teodoro Petkoff, former guerrilla leader, Caracas and Bogotá, 1992, 1993, 1994, 1995, and 1999; and the collection of interviews by Agustín Blanco Muñoz (1980, 1981, 1982).

60. See Gallón 1989; Archila 1996; Medina 1980. See also my interview with Gilberto Vieira, former secretary general of the Colombian Communist Party, Bogotá, June 1996.

61. The Communists, together with the Liberals, had taken up arms and formed as guerrillas since 1949, when President Ospina closed Congress, and the worst phase of La Violencia began. For a history of the cycles of Communist resistance and disarmament and the origins of the FARC, see Pizarro 1991b, 1996a.

62. Encarnación (2005) makes a similar point with regard to Spain: a key to Spain's successful transition and rapid democratic consolidation, he argues, was the inclusion of the left, not only the Socialists (PSOE), but also the Communist Party (PCE).

63. This section is based on a careful reading of the written documents that contain the agreements reached by the parties in the two cases. For Colombia the analysis includes the pacts of Benidorm, March, and Sitges, the text of the plebiscite voted on December 1, 1957, and the text of the Acto Legislativo No 1, approved by Congress on September 15, 1959. For Venezuela it includes the Pact of Punto Fijo, signed on October 31, 1958, by URD, AD, and COPEI; and the Declaración de Principios and the Programa Mínimo de Gobierno, signed by the presidential candidates from AD, URD, and COPEI on December 6, 1958, after the electoral campaign was over.

64. There are, of course, plenty of informal constraints and limitations on political interaction. The point here is that pacts serve to make those limits more visible and firm. I am thankful to Ed Schatz for calling my attention to this important point.

65. Understood, in a restricted sense, as electoral participation.

66. Female suffrage had been introduced in 1954 as part of a populist move by then dictator Rojas Pinilla to attract the female population to his side. However, women did not have the opportunity to vote because there were no elections during the dictatorship. The text of the plebiscite in 1957 ratified this expansion of the franchise and enshrined universal suffrage in the amended constitution. Article No. 1 of the plebiscite read as follows: "Women will have the same political rights as men" (Cámara de Representantes 1959: 42).

67. This is the title of Wilde's (1978) well-known article on Colombia. The point I want to stress here is that Venezuela's pact-making experience fits this label much better than the Colombian one.

68. The pact was signed by Rómulo Betancourt (AD), Rafael Caldera (COPEI), and Jóvito Villalba (URD) in Caldera's home in Caracas, which goes by the name "Punto Fijo."

69. See the transcription from the original pact in López Maya, Gómez Calcaño, and Maingón 1989: 111–12. All citations of the Venezuelan pacts come from this same source. The translation is mine.

70. Apart from the fact that military restiveness remained a threat to be reckoned with, this seems like a special protection clause for AD in case it won the election in the face of resistance on the part of the military.

71. For a similar interpretation of this clause see Corrales's (2005) analysis of the Punto Fijo accords.

72. A full transcription of the MPG can be found in López Maya, Gómez Calcaño, and Maingón 1989: 116–19. Page numbers for quotations from this work are given in parentheses in the text.

73. For example, the need to "defend and value human capital," the need to design a housing policy that would "satisfy the needs of the urban and rural population," or the need to "protect mothers and children" (112).

74. This section closes by affirming that an administrative reform will be undertaken with the aim of enhancing the civil service and that an "implacable struggle" will be waged against embezzlement, influence trading, and all sorts of corrupt practices.

75. First published in *El Nacional,* December 7, 1958, 1.

76. The Declaration reads: "It is necessary to create a wide bipartisan coalition government or a series thereof until the institutions, recreated and consolidated with the decided support of the citizenry, will have the sufficient strength so that the civic struggle can be exercised without fear of coups d'etat or the intervention of external factors, through incorruptible suffrage whose decisions will be definite and respected with no contestation." See the Declaration of Benidorm, signed by Alberto Lleras Camargo and Laureano Gómez in Benidorm, Spain, on July 24, 1956. The full transcription of this pact is in Cámara de Representantes 1959: 12–16.

77. See Manifiesto Conjunto de los Partidos Políticos (Pacto de Marzo), in Cámara de Representantes 1959: 22–23.

78. The Liberal Party had been excluded from power since 1949 when President Ospina Pérez staged a presidential coup and closed Congress, giving rise to a series of authoritarian governments. For the Liberals, supporting a Conservative candidate seemed a small price to pay to be reincorporated in the political game and to have guaranteed access to a coalition government and the power-sharing agreement.

79. See the complete transcription of the Pact of Sitges in Cámara de Representantes 1959: 31–40.

80. Through an act approved following the two-thirds rule, Congress could grant itself exception from that rule for approval of certain legislation and only for periods of a maximum of two years.

81. See the full text of this agreement in Cámara de Representantes 1959: 89–91.

82. This last agreement was later enshrined in the constitution via a constitutional amendment approved by the newly elected Congress on September 15, 1959. The entire pact-making sequence is described in detail and documented in Hartlyn 1993: 81–90. A useful description and analysis is Dávila 2002: 47–75.

83. Article 11 of Legislative Decree No. 247 of 1957 (October 4) about a plebiscite for constitutional reform in Cámara de Representantes 1959: 44.

84. The restrictive effects of this institutional feature can be observed in the congressional discussion of certain important reforms such as the agrarian reform, during the first Frente Nacional government. See *Revista Javeriana,* years 1958, 1959, 1960, 1961, and 1962.

85. See Article 13, "Decreto Legislativo Número 247 de 1957," in Cámara de Representantes 1959: 44.

86. La Violencia of the 1940s stemmed in part from the Conservatives' reaction to the process of incorporation triggered by the República Liberal in the 1930s. See Collier and Collier 1991.

87. See Oquist 1978; Deas 1995; Pécaut 1987; and especially Sánchez 1984, 1985, and 1986; Sánchez and Meertens 1983; and Sánchez and Peñaranda 1986. See also Palacios 1995.

88. In fact, the Colombian traditional parties agreed to restore the institutions existing prior to the 1949 breakdown, including the Constitutional Amendment of 1947. The only changes incorporated—the point of the whole negotiation process extending from 1956 to 1959—were related to the creation of restrictions that would place limits on those previously existing institutions.

89. One of the few exceptions is the recent work by Encarnación (2005), who has rightly highlighted the range of actors or degree of inclusion as a critical variable.

90. On the distributional effects of institutions, see Przeworski 1988, 1991.

91. Hartlyn (1998: 107) makes the point about viewing transitions as opportunities.

92. In both cases the election of constituent assemblies in charge of drafting new constitutions, in 1991 and 1999, respectively, signaled the end of the political era begun with the pacts signed in the 1950s. In the 1990s the political realities that led to establishing these two pacted democracies had been superseded, and regime arrangements required transformation. The political crises in these two countries during the last decade of the twentieth century have shown the need to adapt these political regimes to new problems and challenges and also the need to replace the old coalitions of the 1950s and 1960s, dominated by

the traditional parties, with a new coalition capable of including those formerly excluded. That the Colombian pacts were amenable to change and renegotiation suggests that even well-entrenched pacts do not have an everlasting, unchangeable character. For details on the recent crises and political reforms, see chapter 6.

93. Here I draw from Samuel Valenzuela's (1992) very useful reflection on democratic consolidation.

94. I thank Scott Mainwaring for the comments that inspired this reflection.

Chapter 4. Subduing the Challengers

1. My thanks to William Shakespeare and Ernest Hemingway, respectively, for these apt designations.

2. "Game board" refers to O'Donnell and Schmitter's (1986) view of democratic transitions as "multi-layered chess games."

3. One can, of course, extend these reflections on the military to other state institutions (e.g., the bureaucracy, hegemonic parties) that need to be tamed, disciplined, controlled, and made accountable in order for democracy to thrive. In the case of Latin America, however, the question of subordinating the military has long been and remains a key democratic task.

4. The term *reserved domains* is drawn from Valenzuela 1992.

5. I wish to thank Francisco Leal and Andrés Dávila for their generous and enlightening comments on the section devoted to the military. Any errors remain entirely my own.

6. At the end of this section I briefly discuss the sudden reversal of this trend with the two attempted coups in Venezuela in February and November 1992. Indeed, Venezuela's 1992 military crisis provides evidence that the assertion of civilian supremacy was never fully complete in that case. This fact notwithstanding, it would be foolish to ignore the significant advances made in the late 1950s and all the way up to the late 1980s. Admittedly, however, advances in this regard, like many other aspects of democratic evolution, are always susceptible of shifting in the opposite direction, that is, of suffering sudden reversals or gradual decay.

7. Military autonomy is understood as the power to define goals and make decisions in crucial policy domains (e.g., internal security and external defense) without major interference, influence, or intervention on the part of civilian authorities. For a discussion on various types of military autonomy see Cruz and Diamint 1998.

8. This was the first time in the history of Venezuela that the military was removed from direct control of the state.

9. In the nineteenth century military caudillos were the norm. Government by the military qua institution started in the twentieth century during Gomez's rule.

10. See their declaration in "Itinerario Histórico" (1957). See also the interview with General Gabriel Paris, who once was Rojas Pinilla's minister of war and then became president of the military junta: "Habla Gabriel París Gordillo, único sobreviviente de junta militar que gobernó el país hace 50 años," May 5, 2007, www.eltiempo.com/politica/2007-05-06.

11. For details about this episode, see Burggraaff 1972: 163–65. See also my interview with Juan Carlos Rey, Caracas, November 1995.

12. Article 4 of the plebiscite reads as follows: "The preceding paragraph notwithstanding, members of the Armed Forces can be called to serve in different capacities in public administration." This article in fact opened the door for the military's permanent participation in the cabinet in the Ministry of War (later called Ministry of Defense). See text of the plebiscite in Cámara de Representantes 1959: 43.

13. See Programa Mínimo de Gobierno under the heading, "Fuerzas Armadas" (Armed Forces), in López Maya, Gómez Calcaño, and Maingón 1989: 118. See also the discussion of military pacts in chapter 3 above.

14. Programa Mínimo de Gobierno, in López Maya, Gómez Calcaño, and Maingón 1989: 118.

15. The chief executive, in his or her role as commander in chief, plays a crucial role in initiating and sustaining the process of civilian control of the military. See the last section of chapter 8 in Stepan 1988 (136–45) where he discusses the tasks that the executive branch of the democratic state must attempt to carry out in order to achieve the restructuring of the management of force within the state.

16. Read under the subtitle "Fuerzas Armadas" in the Programa Mínimo de Gobierno," in López Maya, Gómez Calcaño, and Maingón 1989: 118.

17. I wish to thank Jonathan Hartlyn for bringing this point to my attention.

18. See especially the paragraphs dedicated to the military question in the Declarations of Benidorm and Sitges and in the Pact of March, all reprinted in Cámara de Representantes 1959.

19. Rojas Pinilla was put on trial during 1958 and 1959. The Senate issued its sentence on March 18, 1959. See Senado de la República, Comisión Instructora, *El proceso contra Gustavo Rojas Pinilla ante el Congreso de Colombia*, Bogotá, Imprenta Nacional, 1960, cited in Galvis and Donadio 1988: 545.

20. The main reforms regarding the internal reorganization of the military are detailed by Bigler (1981). They are also discussed in Aguero 1995 and more recently in Trinkunas 2002.

21. For details on these changes, see Dávila 1998.

22. A famous speech that has been widely quoted, among others by Leal (1994).

23. See Leal 1994; Dávila 1998. According to Stepan (1988: 14), the adoption of this national security ideology forms part of what he labels "the new professionalism," which provides justification for the military's expanded role in politics.

24. See my interview with General (ret.) Alberto Muller Rojas, Caracas, November 1995.

25. This motive is cited in most accounts of the military coup attempts of 1992. See, among others, Muller Rojas 1992a. See also the letter signed in prison by Lieutenant Colonel Hugo Chávez and Francisco Arias Cardenas, quoted in Ochoa Antich 1992.

26. The speed and efficacy of its adaptation to this new role can be explained in part as a function of the availability of resources on the part of the Venezuelan state. Interview with General (ret.) Alberto Muller Rojas, Caracas, November 1995.

27. Interview with former President Ramon J. Velásquez, Caracas, November 1995. See also various interviews with the former guerrilla leader and now prominent opposition politician, Teodoro Petkoff, Caracas, 1992, 1994, 1995, and 1999. Below I provide a fuller treatment of the issue of guerrilla insurgency in both countries.

28. See my interview with General (ret.) Muller Rojas, Caracas, November 1995.

29. This is precisely why the violent containment of the popular upheaval of February 1989, known as "el Caracazo," marks such a major turning point in Venezuelan politics. The attempted coups of 1992 should be understood not only as an expression of military discontent vis-à-vis the general situation in the country in the early 1990s but also as the military's concrete rejection of the role that was assigned to them during and after el Caracazo. Chapter 6 more fully addresses the watershed events associated with el Caracazo and its lasting influence in Venezuelan politics.

30. For Venezuela, see Article 132 of the Constitution of 1961. For Colombia, see Dávila 1998.

31. This is what Cruz and Diamint (1998: 116) have called "dedicated autonomy."

32. This changed in Colombia in 1991 when major reforms were introduced to obtain a new balance in civil-military relations, more favorable to the

civilian authorities. For the reforms, see Dávila 1998. See also the very valuable account by Colombia's first civilian minister of defense, Rafael Pardo Rueda, "De primera mano" (1996).

33. Interview with General (ret.) Alberto Muller Rojas, Caracas, November 1995.

34. For the reforms and changes introduced since the early 1990s see Leal 1994; Pizarro 1995; Pardo Rueda 1996; Dávila 1998.

35. See the various reports by Human Rights Watch, especially "The 'Sixth Division': Military and Paramilitary Ties and U.S. Policy in Colombia" (2001).

36. See Leal 1984, 1994, 1999; Dávila 1998; Deas 1999.

37. Paradoxically, as Dávila (1998: 25) has argued, the Colombian armed forces were instrumental to the preservation and stability of the democratic regime while simultaneously acting as an obstacle to the deepening of that democracy.

38. For the evolution of the military and civil-military relations in Colombia, see Leal 1984, 1994, 1999; Pizarro 1987a, 1987b, 1988; Borrero 1990; Dávila 1998.

39. See also Trinkunas 2002.

40. For more on el Caracazo and its aftermath, see chap. 6.

41. See their manifesto, "Nos alzamos por la Constitución . . . ," in Ochoa Antich 1992. See also Trinkunas 2002.

42. In May 1961 the Colombian minister of justice asked the prosecutor general of the armed forces to open a formal investigation into the subversive activities of the Movimiento Obrero Estudiantil-Campesino (MOEC). See *Revista Javeriana* 56, no. 276 (July 1961): 10–11. I am referring explicitly to the emergence of revolutionary guerrillas with a distinctly Marxist ideology, program, and strategy, as opposed to the liberal guerrillas who appeared in 1949 and were active until the late 1950s, evolving later into groups of bandits, even with a social or political justification. This last stage was called the "bandolerización" of the guerrilla movement and came to an end by the mid-1960s. See the excellent work by Sánchez and Meertens (1983).

43. The first major Venezuelan guerrilla group, the Movimiento de Izquierda Revolucionaria, formed as a breakaway from the then-dominant political party, Acción Democrática, as a response to the latter's rightward shift. A militant faction of AD, joined later by the excluded PCV, then opted for guerrilla warfare. In March 1962 the minister of defense recognized for the first time the existence of armed guerrilla groups in Aroa, Guanare, and Coro. See *Revista SIC,* no. 244 (March–April 1962).

44. The left was not only made up of their respective Communist Parties. In Colombia there was a small Socialist Party, led by Antonio Garcia and Luis Emiro Valencia and formed mainly by intellectuals, with no mass following of

considerable size. It was severely discredited, however, because of its close collaboration with the populist military regime of Rojas Pinilla. In contrast, the Communist Party opposed the military dictatorship from the beginning. See Zuluaga 1995: 21–22; Archila 1996: 31; as well as my interviews with Gilberto Vieira, Bogotá, 1996; and Jaime Zuluaga, Bogotá, 1996. In Venezuela the left had historically been more diverse; by the time of the transition it was mainly divided between URD, a signatory to the pacts, and the Communist Party, which played a crucial role in the resistance against the military government but ended up excluded from the pacts. See Ellner 1988; Martinez 1980; and my interviews with Teodoro Petkoff, Caracas, multiple occasions.

45. Declaration from the PCC in the 8th meeting of its Plenum, which opened on December 7, 1959, with the attendance of 148 delegates from all over the country, in *Semana,* January 13, 1959, as cited in *Revista Javeriana* 51, nos. 251–52 (February–March 1959): 10. See also my interview with Gilberto Vieira, former secretary general of the PCC, Bogotá, June 5, 1996.

46. The PCV had played a crucial role in the resistance against the Pérez Jiménez dictatorship, especially in the formation of the Junta Patriótica, the party coalition that led the resistance and the popular upheaval before the dictator's downfall. Thus it was deeply resentful about its exclusion from the pacts. Of particular importance is the fact that in the clandestine resistance movement strong links had been built between the rank and file of the parties, especially AD and PCV. When the party leadership, especially Rómulo Betancourt from AD, decided on the exclusion of the PCV, the rank and file of AD reacted against that decision. The young militants who had been together in the underground resistance would join again, a few years later, the guerrilla rebellion against the democratic regime.

47. Interview with Teodoro Petkoff, a leader of the PCV, in Blanco Muñoz 1980: 180.

48. MIR resulted from the first major division of AD, the governing party. It was formed by an important sector of the youth wing of the party that was expelled in 1960 because of its leftist positions and its close relationship with the PCV. See *Revista SIC,* no. 225 (April 1960).

49. As a result of their cooperation in these military rebellions, the PCV and MIR were banned in May 1962.

50. For data on electoral abstention in Venezuela, see fig. 5.1.

51. This group was determined to continue the armed struggle and received the full support of the Cuban government, which viewed the PCV as committing treason against the revolutionary cause. See the book-length interview with Douglas Bravo in Peña 1978; see also the interviews with the most important guerrilla leaders compiled by Blanco Muñoz in a series of volumes titled *La Lucha Armada* (1980, 1981, 1982). See also my last interview with Teodoro Petkoff, Caracas, December 1999.

52. Interview with Gustavo Machado, a leader of the PCV, in Blanco Muñoz 1980: 14.

53. Interview with Guillermo García Ponce, a leader of the PCV, in Blanco Muñoz 1980: 387.

54. Interview with Teodoro Petkoff, in Blanco Muñoz 1980: 235.

55. See interview with Douglas Bravo, in Peña 1978.

56. See Reales et al. 2001 for a comparative study of post-guerrilla politics in Latin America that includes MAS, the Frente Farabundo Martí (FMLN) in El Salvador, the Unión Revolucionaria Nacional Guatemalteca (URNG), and M-19, EPL, Partido Revolucionario de los Trabajadores (PRT), and Movimiento Armado Quintín Lame (MAQL) in Colombia.

57. MAS obtained 5.29 percent of the votes in this election. Together, five leftist parties (URD, PCV, FDP, MEP, and MAS) obtained over 15 percent of the popular vote for legislative elections in 1973. Data is from Kornblith and Levine 1995: 50, table 2.2.

58. According to Gilberto Vieira, former secretary general of the PCC, they asked their supporters to vote for a formula of their own, different from the plebiscite, which called for the reestablishment in Colombia of democratic institutions with freedom and equal rights for all. Votes for that formula were counted as blank votes. Interview, June 5, 1996.

59. According to Vieira, repression against the Communists began during the Ospina administration (1946–50) when then–Minister of the Interior José Antonio Montalvo declared a strategy of "blood and fire" in the Chamber of Representatives. Then came a period of massacres and personal assassinations, until the Communist Party was finally banned from legal politics by the military dictatorship in 1954. Interview, Bogotá, June 5, 1996.

60. See Archila 1991; and sections on Colombia in Collier and Collier 1991.

61. These were located mainly in the Departments of Cundinamarca, Huila, Tolima, Meta, and Caquetá.

62. For details about the intermittent armed mobilization of the Communist peasant communities, see Sánchez and Meertens 1984; Pizarro 1991b. See also my interview with Vieira, June 5, 1996.

63. Although the MRL served as a vehicle for the representation of the excluded left, that was not necessarily an explicit or desired objective of its founding members, especially Alfonso López Michelsen (son of former President Alfonso López Pumarejo). According to López Michelsen, he created the MRL as a group of dissident liberals who opposed the National Front agreements, especially the clause dictating alternation in the presidency. The Communists joined on their own initiative, "dressed up as liberals." Interview, Bogotá, June 18, 1996. See also interview, Vieira, Bogotá, June 5, 1996.

64. Senator Alvaro Gómez Hurtado, the son of former President Laureano Gómez, gave a speech in the Senate on October 25, 1961, in which he explicitly called these areas "independent republics": "It has passed unnoticed that there are in this country a series of independent republics which do not recognize the Colombian State's sovereignty, where the Colombian army cannot go, where it is said that its presence is nefarious, that it scares away the people. . . . National sovereignty is shrinking like a handkerchief: this is one of the most painful phenomena of the National Front." Quoted in Alape 1985: 245; my translation.

65. My translation of the expression, "la combinación de todas las formas de lucha."

66. Commenting on this, Archer (1995: 167) states, "The decision of the major left-wing groups, especially the Communist Party of Colombia (PCC), to play both a military and political role had an extremely negative impact on the long-term growth of the left and other reformist groups as well."

67. For the definition of loyal, semiloyal, and disloyal opposition, see Linz 1978.

68. As noted earlier, Venezuela had a closer relationship to the Caribbean basin than its neighbor, Colombia, which meant that it experienced a stronger impact of the Cuban Revolution in its own domestic politics.

69. As Norbert Lechner (1990) noted, the political debate in Latin America during the 1960s was centered on the question of revolution, not that of democracy. Archila (1996) reminds us that the most divisive debates in the Colombian left during the 1960s and 1970s were about the question of armed rebellion. A true revolutionary was, above all, one who espoused armed rebellion, independently of his or her political project.

70. In Venezuela the radicalization of the left after the Cuban Revolution was especially striking. See Plaza 1978 on the visit of Fidel Castro on January 23, 1959, days before the inauguration of the Betancourt government. After that a radical sector in the PCV was convinced that the road to a socialist revolution had been opened by the overthrow of the military dictatorship and should not stop at the stage of "bourgeois democracy" but should go forward all the way to socialism, as in Cuba.

71. For a schematic presentation of the leftist groups in Colombia (including the guerrillas) during the National Front period, see Archila 1996, esp. fig. p. 32. For a detailed explanation of the emergence of each group and its further evolution, see Pizarro 1986, 1991a, 1991b, 1996a.

72. Mr. Velásquez is a well-known historian and a member of AD who became president in 1993, after the impeachment of President Carlos Andrés Pérez. See interview with Ramon J. Velásquez, Caracas, November 1995.

73. See Pizarro 1996a: esp. chap. 5, "El apoyo campesino y la expansión guerrillera."

74. See Cruz (2005) for a fascinating and related comparison of the Costa Rican and Nicaraguan experiences with democracy and violence. She introduces the concept "prior game"—which is established before the advent and consolidation of democratic politics—as the key to understanding the degree of polarization found in Nicaraguan politics as opposed to the capacity for consensus building among Costa Rican elites.

75. See my discussion in chapter 2 above.

76. See Karl 1986, 1997; España 1989; Rey 1972; Kornblith 1992a, 1992b, 1993c.

77. See my article with Renata Segura, "El fortalecimiento selectivo del Estado durante el Frente Nacional," in *Controversia* (1996).

78. Collier and Collier (1991) have classified the Venezuelan parties, especially AD, as "radical populist" parties, mainly because they acted as the vehicles for the incorporation of both urban workers and peasants. The most compelling work on the links between the Venezuelan parties and the peasantry is Powell 1971.

79. The following remarks on the Venezuelan electoral system draw heavily on Shugart 1992.

80. When asked about why the armed forces had not been able to win the war against the guerrillas during the National Front years, General (ret.) Alvaro Valencia Tovar cited the lack of civilian leadership as the main handicap for a successful counterinsurgency effort. See interview, Bogotá, June 1996.

81. See my interview with Jaime Zuluaga, Bogotá, June 1996.

82. The electoral successes of the M-19 in the 1990s, in particular, its strong showing in the election of the 1991 Constituent Assembly, provide some evidence that there was space for a leftist opposition and that the ongoing armed conflict was, at least in part, the result of a conscious decision on the part of the left to pursue the insurgent strategy—and not simply an inevitable consequence of socioeconomic or political exclusion. More recently, the emergence and relative electoral success of the Polo Democrático Alternativo (PDA) adds weight to this hypothesis.

83. Five guerrilla groups finally negotiated peace agreements with the Colombian government in the early 1990s: M-19, EPL, PRT, MAQL, and the Corriente de Renovación Socialista (CRS). The scenario of the Constituent Assembly provided an unparalleled opportunity for widening the scope of inclusion and representation in the Colombian political system and thus acted as a powerful incentive for negotiation and reincorporation of these groups. See Bejarano 2003.

84. See, e.g., Linz 1978; Linz and Stepan 1978; Hall 1993.

Chapter 5. Institutionalizing Inclusion and Contestation

1. Rather than focus on its components separately, "political society" nicely captures the complex interplay between these institutions.

2. According to Mainwaring and Scully's (1995) count, Colombia had a mean number of parties of 2.1 between 1970 and 1990, and Venezuela's mean number of parties between 1973 and 1993 was 3.0 (see p. 30, table 1.7). By Payne et al.'s measure, between 1978 and 1998 Colombia's effective number of parties was, on average, 2.51; Venezuela's, on the other hand, was 3.69 (see Payne et al. 2002: 145, table 6.10). Venezuela could therefore be classified as a two-and-one-half-party system, standing between bipartism and multipartism, according to Blondel's classification (cited in Mainwaring and Scully 1995: 32).

3. Contrast these figures with Peru's (54.2 percent) and Brazil's (70.0 percent). See Mainwaring and Scully 1995: 8, table 1.1.

4. See Mainwaring and Scully 1995: 17, table 1.6.

5. As Coppedge (1994a, 1994b) has insisted with regard to Venezuela, the overinstitutionalization of a party system may be as problematic as the underinstitutionalization stressed by Mainwaring and Scully (see also Crisp 2000; Corrales 2000; Roberts 2003). Looking at Colombia, Hartlyn (1996a: 176) also noted that "certain kinds of institutionalization over time may become problematic for democracy."

6. For the centrality of parties to Venezuela's political life, see, e.g., Coppedge 1994; Kornblith and Levine 1995: 37.

7. As noted previously, the Communist Party of Venezuela was excluded from the party pacts signed in 1957–58. However, it was not barred from participating in elections. In fact, it participated in presidential and legislative elections in 1958, as well as in the drafting of a new constitution in 1961. It was only after the emergence of the guerrillas in 1962 that the PCV and the MIR (the splinter youth wing of AD) were banned because of their support for the armed insurgency.

8. By "personalistic electoral vehicles," I mean fleeting electoral movements built around a prominent personality, for example, Admiral Wolfgang Larrazábal or Arturo Uslar Pietri.

9. See Kornblith and Levine 1995: 45. They add, "The use of coalitions extended beyond national politics to all levels of organized activity," including trade unions and secondary associations.

10. In 1969 AD's Leoni gave way to COPEI's Caldera; in 1974 Caldera transferred power to AD's Carlos Andrés Pérez. In 1979 Pérez handed the presidency to COPEI's Herrera Campins; again in 1984, Herrera Campins gave way

to the presidency of AD's Lushinchi. With the election of Carlos Andrés Pérez, power remained in the hands of AD for a second period (1989–94) but had to be transferred finally in 1994 to President Caldera who ran this time, not as the candidate of his party, COPEI, but as the candidate of a coalition of opposition parties called Convergencia. The last transfer of power, between Caldera and Hugo Chávez, in 1998, was also peaceful. However, it did not happen between AD and COPEI.

11. The D'Hondt formula uses a system of successive divisors (1, 2, 3 . . .) to allocate seats in sequential order to the political party with the highest average at each iteration until all seats are allocated. The system remained unaltered until 1993, when a mixed-proportional system was introduced: half the national deputies are now elected in single member districts while the other half is still elected according to the rules of the previous PR system. I wish to acknowledge Laura Wills's help clarifying many of the details of the Venezuelan and Colombian electoral systems. For a comparative assessment of Latin America's electoral systems, see Wills Otero and Pérez-Liñán 2005.

12. The closed-list PR system meant that voters selected a party list without the possibility of expressing a preference for individual candidates as no candidates' names were listed on the ballot. Party authorities controlled candidate selection, as well as the order in which candidates were listed. The electorate therefore only had a choice between parties. This centralization of party politics impeded intraparty competition and made legislators accountable to the leadership of their parties rather than to the electorate. The reform introduced in 1993 was conceived as an attempt to bring legislators closer to voters and as a means to reduce the authority of party leaders and the legislators' party-centered behavior.

13. In 1993 MAS became a partner in a coalition government with Convergencia, and the role of the opposition on the left was occupied by la Causa R, which thrived in the late 1980s and early 1990s as a result of political decentralization. In the 1990s, with the decline of the traditional parties and the changes brought about by decentralization and electoral reform, several parties and movements on the left gained a new salience. For a detailed account of the rise of la Causa R, see López Maya 1994; Boudon 1997.

14. See Petkoff 2000, as well as his editorial pieces in the opposition newspaper *Tal Cual*.

15. Indeed, the sudden and steep decline in electoral participation since 1988 was one of the first warning signs of the impending crisis.

16. This realignment occurred around the polarizing figure of President Alvaro Uribe Velez, who took office in 2002. In the longer run, however, after Uribe leaves center stage, this might prove an ephemeral phenomenon.

17. In creating the National Front the political elite sought to break the pattern of partisan competition and violence that began a century before. See

Archer 1995: 177. For a detailed description of this fascinating process, see chapter 3 above as well as Hartlyn 1988; Dávila 2002.

18. To be sure, the transformation of the traditional parties owes a great deal to longer-term transformations of the Colombian state and society since the mid-twentieth century. My main interest here is to emphasize the degree to which they responded to the institutional transformations brought about by the National Front pacts of 1957–59.

19. See Mainwaring and Scully 1995: n. 52; Mainwaring 1993; Hartlyn 1994.

20. Local and regional elections were opened up to free competition in 1972 thanks to the constitutional reform carried out in 1968. National elections had to wait until 1974 to be reopened again.

21. Some have assimilated the Colombian two-party coalition of those years with the Mexican PRI.

22. Until 2003 the members of the Colombian legislature were elected using a proportional representation system with districts of varying magnitude. Candidates were presented in party lists, and each political party could present simultaneously an unlimited number of lists as well as an unlimited number of candidates on each list. Electors voted for the entire list rather than for individual candidates and could not select their preferred candidate on the list. Technically, the lists were closed and blocked. Seats were allocated using the Hare (quotient) formula, a set of quotas (calculated by dividing valid votes between number of seats) to distribute seats, with parties receiving one seat for every full quota won. There was no electoral threshold. See Wills Otero and Pérez-Liñán 2005.

23. Because of these features, Coppedge (1994a) has aptly labeled the Venezuelan regime a "partyarchy."

24. For similar views of the Colombian party system, see Hartlyn 1988, 1998.

25. One of the most important institutional legacies from the transition is of course the electoral system enshrined in the pacts. Electoral rules, as we know, are quite effective at shaping the parties and the party system.

26. For more on this issue, see the discussion by Hartlyn in *Presidentialism and Colombian Politics* (1994).

27. A cursory look at the list of decrees issued under a state of siege by the Colombian Executive during the National Front years gives the impression that the emergency powers given to the president by this constitutional emergency figure were used as frequently to solve the deadlock between the presidency and Congress as they were used to repress the mounting social and political opposition to the National Front coalition. This impression seems to be corroborated by the fact that one of the main objectives of the 1968 constitutional reform was

to further strengthen the presidency, endowing it with the mechanisms to solve stalemates with Congress in its favor. On the uses and abuses of emergency powers in Colombia, see Gallón 1979.

28. For an excellent discussion of the relationship between the president and Congress in Colombia, see Archer and Shugart 1997.

29. For a longer discussion on this point, see Kornblith and Levine 1995.

30. This expression is used in reference to Huntington's (1968) treatment of the concept of institutionalization. For a searing critique of the mode of institutionalization of Venezuela's parties and party system, see Coppedge 1994a.

31. It was the coincidence of the oil boom with the central role assigned to the parties that reinforced a perverse pattern of institutionalization of the party system in Venezuela. See Karl 1997; Roberts 2003.

32. For a lengthier discussion of the elements leading to Venezuela's recent political crisis, see chapter 6.

33. The effective number of parties measure climbed from 2.51 to 3.17 in the late 1990s. See Payne et al. 2002: 145, table 6.10; see also Pizarro 2006; Pizarro and Bejarano 2007.

34. See Kornblith 1998 and Penfold-Becerra 2001 on Venezuela's electoral reforms.

35. Since his second reelection in late 2006, Chávez began turning his electoral vehicle, MVR, into the Venezuelan United Socialist Party (PSUV). The effort to build a single party of the left was resisted by many members of his coalition, including the PCV and Podemos (the splinter group from MAS that has supported Chávez's government).

36. In the latest presidential election (December 2006), the opposition managed to agree on a single candidate, Manuel Rosales, and obtained 38 percent of the vote. In a recent referendum to decide on a constitutional reform proposed by President Chávez (December 2007), the opposition came together and defeated the government's proposal with 51 percent of the vote. Again in September 2010 the opposition gathered together to win 51 percent of the vote in legislative elections.

37. Combined, AD and COPEI went from controlling 86.4 percent of legislative seats in 1978 to controlling 22.4 percent in 2000 (Payne, Zovatto G., and Díaz 2006: 173, table 6.2).

38. Together these two parties controlled 97.5 of legislative seats in 1978 and just 46.3 in 2002 (Payne, Zovatto G., and Díaz 2006: 173, table 6.2).

39. The percentage of those answering "not close" was 59.16 in Colombia and 61.96 in Venezuela (data from Payne et al. 2002: 136, table 6.3).

40. See also the volume edited by Mainwaring, Bejarano, and Pizarro Leongómez, *The Crisis of Democratic Representation in the Andes* (2006), especially the chapters by Tanaka (47–77) and Pizarro (77–99).

Chapter 6. From Exceptions to Rules?

1. From the early 1980s there was a rapid expansion of the so-called para-military groups, best characterized as vigilantes in that they are organized, extra-legal groups that take the law into their own hands (Cubides 1999). These groups employ different operational tactics and are of diverse social origin, rang-ing from peasants legitimately organized in "self-defense" against the guerrilla's predatory practices to random hired killers and mercenaries. There are also so-cial "cleansing" groups (primarily in urban areas), death squads, and bands of right-wing rural guerrillas (in the style of the Nicaraguan Contras). A noticeable change in the development of paramilitary groups—apart from their unusual growth (estimates are that they increased their ranks from 650 men in 1987 to 8,000 in 2000)—was the emergence of an organization that tried to centralize and control these unruly vigilante groups. Since the mid-1990s the United Self-Defense Groups of Colombia (AUC) emerged as a coordinator of antiguerrilla forces (similar to the former Simon Bolívar Guerrilla Coordinating Group). The AUC served as an umbrella organization for small and large vigilante groups act-ing with similar intentions: to combat the guerrillas and defend the "establish-ment" at all costs. Since 2003 the AUC was involved in a controversial negotiation with the government of President Uribe.

2. "Most analysts have viewed Colombia since 1958 as a qualified democ-racy, using adjectives such as 'controlled,' 'oligarchic,' 'traditional bipartisan elit-ist,' 'near polyarchy,' or 'restricted'" (Hartlyn and Dugas 1999: 251).

3. This section draws on several of my previous works on Colombia's po-litical development. In particular, see Bejarano 2001, 2003, 2006; Bejarano and Pizarro 2004, 2005; Pizarro and Bejarano 2007.

4. "A semi-democratic government or restricted democracy refers to a ci-vilian government elected under reasonably fair conditions, but with significant restrictions in participation, competition and/or the observance of civil liber-ties" (Mainwaring 1999a: 14).

5. Mainwaring (1999a), for example, correctly classifies the Colombian re-gime as "semidemocratic" in two different periods of its contemporary history. His decision to classify the Colombian regime as "democratic" between 1974 and 1990 is somewhat questionable, given that many of the formal and informal restrictions put in place by the National Front were still in place after 1974 and were only abolished with the 1991 Constitution. Despite this, I basically agree with his classification of Colombia as semidemocratic during most of the second half of the twentieth century. The problem lies in the lack of differentiation be-tween these two periods, which seems critical in my opinion.

6. Colombia's Freedom House scores are a case in point. A careful look at table 8.1 in Bejarano and Pizarro 2005 clearly shows that while the country's general rating has worsened notably since 1989–90, the deterioration of civil liberties has been more marked and sustained than that of political rights. In fact, the latter dimension presents variations that are difficult to interpret as a steadily worsening trend: there have been improvements after 1991 and irregular variations since 1994.

7. "The claim of liberal democracies to be such rests on their well established and accessible procedures for protecting the liberties of individual citizens" (Ware 1992, cited in O'Donnell 1999a: 156 n.16).

8. Let us recall the definition offered in the introduction to this book: the four attributes that constitute the core of the contemporary consensus about democracy are (1) inclusion of the majority of the adult population through universal suffrage; (2) selection of top political leaders (president and parliament, at least) through competitive, free, clean, and regular elections; (3) respect for and effective protection of civil rights and liberties; (4) the ability of elected authorities to govern without being subject to external controls or vetoes by nonelected actors (such as the military). See Dahl 1971; Collier and Levitsky 1997; Mainwaring 1999a; Mainwaring, Brinks, and Pérez-Liñán 2001.

9. For a summary of party reforms, see Dugas 2000. For an evaluation of two decades of political reform, see Pizarro and Bejarano 2007. On the 1991 Constitution, see Dugas 1993; Gómez 2000; Bejarano 2001.

10. Only two guerrilla groups remain active, the FARC (formed in 1964) and the ELN (formed in 1965).

11. Another troubling figure is the number of people (4.7 million) who have migrated abroad in the past few years. This represents over 10 percent of the total population. Both data on migration were found at the International Organization for Migration (IOM) webpage: www.iom.int/jahia/page451.html (accessed June 7, 2007).

12. The process became evident from 1977 on and continued without pause during the Turbay Ayala administration (1978–82). Efforts by the next three governments (1982–1994) to subordinate the military were only partly successful and not without reversals. See Pardo Rueda 1996; Dávila 1998; Leal 1994, 1999.

13. In contrast to those who argue that the exercise of citizenship is incomplete or impractical when there is socioeconomic exclusion or inequality, I argue that universal access to certain basic rights (e.g., the right to life, to physical integrity, and to safety)—distinct from the distribution of socioeconomic rights and opportunities—is also a fundamental dimension of citizenship.

14. According to Echandía (1999), between 1989 and 1999, 138 mayors and 569 members of Congress, departmental assemblies, or city councils were

assassinated, along with 174 public officials in other positions. More recently, starting in 2002 and again in the 2006 electoral contest, there have been denunciations of widespread electoral manipulation by the paramilitaries in local, regional, and even national elections, especially in the Atlantic Coast region of the country.

15. The Colombian case is clearly one of gradual democratic erosion and not one of an unexpected breakdown leading to an authoritarian reversal. Mainwaring (1999a: 37) has underlined the relevance of distinguishing between processes of breakdown and erosion of democracy.

16. Between August 1989 and April 1990 three presidential candidates were assassinated. Among these was the Liberal candidate with the greatest chance of becoming president, Luis Carlos Galán. After his assassination, apparently planned by the drug mafia, the Barco government unleashed a major offensive against drug trafficking (the "war on drugs"). This in turn led to a bloody wave of narcoterrorism against the Colombian government and society. In Coppedge and Reinicke's (1990: 63) analysis of the year 1985, Colombia was classified as a democracy. Some years later Mainwaring (1999a: 16) classified it as a "semidemocracy," marking the turning point at 1990. Freedom House's data indicate that the passage from "free" to "partially free" status took place between 1989 and 1990. According to Hartlyn and Dugas (1999), the period of crisis began in the mid-1980s, with some ultimately failed attempts at recuperation in the early 1990s.

17. *Particularism* is the term coined by O'Donnell to name these political practices, which are so common throughout Latin America.

18. Moreover, recent studies show that the independent ("untied") urban vote has increased, especially but not exclusively in presidential elections. In addition, political, ethnic, and religious minorities—which do not base their vote on clientelism or the use of public resources—have had increasing access to the representative system since 1991. See Bejarano and Dávila 1998.

19. Until 2003 (when a new reform was passed) the Colombian electoral system was based on proportional representation, closed and blocked lists, and a Hare distribution formula (see chap. 5). However—and herein lies the main problem—each party or movement could put forth an indefinite number of lists or candidates in each electoral district. In a context of party disorganization, this led to a widespread "war of residuals" that aimed to obtain the largest possible number of seats with the least number of votes. By presenting multiple lists in various electoral districts, each party or movement split its own vote, "giving up the possibility of obtaining seats by quotient (but maximizing) the possibility of obtaining them by residual" (Gutiérrez 1998: 222). A document commissioned by the Ministry of the Interior, authored by a prestigious group of consultants (Arturo Valenzuela, Josep Colomer, Arend Lijphart, and Matthew Shugart),

stated in 1999 that "Colombia's current electoral system is the most 'personalistic' in the world" ("Informe de la Consultoría Internacional" 1999: 237).

20. According to the norms regulating party activity, a party only needed the support of one member of Parliament, 50,000 votes, or 50,000 signatures to be legally recognized by the National Electoral Council. Thanks to this lax requirement, any electoral micro-enterprise (whether a Liberal or Conservative personalistic faction or a "third force") could have free access to television, obtain state financing, and indiscriminately gather endorsements for electoral campaigns. See Pizarro 1996b, 2006; Pizarro and Bejarano 2007.

21. Both the numbers of political parties and the movements registered with the National Electoral Council as well as the number of lists for the Senate and the Chamber of Deputies dramatically increased in the decade between 1991 and 2000. See chap. 5, esp. table 5.5.

22. Between 1963 and 1983 the homicide rate per 100,000 inhabitants averaged 24.8.

23. Colombia's levels of violence are unusually high, even compared to other Latin American countries. In the 1990s only El Salvador's homicide rate surpassed that of Colombia. See Levitt and Rubio 2000: 3–4.

24. As suggested by Mauceri (2004: 146–47, 156–59), the absence of a coherent political project shared by the elites is perhaps one of the most important causes of the weakness of the Colombian state. Starting with the Betancur government (1982–86), and because of the negotiation policy advocated by the president, a deep division among the elites became evident: while some sectors insisted on a negotiated settlement to the armed conflict, others preferred to privatize and decentralize the counterinsurgency effort by supporting paramilitary groups and bypassing the role of the state in keeping order within its borders. The so-called paramilitary armies in Colombia and the abdication of power by some sectors within the state are the consequence of a political split among the elites.

25. By making an argument about the "partial collapse" of the state, I wish to differentiate Colombia from those cases where there has been a total collapse of the state such as Somalia and other cases treated in the contemporary literature on "failed states" (see Zartman 1995; Rotberg 2002). The only case in Latin America that comes close to being classified as a failed or collapsed state is Haiti.

26. This was the case in various regions within the mid-Magdalena, in the north of Antioquia, the Department of Córdoba, and most of the Atlantic coast.

27. The most renowned case but by no means the only one was the presidential campaign of Ernesto Samper in 1994, which was partially funded by the Cali Cartel. More recently more than seventy members of Congress have been indicted for their ties with paramilitary groups and narcotrafficking networks in what has become known as the "parapolítica" scandal. At least half of them are undergoing trial.

28. This trend toward militarization of the fight against drugs has gone even further since the U.S. Congress approved funding for "Plan Colombia" in year 2000. For the deleterious impact of U.S. policy on the Andean states, including Colombia, see Mason 2000; Youngers 2004; Mason and Tickner 2006.

29. Since 2000 Colombia has received close to $5 billion in security aid from the United States, making it the largest recipient of military aid outside of the Middle East.

30. In terms of the "war on drugs"—allegedly the main goal of U.S. aid—the results have been far more disappointing.

31. For a similar approach, see Tanaka's account of the crisis of democracy in Peru under Fujimori, "Peru 1980-2000: Chronicle of a Death Foretold?" (2005).

32. See "Boletín Demográfico. Edición Especial. Urbanización y Evolución de la Población Urbana de América Latina, 1950–1990," CELADE, May 2001, Cuadro 32, p. 135.

33. See Naím 1993: 24; 2001: 21. It seems increasingly difficult to have access to credible social indicators data on Venezuela. Despite increased social spending during Hugo Chávez's over ten years in office, poverty indicators seem to have remained relatively unchanged. See Penfold-Becerra 2007.

34. There is, of course, plenty of corruption in Venezuela, as in many other developing countries, especially those where the state has direct access to abundant resources. Nevertheless, while corruption remains a problem and poses an obstacle to development, the diagnosis of Venezuela's ills as caused entirely or mainly by corruption has been exaggerated to the point of becoming a hindrance to understanding the real causes behind the crisis. As Naím (2001: 23) has pointed out, "Corruption is a symptom, not a cause, of the country's problems."

35. On the dramatic events of February 27 and 28, 1989, see the special editions of *Cuadernos del Cendes,* no. 10, Segunda Epoca (January–April 1989); and *Politeia,* no. 13 (1989). See Kornblith 1998: chap. 1. A careful consideration of the policy dilemmas of the second Pérez administration is in Naím 1993. For an explanation of the failure of market reforms in Venezuela that puts the accent on the relations between the president and his party, see Corrales 2002.

36. Translation is mine. For dramatic testimonies on the events of February 27 and 28, 1989, see Araujo et al. 1989.

37. See table 1 in Briceño-Leon 2006 (p. 321). The same author reports that the official data on the homicide rate have not been made available by the authorities since 2004 (323).

38. To a great extent this progressive corrosion of the Venezuelan state is attributable to the pernicious dependence on oil revenues. Rather than the fall in oil prices, it is the boom-and-bust cycles that introduce major economic and policy distortions. As argued by Karl (1997), booms contribute to creating and

consolidating certain perverse policy practices that are hardly reversible when the rents stop flowing.

39. The solution to this impasse was eventually achieved thanks to a providential provision that allowed for the enactment of a judicial process against President Pérez. In Colombia also, the presidential system had a lot to do with the crisis unleashed after the tainted 1994 election of Ernesto Samper. This dimension of these crises could have been avoided had the regime counted on a safety valve to avoid the problems created by the fixed presidential term. As Linz and Valenzuela (1994a, 1994b) and others have argued, the rigidities of presidentialism play a significant role in fostering an "impossible" political game that may put democracy in peril. See also Coppedge 1994b: 158.

40. Following O'Donnell's (1992) way of labeling a rapid and unexpected breakdown of democracy. On the coup, see the coup plotters' manifesto, "Nos alzamos por la constitución. Carta de los oficiales del MBR200," dated June 24, 1992, and signed by the leaders of the attempted coup, then in jail. It is included in Ochoa 1992: 7–33. See also the analysis offered by Sonntag and Maingón (1992).

41. This was well captured at the time in the title of a book that labeled the Venezuelan political regime as a "democracy under stress" *(democracia bajo presion)*. The Spanish version was edited in Venezuela by Andrés Serbín, Andrés Stambouli, Jennifer McCoy, and William C. Smith (1993). The English version is titled *Venezuelan Democracy under Stress* (1995). Another compilation of articles useful for comprehending the Venezuelan crisis is Goodman 1995.

42. According to the interim president, Ramón J. Velásquez, when he assumed the presidency Venezuela "was a country that had its institutional bases destroyed" after the two attempted coups. His principal objectives, thus, were to make it to the elections in December, establish the new Congress (January 1994), and inaugurate the new president (February 4, 1994). In his own words, the aim was "to reach the other side of the institutional bridge." See my interview with Velásquez, Caracas, November 10, 1995.

43. The concept "re-equilibration" is taken from Linz 1978.

44. Corrales and Penfold (2007) have characterized it as a "transition toward authoritarianism."

45. An evaluation of Chávez's controversial government is clearly beyond the scope of this book. It is obvious, however, that his election in 1998 (amid the collapse of the party system) and the changes introduced during the constitutional reform of 1999 put an end to an era of Venezuelan democracy, inaugurating a new period in which, despite the president's popularity, the democratic credentials of the regime have been thrown into question. On Chávez, see Gott 2005. For an attempt to explain the rise of Chávez and his hold on power, see Ellner and Hellinger 2004.

46. With good reason, Venezuelans have called the system formed by these two parties "la partidocracia," a term that Coppedge (1994a) translated as "partyarchy."

47. In January 2007, after his second reelection in 2006, Chávez announced his intention to create a new single party, Partido Único de la Revolución Venezolana (later Partido Socialista Unido de Venezuela). Many of his smaller allies, including the Communist Party of Venezuela, balked at the proposal.

48. See Manifesto, in Ochoa 1992: 30.

49. This section on the Constituent Assembly draws heavily from my article with Renata Segura, "Ni una asamblea más sin nosotros!" (2004).

50. For a discussion of the type of regime promised and then created by Chávez, see Coppedge 2003.

51. The PCV was founded in the 1930s; MEP dated from the early 1960s; MAS, a socialist dissidence from the PCV, was founded in the early 1970s; and the PPT was a splinter party from la Causa Radical, a Marxist party founded in the early 1960s.

52. This is a crucial difference separating the Venezuelan experience in constitution making from the Colombian, Ecuadorean, and Bolivian cases.

53. The idea of the "cheering crowd" as applied to Venezuela comes from Scott's quote in García-Guadilla and Hurtado (2000).

54. It must be noted, however, that abstention in this election was 62.4 percent. See García-Guadilla and Hurtado 2000: 19.

55. Whereby some seats are filled in single-member districts by plurality and others are filled in multimember districts by proportional representation (PR). An account of the controversy surrounding the drafting of the electoral rules for the assembly can be found in García-Guadilla and Hurtado 2000: 17–18. See also Coppedge 2003: 167.

56. "This is a variant of a system known as the bloc vote, which has strongly majoritarian tendencies, that is, it tends to exaggerate the margin of victory of the largest party" (Coppedge 2003: 187).

57. All the Polo Patriótico candidates ran on a single Polo ticket. Because the parties in the alliance had negotiated to prevent competition within the alliance, they succeeded in pooling their votes efficiently. See Coppedge 2003: 187.

58. In part because of the discredit affecting the parties, the opposition candidates ran independently, avoiding any resemblance with the party lists of the past. The negative effect of this was that they competed against each other and divided the opposition vote.

59. Later on, on February 15, 2009, Chávez proposed and won a referendum lifting all limits on the reelection of the president.

60. Corrales and Penfold (2007: 101) have called it "the most heavily presidentialist constitution in contemporary Latin America." See my evaluation of the 1999 Constitution (2005), as well as Corrales 2006b. On the constitution-making process, see Segura and Bejarano 2004.

61. "The executive, legislative, and judicial branches of government, most state and local governments, the central bank and the oil industry . . . are all under the direct and active control of the presidency" (Naím 2001: 19).

REFERENCES

Documents

Colombia

Declaración de Benidorm. July 24, 1956.
Manifiesto Conjunto de los Partidos Políticos o "Pacto de Marzo." March 20, 1957.
Declaración de Sitges. July 20, 1957.
Decreto Nº 0247 por el cual se convoca al Plebiscito Nacional del 1º de diciembre de 1957 (including text of Plebiscite). October 4, 1957.
Pacto de San Carlos. November 1957.
Acto Legislativo Nº 1 del 15 de septiembre de 1959 por el cual se crea la Alternación Presidencial. September 15, 1959.
Constitución Política de Colombia (with reforms). 1886.
Constitución Política de Colombia. 1991.

Venezuela

Pacto de Avenimiento Obrero-Patronal. April 24, 1958.
Pacto de Punto Fijo. October 31, 1958.
Declaración de Principios. December 6, 1958.
Programa Mínimo de Gobierno. December 6, 1958.
Constitución de la República de Venezuela. 1961.
Constitución de la República Bolivariana de Venezuela. 1999.

Journals and Newspapers

Análisis Político. Instituto de Estudios Políticos y Relaciones Internacionales, Universidad Nacional (Colombia).
Controversia. CINEP (Colombia).
Cuadernos del Cendes. Centro de Estudios del Desarrollo, UCV (Venezuela).
Politeia. Instituto de Estudios Políticos, UCV (Venezuela).
Revista Javeriana. Universidad Javeriana, Bogotá, Colombia (1956–74).
Revista SIC. Centro Gumilla, Caracas, Venezuela (1957–74).

Interviews

Venezuela
Allan Brewer-Carias, delegate to the Constituent Assembly. New York, April 23, 2003.
Manuel Caballero, historian, Caracas and Bogotá. Numerous occasions.
Ocarina Castillo D'Imperio, historian. November 10, 1995.
Luis Pedro España, sociologist. Caracas, October 18, 1994.
Luis Gómez Calcaño, sociologist. 1992–2000.
Miriam Kornblith, political scientist. Bogotá, Caracas, Notre Dame, San Juan, 1992–2006.
Edgardo Lander, sociologist. Caracas and New York, 1993–99.
Luis Lander, social scientist. Caracas and New York, 1993–2000.
Margarita López Maya, historian. Bogotá, Caracas, New York, 1992–2000.
Thaís Maingón, sociologist. Caracas, July 1992.
General (ret.) Alberto Müller Rojas. Caracas, November 8, 1995.
Juan Carlos Navarro, political scientist. November 9, 1995.
Dick Parker, historian. June 9 and 14, 1995.
Carlos Andrés Pérez, former president of Venezuela. La Ahumada, November 9, 1995.
Teodoro Petkoff, politician and founder of MAS. 1992–99.
Manuel Rachadell, law professor and member of COPRE. 1992–95.
Juan Carlos Rey, political scientist. Caracas, November 9, 1995.
Rafael Rodríguez, economist. June 1995.
Carlos Romero, political scientist. 1992–2000.
Ana María San Juan, sociologist. 1992–2007.
Heinz Sonntag, sociologist. Caracas, July 1992.
Arturo Sosa, historian and director of Centro Gumilla. June 14, 1995.
Ramón J. Velásquez, former president of Venezuela. Caracas, November 10, 1995.

Colombia
Mauricio Archila, historian. Bogotá, 1994–2000.
Belisario Betancur, former president of Colombia. Bogotá, June 4 and 12, 1996.
Andrés Dávila, political scientist. 1992–2000.
Fernán González, historian. 1992–2000.
Francisco Leal Buitrago, sociologist. 1992–2000.
Rodrigo Llorente, Conservative Party. Bogotá, May 21, 1996.
Alfonso López Michelsen, former president of Colombia. Bogotá, June 18, 1996.
Marco Palacios, historian. 1993–2000.

Carlos Mario Perea-Restrepo, historian. 1995–2000.
General (ret.) Juan Salcedo Lora. Bogotá, June 1996.
Horacio Serpa Uribe, Liberal Party. Bogotá, August 8 and 15, 2006.
General (ret.) Alvaro Valencia Tovar. Bogotá, May 24, 1996.
Gilberto Vieira, former secretary general of the PCC. Bogotá, June 5, 1996.
Jaime Zuluaga, economist. Bogotá, June 1996.

Books, Chapters, and Journal Articles

Abel, Christopher. 1987. *Política, iglesia y partidos en Colombia.* Bogotá: FAES and Universidad Nacional de Colombia.
Acedo de Sucre, María Lourdes, and Carmen Margarita Nones Mendoza. 1994. *La generación venezolana de 1928: Estudio de una élite política.* 2nd ed. Caracas: Fundación Carlos Eduardo Frías.
Acemoglu, Daron, and James A. Robinson. 2006. *Economic Origins of Dictatorship and Democracy.* Cambridge: Cambridge University Press.
Acuña, Carlos, and Catalina Smulovitz. 1996. "Adjusting the Armed Forces to Democracy: Successes, Failures and Ambiguities in the Southern Cone." In *Constructing Democracy: Human Rights, Citizenship, and Society in Latin America,* ed. Elizabeth Jelin and Eric Hershberg, 13–37. Boulder: Westview Press.
Adelman, Jeremy. 1999. *Colonial Legacies: The Problem of Persistence in Latin American History.* New York: Routledge.
———. 2006. "Unfinished States: Historical Perspectives on the Andes." In *State and Society in Conflict: Comparative Perspectives on the Andean Crises,* ed. Paul W. Drake and Eric Hershberg, 41–73. Pittsburgh: University of Pittsburgh Press.
Agüero, Felipe. 1990. "The Military and Democracy in Venezuela." In *The Military and Democracy: The Future of Civil-Military Relations in Latin America,* ed. Louis Wolf Goodman, Johanna S. R. Mendelson, and Juan Rial, 257–75. New York: Lexington Books.
———. 1992. "The Military and the Limits to Democratization in South America." In *Issues in Democratic Consolidation: The New South American Democracies in Comparative Perspective,* ed. Scott Mainwaring, Guillermo O'Donnell, and J. Samuel Valenzuela, 153–98. Notre Dame: University of Notre Dame Press.
———. 1993. "Las fuerzas armadas y el debilitamiento de la democracia en Venezuela." In *Venezuela: La democracia bajo presión,* ed. Andrés Serbín, Andrés Stambouli, Jennifer McCoy, and William Smith, 187–203. Caracas: INVESP and Nueva Sociedad.

————. 1995a. "Debilitating Democracy: Political Elites and Military Rebels." In *Lessons of the Venezuelan Experience,* ed. Louis W. Goodman, Johanna Mendelson Forman, Moisés Naím, Joseph S. Tulchin, and Gary Bland, 136–62. Washington, DC, and Baltimore: Woodrow Wilson Center Press and Johns Hopkins University Press.

————. 1995b. "Democratic Consolidation and the Military in Southern Europe and South America." In *The Politics of Democratic Consolidation: Southern Europe in Comparative Perspective,* ed. Richard Gunther, P. Nikiforos Diamandouros, and Hans-Jürgen Puhle, 124–65. Baltimore: Johns Hopkins University Press.

Alape, Arturo. 1985. *La paz, la violencia: Testigos de excepción.* Bogotá: Planeta.

Altman, David, and Aníbal Pérez-Liñán. 2002. "Assessing the Quality of Democracy: Freedom, Competitiveness and Participation in Eighteen Latin American Countries." *Democratization* 9, no. 2 (Summer): 85–100.

Anderson, Lisa. 1986. *The State and Social Transformation in Tunisia and Libya.* Princeton: Princeton University Press.

————. 1987. "The State in the Middle East and North Africa." *Comparative Politics* 20, no. 1 (October): 1–18.

————. 1999a. "A Review of Recent Studies on Oil and State Formation in the Middle East." *Journal of International Affairs* 53, no. 1 (Fall): 351–54.

————, ed. 1999b. *Transitions to Democracy.* New York: Columbia University Press.

Andrews, George Reid, and Herrick Chapman, eds. 1995. *The Social Construction of Democracy, 1870–1990.* New York: New York University Press.

Araujo, Elizabeth, Roberto Giusti, Fabricio Ojeda, and Régulo Párraga. 1989. *El día que bajaron los cerros: El saqueo de Caracas.* Caracas: Editorial Ateneo de Caracas and C.A. Editora El Nacional.

Archer, Ronald P. 1995. "Party Strength and Weakness in Colombia's Besieged Democracy." In *Building Democratic Institutions: Party Systems in Latin America,* ed. Scott Mainwaring and Timothy R. Scully, 164–99. Stanford: Stanford University Press.

Archer, Ronald P., and Matthew Soberg Shugart. 1997. "The Unrealized Potential of Presidential Dominance in Colombia." In *Presidentialism and Democracy in Latin America,* ed. Scott Mainwaring and Matthew Soberg Shugart, 110–59. Cambridge: Cambridge University Press.

Archila, Mauricio. 1991. *Cultura e identidad obrera: Colombia 1910–1945.* Bogotá: CINEP.

————. 1996. "¿Utopía armada? Oposición política y movimientos sociales durante el Frente Nacional." *Controversia* 68 (May): 25–53.

————, ed. 2002. *25 años de luchas sociales en Colombia, 1975–2000.* Bogotá: CINEP.

————. 2003. *Idas y venidas, vueltas y revueltas: Protestas sociales en Colombia, 1958–1990.* Bogotá: Instituto Colombiano de Antropología e Historia.

Arnson, Cynthia J., and Teresa Whitfield. 2005. "Third Parties and Intractable Conflicts: The Case of Colombia." In *Grasping the Nettle: Analyzing Cases of Intractable Conflict,* ed. Charles A. Crocker, Fen Osler Hampson, and Pamela Aall, 231–60. Washington, DC: U.S. Institute of Peace Press.

Arroyo Talavera, Eduardo. 1988. *Elecciones y negociaciones: Los límites de la democracia en Venezuela.* Caracas: Fondo Editorial CONICIT and Pomaire.

Bagley, Bruce. 1984. "Colombia: National Front and Economic Development." In *Politics, Policies, and Economic Development in Latin America,* ed. Robert Wesson, 124–60. Stanford: Hoover Institution Press.

Bailey, John J. 1977. "Pluralist and Corporatist Dimensions of Interest Representation in Colombia." In *Authoritarianism and Corporatism in Latin America,* ed. James M. Malloy, 259–301. Pittsburgh: University of Pittsburgh Press.

Baptista, Asdrúbal, and Bernard Mommer. 1992. *El petróleo en el pensamiento económico Venezolano: Un ensayo.* 2nd ed. Caracas: Ediciones IESA.

Bates, Robert. 1997. *Open-Economy Politics: The Political Economy of the World Coffee Trade.* Princeton: Princeton University Press.

Beblawi, Hazem. 1987. "The Rentier State in the Arab World." In *The Rentier State: Essays in the Political Economy of Arab Countries,* ed. Hazem Beblawi and Giacomo Luciani, 49–62. London: Croom Helm.

Beblawi, Hazem, and Giacomo Luciani, eds. 1987. *The Rentier State.* London: Croom Helm.

Bejarano, Ana María. 1994. "Recuperar el Estado para fortalecer la democracia." *Análisis Político* 22 (May–August): 51–88.

————. 2001. "The Constitution of 1991: An Institutional Evaluation Seven Years Later." In *Violence in Colombia, 1990–2000: Waging War and Negotiating Peace,* ed. Charles Bergquist, Ricardo Peñaranda, and Gonzalo Sánchez, 53–74. Wilmington, DE: Scholarly Resources.

————. 2002. "Buenas intenciones y efectos perversos: Los límites del reformismo institucional en Colombia y Venezuela." *Comentario Internacional: Revista del Centro Andino de Estudios Internacionales* 4: 177–86.

————. 2003. "Protracted Conflict, Multiple Protagonists and Staggered Negotiations: Colombia, 1982–2002." *Canadian Journal of Latin American and Caribbean Studies* 28 (55–56): 223–47.

————. 2005. "Transformaciones de la democracia en Venezuela: Una lectura crítica de la Constitución de 1999." *Desafíos* 12: 132–44.

————. 2006. "Stuck in the Gray Zone: States, Societies and Democracy in the Andes: A Review Essay." *Canadian Journal of Latin American and Caribbean Studies* 31 (62): 259–74.

Bejarano, Ana María, Felipe Botero, Laura Wills, and Laura Zambrano. 2001. "Que hace funcionar al Congreso? Una aproximación inicial a las fallas y los aciertos de la institución legislativa." In *Estudios Ocasionales CIJUS,* 201–305. Bogotá: Ediciones Uniandes and COLCIENCIAS.

Bejarano, Ana María, and Andrés Dávila, eds. 1998. *Elecciones y democracia en Colombia, 1997–1998.* Bogotá: Universidad de Los Andes, Fundación Social and Veeduría Ciudadana a la Elección Presidencial.

Bejarano, Ana María, and Eduardo Pizarro. 2004. "Colombia: The Partial Collapse of the State and the Emergence of Aspiring State-Makers." In *States-within-States: Incipient Political Entities in the Post–Cold War Era,* ed. Ian Spears and Paul Kingston, 99–118. New York: Palgrave–St. Martin's Press.

———. 2005. "From 'Restricted' to 'Besieged': The Changing Nature of the Limits to Democracy in Colombia." In *The Third Wave of Democratization in Latin America: Advances and Setbacks,* ed. Frances Hagopian and Scott Mainwaring, 235–60. Cambridge: Cambridge University Press.

Bejarano, Ana María, and Renata Segura-Bonnet. 1996. "El fortalecimiento selectivo del Estado durante el Frente Nacional." *Controversia* 169 (November): 9–37.

Bejarano, Ana María, Laura Wills, Catalina Acevedo, Felipe Botero, and Aquiles Arrieta. 2001. "La fragmentación interna del Estado y su impacto sobre la formulación e implementación de una política estatal de paz y convivencia ciudadana." In *Estudios Ocasionales CIJUS.* Bogotá: Ediciones Uniandes and COLCIENCIAS.

Bergquist, Charles W. 1986a. *Coffee and Conflict in Colombia, 1886–1910.* Durham: Duke University Press.

———. 1986b. *Labor in Latin America: Comparative Essays on Chile, Argentina, Venezuela and Colombia.* Stanford: Stanford University Press.

Bermeo, Nancy. 1990. "Rethinking Regime Change." *Comparative Politics* 22, no. 3 (April): 359–77.

———. 1992. "Democracy and the Lessons of Dictatorship." *Comparative Politics* 24, no. 3 (April): 273–91.

Berry, R. Albert, Ronald G. Hellman, and Mauricio Solaún, eds. 1980. *Politics of Compromise: Coalition Government in Colombia.* New Brunswick, NJ: Transaction.

Betancourt, Rómulo. 1969. *Venezuela: Política y petróleo.* 3rd ed. Bogotá: Editorial Senderos.

Bigler, Gene E. 1981. "La restricción política y la profesionalización militar en Venezuela." *Politeia* 10: 85–142.

Blanco Muñoz, Agustín. 1980. *La lucha armada: Hablan 5 jefes.* Caracas: UCV-FACES.

———. 1981. *La lucha armada: La izquierda revolucionaria insurge.* Caracas: UCV-FACES.

———. 1982. *La lucha armada: Hablan tres comandantes de la izquierda revolucionaria.* Caracas: UCV-FACES.

Boudon, Lawrence. 1997. "New Party Persistence and Failure: A Comparative Analysis of Colombia's M-19 Democratic Alliance and Venezuela's Radical Cause." Ph.D. diss., University of Miami.

———. 1998. "Los partidos y la crisis de representación en América Latina: Los casos de Colombia, México y Venezuela." *Contribuciones* 15, no. 1 (January–March): 7–28.

Braudel, Fernand. 1980. *On History.* Trans. Sarah Matthews. Chicago: University of Chicago Press.

Brewer-Carías, Allan R. 1985. *Instituciones políticas y constitucionales.* Caracas–San Cristóbal: Editorial Jurídica Venezolana–Universidad Católica del Táchira.

Briceño-Leon, Roberto. 2006. "Violence in Venezuela: Oil Rent and Political Crisis." *Ciência e Saúde Coletiva* 11 (2): 315–25.

Burggraaff, Winfield J. 1972. *The Venezuelan Armed Forces in Politics: 1935–1959.* Columbia: University of Missouri Press.

Burggraaff, Winfield J., and Richard L. Millet. 1995. "More than Failed Coups: The Crisis in Venezuelan Civil-Military Relations." In *Lessons of the Venezuelan Experience,* ed. Louis W. Goodman, Johanna Mendelson Forman, Moisés Naím, Joseph S. Tulchin, and Gary Bland, 57–78. Washington, DC, and Baltimore: Woodrow Wilson Center Press and Johns Hopkins University Press.

Burt, Jo-Marie, and Philip Mauceri, eds. 2004. *Politics in the Andes: Identity, Conflict, Reform.* Pittsburgh: University of Pittsburgh Press.

Burton, Michael, Richard Gunther, and John Higley. 1992. "Introduction." In *Elites and Democratic Consolidation in Latin America and Southern Europe,* ed. John Higley and Richard Gunther, 1–35. Cambridge: Cambridge University Press.

Bushnell, David. 1993. *The Making of Modern Colombia: A Nation Despite Itself.* Berkeley: University of California Press.

Caballero, Manuel. 1979. *Rómulo Betancourt.* 2nd ed. Caracas: Ediciones Centauro.

———. 1987a. *El discurso del desorden.* Caracas: Alfadil Ediciones.

———. 1987b. *La Internacional Comunista y la revolución latinoamericana, 1919–1943.* Caracas: Editorial Nueva Sociedad.

———. 1988. *Las Venezuelas del siglo veinte.* Caracas: Grijalbo.

———. 1989. *Entre Gómez y Stalin (La sección venezolana de la Internacional Comunista).* 2nd ed. Caracas: Universidad Central de Venezuela.

———. 1991. *El poder brujo: Ensayos de polémicas y otras tintas.* Caracas: Monte Ávila Editores.

Caldera, Rafael. 1992. "Discursos parlamentarios del doctor Rafael Caldera con motivo de los hechos del 27 de febrero de 1989 y del 4 de febrero de 1992." *Politeia* 15: 423–42.

Camacho, Alvaro. 1988. *Droga y sociedad en Colombia: El poder y el estigma.* Cali: CEREC/CIDSE.

———. 1996. "Narcotráfico, Coyuntura y Crisis." In *Tras las huellas de la crisis política,* ed. Francisco Leal, 129–51. Bogotá: Tercer Mundo Editores, FESCOL, and IEPRI.

Cámara de Representantes. 1959. *Por qué y cómo se forjó el Frente Nacional.* Bogotá: Imprenta Nacional.

Cardoso, Fernando Henrique. 1986. "Entrepreneurs and the Transition Process: The Brazilian Case." In *Transitions from Authoritarian Rule: Comparative Perspectives,* ed. Guillermo O'Donnell, Philippe C. Schmitter, and Laurence Whitehead, 137–53. Baltimore: Johns Hopkins University Press.

Cardoso, Fernando Henrique, and Enzo Faletto. 1971. *Dependencia y desarrollo en América Latina.* 3rd ed. Mexico: Siglo XXI.

Carrera Damas, Germán. 1984. *Una nación llamada Venezuela.* Caracas: Monte Ávila Editores.

———. 1994. *Emergencia de un líder: Rómulo Betancourt y el Plan de Barranquilla.* Caracas: Fundación Rómulo Betancourt.

Castillo D'Imperio, Ocarina. 1985. *Agricultura y política en Venezuela, 1948–1958.* Caracas: Ediciones de la Facultad de Ciencias Económicas y Sociales, UCV.

———. 1990. *Los años del buldozer: Ideología y política, 1948–1958.* Caracas: Fondo Editorial Tropikos and Asociación de Profesores UCV-CENDES.

Castro, Luis. 1988. *El dilema octubrista, 1945–1987.* Serie Cuatro Repúblicas. Caracas: Cuadernos LAGOVEN.

Cavarozzi, Marcelo. 1991. "Más allá de las transiciones a la democracia en América Latina." *Revista de Estudios Políticos* 74 (October–December): 85–111.

Centeno, Miguel Angel. 2002. *Blood and Debt: War and State-Making in Latin America.* University Park: Pennsylvania State University Press.

Chalmers, Douglas A. 1977. "The Politicized State in Latin America." In *Authoritarianism and Corporatism in Latin America,* ed. James A. Malloy, 23–45. Pittsburgh: University of Pittsburgh Press.

Chalmers, Douglas A., María Do Carmo Campello de Souza, and Atilio Borón, eds. 1992. *The Right and Democracy in Latin America.* New York: Praeger.

Chalmers, Douglas A., Carlos M. Vilas, Katherine Hite, Scott B. Martin, Kerianne Piester, and Monique Segarra, eds. 1997. *The New Politics of Inequality in Latin America: Rethinking Participation and Representation.* Oxford: Oxford University Press.

Chaudhry, Kiren Aziz. 1997. *The Price of Wealth: Economies and Institutions in the Middle East.* Ithaca: Cornell University Press.

Chávez Frías, Hugo, Francisco José Arias Cárdenas, et al. 1998. "Manifiesto." In *La rebelión de los ángeles,* ed. Angela Zago, 99–108. Caracas: Fuente Editores.

Chernick, Marc W. 1988. "Negotiated Settlement to Armed Conflict: Lessons from the Colombian Peace Process." *Journal of Interamerican and World Affairs* 30, no. 4 (Winter): 53–88.

Collier, David, ed. 1979. *The New Authoritarianism in Latin America.* Princeton: Princeton University Press.

Collier, David, and Steven Levitsky. 1997. "Democracy with Adjectives." *World Politics* 49 (April): 430–51.

Collier, Ruth Berins. 1999. *Paths toward Democracy: The Working Class and Elites in Western Europe and South America.* Cambridge: Cambridge University Press.

Collier, Ruth Berins, and David Collier. 1991. *Shaping the Political Arena: Critical Junctures, the Labor Movement and Regime Dynamics in Latin America.* Princeton: Princeton University Press.

Collier, Ruth Berins, and James Mahoney. 1999. "Adding Collective Actors to Collective Outcomes: Labor and Recent Democratization in South America." In *Transitions to Democracy,* ed. Lisa Anderson, 97–119. New York: Columbia University Press.

Colmenares, Germán. 1968. *Partidos políticos y clases sociales.* Bogotá: Ediciones Universidad de los Andes.

Colomer, Joseph. 1990. *El arte de la manipulación política: Votaciones y teoría de juegos en la política española.* Barcelona: Editorial Anagrama.

———. 1991. "Transitions by Agreement: Modeling the Spanish Way." *American Political Science Review* 85, no. 4 (December): 1283–1302.

Comisión Colombiana de Juristas. 2000. *Panorama de Derechos Humanos y derecho humanitario en Colombia. Informe de Avance sobre 2000.* Bogotá: Comisión Colombiana de Juristas.

Cooley, Alexander A. 2001. "Booms and Busts: Theorizing Institutional Formation and Change in Oil States." *Review of International Political Economy* 8, no. 1 (Spring): 163–80.

Coppedge, Michael. 1992. "Venezuela's Vulnerable Democracy." *Journal of Democracy* 3, no. 4 (October): 32–44.

———. 1994a. *Strong Parties and Lame Ducks: Presidential Partyarchy and Factionalism in Venezuela.* Stanford: Stanford University Press.

———. 1994b. "Venezuela: Democratic despite Presidentialism." In *The Failure of Presidential Democracy: The Case of Latin America,* vol. 2, ed. Juan J. Linz and Arturo Valenzuela, 322–47. Baltimore: Johns Hopkins University Press.

————. 1998. "The Evolution of Latin American Party Systems." In *Politics, Society and Democracy: Latin America,* ed. Scott Mainwaring and Arturo Valenzuela, 171–206. Boulder: Westview Press.

————. 2003. "Venezuela: Popular Sovereignty versus Liberal Democracy." In *Constructing Democratic Governance in Latin America,* 2nd ed., ed. Jorge I. Dominguez and Michael Shifter, 165–92. Baltimore: Johns Hopkins University Press.

————. 2005. "Explaining Democratic Deterioration in Venezuela through Nested Inference." In *The Third Wave of Democratization in Latin America: Advances and Setbacks,* ed. Frances Hagopian and Scott Mainwaring, 289–316. Cambridge: Cambridge University Press.

Coppedge, Michael, and Wolfgang H. Reinicke. 1990. "Measuring Polyarchy." *Studies in Comparative International Development* 25, no. 1 (Spring): 51–72.

Coronil, Fernando. 1997. *The Magical State: Nature, Money and Modernity in Venezuela.* Chicago: University of Chicago Press.

Corrales, Javier. 2000. "Presidents, Ruling Parties, and Party Rules: A Theory on the Politics of Economic Reform in Latin America." *Comparative Politics* 32, no. 2 (January): 127–49.

————. 2002. *Presidents without Parties: The Politics of Economic Reform in Argentina and Venezuela in the 1990s.* University Park: Pennsylvania State University Press.

————. 2005. "Power Assymetries and Post-Pact Stability: Revisiting and Updating Venezuela's Pacts." Unpublished manuscript.

————. 2006a. "Hugo Boss: How Chávez Is Refashioning Dictatorship for a Democratic Age." *Foreign Policy* 152 (January–February): 32–40.

————. 2006b. "Power Asymmetries and the Rise of Presidential Constitutions." Paper presented at the annual meeting of the American Political Science Association, August 31–September 3, Philadelphia, PA.

Corrales, Javier, and Michael Penfold. 2007. "Venezuela: Crowding out the Opposition." *Journal of Democracy* 18, no. 2 (April): 99–113.

Crisp, Brian F. 1992. "Tyranny by the Minority: Institutional Control of Participation in the Venezuelan Democracy." Ph.D. diss., University of Michigan.

————. 1997. "Presidential Behavior in a System with Strong Parties: Venezuela, 1958–1995." In *Presidentialism and Democracy in Latin America,* ed. Scott Mainwaring and Matthew Soberg Shugart, 160–98. Cambridge: Cambridge University Press.

————. 2000. *Democratic Institutional Design: The Powers and Incentives of Venezuelan Politicians and Interest Groups.* Stanford: Stanford University Press.

Cruz, Consuelo. 1996. "Historical Memory and Political Imagination: Democratization on a Polarized Field." Unpublished manuscript, Columbia University.

———. 2005. *Political Culture and Institutional Development in Costa Rica and Nicaragua: World Making in the Tropics.* Cambridge: Cambridge University Press.

Cruz, Consuelo, and Rut Diamint. 1998. "The New Military Autonomy in Latin America." *Journal of Democracy* 9, no. 4: 115–27.

Cubides, Fernando. 1999. "Los paramilitares y su estrategia." In *Reconocer la guerra para construir la paz,* ed. Malcolm Deas and María Victoria Llorente, 151–99. Bogotá: CEREC, Ediciones Uniandes, and Editorial Norma.

Dahl, Robert A. 1971. *Polyarchy: Participation and Opposition.* New Haven: Yale University Press.

———. 1982. *Dilemmas of Pluralist Democracy: Autonomy vs. Control.* New Haven: Yale University Press.

Dávila, Andrés. 1998. *El juego del poder: Historia, armas y votos.* Bogotá: Fondo Editorial CEREC and Ediciones Uniandes.

———. 2002. *Democracia pactada: El Frente Nacional y el proceso constituyente del 91.* Bogotá: Universidad de Los Andes, CESO, Departamento de Ciencia Política, Alfaomega, and IFEA.

Deas, Malcolm. 1985. "Venezuela, Colombia, and Ecuador: The First Half-Century of Independence." In *The Cambridge History of Latin America,* vol. 3, *From Independence to c. 1870,* ed. Leslie Bethell, 507–38. Cambridge: Cambridge University Press.

———. 1986. "Colombia, Ecuador, and Venezuela, c. 1880–1930." In *The Cambridge History of Latin America,* vol. 5, *C. 1870–1930,* ed. Leslie Bethell, 641–82. Cambridge: Cambridge University Press.

———. 1993. *Del poder y la gramática, y otros ensayos sobre historia, política y literatura colombiana.* Bogotá: Tercer Mundo Editores.

———. 1995. "Venezuela, Colombia and Ecuador." In *The Cambridge History of Latin America,* vol. 11, *Bibliographical Essays,* ed. Leslie Bethell, 274–83. Cambridge: Cambridge University Press.

———. 1999. "A propósito de un demorado esfuerzo civil." In *Reconocer la guerra para construir la paz,* ed. Malcolm Deas and María Victoria Llorente, 9–20. Bogotá: CEREC, Ediciones Uniandes and Grupo Editorial Norma.

———. 2002. "The Man on Foot: Conscription and the Nation-State in Nineteenth-Century Latin America." In *Studies in the Formation of the Nation State in Latin America,* ed. James Dunkerley, 77–93. London: Institute of Latin American Studies, University of London.

Di Palma, Giuseppe. 1990. *To Craft Democracies: An Essay on Democratic Transitions.* Berkeley: University of California Press.

Diamond, Jared. 1999. *Guns, Germs and Steel: The Fates of Human Societies.* New York: Norton.

Diamond, Larry. 1993. "Three Paradoxes of Democracy." In *The Global Resurgence of Democracy,* ed. Larry Diamond and Marc F. Plattner, 95–107. Baltimore: Johns Hopkins University Press.

———. 1996. "Is the Third Wave Over?" *Journal of Democracy* 7, no. 3 (July): 20–37.

Diamond, Larry, and Richard Gunther. 2001. "Types and Functions of Parties." In *Political Parties and Democracy,* ed. Larry Diamond and Richard Gunther, 3–39. Baltimore: Johns Hopkins University Press.

Diamond, Larry, Jonathan Hartlyn, Juan J. Linz, and Seymour Martin Lipset, eds. 1999. *Democracy in Developing Countries: Latin America.* 2nd ed. Boulder: Lynne Rienner.

Diamond, Larry, and Juan J. Linz. 1989. "Introduction: Politics, Society and Democracy in Latin America." In *Democracy in Developing Countries: Latin America,* ed. Larry Diamond, Juan J. Linz, and Seymour Martin Lipset, 1–58. Boulder: Lynne Rienner.

Diamond, Larry, and Leonardo Morlino. 2004. "The Quality of Democracy: An Overview." *Journal of Democracy* 15 (4): 20–31.

———. 2005. *Assessing the Quality of Democracy.* Baltimore: Johns Hopkins University Press.

Diamond, Larry, and Marc F. Plattner, eds. 1993. *The Global Resurgence of Democracy.* Baltimore: Johns Hopkins University Press.

Dix, Robert H. 1967. *Colombia: The Political Dimensions of Change.* New Haven: Yale University Press.

———. 1980. "Consociational Democracy: The Case of Colombia." *Comparative Politics* 12, no. 3 (April): 303–21.

———. 1994. "History and Democracy Revisited." *Comparative Politics* 27, no. 1 (October): 91–105.

Dugas, John, ed. 1993. *La Constitución de 1991. ¿Un pacto político viable?* Bogotá: Universidad de los Andes and Fondo Editorial CEREC.

———. 2000. "Sisyphus in the Andes? The Quest for Political Party Reform in Columbia." Unpublished manuscript, Kalamazoo College.

Dunkerley, James, ed. 2002. *Studies in the Formation of the Nation-State in Latin America.* London: Institute of Latin American Studies, University of London.

Echandía, Camilo. 1999. *El conflicto armado y las manifestaciones de violencia en las regiones de Colombia.* Bogotá: Oficina del Alto Comisionado para la Paz, Presidencia de la República de Colombia.

Eckstein, Susan, ed. 1989. *Power and Popular Protest: Latin American Social Movements.* Berkeley: University of California Press.

Economist. 2001. "Drugs, War and Democracy: A Survey of Colombia." April 21, 1–16.

———. 2008. "Venezuela: Deadly Massage." July 19, 47.

Economist Intelligence Unit. 2001. "Country Profile: Colombia." www .economist.com/countries.

———. 2001. "Country Profile: Venezuela." www.economist.com/countries.

Ellner, Steve. 1980. "Acción Democrática-Partido Comunista de Venezuela: Rivalry on the Venezuelan Left and in Organized Labor, 1936–1948." Ph.D. diss., University of New Mexico.

———. 1988. *Venezuela's Movimiento al Socialismo: From Guerrilla Defeat to Innovative Politics.* Durham: Duke University Press.

———. 1995. "Venezuelan Revisionist Political History, 1908–1958: New Motives and Criteria for Analyzing the Past." *Latin American Research Review* 30 (2): 91–121.

Ellner, Steve, and Daniel Hellinger, eds. 2004. *Venezuelan Politics in the Chávez Era: Class, Polarization, and Conflict.* Boulder: Lynne Rienner.

Elster, Jon. 1991. *Tuercas y tornillos: Una introducción a los conceptos básicos de las ciencias sociales.* 2nd ed. Barcelona: Editorial Gedisa.

———. 1996. "Ulysses Revisited: Precommitment and Constitutionalism." Unpublished manuscript, Columbia University.

Elster, Jon, and Rune Slagstad, eds. 1988. *Constitutionalism and Democracy.* Cambridge: Cambridge University Press.

Encarnación, Omar G. 2005. "Do Political Pacts Freeze Democracy? Spanish and South American Lessons." *West European Politics* 28, no. 1 (January): 182–203.

España, Luis Pedro. 1987. "30 años de 'vida nacional.'" *Revista SIC* 500 (December): 564–70.

———. 1989. *Democracia y renta petrolera.* Caracas: Universidad Católica "Andres Bello," Instituto de Investigaciones Económicas y Sociales.

Evans, Peter. 1995. *Embedded Autonomy: States and Industrial Transformation.* Princeton: Princeton University Press.

Evans, Peter B., Dietrich Rueschemeyer, and Theda Skocpol, eds. 1985. *Bringing the State Back In.* New York: Cambridge University Press.

Fishman, Robert M. 2002. "Rethinking Iberian Democracy Twenty-Five Years after the Transitions." Paper presented at the annual meeting of the American Political Science Association, August 29–September 1, Boston, MA.

Font, Mauricio A. 1990. *Coffee, Contention and Change in the Making of Modern Brazil.* Oxford: Basil Blackwell.

Forero, Juan. 2000. "Behind Colombia's Election Hoopla, Rebels Wield Power." *New York Times,* October 29.

Friedman, Edward. 1999. "The Painful Gradualness of Democratization: Proceduralism as a Necessarily Discontinuous Revolution." In *Democracy and Its Limits: Lessons from Asia, Latin America, and the Middle East,* ed. Howard Handelman and Mark Tessler, 321–40. Notre Dame: University of Notre Dame Press.

Fuenmayor, Juan Bautista. 1979. *1928–1948: Veinte años de política.* 2nd ed. Caracas: Talleres Tipográficos Miguel Ángel García e Hijo.

Gaitán, Pilar, Ricardo Peñaranda, and Eduardo Pizarro, eds. 1996. *Democracia y reestructuración económica en América Latina.* Bogotá: IEPRI and CEREC.

Gallón Giraldo, Gustavo. 1979. *Quince años de Estado de sitio en Colombia, 1958–1978.* Bogotá: Editorial América Latina.

———, ed. 1989. *Entre movimientos y caudillos: 50 años de bipartidismo, izquierda y alternativas populares en Colombia.* Bogotá: CINEP and CEREC.

Galvis, Sylvia, and Alberto Donadio. 1988. *El jefe supremo: Rojas Pinilla en la Violencia y el poder.* Bogota: Planeta Editorial Colombiana.

Gandour, Miguel, and Luis Bernardo Mejía, eds. 1999. *Hacia el rediseño del Estado.* Bogotá: Tercer Mundo Editores and Departamento Nacional de Planeación.

García, Mauricio. 1992. *De La Uribe a Tlaxcala: Procesos de paz.* Bogotá: CINEP.

———. 1995. "Política de negociación con la guerrilla: Cambios de la administración Gaviria a la administración Samper." *Controversia* 167 (October–November): 35–61.

García, Miguel, and Gary Hoskin, eds. 2006. *La reforma política de 2003. ¿La salvación de los partidos políticos colombianos?* Bogotá: Universidad de los Andes and Fundación Konrad Adenauer.

García-Guadilla, María Pilar, and Mónica Hurtado. 2000. "Participation and Constitution Making in Colombia and Venezuela: Enlarging the Scope of Democracy?" Paper presented at the XXII International Congress of the Latin American Studies Association, March 16–18, Miami, FL.

García Santesmases, Antonio. 1988. "Cesión y claudicación: La transición política española." *Pensamiento Iberoamericano: Revista de Economía Política* 14: 273–83.

García Villegas, Mauricio. 2009. "Caracterización del régimen político colombiano (1956–2008)." In *Mayorías sin democracia: Desequilibrio de poderes y estado de derecho en Colombia, 2002–2009,* ed. Mauricio García Villegas and J. E. Revelo Rebolledo, 16–82. Bogotá: Centro de Estudios de Derecho, Justicia y Sociedad, Dejusticia.

Gause III, F. Gregory. 1994. *Oil Monarchies: Domestic and Security Challenges in the Arab Gulf States.* New York: Council on Foreign Relations Press.

Gibson, Edward. 1989. "Nine Cases of the Breakdown of Democracy." In *Democracy in the Americas: Stopping the Pendulum,* ed. Robert A. Pastor, 159–203. New York: Holmes and Meier.

Gillespie, Charles G. 1986. "Uruguay's Transition from Collegial Military-Technocratic Rule." In *Transitions from Authoritarian Rule: Latin America,* ed. Guillermo O'Donnell, Philippe C. Schmitter, and Laurence Whitehead, 173–95. Baltimore: Johns Hopkins University Press.

Gómez Albarello, Juan Gabriel. 2000. "Sobre las constituciones de Colombia (incluida la de papel)." In Instituto de Estudios Políticos, *Colombia cambio de siglo: Balances y perspectivas,* 255–92. Bogotá: Planeta Colombiana.

Gómez Calcaño, Luis, ed. 1987a. *Crisis y movimientos sociales en Venezuela.* Caracas: Fondo Editorial Tropykos.

———. 1987b. "Los movimientos sociales: Democracia emergente en el sistema politico venezolano." In *Venezuela hacia el 2000: Desafíos y opciones,* ed. José Agustín Silva Michelena, 337–67. Caracas: Editorial Nueva Sociedad-ILDIS-UNITAR-PROFAR.

———. 1988. "La democracia venezolana entre la renovación y el estancamiento." *Pensamiento Iberoamericano: Revista de Economía Política* 14 (July–December): 181–95.

Gómez Calcaño, Luis, and Margarita López Maya. 1990. *El tejido de Penélope: La reforma del Estado en Venezuela (1984–1988).* Caracas: CENDES and APUCV-IPP.

González, Fernán. 1989a. "Aproximación a la configuración política de Colombia." *Controversia* 153–54 (June): 20–72.

———. 1989b. "La Iglesia Católica y el Estado colombiano." In *Nueva Historia de Colombia,* vol. 2, ed. Alvaro Tirado Mejía, 371–96. Bogotá: Planeta Colombiana.

———. 1997a. *Para leer la política: Ensayos de historia política colombiana.* 2 vols. Bogotá: CINEP.

———. 1997b. *Poderes enfrentados: Iglesia y Estado en Colombia.* Bogotá: CINEP.

Goodin, Robert E., ed. 1996. *The Theory of Institutional Design.* Cambridge: Cambridge University Press.

Goodman, Louis W., Johanna Mendelson Forman, Moisés Naím, Joseph S. Tulchin, and Gary Bland, eds. 1995. *Lessons of the Venezuelan Experience.* Washington, DC, and Baltimore: Woodrow Wilson Center Press and Johns Hopkins University Press.

Gott, Richard. 2005. *Hugo Chávez and the Bolivarian Revolution.* London: Verso.

Gros, Christian. 1991. *Colombia indígena: Identidad cultural y cambio social.* Bogotá: CEREC.

Guevara, Pedro. 1989. *Concertación y conflicto: El pacto social y el fracaso de las respuestas consensuales a la crisis del sistema político venezolano.* Caracas: Universidad Central de Venezuela, Facultad de Ciencias Jurídicas y Políticas, Escuela de Estudios Políticos y Administrativos.

Gunther, Richard, P. Nikiforos Diamandouros, and Hans-Jürgen Puhle, eds. 1995. *The Politics of Democratic Consolidation: Southern Europe in Comparative Perspective.* Baltimore: Johns Hopkins University Press.

——. 1996. "O'Donnell's 'Illusions': A Rejoinder." *Journal of Democracy* 7, no. 4 (October): 151–59.

Gutiérrez, Francisco. 1998. "Rescate por un elefante: Congreso, sistema y reforma política." In *Elecciones y democracia en Colombia, 1997–1998,* ed. Ana María Bejarano and Andrés Dávila, 215–53. Bogotá: Universidad de los Andes.

——. 2006. "Checks and Imbalances: Problems with Congress in Colombia and Ecuador, 1978–2003." In *State and Society in Conflict: Comparative Perspectives on Andean Crises,* ed. Paul W. Drake and Eric Hershberg, 257–87. Pittsburgh: University of Pittsburgh Press.

——. 2007. *¿Lo que el viento se llevó? Los partidos políticos y la democracia en Colombia, 1958–2002.* Bogotá: Grupo Editorial Norma.

Gutiérrez, Francisco, and Luisa Ramírez Rueda. 2004. "The Tense Relationship between Democracy and Violence in Colombia, 1974–2001." In *Politics in the Andes: Identity, Conflict, Reform,* ed. Jo-Marie Burt and Philip Mauceri, 228–46. Pittsburgh: University of Pittsburgh Press.

Haggard, Stephan, and Robert R. Kaufman. 1995. *The Political Economy of Democratic Transitions.* Princeton: Princeton University Press.

Hagopian, Frances. 1990. "'Democracy by Undemocratic Means'? Elites, Political Pacts and Regime Transition in Brazil." *Comparative Political Studies* 23, no. 2 (July): 147–70.

——. 1992. "The Compromised Consolidation: The Political Class in the Brazilian Transition." In *Issues in Democratic Consolidation: The New South American Democracies in Comparative Perspective,* ed. Scott Mainwaring, Guillermo O'Donnell, and J. Samuel Valenzuela, 243–93. Notre Dame: University of Notre Dame Press.

——. 1993. "After Regime Change: Authoritarian Legacies, Political Representation and the Democratic Future of South America." *World Politics* 45, no. 3 (April): 464–500.

——. 1994. "Traditional Politics against State Transformation." In *State Power and Social Forces: Domination and Transformation,* ed. Joel Migdal, Atul Kohli, and Vivienne Shue, 37–64. Cambridge: Cambridge University Press.

——. 1996a. *Traditional Politics and Regime Change in Brazil.* Cambridge: Cambridge University Press.

——. 1996b. "Traditional Power Structures and Democratic Governance in Latin America." In *Constructing Democratic Governance: Latin America and the Caribbean in the 1990s,* ed. Jorge I. Domínguez and Abraham F. Lowenthal, 64–86. Baltimore: Johns Hopkins University Press.

————. 1998. "Democracy and Political Representation in Latin America in the 1990s: Pause, Reorganization, or Decline?" In *Fault Lines of Democracy in Post-Transition Latin America,* ed. Felipe Agüero and Jeffrey Stark, 99–143. Miami: North-South Center Press, University of Miami.

Hagopian, Frances, and Scott Mainwaring, eds. 2005. *The Third Wave of Democratization in Latin America: Advances and Setbacks.* Cambridge: Cambridge University Press.

Hall, John A. 1993. "Consolidations of Democracy." In *Prospects for Democracy: North, South, East, West,* ed. David Held, 271–90. Stanford: Stanford University Press.

Hall, John A., and G. John Ickenberry. 1993. *El Estado.* Madrid: Alianza Editorial.

Hall, Peter A., and Rosemary Taylor. 1994. "Political Science and the Four New Institutionalisms." Unpublished manuscript, Harvard University.

Hartlyn, Jonathan. 1988. *The Politics of Coalition Rule in Colombia.* Cambridge: Cambridge University Press.

————. 1989. "Colombia: The Politics of Violence and Accommodation." In *Democracy in Developing Countries: Latin America,* ed. Larry Diamond, Juan J. Linz, and Seymour Martin Lipset, 291–334. Boulder: Lynne Rienner.

————. 1993. *La política del régimen de coalición: La experiencia del Frente Nacional en Colombia.* Bogotá: Tercer Mundo Editores, CEI, and Ediciones Uniandes. [Spanish-language edition of Hartlyn 1988.]

————. 1994. "Presidentialism and Colombian Politics. In *The Failure of Presidential Democracy: The Case of Latin America,* ed. Juan J. Linz and Arturo Valenzuela, 220–53. Baltimore: Johns Hopkins University Press.

————. 1996a. "Las democracias hoy en América Latina: Convergencias y divergencias." In *Democracia y reestructuración económica en América Latina,* ed. Pilar Gaitán, Ricardo Peñaranda, and Eduardo Pizarro, 25–66. Bogotá: CEREC-IEPRI.

————. 1996b. "Latin America's Parties." Review of *Building Democratic Institutions: Party Systems in Latin America* by Scott Mainwaring and Timothy R. Scully. *Journal of Democracy* 7, no. 4 (October): 174–77.

————. 1998. "Political Continuities, Missed Opportunities and Institutional Rigidities: Another Look at Democratic Transitions in Latin America." In *Politics, Society and Democracy: Latin America: Essays in Honor of Juan J. Linz,* ed. Scott Mainwaring and Arturo Valenzuela, 101–20. Boulder: Westview Press.

Hartlyn, Jonathan, and John Dugas. 1999. "Colombia: The Politics of Violence and Democratic Transformation." In *Democracy in Developing Countries: Latin America,* 2nd ed., ed. Larry Diamond, Jonathan Hartlyn, Juan J. Linz, and Seymour Martin Lipset, 249–307. Boulder: Lynne Rienner.

Held, David, ed. 1993. *Prospects for Democracy: North, South, East, West.* Stanford: Stanford University Press.

Herbst, Jeffrey. 2000. *States and Power in Africa: Comparative Lessons in Authority and Control.* Princeton: Princeton University Press.

Herman, Donald L., ed. 1988. *Democracy in Latin America: Colombia and Venezuela.* New York: Praeger.

Hernández, Ramón. 1983. *Teodoro Petkoff: Viaje al fondo de sí mismo.* Caracas: Editorial Fuentes.

Higley, John, and Richard Gunther, eds. 1992. *Elites and Democratic Consolidation in Latin America and Southern Europe.* Cambridge: Cambridge University Press.

Holmes, Stephen. 1988. "Gag Rules or the Politics of Omission." In *Constitutionalism and Democracy,* ed. Jon Elster and Rune Slagstad, 19–58. Cambridge: Cambridge University Press.

Hoskin, Gary, and Miguel García. 2006. *La reforma política de 2003. ¿La salvación de los partidos politicos colombianos?* Bogotá: Universidad de Los Andes, Facultad de Ciencias Sociales, CESO, Departamento de Ciencia Politica.

Huber Stephens, Evelyne. 1989. "Capitalist Development and Democracy in South America." *Politics & Society* 17, no. 3: 281–352.

Human Rights Watch. 2001. *The "Sixth Division": Military-Paramilitary Ties and U.S. Policy in Colombia.* New York: Human Rights Watch.

Huntington, Samuel P. 1968. *Political Order in Changing Societies.* New Haven: Yale University Press.

———. 1984. "Will More Countries Become Democratic?" *Political Science Quarterly* 99, no. 2 (Summer): 193–218.

———. 1991a. "Democracy's Third Wave." *Journal of Democracy* 2, no. 2 (Spring): 12–36.

———. 1991b. *The Third Wave: Democratization in the Late Twentieth Century.* Norman: University of Oklahoma Press.

Jackish, Carlota, ed. 1998. *Representación política y democracia.* Buenos Aires: CIEDLA.

Jacome, Francine. 1998. "Los militares en Venezuela ¿Ruptura o continuidad del pacto tácito?" *Revista Venezolana de Economía y Ciencias Sociales* 4, no. 2–3 (April–September): 259–77.

———. 1999. "Las relaciones cívico-militares en Venezuela (1992–1997)." In *Control civil y Fuerzas Armadas en las nuevas democracias lationamericanas,* ed. Rut Diamint, 401–32. Buenos Aires: Universidad Torcuato di Tella and Grupo Editor Latinoamericano.

Jelin, Elizabeth, and Eric Hershberg, eds. 1996. *Constructing Democracy: Human Rights, Citizenship and Society in Latin America.* Boulder: Westview Press.

Joseph, Gilbert M., and Daniel Nugent, eds. 1994. *Everyday Forms of State Formation: Revolution and the Negotiation of Rule in Modern Mexico.* Durham: Duke University Press.

Junta Militar de Gobierno. 1957. *Itinerario histórico.* Bogotá: n.p.

Kalmanovitz, Salomón. 1982. *Economía y nación: Una breve historia de Colombia.* Bogotá: CINEP.

Karl, Terry Lynn. 1986. "Petroleum and Political Pacts: The Transition to Democracy in Venezuela." In *Transitions from Authoritarian Rule: Latin America,* ed. Guillermo O'Donnell, Philippe C. Schmitter, and Laurence Whitehead, 196–219. Baltimore: Johns Hopkins University Press.

———. 1987. "Petroleum and Political Pacts: The Transition to Democracy in Venezuela." *Latin American Research Review* 22 (1): 63–94.

———. 1990. "Dilemmas of Democratization in Latin America." *Comparative Politics* 23 (1): 1–21.

———. 1995. "The Venezuelan Petro-State and the Crisis of 'Its' Democracy." In *Venezuelan Democracy under Stress,* ed. Jennifer McCoy, Andrés Serbin, William C. Smith, and Andrés Stambouli, 33–58. Miami: North-South Center, University of Miami.

———. 1997. *The Paradox of Plenty: Oil Booms and Petro-States.* Berkeley: University of California Press.

Karl, Terry Lynn, and Philippe Schmitter. 1991. "Modes of Transition in Latin America, Southern and Eastern Europe." *International Social Science Journal* 128 (May): 269–84.

Kaufman, Robert, and Stephan Haggard. 1995. *The Political Economy of Democratic Transitions.* Princeton: Princeton University Press.

Kitschelt, Herbert P. 1992. "Structure or Process Driven Explanations of Political Regime Change? (Review Essay)." *American Political Science Review* 86, no. 4 (December): 1028–34.

Kline, Harvey. 1995. *Colombia: Democracy under Assault.* 2nd ed. Boulder: Westview.

———. 1999. *State Building and Conflict Resolution in Colombia: 1986–1994.* Tuscaloosa: University of Alabama Press.

Kornblith, Miriam. 1988. "Concepción de la política y conflicto antagónico en el Trienio: Su estudio a través de los debates de la Asamblea Constituyente de 1946–47." Unpublished manuscript, Instituto de Estudios Políticos, Universidad Central de Venezuela.

———. 1989a. "Deuda y democracia en Venezuela: Los sucesos del 27 y 28 de febrero de 1989." *Cuadernos del Cendes* 10: 17–34.

———. 1989b. "Proceso constitucional y consolidación de la democracia en Venezuela: Las constituciones de 1947 y 1961." *Politeia* 13: 283–329.

————. 1991. "The Politics of Constitution-Making: Constitutions and Democracy in Venezuela." *Journal of Latin American Studies* 23 (1): 661–89.

————. 1992a. "Reforma constitucional, crisis política y estabilidad de la democracia en Venezuela." *Politeia* 15: 121–69.

————. 1992b. "Sistema de partidos y reforma electoral en Venezuela." In *Los partidos políticos en el inicio de los noventa. Seis casos latinoamericanos,* ed. Garretón Manuel, 27–48. Santiago: Ediciones FLACSO-Chile.

————. 1993a. "Estado, políticos y empresarios: Nuevas reglas del juego y democracia en Venezuela." Paper presented at the XIX Venezuelan Congress of Sociology of the Latin American Sociology Association (ALAS), June, Caracas.

————. 1993b. "Reflexiones críticas en torno al intento de reforma constitucional en Venezuela de 1989–1992." In *Venezuela: Crisis política y reforma constitucional,* ed. Ricardo Combellas. Caracas: Instituto de Estudios Políticos, UCV.

————. 1993c. "Venezuela: Crisis socio-política, nuevas reglas de juego y estabilidad de la democracia." In *Hacia la consolidación democrática andina: Transición o desestabilización,* ed. Murillo Gabriel, 241–92. Bogotá: Departamento de Ciencia Política, Universidad de los Andes and Tercer Mundo Editores.

————. 1994. "La crisis del sistema político venezolano." *Revista Nueva Sociedad* 34: 142–57.

————. 1995. "Political Crisis and Constitutional Reform." In *The Lessons of the Venezuelan Experience,* ed. Louis W. Goodman, Johanna Mendelson Forman, Moisés Naím, Joseph S. Tulchin, and Gary Bland, 334–61. Washington, DC, and Baltimore: Woodrow Wilson Center Press and Johns Hopkins University Press.

————. 1998. *Venezuela en los noventa: Las crisis de la democracia.* Caracas: UCV and Ediciones IESA.

————. 2006. "Sowing Democracy in Venezuela: Advances and Challenges in a Time of Change." In *State and Society in Conflict: Comparative Perspectives on Andean Crises,* ed. Paul W. Drake and Eric Hershberg, 288–314. Pittsburgh: University of Pittsburgh Press.

Kornblith, Miriam, and Daniel H. Levine. 1995. "Venezuela: The Life and Times of the Party System." In *Building Democratic Institutions: Party Systems in Latin America,* ed. Scott Mainwaring and Timothy R. Scully, 37–71. Stanford: Stanford University Press.

Kornblith, Miriam, and Thaís Maingón. 1985. *Estado y gasto público en Venezuela, 1936–1980.* Caracas: Ediciones de la Biblioteca UCV.

Kornblith, Miriam, and Luken Quintana. 1981. "Gestión fiscal y centralización del poder político en los gobiernos de Cipriano Castro y Juan Vicente Gómez." *Politeia* 10: 143–238.

Krasner, Stephen D. 1988. "Sovereignty: An Institutional Perspective." *Comparative Political Studies* 21, no. 1 (April): 66–94.

Leal, Claudia. 2003. "Mapping the Colombian Conflict." *Canadian Journal of Latin American and Caribbean Studies* 28 (55–56): 211–22.

Leal, Francisco, and Andrés Dávila. 1990. *Clientelismo: El sistema político y su expresión regional.* Bogotá: IEPRI and Tercer Mundo Editores.

Leal, Francisco, and León Zamosc, eds. 1991. *Al filo del caos: Crisis política en la Colombia de los años 80.* Bogotá: Tercer Mundo Editores and IEPRI Universidad Nacional.

Leal Buitrago, Francisco. 1984. *Estado y política en Colombia.* Bogotá: Siglo XXI.

———. 1994. *El oficio de la guerra: La seguridad nacional en Colombia.* Bogotá: Tercer Mundo Editores and IEPRI.

———, ed. 1995. *En búsqueda de la estabilidad perdida.* Bogotá: Tercer Mundo Editores.

———, ed. 1996. *Tras las huellas de la crisis política.* Bogotá: Tercer Mundo Editores, FESCOL, and IEPRI.

———, ed. 1999. *Los laberintos de la guerra: Utopías e incertidumbres sobre la paz.* Bogotá: Tercer Mundo Editores and Universidad de los Andes, Facultad de Ciencias Sociales.

Lechner, Norbert. 1990. *Los patios interiores de la democracia: Subjetividad y política.* 2nd ed. Santiago: Fondo de Cultura Económica–FLACSO.

Le Grand, Catherine C. 2003. "The Colombian Crisis in Historical Perspective." *Canadian Journal of Latin American and Caribbean Studies* 28 (55–56): 165–209.

Levine, Daniel H. 1973. *Conflict and Political Change in Venezuela.* Princeton: Princeton University Press.

———. 1978. "Venezuela since 1958: The Consolidation of Democratic Politics." In *The Breakdown of Democratic Regimes: Latin America,* ed. Juan J. Linz and Alfred Stepan, 82–107. Baltimore: Johns Hopkins University Press.

———. 1981. *Religion and Politics in Latin America: The Catholic Church in Venezuela and Colombia.* Princeton: Princeton University Press.

———. 1985. "The Transition to Democracy: Are There Lessons from Venezuela?" *Bulletin of Latin American Research* 4 (2): 47–61.

———. 1988. "Paradigm Lost: From Dependency to Democracy." *World Politics* 40, no. 3 (April): 377–94.

———. 1989. "Venezuela: The Nature, Sources, and Future Prospects of Democracy." In *Democracy in Developing Countries: Latin America,* ed. Larry Diamond, Juan J. Linz, and Seymour Martin Lipset, 247–89. Boulder: Lynne Rienner.

Levine, Daniel H., and Brian F. Crisp. 1999. "Venezuela: The Character, Crisis, and Posible Future of Democracy." In *Democracy in Developing Countries:*

Latin America, 2nd ed., ed. Larry Diamond, Jonathan Hartlyn, Juan J. Linz, and Seymour Martin Lipset, 367–428. Boulder: Lynne Rienner.

Levitsky, Steven, and Lucan Way. 2002. "Elections without Democracy: The Rise of Competitive Authoritarianism." *Journal of Democracy* 13 (2): 51–66.

Levitt, Steven, and Mauricio Rubio. 2000. "Understanding Crime in Colombia and What Can Be Done About It." Working Paper Series No. 20, August, Fedesarrollo, Bogotá.

Lieuwen, Edwin. 1954. *Petroleum in Venezuela: A History.* Berkeley: University of California Press.

Lijphart, Arend. 1969. "Consociational Democracy." *World Politics* 21, no. 2 (January): 207–25.

———. 1971. "Comparative Politics and the Comparative Method." *American Political Science Review* 65, no. 3 (September): 682–93.

———. 1975. "The Comparable-Cases Strategy in Comparative Research." *Comparative Political Studies* 8, no. 2 (July): 158–77.

Linz, Juan J. 1973. "The Future of an Authoritarian Situation or the Institutionalization of an Authoritarian Regime." In *Authoritarian Brazil: Origins, Policies and Future,* ed. Alfred Stepan, 233–54. New Haven: Yale University Press.

———. 1975. "Totalitarian and Authoritarian Regimes." In *Handbook of Political Science,* vol. 3, ed. Fred I. Greenstein and Nelson W. Polsby, 175–411. Reading, MA: Addison-Wesley.

———. 1978. *The Breakdown of Democratic Regimes: Crisis, Breakdown and Reequilibration.* Baltimore: Johns Hopkins University Press.

Linz, Juan J., and Alfred Stepan, eds. 1978. *The Breakdown of Democratic Regimes: Latin America.* Baltimore: Johns Hopkins University Press.

———. 1996a. *Problems of Democratic Transition and Consolidation: Southern Europe, South America and Post-Communist Europe.* Baltimore: Johns Hopkins University Press.

———. 1996b. "Towards Consolidated Democracies." *Journal of Democracy* 7, no. 2 (April): 13–33.

Linz, Juan J., Alfred Stepan, and Richard Gunther. 1995. "Democratic Transition and Consolidation in Southern Europe, with Reflections on Latin America and Eastern Europe." In *The Politics of Democratic Consolidation: Southern Europe in Comparative Perspective,* ed. Richard Gunther, P. Nikiforos Diamandouros, and Hans-Jürgen Puhle, 77–123. Baltimore: Johns Hopkins University Press.

Linz, Juan J., and Arturo Valenzuela, eds. 1994a. *The Failure of Presidential Democracy: The Case of Latin America,* vol. 1. Baltimore: Johns Hopkins University Press.

———, eds. 1994b. *The Failure of Presidential Democracy: Comparative Perspectives,* vol. 2. Baltimore: Johns Hopkins University Press.

Lleras, Alberto. 1997. *Memorias.* Bogotá: Banco de la República and El Ancora Editores.

López-Alves, Fernando. 2000. *State Formation and Democracy in Latin America, 1810–1900.* Durham: Duke University Press.

López Maya, Margarita. 1994. "El ascenso en Venezuela de la Causa R." Paper presented at the conference "Inequality and New Forms of Popular Representation," Institute of Latin American and Iberian Studies (ILAIS), Columbia University, March 3–5, New York.

———. 1996. *EE.UU. en Venezuela, 1945–1948: Revelaciones de los archivos estadounidenses.* Caracas: Ediciones CDCH and Universidad Central de Venezuela.

———. 1997. "The Rise of Causa R in Venezuela." In *The New Politics of Inequality in Latin America,* ed. Douglas Chalmers, Carlos Vilas, Katherine Hite, Scott Martin, Kerianne Piester, and Monique Segarra, 117–43. New York: Oxford University Press.

———. 1998. "Problemas de los partidos populares en la transición (tras una alternativa política en Venezuela)." *Contribuciones* 15, no. 1 (January–March): 79–106.

———, ed. 1999. *Lucha popular, democracia, neoliberalismo: protesta popular en América Latina en los años del ajuste.* Caracas: UCV and Editorial Nueva Sociedad.

López Maya, Margarita, and Luis Gómez Calcaño. 1989. "Desarrollo y hegemonía en la sociedad venezolana: 1958–1985." In *De Punto Fijo al pacto social: Desarrollo y hegemonía en Venezuela (1958–1985),* ed. Margarita López Maya, Luis Gómez Calcaño, and Thaís Maingón, 13–124. Caracas: Fondo Editorial Acta Científica Venezolana.

López Maya, Margarita, Luis Gómez Calcaño, and Thaís Maingón, eds. 1989. *De Punto Fijo al pacto social: Desarrollo y hegemonía en Venezuela (1958–1985).* Caracas: Fondo Editorial Acta Científica Venezolana.

López Maya, Margarita, and Edgardo Lander. 1996. "La transformación de una sociedad 'petrolero-rentista': Desarrollo económico y viabilidad democrática en Venezuela." In *Democracia y reestructuración económica en América Latina,* ed. Pilar Gaitán, Ricardo Peñaranda, and Eduardo Pizarro, 159–88. Bogotá: IEPRI and CEREC.

López Maya, Margarita, and Luis E. Lander. 2004. "The Struggle for Hegemony in Venezuela." In *Politics in the Andes: Identity, Conflict, Reform,* ed. Jo-Marie Burt and Philip Mauceri, 207–27. Pittsburgh: University of Pittsburgh Press.

López Maya, Margarita, and Carlos Meléndez. 2007. "Partidos y sistema de partidos en Venezuela." In *La política por dentro: Cambios y continuidades en las organizaciones políticas de los países andinos,* ed. Rafael Roncagliolo and Carlos Meléndez, 273–302. Lima: IDEA and Asociación Civil Transparencia.

López Michelsen, Alfonso. 2001. *Palabras pendientes: Conversaciones con Enrique Santos Calderón.* Bogotá: El Ancora Editores.

López-Restrepo, Andrés. 1998. "Narcotráfico y elecciones: Delincuencia y corrupción en la reciente vida política colombiana." In *Elecciones y democracia en Colombia, 1997–1998,* ed. Ana María Bejarano and Andrés Dávila, 35–50. Bogotá: Fundación Social Departamento de Ciencia Política de la Universidad de los Andes and Veeduría Ciudadana a la Elección Presidencial.

López-Restrepo, Andrés, and Álvaro Camacho-Guizado. 2003. "From Smugglers to Warlords: Twentieth-Century Colombia Drug Traffickers." *Canadian Journal of Latin American and Caribbean Studies* 28 (55–56): 249–76.

Luciani, Giacomo. 1987. "Allocation vs. Production States: A Theoretical Framework." In *The Rentier State,* ed. Hazem Beblawi and Giacomo Luciani, 63–82. London: Croom Helm.

———. 1994. "The Oil Rent, the Fiscal Crisis of the State and Democratization." In *Democracy Without Democrats? The Renewal of Politics in the Muslim World,* ed. Ghassan Salamé, 130–55. London: I. B. Tauris.

Luque, Guillermo. 1986. *De la Acción Católica al partido COPEI, 1936–1946.* Caracas: Ediciones de la Facultad de Humanidades y Educación, UCV.

Machillanda Pinto, José. 1988. *Poder político y poder militar en Venezuela, 1958–1986.* Caracas: Ediciones Centauro.

Mahoney, James. 2001. *The Legacies of Liberalism: Path-Dependence and Political Regimes in Central America.* Baltimore: Johns Hopkins University Press.

———. 2003. "Knowledge Accumulation in Comparative Historical Research: The Case of Democracy and Authoritarianism." In *Comparative Historical Analysis in the Social Sciences,* ed. James Mahoney and Dietrich Rueschemeyer, 131–74. Cambridge: Cambridge University Press.

Mainwaring, Scott. 1992. "Transitions to Democracy and Democratic Consolidation: Theoretical and Comparative Issues." In *Issues in Democratic Consolidation: The New South American Democracies in Comparative Perspective,* ed. Scott Mainwaring, Guillermo O'Donnell, and J. Samuel Valenzuela, 294–335. Notre Dame: University of Notre Dame Press.

———. 1993. "Presidentialism, Multipartism, and Democracy: The Difficult Combination." *Comparative Political Studies* 26 (2): 198–228.

———. 1999a. "Democratic Survivability in Latin America." In *Democracy and Its Limits: Lessons from Asia, Latin America, and the Middle East,* ed. Howard Handelman and Mark Tessler, 11–68. Notre Dame: University of Notre Dame Press.

———. 1999b. *Rethinking Party Systems in the Third Wave of Democratization: The Case of Brazil.* Stanford: Stanford University Press.

Mainwaring, Scott, Ana María Bejarano, and Eduardo Pizarro. 2006. "The Crisis of Democratic Representation in the Andes: An Overview." In *The Crisis of Democratic Representation in the Andes,* ed. Scott Mainwaring, Ana María Bejarano, and Eduardo Pizarro, 1–44. Stanford: Stanford University Press. [Spanish-language edition: *La crisis de la representación democrática en los países andinos.* Bogotá: Grupo Editorial Norma, 2008.]

Mainwaring, Scott, Daniel Brinks, and Aníbal Pérez-Liñán. 2001. "Classifying Political Regimes in Latin America, 1945–1999." *Studies in Comparative International Development* 36 (1): 37–65.

Mainwaring, Scott, Guillermo O'Donnell, and J. Samuel Valenzuela, eds. 1992. *Issues in Democratic Consolidation: The New South American Democracies in Comparative Perspective.* Notre Dame: University of Notre Dame Press.

Mainwaring, Scott, and Aníbal Pérez-Liñán. 2005. "Latin American Democratization since 1978: Democratic Transitions, Breakdowns, and Erosions." In *The Third Wave of Democratization in Latin America: Advances and Setbacks,* ed. Frances Hagopian and Scott Mainwaring, 14–59. Cambridge: Cambridge University Press.

Mainwaring, Scott, and Timothy R. Scully, eds. 1995. *Building Democratic Institutions: Party Systems in Latin America.* Stanford: Stanford University Press.

Mainwaring, Scott, and Matthew Soberg Shugart, eds. 1997. *Presidentialism and Democracy in Latin America.* Cambridge: Cambridge University Press.

Malloy, James M., ed. 1977. *Authoritarianism and Corporatism in Latin America.* Pittsburgh: University of Pittsburgh Press.

Malloy, James M., and Mitchell Seligson, eds. 1987. *Authoritarians and Democrats: Regime Transition in Latin America.* Pittsburgh: University of Pittsburgh Press.

Mann, Michael. 1984. "The Autonomous Power of the State: Its Origins, Mechanisms, and Results." *Archives Europeénes de Sociologie* 25 (2): 185–213.

Maravall, José María, and Julián Santamaría. 1986. "Political Change in Spain and the Prospects for Democracy." In *Transitions from Authoritarian Rule: Southern Europe,* ed. Guillermo O'Donnell, Philippe C. Schmitter, and Laurence Whitehead, 71–108. Baltimore: Johns Hopkins University Press.

March, James G., and Johan P. Olsen. 1984. "The New Institutionalism: Organizational Factors in Political Life." *American Political Science Review* 78 (September): 734–49.

———. 1989. *Rediscovering Institutions: The Organizational Basis of Politics.* New York: Free Press.

Martínez, Pedro José. 1980. "La unidad de la izquierda en Venezuela." *Politeia* 9: 311–93.

Martz, John D. 1962. *Colombia: A Contemporary Political Survey.* Chapel Hill: University of North Carolina Press.

———. 1966. *Accion Democrática: Evolution of a Modern Political Party in Venezuela.* Princeton: Princeton University Press.

————. 1992. "Party Elites and Leadership in Colombia and Venezuela." *Journal of Latin American Studies* 24 (1): 87–121.

————. 1997. *The Politics of Clientelism: Democracy and the State in Colombia.* New Brunswick, NJ: Transaction.

Mason, Ann. 2000. "La crisis de seguridad en Colombia: Causas y consecuencias internacionales de un Estado en vía de fracaso." *Colombia Internacional* 49–50: 82–102.

Mason, Ann, and Arlene Tickner. 2006. "A Transregional Security Cartography of the Andes." In *State and Society in Conflict: Comparative Perspectives on Andean Crises,* ed. Paul Drake and Eric Hershberg, 74–98. Pittsburgh: University of Pittsburgh Press.

Mauceri, Philip. 2004. "States, Elites, and the Response to Insurgency." In *Politics in the Andes: Identity, Conflict, Reform,* ed. Jo-Marie Burt and Philip Mauceri, 146–63. Pittsburgh: University of Pittsburgh Press.

McCoy, Jennifer L., and David J. Myers, eds. 2004. *The Unraveling of Representative Democracy in Venezuela.* Baltimore: Johns Hopkins University Press.

McCoy, Jennifer L., Andrés Serbin, William C. Smith, and Andrés Stambouli, eds. 1995. *Venezuelan Democracy under Stress.* Coral Gables, FL: North-South Center, University of Miami.

Medina, Medófilo. 1980. *Historia del Partido Comunista de Colombia,* vol. 1. Bogotá: Centro de Estudios e Investigaciones Sociales.

————. 1984. *La protesta urbana en Colombia en el siglo veinte.* Bogotá: Ediciones Aurora.

Méndez, Juan E. 1999. "Problems of Lawless Violence: Introduction." In *The (Un)Rule of Law and the Underprivileged in Latin America,* ed. Juan E. Méndez, Guillermo O'Donnell, and Paulo Sergio Pinheiro, 19–24. Notre Dame: University of Notre Dame Press.

Mesa, Darío. 1980. "La vida política después de Panamá." In *Manual de Historia de Colombia,* vol. 3, ed. Jaime Jaramillo Uribe et al., 83–176. Bogotá: Instituto Colombiano de Cultura.

Michels, Robert. 1968. *Political Parties: A Sociological Study of the Oligarchical Tendencies of Modern Democracy.* 2nd ed. New York: Free Press.

Mitchell, Brian R. 2003. *International Historical Statistics: The Americas, 1750–2000.* 5th ed. New York: Palgrave Macmillan.

Molina Vega, José Enrique. 1991a. "El nuevo sistema electoral municipal. ¿Exito o fracaso?" In *Liderazgo e ideología,* ed. Magallanes Manuel Vicente. Caracas: Consejo Supremo Electoral.

————. 1991b. *El sistema electoral venezolano y sus consecuencias políticas.* Valencia: IIDH, CAPEL, and Vadell Hermanos Editores.

Molina Vega, José Enrique, and Carmen Pérez-Baralt. 1996. "El comportamiento electoral en Venezuela (1946–1993): Factores explicativos." *Cuestiones Políticas,* no. 17: 25–60.

Montenegro, Santiago. 2006. *Sociedad abierta, geografía y desarrollo: Ensayos de economía política.* Bogotá: Editorial Norma.

Moore, Barrington. 1966. *The Social Origins of Dictatorship and Democracy.* Boston: Beacon Press.

Müller Rojas, Alberto. 1989. "Las fuerzas del orden en la crisis de febrero." *Politeia* 13: 115–54.

———1992a. *Relaciones peligrosas: Militares, política y Estado.* Caracas: Fondo Editorial APUCV/IPP, Fondo Editorial Tropykos and Fundación Gual y España.

———. 1992b. "Venezuela: Trancas y salidas. Factores militares de la crisis del régimen político." *Politeia* 15: 93–107.

Munck, Gerardo L., and Carol Skalnik Leff. 1999. "Modes of Transition and Democratization: South America and Eastern Europe in Comparative Perspective." In *Transitions to Democracy,* ed. Lisa Anderson, 193–216. New York: Columbia University Press.

Naím, Moisés. 1993. *Paper Tigers and Minotaurs: The Politics of Venezuela's Economic Reforms.* Washington, DC: Carnegie Endowment for International Peace.

———. 2001. "The Real Story behind Venezuela's Woes." *Journal of Democracy* 12, no. 2 (April): 17–31.

Naím, Moisés, and Ramón Piñango. 1984. *El caso Venezuela: Una ilusión de armonía.* Caracas: Ediciones IESA.

Nelson, Joan M. 1994. *A Precarious Balance: An Overview of Democracy and Economic Reforms in Eastern Europe and Latin America.* San Francisco: International Center for Economic Growth and Overseas Development Council.

Nettl, J. P. 1968. "The State as a Conceptual Variable." *World Politics* 20, no. 4 (July): 559–92.

North, Douglas. 1990. *Institutions, Institutional Change and Economic Performance.* Cambridge: Cambridge University Press.

Ocampo, José Antonio, ed. 1987. *Historia económica de Colombia.* Bogotá: Siglo XXI.

Ochoa Antich, Enrique. 1992. *Carta a los militares de nuestra generación.* Caracas: Fuentes Editores.

O'Donnell, Guillermo. 1973. *Modernization and Bureaucratic-Authoritarianism: Studies in South American Politics.* Berkeley: Institute of International Studies.

———. 1992. "Transitions, Continuities and Paradoxes." In *Issues in Democratic Consolidation: The New South American Democracies in Comparative Perspective,* ed. Scott Mainwaring, Guillermo O'Donnell, and J. Samuel Valenzuela, 17–56. Notre Dame: University of Notre Dame Press.

———. 1994a. "Delegative Democracy." *Journal of Democracy* 5, no. 1 (January): 56–69.

————. 1994b. "The State, Democratization and Some Conceptual Problems." In *Latin American Political Economy in the Age of Neoliberal Reform: Theoretical and Comparative Perspectives for the 1990s,* ed. William Smith et al., 157–80. New Brunswick, NJ: Transaction.

————. 1996a. "Illusions about Consolidation." *Journal of Democracy* 7, no. 2 (April): 34–51.

————. 1996b. "Illusions and Conceptual Flaws." *Journal of Democracy* 7, no. 4 (October): 160–68.

————. 1996c. "Otra institucionalización." *Política y Gobierno* 3 (2): 219–44.

————. 1999a. "On the State, Democratization and some Conceptual Problems: A Latin American View with Glances at some Post-Communist Countries." In *Counterpoints: Selected Essays on Authoritarianism and Democratization,* 133–57, Notre Dame: University of Notre Dame Press.

————. 1999b. "Polyarchies and the (Un)rule of Law in Latin America: A Partial Conclusion." In *The (Un)Rule of Law and the Underprivileged in Latin America,* ed. Juan E. Méndez, Guillermo O'Donnell, and Paulo Sérgio Pinheiro, 303–37. Notre Dame: University of Notre Dame Press.

————. 2004. "Human Development, Human Rights and Democracy." In *The Quality of Democracy: Theory and Applications,* ed. Guillermo O'Donnell, Jorge Vargas Cullell, and Osvaldo M. Iazzetta, 9–92. Notre Dame: University of Notre Dame Press.

O'Donnell, Guillermo, and Philippe Schmitter. 1986. "Tentative Conclusions about Uncertain Democracies." In *Transitions from Authoritarian Rule: Comparative Perspectives,* ed. Guillermo O'Donnell, Philippe C. Schmitter, and Laurence Whitehead, 3–78. Baltimore: Johns Hopkins University Press.

O'Donnell, Guillermo, Philippe C. Schmitter, and Laurence Whitehead, eds. 1986. *Transitions from Authoritarian Rule: Comparative Perspectives.* Baltimore: Johns Hopkins University Press.

Oquist, Paul. 1978. *Violencia, conflicto y política en Colombia.* Bogotá: IEC and Biblioteca del Banco Popular.

Paige, Jeffery. 1997. *Coffee and Power: Revolution and the Rise of Democracy in Central America.* Cambridge, MA: Harvard University Press.

Palacios, Marco. 1983. *El café en Colombia: 1850–1970.* Bogotá: Universidad Nacional de Colombia.

————. 1995. *Entre la legitimidad y la violencia: Colombia, 1875–1994.* Bogotá: Grupo Editorial Norma.

————. 1999. "Presencia y ausencia de populismo: Para un contrapunto colombo-venezolano." Paper presented at the workshop "Del populismo de los antiguos al populismo de los modernos," Colegio de México and Instituto de Estudios Políticos de París, October 20–21, Mexico City.

————. 2000. "La solución política al conflicto armado, 1982–1997." In *Armar la paz es desarmar la guerra,* ed. Alvaro Camacho and Francisco Leal,

345–401. Bogotá: CEREC, DNP, PNUD, FESCOL, IEPRI, Presidencia de la Republica.

Palacios, Marco, and Frank Safford. 2002. *Colombia: País fragmentado, sociedad dividida.* Bogota: Editorial Norma.

Paramio, Ludolfo. 1988. "Algunos rasgos de las transiciones pactadas a la democracia." *Pensamiento Iberoamericano: Revista de Economía Política* 14: 39–45.

Pardo Rueda, Rafael. 1996. *De primera mano: Colombia 1986–1994: Entre conflictos y esperanzas.* Bogotá: CEREC and Grupo Editorial Norma.

Pastor, Robert A., ed. 1989. *Democracy in the Americas: Stopping the Pendulum.* New York: Holmes and Meier.

Payne, J. Mark, Daniel Zovatto G., Fernando Carrillo Flórez, and Andrés Allamand Zavala. 2002. *Democracies in Development: Politics and Reform in Latin America.* Washington, DC: Inter-American Development Bank and International Institute for Democracy and Electoral Assistance.

Payne, Mark J., Daniel Zovatto G., and Mercedes Mateo Díaz, eds. 2006. *La política importa. Democracia y desarrollo en América Latina.* México: Banco Interamericano de Desarrollo and Instituto Internacional para la Democracia y la Asistencia Electoral.

Pécaut, Daniel. 1987. *Orden y violencia: Colombia 1930–1954.* Bogotá: Siglo XXI and Fondo Editorial CEREC.

———. 1989. *Crónica de dos décadas de política colombiana, 1968–1988.* 2nd ed. Bogotá: Siglo XXI.

Peeler, John A. 1992. "Elite Settlement and Democratic Consolidation: Colombia, Costa Rica and Venezuela." In *Elites and Democratic Consolidation in Latin America and Southern Europe,* ed. John Higley and Richard Gunther, 81–112. Cambridge: Cambridge University Press.

———. 1995. "Decay and Renewal in Democratic Regimes: Colombia and Venezuela." Paper presented at the XVI Annual Conference of the Middle Atlantic Council of Latin American Studies (MACLAS), Albright College, March 31–April 1, Reading, PA.

Peña, Alfredo. 1978. *Conversaciones con Douglas Bravo.* Caracas: Editorial Ateneo de Caracas.

Peñarando, Ricardo, and Javier Guerrero, eds. 1999. *De las armas a la política.* Bogotá: TM Editores and IEPRI, Universidad Nacional.

Penfold-Becerra, Michael A. 1999. "Institutional Electoral Incentives and Decentralization Outcomes: Comparing Colombia and Venezuela." Ph.D. diss., Columbia University.

———. 2001. "El colapso del sistema de partidos en Venezuela: Explicación de una muerte anunciada." In *Venezuela en transición: Elecciones y democracia, 1998–2000,* ed. José Vicente Carrasquero, Thaís Maingón, and Friedrich Welsch, 36–51. Caracas: CDB Publicaciones.

―――. 2004a. "Electoral Dynamics and Decentralization in Venezuela." In *Decentralization and Democracy in Latin America,* ed. Alfred Montero and David Samuels, 155–79. Notre Dame: University of Notre Dame Press.

―――. 2004b. "Federalism and Institutional Change in Venezuela." In *Federalism and Democracy in Latin America,* ed. Edward L. Gibson, 197–225. Baltimore: Johns Hopkins University Press.

―――. 2007. "Clientelism and Social Funds: Evidence from Chávez's Misiones." *Latin American Politics and Society* 49 (4): 63–84.

Perea-Restrepo, Carlos Mario. 1996. *Porque la sangre es espíritu: Imaginario y discurso político de las élites capitalinas,* 1942–1949, Bogotá: Aguilar.

―――. 1998. "La segunda república: Un proyecto cultural. El Frente Nacional en Colombia: Origenes y Primera Administración, 1956–1962." Unpublished manuscript, Instituto de Estudios Políticos y Relaciones Internacionales, Bogotá.

Petkoff, Teodoro. 1976. *Proceso a la izquierda.* Bogotá: Editorial La Oveja Negra.

―――. 1986. "Intervención de Venezuela." In *Procesos de reconciliación nacional en América Latina,* ed. Instituto de Estudios Liberales. Bogotá: Editora Guadalupe.

―――. 1990. *Checoeslovaquia: El Socialismo como problema.* Caracas: Monte Ávila Editores.

―――. 1997. *Por qué hago lo que hago.* Caracas: Alfadil Ediciones.

―――. 2000. *La Venezuela de Chávez: Una segunda opinión.* Caracas: Grijalbo.

Pitkin, Hannah Fenichel. 1967. *The Concept of Representation.* Berkeley: University of California Press.

Pizarro, Eduardo. 1986. "La guerrilla revolucionaria en Colombia." In *Pasado y presente de la violencia en Colombia,* ed. Gonzalo Sánchez and Ricardo Peñaranda, 391–411. Bogotá: CEREC.

―――. 1987a. "La profesionalización militar en Colombia (I)." *Análisis Político* 1 (May–August): 27–54.

―――. 1987b. "La profesionalización militar en Colombia (II)." *Análisis Político* 2 (September–December): 7–39.

―――. 1988. "La profesionalización militar en Colombia (III): Los regímenes militares (1953–1958)." *Análisis Político* 3 (January–April): 3–37.

―――. 1991a. "La insurgencia armada: raíces y perspectivas." In *Al filo del caos: Crisis política en la Colombia de los años 80,* ed. Francisco Leal and León Zamosc, 159–208. Bogotá: Tercer Mundo Editores and Universidad Nacional.

―――. 1991b. *Las Farc 1949–1966: De la autodefensa a la combinación de todas las formas de lucha.* Bogotá: Tercer Mundo Editores and IEPRI.

―――. 1995. "La reforma militar en un contexto de democratización política." In *En búsqueda de la estabilidad perdida: Actores políticos en la Colombia de los 90,* ed. Francisco Leal. Bogotá: Tercer Mundo Editores and IEPRI.

———. 1996a. *Insurgencia sin revolución: La guerrilla en Colombia en una perspectiva comparada.* Bogotá: Tercer Mundo Editores and IEPRI.

———. 1996b. "La crisis de los partidos y los partidos en la crisis." In *Tras las huellas de la crisis política,* ed. Francisco Leal. Bogotá: Tercer Mundo Editores, FESCOL, and IEPRI.

———. 2004. *Democracia asediada.* Bogotá: Editorial Norma.

———. 2006. "Giants with Feet of Clay: Political Parties in Colombia." In *The Crisis of Democratic Representation in the Andes,* ed. Scott Mainwaring, Ana María Bejarano, and Eduardo Pizarro Leongómez, 78–99. Stanford: Stanford University Press.

Pizarro, Eduardo, and Ana María Bejarano. 2007. "Political Reform after 1991: What Still Needs to Be Reformed?" In *Peace, Democracy, and Human Rights in Colombia,* ed. Christopher Welna and Gustavo Gallón, 219–67. Notre Dame: University of Notre Dame Press.

Plaza, Helena. 1978. *El 23 de enero de 1958 y el proceso de consolidación de la democracia representativa en Venezuela.* Caracas: Garbizu and Todtmann Editores.

Posada-Carbó, Eduardo. 2006. *La nación soñada: Violencia, liberalismo y democracia en Colombia.* Bogotá: Grupo Editorial Norma.

Powell, John D. 1971. *Political Mobilization of the Venezuelan Peasant.* Cambridge, MA: Harvard University Press.

Powell, Walter W., and Paul J. DiMaggio, eds. 1991. *The New Institutionalism in Organizational Analysis.* Chicago: University of Chicago Press.

Preuss, Ulrich K. 1991. "The Politics of Constitution Making: Transforming Politics into Constitutions." *Law and Policy* 13, no. 2 (April): 107–23.

Pridham, Geoffrey. 1995. "The International Context of Democratic Consolidation: Southern Europe in Comparative Perspective." In *The Politics of Democratic Consolidation: Southern Europe in Comparative Perspective,* ed. Richard Gunther, P. Nikiforos Diamandouros, and Hans-Jürgen Puhle, 166–203. Baltimore: Johns Hopkins University Press.

Przeworski, Adam. 1986. "Some Problems in the Study of the Transition to Democracy." In *Transitions from Authoritarian Rule: Comparative Perspectives,* ed. Guillermo O'Donnell, Philippe Schmitter, and Laurence Whitehead, 47–63. Baltimore: Johns Hopkins University Press.

———. 1988. "Democracy as a Contingent Outcome of Conflicts." In *Constitutionalism and Democracy,* ed. Jon Elster and Rune Slagstad, 59–80. Cambridge: Cambridge University Press.

———. 1991. *Democracy and the Market: Political and Economic Reforms in Eastern Europe and Latin America.* Cambridge: Cambridge University Press.

———. 1992. "The Games of Transition." In *Issues in Democratic Consolidation: The New South American Democracies in Comparative Perspective,* ed. Scott Mainwaring, Guillermo O'Donnell, and J. Samuel Valenzuela, 105–52. Notre Dame: University of Notre Dame Press.

Przeworski, Adam, ed. 1995. *Sustainable Democracy.* Cambridge: Cambridge University Press.

Przeworski, Adam, Michael Alvarez, José Antonio Cheihub, and Fernando Limongi. 1996. "What Makes Democracy Endure?" *Journal of Democracy* 7, no. 1 (January): 39–55.

Putnam, Robert D., with Robert Leonardi and Raffaella Y. Nanetti. 1993. *Making Democracy Work: Civic Traditions in Modern Italy.* Princeton: Princeton University Press.

Ragin, Charles C. 1989. *The Comparative Method: Moving Beyond Qualitative and Quantitative Strategies.* Berkeley: University of California Press.

Ramos Jiménez, Alfredo, ed. 1987. *Venezuela: Un sistema político en crisis.* Mérida: Kappa Editores.

Rangel Rojas, Remigio. 1993. "El papel de las fuerzas armadas: Renovación democrática, apertura económica y nuevas relaciones cívico-militares." In *Venezuela: Democracia bajo presión,* ed. Andrés Serbin, Andrés Stambouli, Jennifer McCoy, and William Smith, 177–85. Caracas: Instituto Venezolano de Estudios Sociales y Políticos (INVESP) and Editorial Nueva Sociedad.

Rangel Suárez, Alfredo. 1998. *Colombia: Guerra en el fin de siglo.* Bogotá: TM Editores and Universidad de los Andes, Facultad de Ciencias Sociales.

Reales, Clara Elena, Ana María Bejarano, Laura Wills, Catalina Acevedo, Aquiles Arrieta, and Gustavo Salazar. 2001. "Política después de la guerra: La reincorporación de grupos guerrilleros en América Latina y su impacto en la consolidación de una oposición democrática viable." In *Estudios Ocasionales CIJUS.* Bogotá: Ediciones Uniandes, Facultad de Derecho, and National Endowment for Democracy.

Rey, Juan Carlos. 1972. "El sistema de partidos venezolano." *Politeia* 1: 175–230.

———. 1986. "Reformas del sistema electoral venezolano." In *Reformas electorales y partidos políticos,* ed. Manuel Vicente Magallanes. Caracas: Publicaciones del Consejo Electoral Supremo.

———. 1987. "El futuro de la democracia en Venezuela." In *Venezuela hacia el 2000: Desafíos y opciones,* ed. José Agustín Silva Michelena, 183–245. Caracas: Editorial Nueva Sociedad, ILDIS, and UNITAR/PROFAR.

———. 1989. *El futuro de la democracia en Venezuela.* Caracas: Serie Estudios Colección IDEA.

Roberts, Kenneth M. 2003. "Social Correlates of Party System Demise and Populist Resurgence in Venezuela." *Latin American Politics and Society* 45, no. 3 (Autumn): 35–57.

Rodríguez Iturbe, José. 1984. *Crónica de la década militar.* Caracas: Ediciones Nueva Política.

Romero, Aníbal. 1986. *La miseria del populismo: Mitos y realidades de la democracia en Venezuela.* Caracas: Ediciones Centauro.

———. 1996. "Venezuela: Democracy Hangs On." *Journal of Democracy* 7, no. 4 (October): 30–42.

Roncagliolo, Rafael, and Carlos Meléndez, eds. 2007. *La política por dentro: Cambios y continuidades en las organizaciones políticas de los países andinos.* Lima: IDEA and Asociación Civil Transparencia.

Ross, Michael L. 1999. "The Political Economy of the Resource Curse." *World Politics* 51 (2): 297–322.

———. 2001. "Does Oil Hinder Democracy?" *World Politics* 53 (3): 325–61.

Ross-Schneider, Ben. 1995. "Democratic Consolidations: Some Broad Comparisons and Sweeping Arguments." *Latin American Research Review* 30 (2): 215–34.

Rotberg, Robert I. 2002. "The New Nature of Nation-State Failure." In *The Washington Quarterly* 25, no. 3 (Summer): 85–96.

Rotker, Susana. 2000. "Nosotros somos los otros." In *Ciudadanías del miedo,* ed. Susana Rotker, 217–29. Caracas: Editorial Nueva Sociedad.

Rubio, Mauricio. 1999. "La Justicia en una sociedad violenta." In *Reconocer la guerra para construir la paz,* ed. Malcolm Deas and Maria Victoria Llorente, 201–35. Bogotá: CEREC, Ediciones Uniandes, Grupo Editorial Norma.

Rueschemeyer, Dietrich, Evelyne Huber Stephens, and John D. Stephens. 1992. *Capitalist Development and Democracy.* Chicago: University of Chicago Press.

Ruhl, Mark J. 1980. "The Military." In *Politics of Compromise: Coalition Government in Colombia,* ed. R. Albert Berry, Mauricio Solaún, and Ronald G. Hellman, 181–206. New Brunswick, NJ: Transaction.

Rustow, Dankwart A. 1970. "Transitions to Democracy: Toward a Dynamic Model." *Comparative Politics* 2 (3): 330–67.

Safford, Frank. 1977. *Aspectos del siglo XIX en Colombia.* Medellín: Ediciones Hombre Nuevo.

———. 1992. "The Problem of Political Order in Early Republican Spanish America." *Journal of Latin American Studies* 24: 83–97.

Salamanca, Luis. 1982. "El papel de la CTV en el sistema politico venezolano: La hipótesis corporativista." *Politeia* 11: 173–95.

Salcedo Bastardo, José Luis, Luis Herrera Campins, and Benito Raul Losada. 1978. *1958: Tránsito de la dictadura a la democracia en Venezuela.* Barcelona: Editorial Ariel.

Sánchez, Gonzalo. 1984. *Ensayos de historia social y política del siglo XX.* Bogotá: El Ancora Editores.

———. 1985. "La Violencia y sus efectos en el sistema político colombiano." In *Once ensayos sobre la Violencia,* ed. Marta Cárdenas. Bogotá: Centro Gaitán and Fondo Editorial CEREC.

———. 1986. "Los estudios sobre la Violencia: Balance y perspectivas." In *Pasado y presente de la violencia en Colombia,* ed. Gonzalo Sánchez and Ricardo Peñaranda, 11–30. Bogotá: Fondo Editorial CEREC.

————. 1996. "Introducción: Los intelectuales y la democracia en Colombia y América Latina, ayer y hoy." In *Democracia y reestructuración económica en América Latina,* ed. Pilar Gaitán, Ricardo Peñaranda, and Eduardo Pizarro, 11–21. Bogotá: CEREC and IEPRI.

Sánchez, Gonzalo, and Donny Meertens. 1983. *Bandoleros, gamonales y campesinos: El caso de la Violencia en Colombia.* Bogotá: El Ancora Editores.

Sánchez, Gonzalo and Ricardo Peñaranda, eds. 1986. *Pasado y presente de la Violencia en Colombia.* Bogotá: CEREC.

Sánchez, Omar. 2003. "Beyond Pacted Transitions in Spain and Chile: Elite and Institutional Differences." *Democratization* 10, no. 2 (Summer): 65–86.

Sartori, Giovanni. 1976. *Parties and Party Systems: A Framework for Analysis.* New York: Cambridge University Press.

————. 1984. *La política: Lógica y método en las ciencias sociales.* Mexico City: Fondo de Cultura Económica.

————. 1987. *The Theory of Democracy Revisited.* 2 vols. Chatham, NJ: Chatham House.

————. 1991. "Comparing and Miscomparing." *Journal of Theoretical Politics* 3 (3): 243–57.

————. 1994. *Ingeniería constitucional comparada.* Mexico City: Fondo de Cultura Económica.

Sartori, Giovanni, and Leonardo Morlino, eds. 1994. *La comparación en las ciencias sociales.* Madrid: Alianza Editorial.

Schedler, Andreas. 1998. "What Is Democratic Consolidation?" *Journal of Democracy* 9, no. 2 (April): 91–107.

Schmitter, Philippe C. 1994. "Dangers and Dilemmas of Democracy." *Journal of Democracy* 5, no. 2 (April): 57–74.

————. 1995. "More Liberal, Preliberal or Postliberal?" *Journal of Democracy* 6, no. 1 (January): 15–22.

Schmitter, Philippe C., and Terry Lynn Karl. 1993. "What Democracy Is . . . and Is Not." In *The Global Resurgence of Democracy,* ed. Larry Diamond and Marc F. Plattner, 39–52. Baltimore: Johns Hopkins University Press.

Schumpeter, Joseph A. 1950. *Capitalism, Socialism and Democracy.* New York: Harper and Row.

Segura, Renata, and Ana María Bejarano. 2004. "Ni una asamblea más sin nosotros! Exclusion, Inclusion and the Politics of Constitution-Making in the Andes." *Constellations* 11, no. 2 (June): 217–36.

Serbin, Andrés, Andrés Stambouli, Jennifer McCoy, and William Smith, eds. 1993. *Venezuela: La democracia bajo presión.* Caracas: INVESP and Nueva Sociedad.

Shain, Yossi, and Juan Linz. 1992. "The Role of Interim Governments." *Journal of Democracy* 3, no. 1 (January): 73–89.

————, eds. 1995. *Between States: Interim Governments in Democratic Transitions.* Cambridge: Cambridge University Press.

Shefter, Martin. 1994. *Political Parties and the State: The American Historical Experience.* Princeton: Princeton University Press.

Shepsle, Kenneth A. 1989. "Studying Institutions: Some Lessons from the Rational Choice Approach." *Journal of Theoretical Politics* 1: 131–47.

————. 1999. "La economía política de la reforma estatal: Política hasta la médula." In *Hacia el rediseño del Estado,* ed. Miguel Gandour Pordominsky and Luis Bernardo Mejía Guinand, 79–103. Bogotá: Tercer Mundo Editores and Departamento Nacional de Planeación.

Shepsle, Kenneth A., and Mark S. Bonchek. 1997. *Analyzing Politics: Rationality, Behavior and Institutions.* New York: Norton.

Shin, Doh Chull. 1994. "On the Third Wave of Democratization: A Synthesis and Evaluation of Recent Theory and Research." *World Politics* 47 (October): 135–70.

Shugart, Matthew Soberg. 1992. "Guerrillas and Elections: An Institutionalist Perspective on the Costs of Conflict and Competition." *International Studies Quarterly* 36, no. 2 (June): 121–52.

————. 2005. "The Unraveling of Representative Democracy in Venezuela." Review of *The Unraveling of Representative Democracy in Venezuela* by Jennifer L. McCoy and David J. Myers. *Perspectives on Politics* 3, no. 4 (December): 925–26.

Silva, Gabriel. 1989. "El origen del Frente Nacional y el gobierno de la Junta Militar." In *Nueva Historia de Colombia,* vol. 2, ed. Alvaro Tirado Mejía, 179–210. Bogotá: Planeta Colombiana Editorial.

Silva Michelena, José Agustín, ed. 1987. *Venezuela hacia el 2000: Desafíos y opciones.* Caracas: Editorial Nueva Sociedad, ILDIS, and UNITAR/PROFAR.

Skocpol, Theda. 1979. *States and Social Revolutions: A Comparative Analysis of France, Russia and China.* Cambridge: Cambridge University Press.

————. 1982. "Rentier State and Shi'a Islam in the Iranian Revolution." *Theory and Society* 2, no. 3 (May): 265–83.

————. 1985. "Bringing the State Back In: Strategies of Analysis in Current Research." In *Bringing the State Back In,* ed. Peter Evans, Dietrich Rueschemeyer, and Theda Skocpol, 3–38. Cambridge: Cambridge University Press.

Skocpol, Theda, and Margaret Somers. 1980. "The Uses of Comparative History in Macrosocial Inquiry." *Comparative Studies in Society and History* 22, no. 2 (April): 174–97.

Smith, William C., Carlos H. Acuña, and Eduardo A. Gamarra, eds. 1994. *Latin American Political Economy in the Age of Neoliberal Reform: Theoretical and Comparative Perspectives for the 1990s.* New Brunswick, NJ: Transaction.

Solaún, Mauricio. 1980. "Colombian Politics: Historical Characteristics and Problems." In *Politics of Compromise: Coalition Government in Colombia,* ed. R. Albert Berry, Ronald G. Hellman, and Mauricio Solaún, 1–57. New Brunswick, NJ: Transaction.

Solé Tura, Jordi. 1988. "Transición a la democracia y estabilidad: El caso de España." *Pensamiento Iberoamericano: Revista de Economía Política* 14: 263–71.

Sonntag, Heinz, and Thaís Maingón. 1992. *Venezuela 4-F 1992: Un análisis sociopolítico.* Caracas: Editorial Nueva Sociedad.

Sosa, Arturo. 1988. "Iglesia y democracia en Venezuela." *Revista SIC* 501 (January): 14–19.

Stambouli, Andrés. 1980. *Crisis política: Venezuela, 1945–1958.* Caracas: Editorial Ateneo de Caracas.

Stein, Stanley J., and Barbara Stein. 1970. *The Colonial Heritage of Latin America: Essays on Economic Dependence in Perspective.* New York: Oxford University Press.

Steinmo, Sven, Kathleen Thelen, and Frank Longstreth. 1992. *Structuring Politics: Historical Institutionalism in Comparative Analysis.* Cambridge: Cambridge University Press.

Stepan, Alfred. 1978. *The State and Society: Peru in Comparative Perspective.* Princeton: Princeton University Press.

———. 1986. "Paths toward Redemocratization: Theoretical and Comparative Considerations." In *Transitions from Authoritarian Rule: Comparative Perspectives,* ed. Guillermo O'Donnell, Philippe Schmitter, and Laurence Whitehead, 64–84. Baltimore: Johns Hopkins University Press.

———. 1988. *Rethinking Military Politics.* Princeton: Princeton University Press.

———. 1993. "On the Tasks of a Democratic Opposition." In *The Global Resurgence of Democracy,* ed. Larry Diamond and Marc F. Plattner, 61–69. Baltimore: Johns Hopkins University Press.

Tanaka, Martín. 2002. *La situación de la democracia en Colombia, Perú y Venezuela a inicios de siglo.* Lima: Comision Andina de Juristas.

———. 2005. "Peru 1980–2000: Chronicle of a Death Foretold? Determinism, Political Decisions and Open Outcomes." In *The Third Wave of Democratization in Latin America: Advances and Setbacks,* ed. Frances Hagopian and Scott Mainwaring, 261–88. Cambridge: Cambridge University Press.

———. 2006. "From Crisis to Collapse of the Party Systems and Dilemmas of Democratic Representation: Peru and Venezuela." In *The Crisis of Democratic Representation in the Andes,* ed. Scott Mainwaring, Ana María Bejarano, and Eduardo Pizarro Leongómez, 47–77. Stanford: Stanford University Press.

Tarrow, Sidney. 1994. *Power in Movement: Social Movements, Collective Action and Politics.* Cambridge: Cambridge University Press.

—————. 1995. "Mass Mobilization and Regime Change: Pacts, Reform and Popular Power in Italy (1918–1922) and Spain (1975–1978)." In *The Politics of Democratic Consolidation: Southern Europe in Comparative Perspective,* ed. Richard Gunther, P. Nikiforos Diamandouros, and Hans-Jürgen Puhle, 204–30. Baltimore: Johns Hopkins University Press.

Thelen, Kathleen. 2003. "How Institutions Evolve: Insights from Comparative Historical Analysis." In *Comparative Historical Analysis in the Social Sciences,* ed. James Mahoney and Dietrich Rueschemeyer, 208–40. Cambridge: Cambridge University Press.

Thelen, Kathleen, and Sven Steinmo. 1992. "Historical Institutionalism in Comparative Politics." In *Structuring Politics: Historical Institutionalism in Comparative Analysis,* ed. Sven Steinmo, Kathleen Thelen, and Frank Longstreth, 1–30. Cambridge: Cambridge University Press.

Thorp, Rosemary. 1998. *Progress, Poverty and Exclusion: An Economic History of Latin America in the 20th Century.* Washington, DC: Inter-American Development Bank.

Thoumi, Francisco. 1994. *Economía política y narcotráfico.* Bogotá: Tercer Mundo Editores.

—————, ed. 1997. *Drogas ilícitas en Colombia: Su impacto económico, político y social.* Bogotá: Planeta Colombiana Editorial.

Tilly, Charles. 1978. *From Mobilization to Revolution.* Reading, MA: Addison-Wesley.

—————. 1984. *Big Structures, Large Processes, Huge Comparisons.* New York: Russell Sage Foundation.

—————. 1994. "Democracy Is a Lake." Working Paper No. 185. Center for Studies of Social Change, New School for Social Research, New York.

—————. 2007. *Democracy.* Cambridge: Cambridge University Press.

Tirado Mejía, Alvaro, ed. 1989. *Nueva historia de Colombia.* Bogotá: Planeta Colombiana Editorial.

Trinkunas, Harold A. 2002. "The Crisis in Venezuelan Civil-Military Relations: From Punto Fijo to the Fifth Republic." *Latin American Research Review* 37 (1): 41–76.

Tugwell, Franklin. 1975. *The Politics of Oil in Venezuela.* Stanford: Stanford University Press.

United Nations Development Programme (UNDP). 2004. *Democracy in Latin America: Towards a Citizens' Democracy.* New York: UNDP.

Urán, Carlos Horacio. 1983. *Rojas y la manipulación del poder.* Bogotá: Carlos Valencia Editores.

Urbaneja, Diego Bautista. 1978. "Introducción histórica al sistema politico venezolano." *Politeia* 7: 11–59.

———. 1992. *Pueblo y petróleo en la política venezolana del siglo XX.* Caracas: Ediciones CEPET.

———. 1993. "Los partidos políticos, el Estado y la sociedad civil." In *Venezuela, democracia y futuro: Los partidos políticos en la década de los 90,* ed. Comisión Presidencial para la Reforma del Estado. Caracas: COPRE.

Uricoechea, Fernando. 1986. *Estado y burocracia en Colombia: Historia y organización.* Bogotá: Universidad Nacional de Colombia.

Valencia Tovar, Alvaro. 1992. *Testimonio de una época.* Bogotá: Planeta Colombiana Editorial.

Valenzuela, Arturo, Josep Colomer, Arend Lijphart and Matthew Shugart. 1999. "Sobre la reforma política en Colombia: Informe de la consultoría internacional." In *Reforma política. Un propósito de nación: Memorias,* ed. Ministerio del Interior. Bogotá: Ministerio del Interior.

Valenzuela, J. Samuel. 1992. "Democratic Consolidation in Post-Transitional Settings: Notion, Process, and Facilitating Conditions." In *Issues in Democratic Consolidation: The New South American Democracies in Comparative Perspective,* ed. Scott Mainwaring, Guillermo O'Donnell, and J. Samuel Valenzuela, 57–104. Notre Dame: University of Notre Dame Press.

Vallenilla Lanz, Laureano. 1961. *Cesarismo democrático: Estudio sobre las bases sociológicas de la constitución efectiva de Venezuela.* 4th ed. Caracas: Tipografía Garrido.

Vallenilla, Luis. 1975. *Oil, the Making of a New Economic Order: Venezuelan Oil and OPEC.* New York: McGraw-Hill.

Valles, Oscar. 1992. "Los antecedentes programáticos del Pacto de Punto Fijo: Proyecto de consolidación democrática, 1946–1948." *Politeia* 15: 289–302.

Van Cott, Donna Lee. 2005. *From Movements to Parties in Latin America: The Evolution of Ethnic Politics.* New York: Cambridge University Press.

Vázquez Carrizosa, Camilo. 1969. *El Frente Nacional, su orden y desarrollo: Memorias de Camilo Vázquez-Cobo Carrizosa.* Ed. Sylvia Wills de Vázquez Carrizosa. Cali: n.p.

Velásquez, Ramón J. 1979. "Aspectos de la evolución política de Venezuela en el último medio siglo." In *Venezuela moderna: Medio siglo de historia, 1926–1976,* ed. Ramón J. Velásquez, Arístides Calvani, Allan Brewer-Carias, Carlos Rafael Silva, Juan Liscano, and Marcel Roche, 11–433. Caracas: Editorial Ariel and Fundación Eugenio Mendoza.

Velásquez, Ramón J., Arístides Calvani, Allan Brewer-Carias, Carlos Rafael Silva, Juan Liscano, and Marcel Roche, eds. 1979. *Venezuela moderna: Medio siglo de historia, 1926–1976.* Caracas: Editorial Ariel and Fundación Eugenio Mendoza.

Vilas, Carlos M. 1997. "Participation, Inequality and the Whereabouts of Democracy." In *The New Politics of Inequality in Latin America: Rethinking*

Participation and Representation, ed. Douglas A. Chalmers, Carlos M. Vilas, Katherine Hite, Scott B. Martin, Kerianne Peister, and Monique Segarra, 3–42. Oxford: Oxford University Press.

Waldmann, Peter. 1986. "La violencia política en América Latina." In *Procesos de reconciliación nacional en América Latina,* ed. Instituto de Estudios Liberales, 23–35. Bogotá: Instituto de Estudios Liberales.

Weingast, Barry R. "The Political Foundations of Democracy and the Rule of Law." *American Political Science Review* 91, no. 2 (June): 245–63.

Weyland, Kurt. 2005. "The Growing Sustainability of Brazil's Low-Quality Democracy." In *The Third Wave of Democratization in Latin America: Advances and Setbacks,* ed. Frances Hagopian and Scott Mainwaring, 90–120. Cambridge: Cambridge University Press.

Whitehead, Laurence. 1986. "International Aspects of Democratization." In *Transitions from Authoritarian Rule: Comparative Perspectives,* ed. Guillermo O'Donnell, Philippe Schmitter, and Laurence Whitehead, 3–46. Baltimore: Johns Hopkins University Press.

———. 1993. "The Alternatives to 'Liberal Democracy': A Latin American Perspective." In *Prospects for Democracy: North, South, East, West,* ed. David Held, 312–29. Stanford: Stanford University Press.

Wickham-Crowley, Timothy. 1989. "Winners, Losers and Also-Rans: Toward a Comparative Sociology of Latin American Guerrilla Movements." In *Power and Popular Protest: Latin American Social Movements,* ed. Susan Eckstein, 132–81. Berkeley: University of California Press.

———. 1992. *Guerrillas and Revolution in Latin America: A Comparative Study of Insurgents and Regimes since 1956.* Princeton: Princeton University Press.

Wilde, Alexander. 1978. "Conversations among Gentlemen: 'Oligarchic' Democracy in Colombia." In *The Breakdown of Democratic Regimes: Latin America,* ed. Juan J. Linz and Alfred Stepan, 28–81. Baltimore: Johns Hopkins University Press.

———. 1980. "The Contemporary Church: the Political and the Pastoral." In *Politics of Compromise: Coalition Government in Colombia,* ed. R. Albert Berry, Ronald Hellman, and Mauricio Solaún, 207–35. New Brunswick, NJ: Transaction.

———. 1982. *Conversaciones de caballeros: La quiebra de la democracia en Colombia.* Bogotá: Ediciones Tercer Mundo.

Williams, Robert G. 1994. *States and Social Evolution: Coffee and the Rise of National Governments in Central America.* Chapel Hill: University of North Carolina Press.

Wills Otero, Laura, and Aníbal Pérez-Liñán. 2005. "La evolución de los sistemas electorales en América: 1900–2004." *Colección* 16: 47–82.

Winson, Anthony. 1989. *Coffee and Democracy in Modern Costa Rica.* Toronto: Between the Lines Press.

Yarrington, Doug. 2003. "Cattle, Corruption and Venezuelan State Formation During the Regime of Juan Vicente Gomez, 1908–35." *Latin American Research Review* 38, no. 2 (June): 9–33.

Yashar, Deborah. 1997. *Demanding Democracy: Reform and Reaction in Costa Rica and Guatemala.* Stanford: Stanford University Press.

———. 2005. *Contesting Citizenship in Latin America: The Rise of Indigenous Movements and the Postliberal Challenge.* Cambridge: Cambridge University Press.

Yépez Daza, Jacobo. 1988. "El realismo militar venezolano." In *El caso Venezuela: Una ilusión de armonía,* 4th ed., ed. Moisés Naím and Ramón Piñango, 328–49. Caracas: Ediciones IESA.

Youngers, Coletta A. 2004. "The U.S. 'War on Drugs' and Its Impact on Democracy in the Andes." In *Politics in the Andes: Identity, Conflict, Reform,* ed. Jo-Marie Burt and Philip Mauceri, 126–45. Pittsburgh: University of Pittsburgh Press.

Zartman, William I. 1995. *Collapsed States: The Disintegration and Restoration of Legitimate Authority.* Boulder: Lynne Rienner.

Zaverucha, Jorge. 1993. "The Degree of Military Autonomy during the Spanish, Argentine, and Brazilian Transitions." *Journal of Latin American Studies* 25 (2): 283–99.

Ziems, Angel. 1979. *El gomecismo y la formación del ejército nacional.* Caracas: Editorial Ateneo de Caracas.

Zuluaga, Jaime. 1995. "Nueva izquierda y guerrilla en Colombia." Unpublished manuscript, Universidad Nacional de Colombia, Instituto de Estudios Políticos y Relaciones Internacionales, Bogotá.

Huntington, Samuel P., 12, 84, 88,
156, 239

"illiberal" democracy, 221
IMF (International Monetary Fund),
237
industrialization, 28
delayed, 39, 40
through import substitution, 26
late, 39
in Southern Cone, 39
institutional factors. *See* political-
institutional factors
institutionalization of democracy, 20,
253
and building of a representative and
competitive party system, 175
as contentious, 8–9, 133, 134
defined, 8–9, 133, 256n15
divergent forms of, 11, 251
and incorporation of the left, 175
limitations on, 150
and pacts, 237
perverse pattern of, 174, 256n16
process of, 134–35
as reversible, 9
and subordination of the military,
175
See also democratic consolidation;
democratization; regime trajectory
institutionalization of party systems.
See party system,
institutionalization of
"iron law of oligarchy," 241

Karl, Terry Lynn, 13, 30, 37, 85, 86

leftist guerrillas. *See* armed challengers
on the left
Liberal Party (PL) (Colombia), 51,
105, 118, 190, 196, 202, 266n41
and Alvaro Uribe, 232
and Catholic Church, 100
concessions made by, 116, 118, 165,
275n78
emergence of, 63

factions within, 209
and Pacto de Marzo (Pact of March),
92
in 2006 elections, 233
violent conflict with Conservative
Party, 123
Lleras Camargo, Alberto, 94, 97, 104,
105, 116, 118, 142, 144, 165,
172, 191
López-Alves, Fernando, 48, 49, 51, 54,
57, 263n12, 264n17
López Contreras, Eleázar, 10, 264n26.
See also Andinos

Mainwaring, Scott, 59, 80, 81, 91,
255n6, 289nn4–5, 291n16
Manifiesto of the Junta Patriótica
(Venezuela), 90, 97
Medina Angarita, Isaías, 10, 264n26.
See also Andinos
military
authoritarian experiments of, 189
autonomy of, 136, 148–57, 220,
239, 249
—defined, 277n7
confronting challenges to democratic
continuity by, 135, 136–42,
175
coup attempts by, 218, 224, 235,
243
defined, 135
establishing and sustaining civilian
control of, 3, 4, 52, 134, 135–42,
142–57, 175, 224, 239, 277n3
influence on policy matters of, 4,
223, 239
intervention in politics of, 239
pacts, 81, 89, 97, 99
prerogatives of, 99, 148–57, 175,
220, 249
"reserved domains" of, 135
subordination of (*see* military,
establishing and sustaining civilian
control of)
United States' support for and
training of, 273n54

ANA MARÍA BEJARANO

is associate professor of political science at the University of Toronto